POLAR DESERTS
and
MODERN MAN

POLAR DESERTS
and
MODERN MAN

Editors:
TERAH L. SMILEY
JAMES H. ZUMBERGE

THE UNIVERSITY OF ARIZONA PRESS
Tucson, Arizona

The chapters of this book
have been adapted from papers presented at
the Polar Deserts Symposium
sponsored by
the Committee on Arid Lands
of the
American Association for the Advancement of Science
at Philadelphia, Pennsylvania
December 29–30, 1971.

THE UNIVERSITY OF ARIZONA PRESS

Copyright © 1974
The Arizona Board of Regents
All Rights Reserved
Manufactured in the U.S.A.

ISBN-0-8165-0383-4
L.C. No. 73-85722

CONTENTS

List of Illustrations   vi

List of Tables   vii

Preface   ix

PART ONE
NATURAL ENVIRONMENT

1. Some Aspects of Climatology in Polar Barrens   3
        I. Winter Temperature Attenuation in High-Latitude Barrens   3
        II. Precipitation in Arctic and Antarctic Coastal Barrens   13
        — Mario B. Giovinetto
2. A Climatological Analysis of North Polar Desert Areas   23
        — Michael J. Bovis and Roger G. Barry
3. Geomorphic Processes in Polar Deserts   33
        — Troy L. Péwé
4. Geological and Limnological Factors of Cold Deserts   53
        — William E. Davies
5. Soils of the High Arctic Landscapes   63
        — J. C. F. Tedrow
6. Application of Low-Latitude Microbial Ecology to
   High-Latitude Deserts   71
        — Roy E. Cameron
7. Macrobiology and Ecology in Polar Deserts   91
        — William S. Benninghoff
8. Indigenous Peoples of Polar Deserts   99
        — Graham W. Rowley

PART TWO
ECONOMIC BASE FOR DEVELOPMENT

9. Processes and Costs Imposed by Environmental Stress   105
        — Arlon R. Tussing
10. Review of Development of Arctic Resources   115
         — John C. Reed
11. Resource Development in Canada's High Arctic   119
         — George Jacobsen

PART THREE
PROBLEMS OF IMMIGRANTS

12. Transportation in the Arctic   125
         — Fletcher C. Paddison and Albert M. Stone
13. Health and Sanitation Problems in the Arctic   151
         — J. W. Grainge and John W. Shaw
14. Behavioral Design of Habitats for Man in Polar Deserts   161
         — William M. Smith

Index   165

ILLUSTRATIONS

ASPECTS OF CLIMATOLOGY
1. 1 Map: Arctic Stations   4
1. 2 Map: Antarctic Stations   5
1. 3 Graph: Monthly mean temperatures   6
1. 4 Graph: Insolation and temperatures   7
1. 5 Graph: Atmospheric cooling above pack ice   8
1. 6 Graph: Cloud cover variations   8
1. 7 Graph: Insolation and temperatures   9
1. 8 Graph: Angstrom-ratio values   9
1. 9 Graph: Aerological data   11
1.10 Graph: Winter turbulent heat flux   11
1.11 Chart: Snow and ice facies   14
1.12 Map: Arctic stations for precipitation
      determinations   16
1.13 Map: Antarctic stations for precipitation
      determinations   17
1.14 Graph: Precipitation phenomena   18
1.15 Map: Stations selected for precipitation
      comparisons   19
1.16 Graph: Precipitation in western
      North America   19
1.17 Graph: Precipitation in northern Africa and
      Middle East   20

CLIMATOLOGICAL ANALYSIS
2. 1 Map: Station locations for climatic records   24
2. 2 Map: Annual water budget   27
2. 3 Map: Distribution of deserts and semideserts   29
2. 4 Map: Distribution of deserts and semideserts   30

GEOMORPHIC PROCESSES
3. 1 Map: Polar deserts in northern hemisphere   33
3. 2 Photo: Polygonal ground formed by
      active ice wedges   34
3. 3 Photo: Wind-swept and wind-truncated
      boulders   35
3. 4 Map: Distribution of permafrost   36
3. 5 Chart: Surface features and permafrost   37
3. 6 Graph: Thermal profile of permafrost   37
3. 7 Photo: Foliated ground-ice mass   39
3. 8 Chart: Ice wedges and fossil ice   40
3. 9 Chart: Diagram of sand wedge   41
3.10 Photo: Sand-wedge polygons in northern
      Greenland   41
3.11 Chart: Geomorphic processes in relation
      to precipitation   42
3.12 Photo: Sand-wedge polygons in Antarctica   43
3.13 Photo: Raised-edge tundra polygons   43
3.14 Photo: Thermokarst pit in pasture land
      in Siberia   44
3.15 Photo: Stone circles in drained pond   44
3.16 Photo: Headwaters of tributary of Nome Creek   46
3.17 Photo: Cavernous weathering in granite
      boulders, Antarctica   47
3.18 Photo: Taffoni in arkosic conglomerate,
      Arizona   48
3.19 Photo: Petroleum camp on ice-wedge
      polygons, Alaska   49
3.20 Photo: Apartment house on permafrost, Siberia   50

GEOLOGY AND LIMNOLOGY
4. 1 Photo: Perennial snowbank in Greenland   54
4. 2 Photo: Small seep issuing from ground ice   54
4. 3 Photo: River fed by melt of Greenland ice sheet   55

4. 4 Photo: Small dimictic lake near Thule,
      Greenland   57
4. 5 Photo: Salt incrustation on silt   58
4. 6 Photo: Rills etched into limestone   59
4. 7 Photo: Caves with entrances up to 15
      meters wide   60

SOILS
5. 1 Map: Major soil zones of northern
      polar regions   64
5. 2 Chart: Major genetic soil zones of the
      High Arctic   64
5. 3 Photo: Polar desert on Prince Patrick Island   64
5. 4 Photo: Polar desert soil in northern Greenland   65
5. 5 Photo: Soils of the hummocky ground   65
5. 6 Photo: Profile of soil of the hummocky ground   65
5. 7 Photo: Soils of the polar desert-tundra
      interjacence   66
5. 8 Photo: Tundra soil in northern Greenland   66
5. 9 Photo: Tundra soil and buried organic fragments   67
5.10 Photo: Bog soil on Prince Patrick Island   67
5.11 Chart: Conditions in the High Arctic   68

MICROBIAL ECOLOGY
6. 1 Photo: Scattered vegetation at desert biome
      study site   72
6. 2 Photo: Close-up of algae soil crust   72
6. 3 Photo: Pebbly, cracked, low, barren area
      with algae crusts   72
6. 4 Photo: Barren, eroded, ventifacted, Antarctic
      dry valley   72
6. 5 Map: Microbial and ecological investigations,
      Antarctica   73
6. 6 Photo: Frozen pond; location of farthest
      south algae   73
6. 7 Photo: Farthest south exposed rock and soil
      in the world   73
6. 8 Photo: Moss, lichen, and grass-covered
      frost-crack polygon   73
6. 9 Photo: Putu dunes, covered with willow   73
6.10 Graph: Soil moisture retention-release curves
      for desert biome   75
6.11 Graph: Soil moisture retention-release curves
      for soil profile   75
6.12 Graph: Thermoluminescence glow curves   78
6.13 Graph: Thermoluminescence glow curves   78
6.14 Graph: Thermoluminescence glow curves   78
6.15 Graph: Thermoluminescence glow curves   79
6.16 Graph: Thermoluminescence glow curves   79
6.17 Graph: Air and soil surface temperatures   85
6.18 Graph: Soil subsurface temperatures   85
6.19 Graph: Soil and air temperature   85
6.20 Photo: Don Juan Pond, Antarctica, contains
      few microorganisms   86
6.21 Graph: Bacterial abundance and
      thermoluminescence   87
6.22 Chart: Population destiny and environmental
      factors, Antarctica   88

TRANSPORTATION
12. 1 Photo: Early snowmobile, Scott's Antarctic
       expedition   126
12. 2 Photo: Siberian ponies pull sleds, Scott's
       Antarctic expedition   126
12. 3 Photo: Men hauling sled, Scott's Antarctic
       expedition   126
12. 4 Map: The Arctic regions   127

12. 5 Photo: Arctic ice pack   128
12. 6 Photo: A new pressure ridge   128
12. 7 Photo: Arctic Research Laboratory Island
          (ARLIS V)   129
12. 8 Photo: Indelible tracks left in the tundra   130
12. 9 Map: Northern transportation routes of the
          U.S.S.R.   132
12.10 Map: Northern air transportation routes
          of the U.S.S.R.   133
12.11 Map: Route of the SS *Manhattan*, autumn 1969   134
12.12 Map: Transportation routes of northern Canada   135
12.13 Map: Commercial airline service of Canada   136
12.14 Photo: Resupply in the Canadian East Arctic   137
12.15 Map: Northern Alaska air transportation routes   137
12.16 Map: Surface transportation routes of Alaska   138
12.17 Photo: Snowmobile and sled on ARLIS V   139
12.18 Photo: Army land-train low-ground-pressure
          vehicle   139
12.19 Photo: Seagoing barge with tug and
          icebreaker support   140
12.20 Photo: Causeway at Prudhoe Bay   140
12.21 Photo: The icebreaker tanker SS *Manhattan*   142
12.22 Diagram: Basic types of air-cushion vehicles   144

12.23 Graph: Footprint pressures of surface transport
          vehicles   144
12.24 Photo: The SRN-4 hovercraft   145
12.25 Photo: SK-5 hovercraft on fast ice   145
12.26 Drawing: One concept of ARPA arctic
          surface-effect vehicle   147

HEALTH AND SANITATION
13. 1 Photo: Log cabin with sod roof   151
13. 2 Photo: A winter scene at Tuktoyaktuk   152
13. 3 Photo: Log cabin, tents, and Hudson Bay
          Company outbuildings   152
13. 4 Photo: Welfare house supplied to family
          at Inuvik   153
13. 5 Photo: An Eskimo girl at Cambridge Bay   153
13. 6 Photo: Eskimo parents and children   153
13. 7 Photo: Log cabin and sleigh dogs at
          Tuktoyaktuk   154
13. 8 Photo: Utilidor under construction at Inuvik   156
13. 9 Photo: Health worker observes a spill of sewage   156
13.10 Photo: Water intake and pump on a raft   157
13.11 Photo: Water pump and delta lake at Aklavik   157
13.12 Photo: A dog team hauls ice for water supplies   158

TABLES

ASPECTS OF CLIMATOLOGY
1. 1 Mean air temperatures   6
1. 2 Generalized seasonal scheme   7
1. 3 Winter cloud cover and harmonic amplitude
          ratios   9
1. 4 Turbulent heat flux in winter in the Antarctic   11
1. 5 Precipitation in high-latitude stations   15
1. 6 Precipitation near ice termini   16
1. 7 Precipitation in low-latitude coastal stations   18
1. 8 Precipitation in middle-latitude stations   19

CLIMATOLOGICAL ANALYSIS
2. 1 Discriminant analysis of Charlier and
          Fillipov maps   25
2. 2 Population rank of stations on Charlier map   25
2. 3 Population rank of stations according
          to temperature   25
2. 4 Population rank of stations on Fillipov maps   26
2. 5 Evaporation and annual water budget
          according to Budyko   26
2. 6 Dryness ratio and Thornwaite-Mather index   28
2. 7 Evaporation and annual water budget
          according to Turc   28

SOILS
5. 1 Geobotanical divisions of northern
          polar landscapes   63

MICROBIAL ECOLOGY
6. 1 Properties of United States arid-zone soils   76
6. 2 Properties of world arid-zone soils   77
6. 3 Microbial groups in Antarctic soils   80
6. 4 Microbiological determinations of arid-zone soils   81

6. 5 Microbiological determinations of arid-zone soils   82
6. 6 Metabolic activity and culturable microorganisms   83
6. 7 Life forms in Antarctic terrestrial ecosystems   84
6. 8 Microbial and cryptogamic populations
          in Antarctic   88

MICROBIOLOGY AND ECOLOGY
7. 1 Productivity data for classes of polar
          vegetation   94

PROCESSES AND COSTS
9. 1 Cost-of-living information for selected cities   106
9. 2 Anchorage family-budget costs   107
9. 3 Anchorage intermediate-level family-budget
          categories   108
9. 4 Gross sales and personal income in
          Anchorage area   110
9. 5 Housing in the Anchorage area   111
9. 6 Cultural amenities at Mirnyy, Yakut A.S.S.R.   111

TRANSPORTATION
12. 1 Icebreaker ships   131
12. 2 Large-payload rotary-wing aircraft   133
12. 3 Marine transport to the Canadian arctic   136
12. 4 Alaskan marine and motor transport   139
12. 5 Air cargo to north of Brooks Range, Alaska   141
12. 6 Large-payload fixed-wing cargo aircraft   141
12. 7 Power requirements for large Arctic cargo ships   143
12. 8 Comparison of hovercraft   145
12. 9 Arctic transportation costs   146
12.10 Overview of Arctic transportation by area   147
12.11 Overview of Arctic transportation by methods   148

PREFACE

The polar regions, especially those in the Antarctic, represent the last of the earth's land areas to be explored and investigated. The frontiers of the planet earth have disappeared; man has penetrated all earthly environments that are amenable to occupancy by human beings, at least within the capabilities of modern technology.

Literature on deserts of the world takes little if any note of the cold, arid polar areas which — in spite of their differences in temperature and solar radiation — are true deserts such as their well-known tropical and temperate zone counterparts wherein the geological, climatological, and biological processes are in a highly delicate balance. The rigorous climate and the geographic isolation of the polar areas have not been amenable to human occupation except for various Eskimo groups living along the shores of the Arctic Ocean. The discovery of resources, especially in the Arctic area, is prompting the movement of man and machinery into this less hospitable region, and the localities which will receive the major impact of development will be those which are free of permanent ice. In general, these are the more arid ones.

This book examines the polar deserts with respect to their physical and biological characteristics in relation to intensified development in the polar areas. Included in this objective is a consideration of the stresses existing between the environment and society, of both yesterday and tomorrow. Experts in a variety of subject matter divisions of polar studies provide the coverage of the major areas of importance relating to polar deserts. In exploring the similarities and differences between the polar deserts and the low-latitude deserts, special note is taken of how man might apply knowledge gained by the long history of occupation of the latter areas. Special reference is made to the problems faced by modern man as the tempo of the economic and scientific interest in polar regions increases.

Analyses are given of the natural setting and the dynamic processes of the polar deserts, including climatology, geology, hydrology, soils, biology, and the indigenous human occupants. Additional information presents costs imposed by environmental stress in the polar deserts; resource development of the past, present, and future; communications and transportation; health and sanitation; and the design of habitats for man in the harsh environment of polar deserts.

No precise definition exists for polar deserts, but generally speaking they can be considered to be glacier-free terrestrial areas wherein the mean annual precipitation is 25 centimeters or less, and the mean temperature for the warmest month is less than 10° Celsius. It is recognized that precipitation or lack thereof is not really a good basis for defining aridity in polar regions. However, we need not wait for a precise definition of a polar desert before we study the areas with respect to their economic value and the impact that exploitation will have on their physical and biological regimes. We have excluded the glacier-covered areas, because their immediate economic significance is small and the likelihood of large permanent settlements ever being established seems remote.

Systematic scientific polar exploration has only recently begun. Even though several scientific studies of the north and south polar regions started before the twentieth century, it was the International Geophysical Year of 1957–58 that launched scientists of many nations into large-scale systematic studies of the physical and biological aspects of the Arctic and Antarctic regions.

The polar regions are no longer the unknowns they once were. For example, the discovery of large oil reserves in northern Alaska and the Northwest Territory has intensified the interests of many groups. This development has become a *cause célèbre* in that it has firmly fixed the views of the various pro and con interests in the extraction and delivery of crude oil to the market.

The indigenous peoples of the Arctic have a stake in the economic development of their lands that is often ignored or overlooked. These populations depend on the Arctic lands for their life support. For centuries they have harvested the wildlife and used other renewable resources of their lands. Such resource utilization did not have much of an environmental impact on either the land or its inhabitants. The indigenous peoples cared little for the mineral wealth beneath them because it had no value to their economy. Not until man and machines from the more complex world appeared to extract the oil and mine the ores did the native population become aware of the interest that their lands held for others.

Thus, economic exploitation in the Arctic raises not only the question of what such activities will do to the land but also the question of the effects on the native population. The sociological implications of the confrontation between the culture of modern technology and the culture of ancient peoples as a result of the insensitivities of man has scarred the human history of the western world since the discovery of the Americas, and we must be mindful that the economic activities in the polar regions of the North could leave scars, both on the land and on its people.

The polar deserts of the Antarctic present a different situation with respect to exploitation and its sociological effects. For one thing, the "desert" areas are small isolated ones; for another, Antarctica never was the "natural" home of man; and for another, the immediate chance, as of the early 1970s, of any minerals of significant economic value being discovered there seems remote.

Antarctica, in the early 1970s, was the only continent on earth controlled by international agreement. This agreement is embodied in the Antarctic Treaty to which twelve nations (Argentina, Australia, Belgium, Chile, France, Japan, New Zealand, Norway, South Africa, United Kingdom, United States of America, and the Soviet Union) were signators in 1959. The treaty became effective on June 23, 1961, the date of ratification by the last nation to do so. The treaty generally provides for peaceful use of Antarctica, freedom of scientific investigation, and free exchange of all information collected there; in addition, it provides for a moratorium on all political claims on the continent, at least until 1991.

While it is generally agreed that the first ten years of the treaty saw its objectives realized, the question of economic exploitation remains moot. Nowhere in the treaty are there any guidelines regarding the exploitation of mineral resources. Even though it is unlikely that imminent exploitation for potential mineral resources will occur on land areas covered by the treaty, the possibility of offshore exploitation for liquid hydrocarbons on the Antarctic continental shelf cannot be shrugged off as an impossibility.

Experience should teach us that no place on earth is likely to escape the probe of the exploratory drill in search of minerals and fossil fuels of economic significance. If mineral resources should be discovered in Antarctica before 1991, the spirit of the signatory nations would be given a real test. Until that occurs, however, the scientific studies in Antarctica will provide important baseline information against which the impact of any economic endeavors involving the extraction of ores or the pumping of oil can be assessed.

Certainly the following pages can in no way be considered exhaustive or definitive of the problems associated with the interaction of man and the polar desert areas. This material is mostly that presented at a Symposium on Polar Deserts held in Philadelphia, Pennsylvania, December 29–30, 1971, during the annual meeting of the American Association for the Advancement of Science. The conveners of the Symposium, the Association's *Committee on Arid Lands,* have a vital interest in the deserts and semideserts of the world because, in these highly sensitive areas, the clarity of changes in natural processes takes place on a time-scale short enough to allow detailed study.

TERAH L. SMILEY
University of Arizona

JAMES H. ZUMBERGE
University of Nebraska

PART ONE

NATURAL ENVIRONMENT

CHAPTER 1

SOME ASPECTS OF CLIMATOLOGY IN POLAR BARRENS

Mario B. Giovinetto
Department of Geography, University of Calgary, Alberta, Canada

The increasing occupancy of ice-free barrens in the Arctic and Antarctic requires that the technology used, and its environmental impact, be appraised within biological, geological, and climatological frameworks. Within a climatological framework, energy and moisture fluxes at the surface are of particular importance for the understanding of geomorphological and biological processes, and for the planning of housing and transportation structures; this is mainly because the fluxes are essential in estimates of the duration and depth of seasonal freeze-thaw phenomena.

All the comprehensive studies of polar and subpolar climates include discussions of temperature and precipitation regimes (Orvig, 1970). Air temperature (instrument shelter) and precipitation (gauge) are among the interrelated variables used in inferring energy and moisture fluxes at the surface. These inferences are hampered from the outset due to the unreliability of solid precipitation gauge-data. Most studies have concentrated on the pack-ice, Greenland ice sheet, and tundra climates of the Arctic, and on the southern oceans and ice-sheet climates of the Antarctic, using combined data from stations in ice-free areas as well as in areas of permanent ice cover.

Two climatic characteristics that have not been discussed fully or exclusively in the regional context of ice-free barrens are (1) the attenuation of winter air-temperatures and (2) the relatively small variability of annual precipitation. The first characteristic is discussed in section I of this chapter; the second characteristic is discussed in section II.

I. WINTER TEMPERATURE ATTENUATION IN HIGH-LATITUDE BARRENS

Station Sampling

In high latitudes the criteria to select localities representative of particular climatic conditions should be based on a consideration of the energy regime combining surface and surface-related atmospheric terms, principally the advective terms. This premise is supported by the fact that at high latitudes, meteorological phenomena and climatological characteristics are dependent during most of the year on the poleward eddy-flux of energy (Holopainen, 1965), with exception of short intervals dominated by particular synoptic situations during summer. To be sure, energy flux estimates are based, among other things, on phase changes of snow, ice, and water at the surface and in the ground, which are at best difficult to assess.

Nevertheless, Vowinckel and Orvig (1971) have estimated the flux of back radiation from atmospheric advection and storage change [RLD(ER); their notation for easy reference] at Sachs Harbour (station 12, fig. 1.1). There RLD(ER) accounted for approximately 10% of the total energy input at the surface during June through August 1967, and 40% during December 1967 through March 1968. RLD(ER) is related to the surface heat budget as follows:

$$SGA + RLD(SAT) + RLD(ER) + RLD$$
$$- [RLD(SAT) + RLD(ER)] =$$
$$RLU + (PR - EW) + QS + FG,$$

where SGA is solar radiation absorbed at the ground; RLD(SAT) is back radiation, originated from solar radiation absorbed in the atmosphere; RLD is downward long-wave flux from the atmosphere; RLU is upward long-wave flux from the ground; PR is heat released on condensation and equivalent to total precipitation; EW is latent heat available to the atmosphere through advection and storage change; QS is sensible heat flux at the surface; and FG is ground heat flux.

It is evident that a typical climatic characteristic in high latitudes is that the advective term remains positive for the surface, at least on a monthly basis. In this context, Sachs Harbour is close to a marginal situation; the contribution of RLD(ER) in July 1967 was only 3% of the total energy input at the surface.

The standard form in which meteorological records are available forces the admittedly cursory approach of selecting, for this report, stations with summer air temperatures approximately equal or lower than those at Sachs Harbour, principally a mean temperature of approximately 6°C for the warmest month (July). This is not to say that RLD(ER) cannot be negative even if the temperature is higher than 6°C; obviously the advective term is not the only one on which surface and near surface air temperatures are dependent.

An examination of standard meteorological records from northern polar and subpolar stations shows that a mean temperature of approximately 6°C or less for the warmest month corresponds well with the following: no

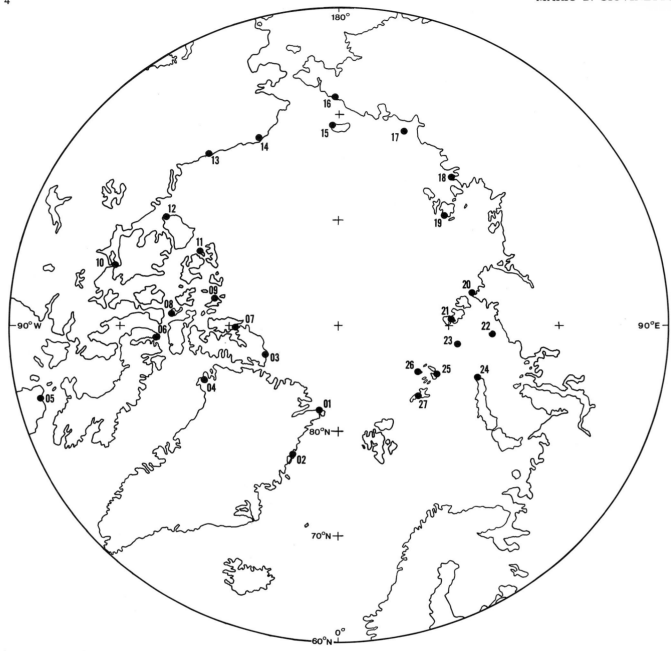

Fig. 1.1. Arctic stations representative of ice-free coastal barrens. Latitude, longitude, elevation (in meters), and harmonic amplitude ratio ($a_2 a_1^{-1}$) are given below.

01	Nord	81°36′N	016°40′W	35m	0.27	17	Os Chetyryekhstolbovy	70°38′N	162°24′E	6m	0.02
02	Danmarkshavn	76 46	018 46	18	0.21	18	Mys Shalaurova	73 11	143 56	10	0.04
03	Alert	82 30	062 20	62	0.22	19	Ostrov Kotelny	76 00	137 54	10	0.06
04	Thule	76 31	068 50	11	0.15	20	Mys Chelyuskin	77 43	104 17	13	0.11
05	Hall Beach	68 47	081 15	10	0.12	21	Ostrov Domashniy	79 30	091 08	3	0.14
06	Arctic Bay	73 00	085 18	11	0.08	22	Ostrov Uyedineniya	77 30	082 14	9	0.09
07	Eureka	80 00	085 56	2	0.20	23	Ostrov Vize	79 30	076 59	18	0.13
08	Resolute	74 43	094 59	64	0.13	24	Mys Zhelaniya	76 57	068 35	8	0.12
09	Isachsen	78 47	103 32	25	0.17	25	Ostrov Heisä	80 37	058 03	20	0.11
10	Cambridge Bay	69 07	105 01	14	0.09	26	Ostrov Rudolfa	81 48	057 57	48	0.23
11	Mould Bay	76 14	119 20	15	0.14	27	Bukhta Tikhaya	80 19	052 48	6	0.20
12	Sachs Harbour	71 57	124 44	84	0.11						
13	Barter Island	70 07	143 40	15	0.07						
14	Barrow	71 18	156 47	7	0.07						
15	Ostrov Vrangelya	70 58	178 32	3	0.09						
16	Mys Shmidta	68 55	179 29	7	0.06						

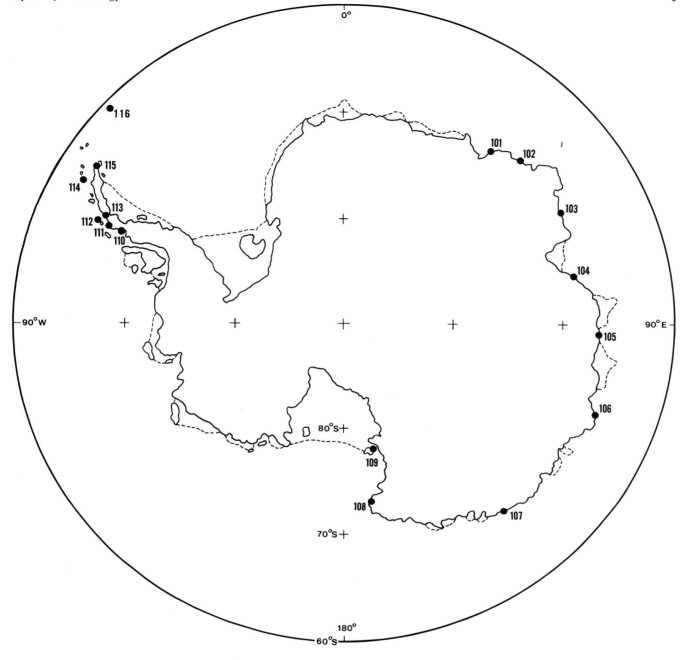

Fig. 1.2.   Antarctic stations representative of ice-free coastal barrens. Latitude, longitude, elevation (in meters), and harmonic amplitude ratio ($a_2a_1^{-1}$) are given below.

101	Syowa	69°00′S	039°35′E	15m	0.22		110	Marguerite Bay	68°11′S	067°01′W	9m	0.19
102	Molodezhnaya	67 40	045 50	42	0.27		111	Argentine Is.	65 15	064 15	11	0.09
103	Mawson	67 36	062 53	8	0.34		112	Melchior	64 20	062 59	8	0.12
104	Davis	68 35	077 58	12	0.27		113	Almirante Brown	64 53	062 52	7	0.08
105	Mirny	66 33	093 01	30	0.32		114	Decepcion	62 59	060 43	8	0.12
106	Wilkes	66 15	110 35	12	0.21		115	Hope Bay	63 24	056 59	11	0.08
107	D. d'Urville	66 42	140 00	41	0.22		116	Orcadas (Laurie I.)	60 44	044 44	4	0.18
108	Hallet	72 18	170 19	5	0.20							
109	McMurdo	77 53	166 44	24	0.37							

more than 3 months with mean temperatures above freezing, and a mean annual temperature lower than −10°C. These are the guidelines used here to select stations.

Most of the forty-three stations selected (figs. 1.1 and 1.2) are located at elevations of 50 meters or less, and at distances from the coastline of less than 100 meters. The latitudinal range is 14° for the Arctic stations, centered at approximately 75°30′N, and 17° for the Antarctic stations, centered at approximately 69°30′S. Locally, differences in distance to ice termini and in seasonal fluctuations of snow cover and/or pack-ice (including polynyas) reduce the similarity between stations. However, these differences in latitude and local conditions between stations in either the Arctic or Antarctic group, and between the groups, are of secondary importance compared with the contrasting features which lie poleward from each station group, namely the Arctic seas and pack-ice, and the Antarctic ice-sheet.

Harmonic Analysis of Air Temperatures

The temperature records of the forty-three stations show that, in general, the difference between consecutive monthly means is smaller in winter than in summer. The smaller winter variation is evident in the distribution of the monthly means (table 1.1 and fig. 1.3). Typically, the departure from the annual mean is smaller for the coldest month than for the warmest (except in stations 17, 18, 22, 25, 111–114, and 116), seven monthly means are colder than the annual mean, and a pronounced minimum is lacking. The described distribution of monthly means is similar to, but does not in every case meet, definitions of the coreless winter phenomenon (comprehensive review, Loewe, 1969). To be sure, daily and monthly ranges of temperature are larger in winter than in summer, in some cases by a factor of two.

In the Arctic the coldest month often is February or March, seldom January; in the Antarctic the coldest month is June, July, or August, with equal frequency. In the Arctic and Antarctic, there is more regularity in the occurrence of the warmest months which, often, are July and January. This is expected because during summer the temperature change follows, with some lag, the change in potential insolation because of variations in the local energy regime, particularly of terms related

TABLE 1.1

Summary of Annual & Monthly Mean Air Temperatures in High-Latitude Coastal Barrens

Item	Arctic			Antarctic		
	Station	Month	°C	Station	Month	°C
Annual mean: (t)						
Maximum	24		− 9.0	113		− 2.7
Minimum	07		−19.1	109		−17.4
Mid-range example	21		−14.0	104		−10.3
Warmest month: (t_w)						
Maximum	10	VII	+ 8.0	114	I	+ 1.4
Minimum	23	VII	+ 0.5	109	I	− 3.4
Mid-range example	01	VII	+ 4.2	101	I	− 1.0
Coldest month: (t_c)						
Maximum	27	I	−17.2	114	VII	− 8.0
Minimum	07	III	−37.6	109	VIII	−27.8
Mid-range example	14	II	−27.7	107	VI	−17.6
Difference: ($t–t_w$)						
Largest	07		24.8	108		14.2
Smallest	27		10.4	114		4.2
Mid-range example	18		17.3	106		9.1
Mean (all stations)	01-27		17.3	101-116		8.5
Difference: ($t–t_c$)						
Largest	10		19.9	108		11.3
Smallest	27		7.9	115		4.6
Mid-range example	21		13.8	102		7.8
Mean (all stations)	01-27		15.2	101-116		7.0

to snow albedo, surface melt runoff, and subsurface temperatures.

The temperature increase from winter to summer is concentrated in April–May (October–November), and the decrease from summer to winter is concentrated in September–November (February–April). This distribution results in "winters" that last approximately four months in the Arctic and five months in the Antarctic (table 1.2; the Antarctic stations in the South American sector are excluded from these generalizations). Relative to a scheme of seasons such as this, the records show that differences of one month in the onset of a season are rare, and the duration of a season is remarkably consistent.

The variation of monthly means can be analyzed using harmonic amplitude ratios (Meinardus, 1938; Loewe, 1969). Following the basic form of Fourier series analysis:

$$t_x \simeq t + A_1 \sin \left(\frac{360°}{P} m \right) + B_1 \cos \left(\frac{360°}{P} m \right) \ldots$$

$$+ A_3 \sin \left(\frac{360°}{P} m \right) + B_3 \cos \left(\frac{360°}{P} m \right),$$

where $t_x(m)$ is the variate, A and B the coefficients, and P the fundamental period (12 months), the amplitude ratio of the first two harmonics ($a_1 a_2^{-1}$) was computed for each series. It ranged from 0.02 to 0.37 (figs. 1.1 and 1.2); as expected in periodic series, the first two harmonics account for a large proportion of the variations: in this case for >98% of the variation in all the stations — together with the third harmonic, they account for >99% in all but two stations.

The amplitude ratio represents an heuristic attenuation-index of winter temperatures. A large ratio indi-

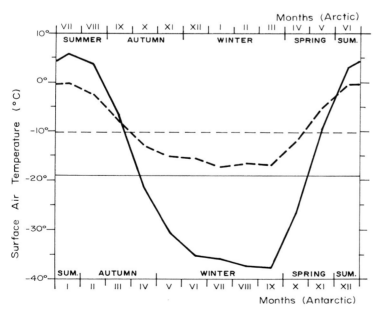

Fig. 1.3. Monthly mean temperatures are shown for station 07 Eureka (solid curve) and for station 104 Davis (broken curve).

cates considerable attenuation (or a coreless winter), and a small ratio indicates little or no attenuation (or a cored winter). Obviously a coreless summer would result in an increase of the amplitude ratio; therefore the appropriate phase must be taken into account.

The latitudinal variation of amplitude ratios is depicted in figure 1.4. (It was stated earlier that all stations are approximately at the same elevation and distance from the coast, and/or probable open leads in the pack-ice.) Linear fits (with 2 degrees of freedom) for station groups 108–116 and 01–27 are close to parallel and clearly exclude stations 101–107. Three features of the distribution are: (1) The ratio increases with increasing latitude. (2) At any given latitude the ratio is smaller in the Arctic than in the Antarctic. (3) The ratio in stations 101–107, the only stations located at the foot of steep terminal ice-sheet slopes, appears to be greater than in other Antarctic locations in ice-free barrens at the same latitude.

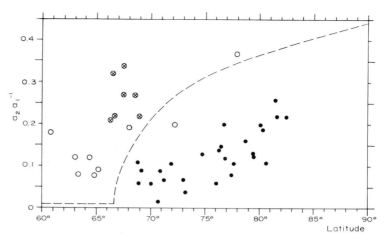

Fig. 1.4. Harmonic amplitude ratios of potential insolation (broken curve) and monthly mean temperatures of Arctic stations (closed circles) and Antarctic stations (open circles and crossed circles, with crossed circles indicating stations 101–107, located at the foot of steep terminal ice-sheet slopes).

Latitude and Potential Insolation

The data for both station groups indicate that the amplitude ratio of temperature follows the general trend of that of potential insolation, which Lettau (1971) proposed as the major cause of coreless winters. He reasoned that the amplitude of the second harmonic should approximate zero at a latitude of 66°30′, increasing to >0.4 of the first harmonic at 90°. Potential insolation data for sixteen evenly spaced dates of the year (List, 1958) result in amplitude ratios of 0.44 at 90°, 0.36 at 80°, and 0.21 at 70° (fig. 1.4). This variation of potential insolation explains the trend of increasing temperature amplitude ratios with increasing latitude.

Atmospheric Heat Advection and Long-wave Energy Fluxes

The second feature of the distribution shown in figure 1.4 is that at a given latitude the amplitude ratio is smaller in the Arctic than in the Antarctic. The amplitude ratios for each group evidently correspond to distinct domains, which can be explained through a discussion of long-wave radiation fluxes in winter. These will be discussed after differences in the rate of meridional heat advection are established.

Poleward Energy Fluxes. Poleward from the sub-

TABLE 1.2

Generalized Seasonal Scheme Applicable to High-Latitude Coastal Barrens

Season	Arctic	Antarctic
Fall	Sept-Nov	Feb-April
Winter	Dec-March	May-Sept
Spring	April-May	Oct-Nov
Summer	June-Aug	Dec-Jan

tropics, and for regular increments in latitude, the decrease of the incoming radiation rate is greater than that of the outgoing radiation rate. In the two-hemisphere composite latitudinal range where the selected stations are located, the deficit increases from 6×10^4 cal cm^{-2} yr^{-1} at 60°, to 9×10^4 cal cm^{-2} yr^{-1} at 85°. Meridional advection of energy compensates for the radiation deficit particularly during the winter.

It was mentioned that the latitudinal range of the Arctic and Antarctic stations are centered at approximately 75°30′N and 69°30′S; for purposes of discussion, consideration of poleward energy fluxes at a latitude of 70° should be adequate. It should be noted that at 70°, atmospheric sensible heat transport — by meridional circulations and eddy fluxes — is an order of magnitude greater than the contributions of latent heat flux and oceanic energy fluxes, each in the order of 10^{21} cal yr^{-1} (Benton, 1954; Budyko, 1956; Malkus, 1962); therefore the latter two are of no concern here.

Palmén and Newton (1969) have estimated the poleward advection of energy at 11.6×10^{21} cal yr^{-1} (70°N) and 12.1×10^{21} cal yr^{-1} (70°S). A wider range of values exists for advection estimates at 70°S than at 70°N. Using smaller amounts of aerological data than Palmén and Newton, advection at 70°S has been estimated at 15×10^{21} cal yr^{-1} by Rubin (1962), and at 16×10^{21} cal yr^{-1} by Gabites (1960). Because energy advected is lost mainly upward, it is of interest that Schwerdtfeger (1970), on the basis of radiation data analyzed by VonderHaar (1968), has indicated that estimates as low as 9×10^{21} cal yr^{-1} are possible. Nevertheless, even a midrange value of 12.5×10^{21} cal yr^{-1} for advection across 70°S suggests that more heat is advected across equivalent latitudes over the southern ice-free barrens than over the northern.

In this context the influence of contrasting physiography poleward from each station group is illustrated

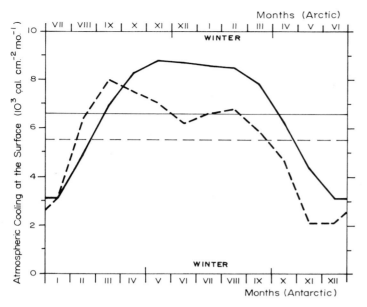

Fig. 1.5. Atmospheric cooling at the surface of Arctic pack-ice (broken curve) and the Antarctic ice-sheet (solid curve). Graph is modified from Fletcher (1965, 1969).

by a comparison of atmospheric cooling at the surface, which Fletcher (1965, 1969) has estimated to be 66×10^3 cal cm^{-2} yr^{-1} for the ice-covered Arctic seas, and 70×10^3 cal cm^{-2} yr^{-1} for the Antarctic ice-sheet (fig. 1.5). This annual difference of approximately 6% is greater when the mean surface cooling in winter is considered: 6.4×10^3 cal cm^{-2} mo^{-1} for the Arctic (December–March), and 8.5×10^3 cal cm^{-2} mo^{-1} for the Antarctic (May–September), or a difference of approximately 28%.

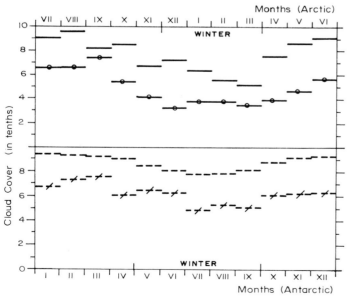

Fig. 1.6. Cloud cover variations at station 07 Eureka (lines with circles), 26 O. Rudolfa (solid lines), 108 Hallet (dash, cross, dash), and 116 Orcadas (triple dash).

Rates of surface cooling such as these generate strong meridional surface-outflow which must be compensated by poleward inflow aloft; it should be expected that in the areas of Antarctic barrens there is a greater meridional advection of energy and, everything else being equal, a greater downward flux than in the Arctic counterparts. Moreover, $a_2a_1^{-1}$ for monthly values of surface cooling are 0.6 for the Arctic and 0.3 for the Antarctic.

An examination of mid-troposphere flow charts for both hemispheres (Lahey and others, 1958a; Van Loon and others, 1971) shows no readily apparent correlation between the winter meridional components and the harmonic amplitude ratios of surface temperature. However, this does not invalidate earlier arguments; the amount of heat advected in winter over an area is not the only determinant agent of its surface temperature regime, and other phenomena inducing long-wave fluxes must be considered.

Vertical Energy Fluxes. The differences between the Arctic and Antarctic vertical energy fluxes during winter can be explained through a consideration of several interrelated variables, each accounting for only a part of the distribution shown in figure 1.4, and certainly for different proportions at each locality. Concerning the general subject of attenuation of winter temperatures in the high latitudes, the principal item is the long-wave radiation budget of the surface. However, the number and distribution of the stations under discussion would require several separate investigations. At present a comparison of downward long-wave fluxes in the Arctic and Antarctic should suffice.

Downward long-wave radiation is highly dependent on temperature differences between particular tropospheric levels and the surface. Vowinckel and Orvig (1970) show that in the Arctic upper air inversions are less frequent in winter (approximately 20%) than in summer (approximately 30%), but in winter the inversion temperature maxima are higher than those of the surface in more than 90% of the observations, a phenomenon common also in the Antarctic (Weyant, 1966).

Since there is correlation between the occurrence of upper air inversions and cloud cover (Vowinckel and Orvig, 1970), it may be inferred that the Antarctic stations, located at the "coast" where cloud cover remains relatively heavy during winter, must have a higher winter frequency of upper air inversions than the Arctic stations.

Cloud cover records for stations representative of extreme values (fig. 1.6) show that mean annual cloud cover ranges approximately from 5/10 to 7/10 in the Arctic stations and from 6/10 to 8/10 in the Antarctic stations; more important is that the decrease from summer to winter is approximately 4/10 in the Arctic but only 2/10 in the Antarctic.

The implication that heavy cloud cover in winter indicates frequent upper air inversions and therefore greater downward energy fluxes is illustrated by a comparison of cloud cover and harmonic amplitude ratios of air temperature at the 500-millibar level (table 1.3, fig. 1.7); accounting for a latitude difference of approximately 10° between the two pair of stations, the attenuation of winter temperature minima in the mid-troposphere is more pronounced in the Antarctic stations. It should also be noted that in both hemispheres the attenuation may be, in some places, more pronounced in the mid-troposphere than at the surface.

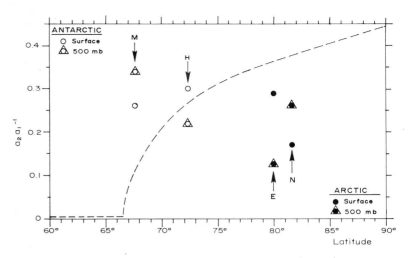

Fig. 1.7. Harmonic amplitude ratios of potential insolation (broken curve) and monthly mean temperatures at the surface and 500-millibar levels. M indicates station 103 Mawson; H, station 108 Hallett; E, station 07 Eureka; and N, station 01 Nord. Data are from table 1.3.

TABLE 1.3

Winter Cloud Cover & Harmonic Amplitude Ratios of Temperatures at the Surface & 500 Millibars

Station	Latitude	Winter Cloud Cover (Tenths)	$a_2 a_1^{-1}$	
			Surface	500 mb *
01	81°36′N	5.3	0.26	0.17
07	80°00′N	3.6	0.13	0.29
103	67°36′S	6.6	0.34	0.26
108	72°18′S	5.2	0.22	0.30

* From Loewe (1969).

Angstrom Ratio Relationships. An alternate method of assessing the difference between Arctic and Antarctic amplitude ratios and energy fluxes is to consider relationships of the Angstrom ratio (A_o) (ratio of effective long-wave radiation to emitted radiation) to advection, surface inversions, cloud cover, and water vapor. Schwerdtfeger (1970) has discussed these relationships in the context of seasonal, and interior versus coastal, differences in Antarctica. Here only the hemispheric differences during winter are of interest. Following the computation

$$A_o \sim (RLU - RLD) \, RLU^{-1}$$

for Sachs Harbour and Wilkes, using the estimates of each term by Vowinckel and Orvig (1971), the distribution of A_o values is shown in figure 1.8. A_o values at Wilkes in winter and spring are smaller than at Sachs Harbour for the same seasons, indicating that at Wilkes the downward flux makes up for a greater proportion of the surface-originated upward flux. The fact that in fall and early winter the A_o is smaller at Sachs Harbour may have to be explained through considerations of synoptic situations, including conditions at the surface, such as the depth of the snow cover. (It has been mentioned that RLU and RLD were estimated on the basis of one-year data.) Moreover, seasonal variations of snow and cloud cover are much larger at Sachs Harbour, generally by a factor of two.

In winter the A_o should increase with decreasing cloud cover and water vapor, and decrease with increasing temperatures above the surface inversion layer. Vowinckel and Orvig (1970) show that in the Arctic basin the surface inversion is more frequent in winter (approximately 80%) than in summer (approximately

30%). As in the case of upper air inversions, both the strength and frequency of surface inversions are related to cloudiness; in winter the surface inversions are very strong and more frequent with clear skies. They commented that on occasions the upper and surface inversions have merged, resulting in a 4-kilometer thick, 25° C inversion. This is, obviously, close to an upper limit for the Arctic basin. Putnins (1970) quotes a maximum inversion strength of 24° C for the Greenland ice-sheet.

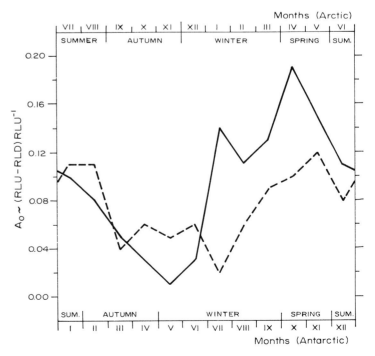

Fig. 1.8. Approximate monthly mean Angstrom-ratio values for station 12 Sachs Harbour (solid curve) and station 106 Wilkes (broken curve).

In the interior of the Antarctic ice-sheet the maximum strength is $\leq 40°$ C (Schwerdtfeger, 1970), the winter mean being $\geq 25°$ C, decreasing outward to $\leq 5°$ C in areas including the ice-free barrens (Phillpot and Zilman, quoted in Schwerdtfeger, 1970). From this it may be inferred that winter mean surface inversion in ice-free barrens is less intense in the Arctic ($<< 5°$ C); although on the basis of cloud cover (fig. 1·6), inversions probably are more frequent than in the Antarctic. This inference concerning a lower frequency is limited to stations 108–116. In the following section it is noted that in stations 101–107 katabatic winds are associated with strong, deep surface inversions and light or no cloud cover, implying a higher frequency in the latter group because katabatic flow frequency in the coastal zone of East Antarctica is $>> 50\%$.

Summary. The larger amplitude ratio domain in the Antarctic barrens can be explained by the greater advection of energy; the stronger, more frequent upper air inversions; and the stronger, although in some sectors less frequent surface inversions.

Air Flow and Vertical Energy Fluxes

The third feature in figure 1.4 indicates that $a_2 a_1^{-1}$ values for stations 101–107 are larger than for other Antarctic ice-free locations at the same latitude; this is significant because they are the only stations at the foot of steep terminal ice-sheet slopes, which is to say in areas of very frequent katabatic flow (Mather and Miller, 1967) supported by quasi steady-state inversion winds of the interior (Lettau, 1966), and where the incoming cyclonic disturbances encounter the steep ice-sheet slopes (Alt and others, 1959).

Due to the peripheral location of stations 101–107 relative to the larger dome of East Antarctica and following the reasoning in the first part of the preceding section, it could be argued that differences in heat advection over East and West Antarctica play a significant role determining the difference in the latitudinal distribution of the ratio between them and stations 108–116. This argument is dismissed for a simple reason; if it were valid, stations 108 and 109 in East Antarctica would have a higher ratio, and station 110 in West Antarctica would have a lower one, which they do not. Moreover, the ratio for stations in *ice-covered* locations should show a difference between east and west Antarctic groups; however, no such difference exists.

Many statements are found in the literature concerning downward turbulent heat flux in winter; among some of the works already used as references, it will be noted that greater windspeeds and stronger surface inversions have been unconditionally related to larger heat fluxes (Loewe, 1969; Rusin, 1961; Palmén and Newton, 1969; Vowinckel and Orvig, 1970) and that the possibility of relatively stratified flow hampering these fluxes exists (Rusin, 1961; Vowinckel and Orvig, 1971). Upon consideration of winter phenomena and energy levels contributing to the larger amplitude ratios in stations 101–107, an attempt is made to estimate the turbulent heat flux *difference* between these stations and stations 108–116. The considerations are based on the facts that katabatic flow is characterized by less vertical mixing than other flow types, and that windspeed and the frequency of flow types are different for each station group.

Reduced vertical mixing is characteristic of katabatic winds in Antarctica. Rusin (1961) discussed this phenomenon using data obtained at station 105, Mirny, where katabatic flow is more intense under conditions of strong, deep surface inversions and light or no cloud cover; these winds are accompanied by a lowering of surface air temperature. However, there are other types of flow which are accompanied by a rising of air temperature. For Mirny, Rusin categorized katabatic winds as "anticyclonic" flow (generally with a S-SE component), to differentiate it from "cyclonic" flow (with an E-NE component) and from "transitional" flow (with an E-SE component), the last type indicating a change from anticyclonic to cyclonic flow and vice versa. Although mesoscale synoptic analyses in Antarctica are at best doubtful because of the great distances between stations, his estimates for segments of the coastal zone characterized by steep ice-sheet slopes suggest frequencies of approximately 0.6 for anticyclonic flow, 0.3 for cyclonic flow, and 0.1 for transitional flow.

Aerological data for Mirny (fig. 1.9) illustrate the conditions prevailing during katabatic flow; the associated surface inversions have been discussed implicitly in the preceding section. It is evident that strong and frequent katabatic flow in stations 101–107 would result, everything else being equal, in larger and more frequent downward radiation fluxes. The data also indicate that vertical mixing should be considerable during conditions dominated by cyclonic and transitional flow types, particularly the latter.

Regardless of the accuracy of synoptic analyses, the fact that mean annual velocities for particular wind types summarized by Rusin differ little from each other at standard anemometer heights (katabatic, 12.7 m sec^{-1}; cyclonic, 12.4 m sec^{-1}; transitional, 11.6 m sec^{-1}) facilitates a discussion of amplitude ratio and turbulent heat flux differences between station groups 101–107 and 108–116 on the basis of mean winter windspeed (using monthly values for May–September), which is 9.4 $\pm$ 3.0 m sec^{-1} in the former and 5.6 $\pm$ 2.0 m sec^{-1} in the latter. The standard errors were computed not accounting for the smallness of the samples; however, biased or unbiased computation of errors does not change the fact that the difference in windspeed is not conclusive, least of all when seasonal mean values are involved. Rather the difference suggests that amplitude ratios for stations at short distances from each other — so that variables such as cloud and snow cover, frequency of wind types, radiation fluxes, and frequency and strength of surface inversions, are assumed to be equal — should show at least a rank

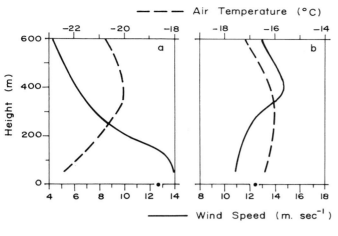
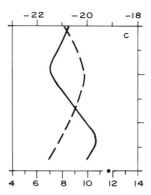

Fig. 1.9.　Aerological data for station 105 Mirny. Means are shown for the year 1956, and conditions of katabatic (a), cyclonic (b), and transitional (c) flow types, and windspeed at a height of 10 meters (black circle). All data are adapted from Rusin (1961).

correspondence between the amplitude ratio, and mean *winter* windspeed and turbulent heat flux. The data from three stations located along a 120 kilometer segment of coastline bear this out (table 1.4 and fig. 1.10; *as a first approximation,* monthly mean values are used; the seasonal means are summarized). There is an almost linear correlation between the amplitude ratio and mean windspeed values at the standard anemometer height of 10 meters (u_{10}, in m sec^{-1}), which is to say with turbulent heat flux (H, negative downward) if a simple relationship such as

$$H = - cu_{10} \text{ cal cm}^{-2} \text{ min}^{-1}$$

is used. In winter, with surface inversions of approximately 5° Celsius, over a relatively smooth ice-shelf surface of negligible slope and $u_{10} > 1$ m sec^{-1}, c has been estimated to be 0.0058 (Liljequist, 1956). The dependence of turbulent heat flux on windspeed is complicated by the strength of the surface inversion, although there seems to be a limit beyond which a stronger inversion does not alter the resultant heat flux (Loewe, 1954). Considerations of this problem are eliminated here because the mean inversion in winter is ≤5° Celsius in all the areas where stations 101–115 are located (station 116 excluded; Phillpot and Zilman, quoted by Schwerdtfeger, 1970). Furthermore, estimates of the monthly mean temperature gradient between heights of 0.5 meters and 2.0 meters from May through August at the three stations listed in table 1.4 differ at most by 0.01° Celsius in any given month (Rusin, 1961).

Using c = 0.006 and considering that katabatic flow hampers turbulent heat flux, say by one-half, an approximation of H during winter months at stations 101–107 ($\overline{u_{10}} = 9.4$ m sec^{-1}) is given by

$$H_{101\text{-}107} (0.6/2 + 0.4) \sim -1.7 \text{ kcal cm}^{-2} \text{ mo}^{-1}$$

where 0.6 and 0.4 are, respectively, the frequencies extrapolated from station 105 for katabatic flow, and the cyclonic and transitional flows characterized by more intense vertical mixing. This approach to estimate H, principally the assumption that stratified flow may account for a 50% reduction of H, is supported by a

TABLE 1.4

Turbulent Heat Flux in Winter in the Antarctic

Station	Period	Latitude	Longitude	Elevation	$a_2a_1^{-1}$
D. d'Urville*	1956-57	66°42′S	140°00′E	41 m	0.22
Port Martin	1950-51	66°49′S	141°24′E	20 m	0.27
Cape Denison	1912-13	67°00′S	142°40′E	6 m	0.30

	May-September			
	u_{10} m sec^{-1}	H kcal cm^{-2} mo^{-1}	u_1† m sec^{-1}	H′† kcal cm^{-2} mo^{-1}
D. d'Urville	11.4	−2.8	9.7	−1.7
Port Martin	19.2	−5.1	15.4	−2.2
Cape Denison	25.5	−6.7	19.6	−3.7

*Also identified as Station 107.
†From Rusin (1961).

comparison with a detailed work of Rusin (1961). The comparison shows that H, weighted by flow type frequencies, approximates turbulent heat fluxes estimated by the eddy diffusion method (H′; table 1.4 and fig. 1.10) after calculating u_1 (windspeed at a height of 1

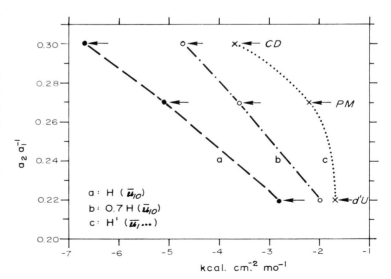

Fig. 1.10.　Winter (May–September) turbulent heat flux, negative downward. CP indicates Cape Denison; PM, Port Martin; and d'U, station 107, Dumont d'Urville. Data are from table 1.4.

meter) by the logarithmic law, and other variables assuming a negligibly small surface roughness parameter.

For stations 108–116 ($\overline{u_{10}} = 5.6$ m sec^{-1}), where the simplest assumption would be that flow type frequencies are reversed, particularly at stations 110–116 (Alt and others, 1959; Van Loon and others, 1971), the approximation is

$$H_{108\text{-}116} (0.4/2 + 0.6) \sim -1.2 \text{ kcal cm}^{-2} \text{ mo}^{-1}.$$

The estimated winter difference in H, approximately 0.5 kcal cm^{-2} mo^{-1}, is of a magnitude sufficiently large to account for a large proportion of the observed difference in amplitude ratios between groups.

Conclusions

The harmonic amplitude ratio ($a_2 a_1^{-1}$) of monthly mean temperatures in high-latitude areas is an heuristic index of winter temperature attenuation, or corelessness. Ratios > 0.2 indicate coreless winters, and < 0.1 indicate relatively well-cored winters. Most of the twenty-seven Arctic and sixteen Antarctic stations in ice-free barrens (or representative of this condition) selected for discussion are located at elevations and distances from the coast of 100 meters or less; the composite two-hemisphere latitudinal range of the stations extends from 60°44′ poleward to 82°30′, and the ratio values range from 0.02 to 0.37. The latitudinal distribution shows that the ratios (1) increase with increasing latitude, (2) are smaller in the Arctic than in the Antarctic, and (3) are greater in East Antarctic stations at the foot of steep terminal ice-sheet slopes than in other Antarctic stations.

The first feature is clearly compatible with the amplitude ratio of potential insolation, which increases from approximately zero at the polar circles to 0.44 at the poles. The second feature is accounted for by comparisons of hemispheric differences (particularly during the winter months) in terms of (1) atmospheric advection of heat across a latitude of 70°, (2) atmospheric cooling at the surface of the Arctic pack-ice and the Antarctic ice-sheet, (3) long wave energy flux ratios, and (4) cloud cover and the strength and frequency of upper air and surface inversions. The third feature is explained by differences in winter windspeed, frequency of surface-flow types with characteristic intensities of vertical mixing, and associated downward turbulent heat fluxes.

Paleoclimatic Implications

Concerning Pleistocene glaciation, Loewe (1969) noted that the area with coreless winters was larger then, and that as the Northern Hemisphere ice-sheets reached middle latitudes, the radiation regime was different from that in polar latitudes, resulting in "less developed" coreless winters. He also noted that "katabatic wind is likely to have prevailed and would have given a descending component to the upper air

layers. This would have led to some mixing with the cold air below the inversion and a reduction of the fall of temperature during the winter." In the context of ice-free areas adjacent to grounded ice-sheet termini (of which stations 101–107 are considered to be representative), the contribution of surface outflow to corelessness would have been greater than at the present whenever Pleistocene glaciation extended into upper midlatitudes (40°–60°); then, as presently, in East Antarctica the contributions would have been limited to a relatively narrow zone parallel to the termini. True "katabatic" flow (unaided by the pressure field) dissipates in a zone of convergence and forced uplift which exists from a few to several kilometers outward from the termini. (For summaries of investigations by Dolganov and Weller among others, refer to Rusin, 1961, and Schwerdtfeger, 1970.) Because of strong winds, it is difficult to think of these narrow segmented zones extending parallel to termini for thousands of kilometers as macrobiotic refugia following the glacial fluctuations; however in the ice-free areas adjacent to termini (say within 10 kilometers) the winters would have been relatively milder than farther away from the ice. Taking into account surface roughness, a role as microbiotic refugia may be postulated for these zones, particularly as it relates to the lee side of rocks.

Coreless Winters in Polar Regions

Poleward from a latitude of 65° there are stations in areas of permanent ice cover at elevations and distances from the coast ranging through at least three orders of magnitude, and complex combinations involving differences in firn and ice types, thickness, and underlying media, should be expected to obscure potentially obvious relationships. Nevertheless, a study (in progress) of the latitudinal distribution of amplitude ratios from thirty-two Arctic and Antarctic stations in ice-covered areas indicates that some explanations of features already discussed for the ice-free locations apply to the ice-covered areas as well.

The amplitude ratios of stations established in grounded ice-sheets, and in ice-shelves and ice-islands, have a distribution similar to those from ice-free areas, this is to say there is a trend of increasing ratios with increasing latitude, and Lettau's proposal relating the amplitude ratios of temperature and potential insolation in general is applicable here; the exceptions appear to be some Arctic stations established in the pack-ice.

The amplitude ratios domain of Arctic stations in ice-covered areas is smaller than that of Antarctic stations in the ice-sheet. Of seventy-five stations located in ice-free and ice-covered areas, only seven stations indicate domain overlap. The overlap is sufficiently restricted that there need be no modification of the conclusions, namely that the larger ratio domain in Antarctica is the result of a greater advection of heat and of stronger upper and surface inversions.

Data Limitations

In the Arctic the temperature records of twenty-seven stations meet the guidelines stated in the discussion of selective criteria. The noticeable asymmetry of their distribution relative to the pole, which excludes much of the Norwegian and Barents seas, and the south-western Kara Sea, is understandable because of the intense warm air advection east of the Icelandic trough, particularly from fall through spring (detailed mean pressure distributions for the mid-troposphere are found in Lahey and others, 1958a; the less important surface distributions are found in Lahey and others, 1958b; and in Prik, 1959). In addition, this is the same sector where oceanic advection of energy into the Arctic basin is at a maximum (Timofeyev, 1964; Panov and Shpaikher, 1964).

The major handicap to an otherwise adequate distribution of the stations is their coastal location. Their records are not representative of phenomena at even relatively short distances inland, which is an important limitation in the case of Arctic ice-free barrens because they extend inland for considerable distances.

In the Antarctic, the temperature guidelines correspond to locations in the southern oceans. The records of sixteen stations established in ice-free areas — including a few in areas that may be considered representative of ice-free conditions, such as Mawson, Mirny, and Dumont d'Urville — show that except for stations in the South American sector, the mean temperature for the warmest month is below freezing. The distribution of stations is satisfactory as a sample of the two principal regimes inferred for the coastal region, that is to say near the margin of the ice-sheet and along the "open" western coast of the Antarctic Peninsula. However, the ice-free areas associated with the inland section of the Transantarctic Mountains (which reach a latitude of 86°S, a latitude 3° higher than Peary Land in Greenland), the mountain ranges in Marie Byrd, Ellsworth, and Queen Maud lands, and the "closed" eastern coast of the Antarctic Peninsula, are not covered by the sample. This is unfortunate because their climatic regime is considerably different from those in the sampled areas.

The data from many of the stations selected comprise a relatively short series for purposes of climatological analysis and are barely adequate for the discussion of annual, seasonal, and monthly means. This limitation applies in particular to the Antarctic stations, where in most cases it was possible to use only five- to ten-year series; shorter series available from ice-free areas, such as those where Oazis (66°18'S, 100°43'E) and Vanda (approximately at 77°35'S, 162°E) stations are located, were excluded from the sampling.

The ecosystems of high latitude barrens are simple; the microbiota and thin soils, if any, have an insignificant role as modifiers of specific energy and moisture fluxes which are then very dependent on small changes of slope angle and orientation. For example, Zakharova (1959) shows that in spring and fall, at a latitude of approximately 70°, a 15°-slope would result in $\pm$ 50% departures from the total radiation input on a horizontal surface, the sign depending on northern or southern exposure. The difference in direct radiation input from that on a horizontal surface is relatively easy to estimate, but the difference in diffuse radiation input is not (Belyaeva, 1961; and Kondrat'ev and Monolova, 1961; cited in Gol'tsberg, 1967). Localized departures of 50% in energy input in spring and fall result in differences of approximately one month in the duration of the snow cover and of the short-term freezing and thawing alternation; they also result in differences of the order of decimeters in the seasonal penetration of the 0° Celsius isotherm, and in the order of 10° Celsius in the maximum temperatures reached by rock surfaces. These variables, among others, determine slope stability, the rate of chemical weathering, and variations in soil moisture (for examples of their significance see: Black and Berg, 1963; Gannutz, 1971; Kelly and Zumberge, 1961; Rudolph, 1966).

In summary, interpretations of particular microclimates based on station data are meaningless unless local adjustments are made for differences in slope angle and orientation during daylight periods. This could be critical in a discussion of the attenuation of winter temperature in localities at latitudes lower than, say, 75°.

II. Precipitation in Arctic and Antarctic Coastal Barrens

Precipitation is one of the principal variables used to infer energy and moisture fluxes at the surface, and therefore of importance in understanding climatological, biological, and geomorphological phenomena. Discrete and sample-mean values of precipitation gauge-data for the Arctic and Antarctic ice-free barrens are available but usually unreliable because of nonsystematic errors varying normally from −50% to +100%. Beyond considerations of instrument design, instrument-induced turbulence, precipitation type (crystals, flakes), status

of surrounding snow cover, and windspeed, it may be stated that gauge-data values in ice-free and firn-covered areas are smaller and larger, respectively, than the probable precipitation rates determined by other methods in pilot studies (Aver'ianov, 1963; Black, 1954; Rusin, 1961).

In the ice-free barrens it is possible to estimate annual precipitation values and the magnitude of their total variability (areal plus temporal) using glaciological data from adjacent glaciated areas. Annual variability

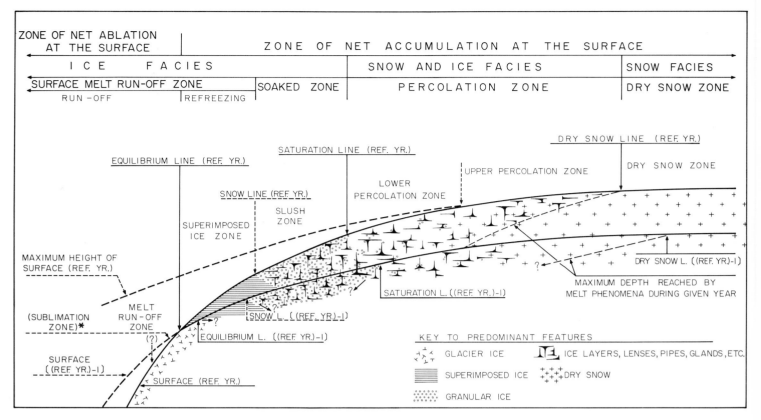

Fig. 1.11   Snow and ice facies [compiled and modified from Benson (1962) and Müller (1962, 1963); for a discussion of facies distribution in Greenland and Antarctica refer to Benson (1962) and Giovinetto (1964a)].

terms expressed as variation coefficients are parameters which can be applied to local determinations of mean annual precipitation in ice-free areas — regardless of the method used in the determinations — reducing inherent research problems presented by the short series common in polar and subpolar regions, where many stations are occupied for a limited time.

Precipitation and Accumulation

In firn areas where surface roughness and slope angle are small, the net surface accumulation or balance (b_n) is considered an approximation of precipitation (Swithinbank, 1960). In large glacier areas above and/or within the saturation line, particularly if the lower percolation zone is excluded (fig. 1.11), the 12-month precipitation (P) is approximated by integrating the specific balance ($\dot{b}$). In and above the upper percolation zone, $\dot{b}$ is the difference between specific accumulation $\dot{c}$ (the summation of precipitation, condensation, vapor to solid sublimation, and drifting snow deposition) and ablation $\dot{a}$ (the summation of evaporation, solid to vapor sublimation, and snow deflation):

$$P \sim b_n = \int_{t_0}^{t_{10-14}} \dot{b}.dt$$

where t_0 and t_{10-14} are respectively the beginning and end of a hydrological balance year which in stratigraphic and isotope-ratio methods of obtaining b_n, evaluated by Bull (1971), has normally a duration of between 10 and 14 months.

In the polar regions, orographic uplift, positive vertical motion in cyclonic circulation systems, and advective cooling, are the main causes of precipitation. Consequently in topographic cross-sections extending through ice-free barrens and for relatively short distances into glaciated areas, the precipitation rate should be larger in the latter. However, a cursory estimate of the mean annual precipitation range which would include most of the Arctic and Antarctic ice-free barrens should suffice for purposes of sample selection in estimates of variation coefficients.

The latest comprehensive reports on the distribution of mean net balance ($\bar{b}_n$) in the Greenland and Antarctic ice-sheets (Benson, 1962; Bull, 1971), and winter snow accumulation in the central Arctic pack-ice (Loshchilov, 1964), indicate that a large part of the polar ice-free areas receives a water equivalent precipitation of between 100 mm yr^{-1} and 500 mm yr^{-1} (in estimates of b_n, millimeters are not significant units but are used here because of later comparisons with low latitude precipitation series given in millimeters). Setting sampling limits for $\bar{b}_n$ on the basis of these rates and for the number of annual values N in each series at ≥ 20, a total of twelve Arctic and Antarctic stations meet the requirements (table 1.5; figs. 1.12 and 1.13); all are located in or above the upper percolation zone and near ice termini.

In the twelve series, $\bar{b}_n$ ranges from 127 to 478 mm yr^{-1}, and the frequency distributions are approximately normal, except for Little America V where the very long series shows, as expected, a marked positive skewness. It should be noted that stations 6 to 8 and 11 and 12 are located in ice-shelves near the termini, where b_n varies by as much as 20% within 1 km from the barrier (see Swithinbank, 1960). This phenomenon does not greatly affect the discussions of variability terms which follow.

Areal and Temporal Variabilities

The variation coefficient for a particular "high" latitude station $C_h = S_h.\bar{b}_n^{-1}$ is estimated by computing the standard deviation S_h, which represents the total variability at a particular station in the polar ice-free barrens, V_h. These are here proposed to relate to the areal (V_{ah}) and temporal (V_{th}) variabilities as follows:

$$S_h \equiv V_h = \sqrt{V_{ah}^2 + V_{th}^2}.$$

The term V_{ah} is estimated for areas of dry loose snow cover typical of polar climates by computing the standard deviation of net balance values obtained at individual stakes (b_{nj}) in particular networks and for particular balance years. In the upper percolation zone or

above, V_{ah} is primarily dependent on windspeed and secondarily on precipitation and/or drifting snow availability. In the snow-facies area mentioned, and near the ice terminus, V_{ah} is approximately 21 mm yr^{-1} (table 1.6), an estimate which agrees well with a previous estimate of 26 mm yr^{-1} based on data from twelve inland and coastal Antarctic stations — including the four coastal stations listed in table 1.6 (Giovinetto, 1964b). The data referred to, obtained at fifteen networks and consisting of nineteen annual samples, indicate that for $\bar{b}_n$ with a range of >8 mm yr^{-1} and <368 mm yr^{-1} there is no significant change of V_{ah}. This study, since its publication in 1964, has been expanded to include analysis of unpublished stake network data collected by W. Long, M. Hochstein, C. Roberts, M. Sponholz, R. Dingle, and M. Kuhn.

Annual mean windspeed at the three stations listed in table 1.6 ranges from 4.8 m sec^{-1} to 7.4 m sec^{-1}, which is to say windspeed values of a magnitude common in the ice-free barrens (see climatic summaries in Orvig, 1970); therefore $V_{ah} \approx 21$ mm yr^{-1} is extrapolated for use in the barrens. The extrapolation must be made with caution, particularly concerning localized studies, because snow deposition in rock-strewn surfaces varies by large factors where the snow depth equivalent of b_n is not much larger than the surface roughness.

The difference between V_h and V_{ah} (fig. 1.14) shows that C_h decreases from 0.30 at 100 mm yr^{-1} to 0.25 at 500 mm yr^{-1} and that the proportionality $100V_{th}.\bar{b}_n^{-1}$ approximates 23% throughout the same range of $\bar{b}_n$. Other relationships should be postulated for the rela-

TABLE 1.5

**Annual Mean and Total Variability of Net Balance
in High-Latitude Stations Near Ice Termini**

	Station	Location	Elevation (m)	N	$b_n \sim P$ (mm yr^{-1})	$S_h \equiv V_{th}$ (mm yr^{-1})	Source
1	Upper Ice (Sta. II)	79°56'N 091°54'W	1920	41	374	110	Müller, 1966
2	Lake Hazen	82°08'N 073°52'W	1805	20	127	35	Hattersley-Smith, 1963
3	Site 2	77°—'N 056°—'W	1992	70	405	84	Bader, 1961
4	Station 2-0	77°15'N 062°22'W	1704	22	214	46	Benson, 1962
5	Sukkertoppen (combined series)	66°01'N 015°52'W	1200	20	332	97	Holland, 1961 Rundle, 1962
6	Maudheim	71°03'S 010°56'W	37	(17)	364	96	Schytt, 1960
7	Norway	70°30'S 002°32'W	55	20	478	121	Lunde, 1961
8	Roi Baudouin	70°26'S 024°19'E	40	25	350	95	Gonfiantini and others, 1963
9	Wilkes S-2	66°30'S 112°20'E	1176	174	133	46	Cameron and others, 1959
10	McMurdo Ice Shelf	77°51'S 167°00'E	22	46	174	49	Stuart and Bull, 1963
11	Camp Michigan (Trough)	78°34'S 163°57'W	28	46	224	48	Giovinetto, in Zumberge and others, 1960
12	Little America V	78°11'S 162°10'W	42	104	221	64	Gow, 1963

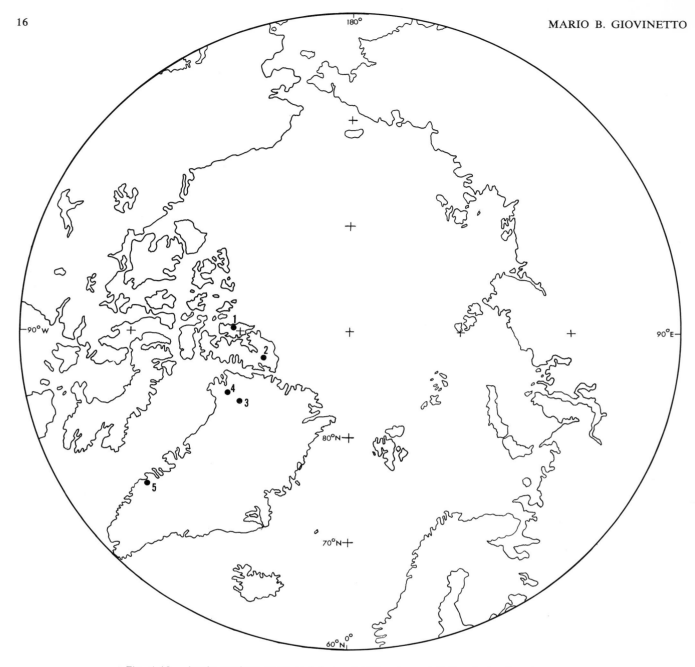

Fig. 1.12.   Arctic stations used to infer variability of precipitation in ice-free barrens.
Stations are: 1, Upper Ice (sta. 11); 2, Lake Hazen; 3, Site 2; 4, Station 2–0; 5, Sukkertoppen combined series. See table 1.5 for additional data.

TABLE 1.6

Annual Areal Variability of Net Balance Near Ice Termini

Station	Location	Elevation (m)	Stakes (no.)	b_{nj} (mm yr^{-1})	V_{ah} (mm yr^{-1})	$t_0 - t_{10-14}$ (days)	Source *
Station 100	78°02′S 154°22′E	2282	32	14	22	412	1
			32	17	14	302	2
Halley Bay	75°36′S 026°41′W	35	9	319	23	363	3
			9	355	19	358	3
Norway	70°30′S 002°32′W	55	37	332	25	315	4
Little America V	78°11′S 162°10′W	42	16	367	23	374	5

* Sources: 1. A. P. Crary, personal communication; 2. Stuart and Heine, 1961;
3. McDowall, 1960 and personal communication; 4. Lunde, 1961; 5. Crary, 1961.

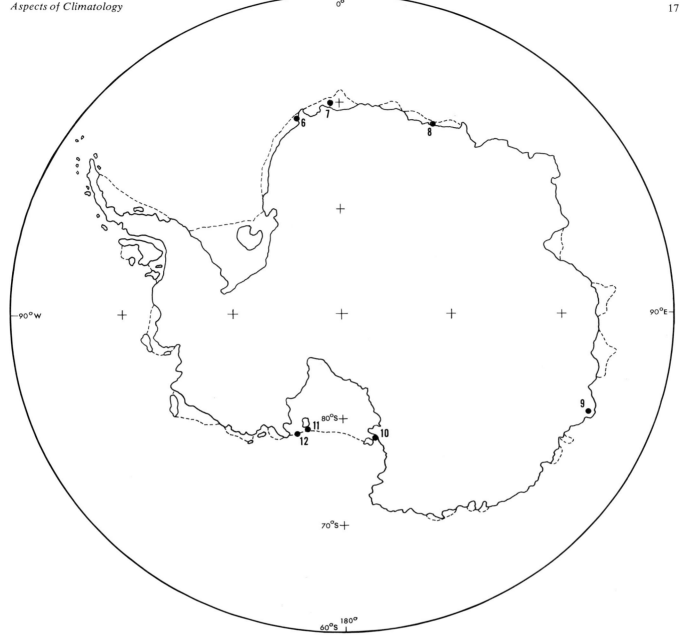

Fig. 1.13. Antarctic stations used to infer the variability of precipitation in ice-free barrens. Stations are: 6, Maudheim; 7, Norway; 8, Roi Baudouin; 9, Wilkes S–2; 10, McMurdo Ice Shelf; 11, Camp Michigan (Trough); 12, Little America V. See table 1.5 for additional data.

tively small areas where $\bar{b}_n$ < 100 mm yr^{-1}, not discussed here.

Rates of precipitation in the order of 100 mm yr^{-1} correspond to arid and semiarid areas of lower latitudes. Considering the sample requirements specified for the polar stations, northern Africa and the Middle East form a continuous area where stations at the coast or near it are found at comparable elevations and in a reasonable number (table 1.7, fig. 1.15). Moreover, in the sampled area, aridity induced by large-scale interaction between features of the circulation and topography may be ignored — this in the context of induced aridity, for example, leeward of the Rockies and the Andes. It should be noted that the following comparisons are not vitally hampered by the present use of calendar year precipitation values.

In analogy with the polar series, in the "low" latitude series,

$$S_l \equiv V_l = \sqrt{V_{al}^2 + V_{tl}^2}$$

An estimate of V_{al} is made by selecting station groups made up of five or more stations located at distances of ≤ 10 km from each other and computing the standard deviation of precipitation values in each station P_j for particular groups and calendar years (table 1.8; fig. 1.16). This estimate is far from ideal and probably

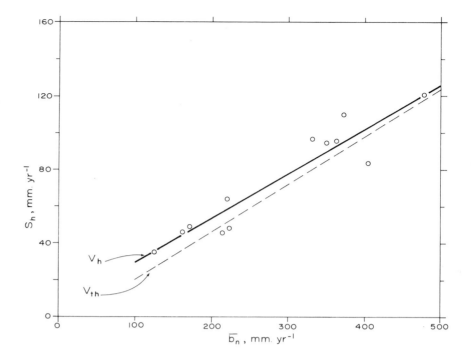

Fig. 1.14. Variability terms of surface balance b_n in glaciated areas near termini, and representative of precipitation phenomena in the coastal ice-free barrens.

TABLE 1.7

Annual Mean & Total Variability of Precipitation in Low-Latitude Arid & Semiarid Coastal Stations

Station	Location	Elevation (m)	N	P (mm yr^{-1})	$S_l \equiv V_{tl}$ (mm yr^{-1})
1 Casablanca	33°34'N 007°40'W	58	27	405	98
2 Marrakech	31°37'N 008°02'W	466	27	242	70
3 Oran	35°38'N 000°37'W	99	25	400	150
4 Biskra	34°48'N 005°44'E	81	26	127	59
5 Alexandria	31°12'N 029°57'E	7	52	190	63
6 Amman	31°57'N 035°57'E	766	38	273	89
7 Rutbah	33°02'N 040°17'E	615	29	121	51
8 Nasiriya	31°01'N 046°14'E	3	(19)	118	51
9 Port Sudan	19°35'N 037°13'E	3	49	100	76
10 Massaua	15°40'N 039°19'E	18	26	198	109
11 Kassala	15°28'N 036°24'E	501	58	325	80
12 Djibouti	11°34'N 043°00'E	3	37	141	78
13 Hargeisa	09°20'N 043°57'E	1370	35	432	118
14 Burao	09°20'N 045°45'E	1040	31	183	80
15 Erigavo	10°37'N 047°22'E	1730	(19)	337	81
16 Belet Uen	04°45'N 045°10'E	173	(19)	184	73
17 Mogadiscio	02°02'N 045°21'E	10	23	371	125
18 Tsavo	03°00'S 038°28'E	460	25	344	130

close to a maximum. A mean closest-neighbor distance between stations of ~3 km for all groups is too large. The density and overall area coverage of gauge networks is less critical in estimates of the areal variability for annual means than for precipitation values of single events or for monthly means, but the elevation differences are not taken into account (although topographic homogeneity within each group was one of the selection criteria). Furthermore, and as implied earlier, the meteorological phenomena associated with small precipitation rates in western North America are not identical with those in northern Africa and the Middle East. Nevertheless a first approximation to low latitude variability terms is made by subtracting V_{al} from V_l (fig. 1.17), obtaining a relative temporal variability $100V_{tl}.\bar{P}^{-1}$ decrease from 57% at 100 mm yr^{-1} to 25% at 500 mm yr^{-1}, which is compatible with the variation coefficient decrease from 0.59 to 0.27, respectively, and for the same increment of $\bar{P}$.

The small sample sizes require a consideration of variance of terms in straight-line equations computed for sample groups and in those probable for their corresponding populations. On this basis the comparisons of least-square fits are inconclusive. However, F-distribution tests in a study including more than one hundred b_n and P series (the latter being for hydrological, not calendar years) show that the difference between $V_h(\bar{b}_n)$ and $V_l(\bar{P})$ is significant and explained by contrasting advective and convective phenomena (Giovinetto, in preparation).

The preceding estimates and comparisons are based principally on two premises: (1) The net surface balance rates in glaciated areas, as qualified, may be equated with precipitation rates. (2) The total varia-

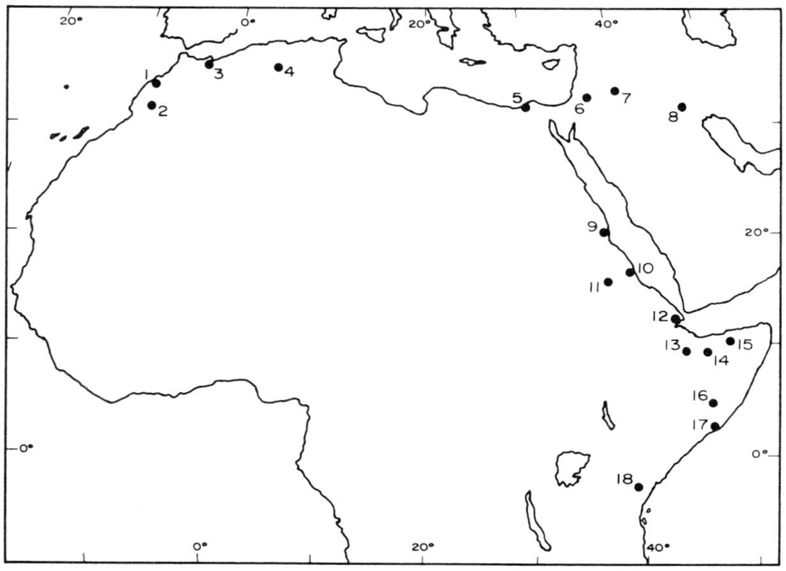

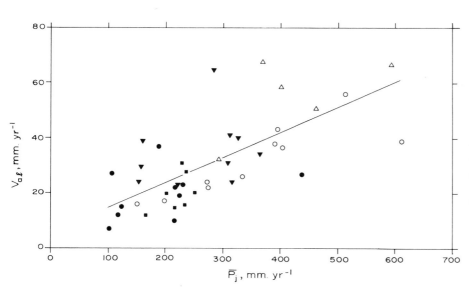

Fig. 1.15. Low-and middle-latitude stations in northern Africa and the Middle East selected for a comparison of precipitation variability terms with Arctic and Antarctic stations. See table 1.7 for identification of stations.

Fig. 1.16. An approximation to the areal variability of precipitation in western North America. Key stations for each station group are Phoenix, Arizona (closed circles); Tucson, Arizona (closed triangles); Brea City, California (open circles); Eastonville, Colorado (open triangles); and Burley, Idaho (closed squares).

TABLE 1.8

Areal Variability of Precipitation in Middle-Latitude Arid & Semiarid Stations*

Key Station		Group Range Lat.	Group Range Long.	Elev.	Stations in Group (no.)	Precip. Years (no.)	Group Range P_j (mm yr^{-1})	Group Range V_{al} (mm yr^{-1})
Phoenix, Arizona								
	from	30°23′N	111°52′W	330m	9	10	102	7
	to	30°30′N	112°04′W	373m			437	37
Tucson, Arizona								
	from	32°12′N	110°49′W	680m	7	10	152	23
	to	32°20′N	111°07′W	796m			363	64
Brea City, California								
	from	33°53′N	117°47′W	101m	15	10	150	16
	to	34°00′N	117°55′W	495m			612	56
Eastonville, Colorado								
	from	39°01′N	104°26′W	1936m	13	5	290	32
	to	39°21′N	104°44′W	2357m			591	68
Burley, Idaho								
	from	42°32′N	113°41′W	1262m	5	7	167	12
	to	42°37′N	113°48′W	1284m			250	28

*A summary from current research (Giovinetto, in preparation)

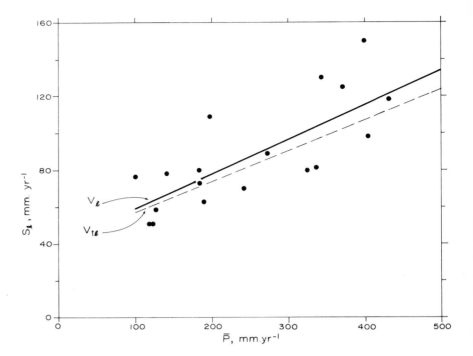

Fig. 1.17. Precipitation variability terms in arid and semiarid locations at or near the coast in northern Africa and the Middle East.

bility of precipitation is the summation of areal and temporal variability terms which can be treated as standard errors.

The findings, some not conclusive, are summarized as follows: (i) The precipitation rates in ice-free barrens near the coast range between 100 mm yr^{-1} and 500 mm yr^{-1} (water equivalent). (ii) The total variability of precipitation, expressed as a variation coefficient, is smaller in the polar barrens (0.25–0.30) than in arid and semiarid coastal areas at lower latitudes (0.27–0.59). (iii) The areal variability in the polar barrens is approximately 21 mm yr^{-1} and does not change with varying precipitation rates; this is in contrast with the relationship hypothesized for the lower latitudes, where the term increases with precipitation. (iv) The temporal variability in the polar barrens amounts to approximately 23% of the mean annual precipitation. This is also in contrast with the relationship hypothesized for the lower latitudes, where the term is of similar magnitude in semiarid locations (20%–30%), increasing by a factor of 2 in the arid locations (40%–60%).

Acknowledgments

It is a pleasure to acknowledge the helpful review of the manuscript for this chapter by Werner Schwerdtfeger, Department of Meteorology, University of Wisconsin at Madison. While the research was in progress, Schwerdtfeger provided some of the temperature series and publications that were difficult to obtain at Berkeley.

For Section I of this chapter, the computer programming by Robert Fromer, Environmental Protection Agency, and data handling by Linda Gummerson, California Aero-Topo Inc., are also gratefully acknowledged.

For Section II of this chapter, J. Monteverdi and A. Morgan helped with the computations and graphics. Their assistance is gratefully appreciated.

BIBLIOGRAPHY

Alt, J., P. Astapenko, and N. J. Ropar, Jr.
    1959   Some aspects of the Antarctic atmospheric circulation in 1958. IGY General Report Series, no. 4, IGY World Data Center A, Washington. 113 pp.
Aver'ianov, V. G.
    1963   On the methods of precipitation measurements in the Central Antarctica. Akademiia Dokladay, USSR, Glaciology Research Section 9 of the International Geophysical Year Program (in English), pp. 195–97.
Bader, H.
    1961   The Greenland ice sheet. United States Army Corps of Engineers Cold Regions Research and Engineering Laboratory. I–B2, 18 pp.

Benson, C. S.
    1962   Stratigraphic studies in the snow and firn of the Greenland ice sheet. United States Army Corps of Engineers Snow, Ice and Permafrost Research Establishment, Research Report 70. 93 pp.
Benton, G. S.
    1954   Comments on the heat balance of the northern hemisphere. Journal of Meteorology 11: 517–18.
Black, R. F.
    1954   Precipitation at Barrow, Alaska, greater than recorded. Transactions, American Geophysical Union 35 (2): 203–07.
Black, R. F., and T. E. Berg
    1963   Hydrothermal regimen of patterned ground, Victoria Land, Antarctica. International Association

of Scientific Hydrology, Publication 61, pp. 121–27.

Budyko, M. I.
1956 Heat balance of the earth's surface. Gidrometeorologicheskoe Izdatel'stvo, Leningrad. 255 pp.

Bull, C.
1971 Snow accumulation in Antarctica. *In* Research in the Antarctic, L. O. Quam (ed.), American Association for the Advancement of Science, pp. 367–421.

Cameron, R., O. H. Løken, and J. R. T. Molholm
1959 Wilkes Station glaciological data. Ohio State University Research Foundation, Report 825–1, 170 pp.

Crary, A. P.
1961 Glaciological studies at Little America Station, Antarctica, 1957 and 1958. 5, American Geographical Society, International Geophysical Year Glaciological Report, 197 pp.

Fletcher, J. O.
1965 Heat budget of the Arctic Basin and its relation to climate. Rand Corporation, R-444-PR, Santa Monica. 179 pp.
1969 Ice extent on the southern ocean and its relation to world climate. Rand Corporation, RM-5793-NSF, Santa Monica. 108 pp.

Gabites, J. F.
1960 Heat balance of the Antarctic through the year. Proceedings of the Symposium in Antarctic Meteorology, Melbourne, pp. 370–77.

Gannutz, T. P.
1971 Ecodynamics of Lichen Communities in Antarctica. *In* Research in the Antarctic, L. O. Quam (ed.), American Association for the Advancement of Science, pp. 213–26.

Giovinetto, M. B.
1964a Distribution of diagenetic snow facies in Antarctica and in Greenland. Arctic 17 (1): 32–40.
1964b The drainage systems of Antarctica: accumulation American Geophysical Union, Antarctic Research Series, vol. 2, Antarctic snow and ice studies, pp. 127–55.
In preparation. The variation coefficient of precipitation in arid and semi-arid areas at different latitudes.

Gol'tsberg, I. A. (ed.)
1967 Microclimate of the USSR. Gidrometeorologicheskoe Izdatel'stvo, Leningrad. Israel Program for Scientific Translations, Jerusalem, 1969. 235 pp.

Gonfiantini, R., V. Togliatti, W. DeBrevek, E. Picciotto, and E. Tongiorgi
1963 Snow stratigraphy and oxygen isotope variations in the glaciological pit of King Baudouin Station, Queen Maud Land, Antarctica. Journal of Geophysical Research 68 (13): 3791–98.

Gow, A. J.
1963 The inner structure of the Ross Ice Shelf at Little America V. as revealed by deep core drilling. International Association of Scientific Hydrology, Pub. 61, pp. 272–84.

Hattersley-Smith, G.
1963 Climatic inferences from firn studies in northern Ellsmere Island. Geografiska Annaler 45 (2–3): 139–51.

Holland, M.
1961 Glaciological observations around Mount Atter, West Greenland. Journal of Glaciology 3 (29): 804–12.

Holopainen, E. O.
1965 On the role of mean meridional circulations in the energy balance of the atmosphere. Tellus 17: 285–94.

Kelly, W. C., and J. H. Zumberge
1961 Weathering of a quartz diorite at Marble Point, McMurdo Sound, Antarctica. Journal of Geology 69: 433–46.

Lahey, J. F., R. A. Bryson, E. W. Wahl, L. H. Horn, and V. D. Henderson
1958a Atlas of 500-mb wind characteristics for the Northern Hemisphere. University of Wisconsin Press, Madison. 99 pp.

Lahey, J. F., R. A. Bryson, and E. W. Wahl
1958b Atlas of five-day normal sea-level pressure charts for the Northern Hemisphere. University of Wisconsin Press, Madison. 76 pp.

Lettau, H.
1966 A case study of katabatic flow on the south polar plateau. *In* Studies in Antarctic Meteorology, Antarctic Research Series, vol. 9, M. J. Rubin (ed.), American Geophysical Union, Washington, pp. 1–11.
1971 Antarctic atmosphere as a test tube for meteorological theories. *In* Research in the Antarctic, L. O. Quam (ed.), American Association for the Advancement of Science, pp. 443–75.

Liljequist, G. H.
1956 Energy exchange of an Antarctic snow field. Norwegian-British-Swedish Expedition 1949–1952, Scientific Results, vol. 2, p. 1, Norsk Polarinstituut, Oslo.

List, R. J. (ed.)
1958 Smithsonian Meteorological Tables. Smithsonian Institution, Washington. 418 pp.

Loewe, F.
1954 Beiträge zur Kenntnis des Antarktis. Erkunde 8 (1): 1–15.
1969 On the coreless winters of the polar regions. Gerlands Beiträge zur Geophysic 78 (6), Akademische Verlagsgesellschaft Geest und Portig K.–G., 701 Leipzig, pp. 453–576.

Loshchilov, V. S.
1964 Snow cover on the ice of the central Arctic. Problemy Arktiki, USSR (in English) 17: 36–45.

Lunde, T.
1961 On the snow accumulation in Dronning Maud Land. Norsk Polarinstitutt, pub. 123, 48 pp.

MacDowall, J.
1960 Some observations at Halley Bay in seismology, glaciology, and meteorology. Proceedings of the Royal Society, London, A, 246, pp. 145–244.

Malkus, J. S.
1962 Large-scale interactions. *In* The Sea, M. N. Hill (ed.), vol. 1, Wiley, New York, pp. 88–294.

Mather, K. B., and G. S. Miller
1967 Notes on topographic factors affecting the surface wind in Antarctica, with special reference to katabatic winds. University of Alaska Technical Report UAG–R–189, College, 125 pp.

Müller, F.
1962 Zonation in the accumulation area of the glaciers of Axel Heiberg Island, NWT, Canada. Journal of Glaciology 4: 302–18.
1963 An Arctic research expedition and its reliance on large-scale maps. Canadian Surveyor 17: 96–112.
1966 Evidence of climatic fluctuations on Axel Heiberg Island, Canadian Arctic Archipelago. *In* Proceed-

Müller, F. *(continued)*
    ings of the Symposium on the Arctic Heat Budget
    and Atmospheric Circulation, J. O. Fletcher (ed.),
    Rand Corporation, RM–5233–NSF, pp. 137–56.
Orvig, S. (ed.)
    1970   Climates of the Polar Regions. World Survey of
           Climatology, vol. 14. Elsevier Publishing Co.,
           370 pp.
Palmén, E., and C. W. Newton
    1969   Atmospheric Circulation Systems. Academic
           Press, New York. 603 pp.
Panov, V. V., and A. O. Shpaikher
    1964   Influence of Atlantic waters on some features of
           the hydrology of the Arctic Basin and adjacent
           seas. Deep Sea Research 11 (2): 275–285.
Prik, Z. M.
    1959   Mean position of surface pressure and tempera-
           ture distribution in the Arctic. Tr. Arkticheskogo
           Nauchn.-Issled. Inst. 217, pp. 5–34.
Putnins, P.
    1970   The climate Greenland. *In* The Climate of the
           Polar Regions, World Survey of Climatology,
           vol. 14, S. Orvig (ed.), Elsevier Publishing Co.,
           New York, pp. 3–128.
Rubin, M. J.
    1962   Atmospheric advection and the Antarctic mass
           and heat budget. Antarctic Research, Geophysical
           Monograph 7, American Geophysical Union,
           Washington, pp. 149–59.
Rudolph, E. D.
    1966   Terrestrial vegetation of Antarctica: Past and
           present studies. *In* Antarctic Soils and Soil Form-
           ing Processes, Antarctic Research Series 8, J. C.
           F. Tedrow (ed.), American Geophysical Union,
           pp. 109–24.
Rundle, A. S.
    1965   Glaciological investigations on Sukkertoppen Ice
           Cap, Southwest Greenland, Summer 1964. Ohio
           State University Research Foundation, Institute
           of Polar Studies Report no. 14, 11 pp.
Rusin, N. P.
    1961   Meteorological and radiational regime of Ant-
           arctica. Gidrometeorologicheskoe Izdatel'stvo,
           Leningrad. Israel Program for Scientific Transla-
           tions, Jerusalem, 1964. 355 pp.
Schwerdtfeger, W.
    1970   The climate of the Antarctic. *In* Climates of the
           Polar Regions, World Survey of Climatology,
           vol. 14, S. Orvig (ed.), Elsevier Publishing Co.,
           New York. pp. 253–55.

Schytt, V.
    1960   Glaciology, 2, Norwegian-British-Swedish Ant-
           arctic Expedition, 1949–52, Scientific Results, vol.
           4. Norsk Polarinstitutt, 179 pp.
Stuart, A. W., and C. Bull
    1963   Glaciological observations on the Ross Ice Shelf
           near Scott Base, Antarctica. Journal of Glaciol-
           ogy 4 (34): 399–414.
Stuart, A. W., and A. J. Heine
    1961   Glaciology, Victoria Land Traverse, 1957–60.
           Ohio State University Research Foundation,
           Report 968-1, 93 pp.
Swithinbank, C. M.
    1960   Glaciology, 2, Norwegian-British-Swedish Ant-
           arctic Expedition, 1949–52, Scientific Results,
           vol. 3, Norsk Polarinstitutt, 158 pp.
Timofeyev, V. T.
    1964   Interaction of waters from the Arctic Ocean with
           those from the Atlantic and Pacific. Deep Sea
           Research 11 (2): 265–74.
Van Loon, H., J. J. Taljaard, R. L. Jenne, and
H. L. Crutcher
    1971   Climate of the upper air: southern hemisphere:
           volume 2, Zonal geostrophic winds. National
           Center for Atmospheric Research, Boulder.
VonderHaar, T.
    1968   Variations of the Earth's radiation budget.
           Department of Meteorology, University of Wis-
           consin Research Report, Madison. 118 pp.
Vowinckel, E., and S. Orvig
    1970   The climate of the north polar basin. *In* Climates
           of the Polar Regions. World Survey of Climatol-
           ogy, vol. 14, S. Orvig (ed.), Elsevier Publishing
           Company, New York, pp. 129–252.
    1971   Synoptic heat budgets at three polar stations.
           Journal of Applied Meteorology 10: 387–96.
Weyant, W. S.
    1966   The Antarctic Atmosphere: Climatology of the
           troposphere and lower stratosphere. Antarctic
           Map Folio Series, Folio 4, American Geographi-
           cal Society, New York.
Zakharova, A. F.
    1959   Radiation regime of north and south slopes of
           different inclinations at various latitudes.
           Uchenye zapiski Leningradskogo Gosudarstven-
           nogo Universiteta, no. 269, Seriya Geografiches-
           kaya, no. 13, Klimatologiya, Izdatel'stvo Lenin-
           gradskogo Gosudarstvennogo Universiteta.
Zumberge, J. H., M. Giovinetto, R. Kehle, and J. Reid
    1960   Deformation of the Ross Ice Shelf near the Bay
           of Whales, Antarctica, American Geographical
           Society, International Geophysical Year Glaciol-
           ogical Report, ser. 3, 148 pp.

CHAPTER 2

A CLIMATOLOGICAL ANALYSIS OF NORTH POLAR DESERT AREAS

Michael J. Bovis and Roger G. Barry

Department of Geography and Institute of Arctic and Alpine Research, University of Colorado, Boulder

Polar deserts have long been identified in high northern latitudes by botanists and soil scientists (Alexandrova, 1960; Tedrow, 1966; and Charlier, 1969). The maps of Charlier as well as those of Dolgin (1970) and Fillipov (1964) depict polar and rock desert as a particular soil or cover-type category, but little attention has been given to its climatological definition. Systems of climatological classification do not include polar desert as a specific type (Blüthgen, 1966), while the review of polar climates by Orvig (1970) makes only passing reference to its occurrence in northern Greenland.

Arctic desert has been defined as "any area in the high latitudes dominated by bare rocks, ice or snow and having a sparse vegetation and low annual rainfall" (Arctic, Desert, Tropic Information Center, 1955).

In a discussion of arctic deserts, Bird (1967) states: "Absence of vegetation is the main characteristic of these areas although sometimes this is more apparent than real. Arctic deserts dominate high arctic areas, but become progressively more restricted farther south. In the middle and southern arctic they are found on uplands, where altitude and wind are major factors in their development. . . ."

Fristrup (1952) makes more reference to their climatological characteristics, noting the occurrence of high temperature, negligible precipitation and strong evaporation, due often to foehn winds, in summer, and the existence of extensive snowfree ground.

The intrinsic property of deserts is aridity, which even in north Greenland can be manifested by salt encrustations and small salt lakes. A primary objective of this analysis therefore is to examine means of estimating moisture balance in the Arctic. In view of the data limitations, however, an alternative strategy is also adopted. On the assumption that vegetation and soil development are more or less in equilibrium with present climate, the limits of polar desert as defined by soil and vegetation criteria are statistically tested with reference to climatic data at existing stations using discriminant analysis. We will discuss this approach first and at the same time outline the botanically and pedologically determined boundaries of deserts in high northern latitudes.

Analysis of Climatic Records

As a preliminary step in the climatological definition of polar deserts, maps in Charlier (1969) and Fillipov (1964) were examined for botanical and pedological limits of desert areas at high latitudes. Stations falling within areas thus classified as deserts were compared statistically with stations in desert-tundra transition zones, by means of a discriminant function for two populations. The program used was based on an algorithm in Krumbein and Graybill, 1965, ch. 14, and checked with data from this source. For some runs, a further check was made by using BMD 04M, from the BMD Series, University of California, Berkeley. The purpose of the analysis was to determine whether or not the two environmental types could be statistically separated on climatological grounds. An advantage of this approach is that no prior climatic definition of polar desert is required.

At each of forty-eight stations shown in figure 2.1, the following variables were determined: (1) mean annual temperature; (2) mean July temperature; (3) annual temperature range; (4) mean annual precipitation; (5) mean number of days with precipitation per annum; (6) summer precipitation (June, July and August); and (7) mean cloud cover. Data sources for the study were Petterssen, Jacobs, and Haynes (1956), Orvig (1970), and Meteorological Office (1958).

Charlier (1969, p. 1991) provides a map for soils of Arctic desert and desert-tundra transition areas. His map restricts polar desert areas to the Canadian archipelago, north of the Viscount Melville and Lancaster Sounds, and to ice-free areas in the extreme north of Greenland. Seven stations from these areas pedologically classified as deserts were compared with seventeen stations from areas mapped as desert-tundra transition. (Most discriminant function routines are flexible as regards number of cases in each population and require only that the same set of variables be determined on each population. In addition, for any population, the number of cases must be greater than or equal to the number of variables measured on that population.) The discriminant analysis of this map is given in table 2.1.

Desert stations are climatologically separable from

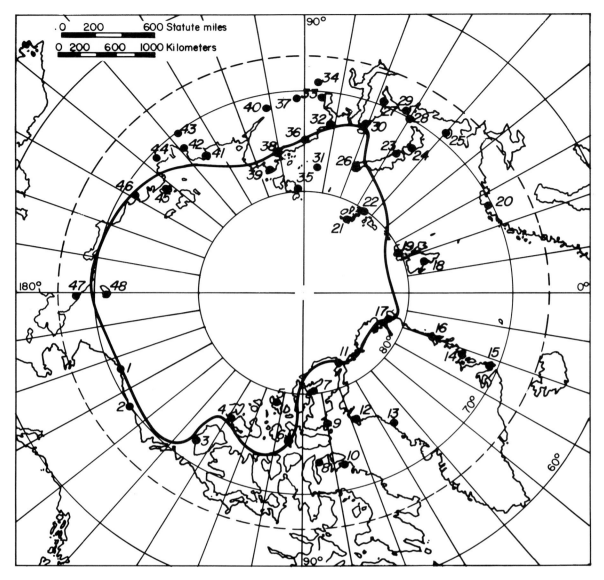

Fig. 2.1. Station locations whose climatic records were analyzed. The heavy line
indicates 40°F (4.4°C) July isotherm. The station numbers are identified as follows:

1. Barrow	13. Upernavik	25. Ostrov Kolguyev	37. Volochanka
2. Barter Island	14. Myggbukta	26. Mys Zhelaniya	38. Ust'ye R. Taimyry
3. Sachs Harbour	15. Scoresbysund	27. Mare Sale	39. Mys Chelyuskin
4. Mould Bay	16. Danmarkshavn	28. Ostrov Vaygach	40. Khatanga
5. Isachsen	17. Nord	29. Yugorskiy Shar	41. Ostrov Sagastyr
6. Resolute	18. Grønfjorden	30. Ostrov Belyy	42. Bukhta Tiksi
7. Eureka	19. Svalbard (Isfjord Radio)	31. Ostrov Uyedineniya	43. Bulun
8. Arctic Bay	20. Kistrand	32. Ostrov Dikson	44. Kazach'ye
9. Craig Harbour	21. Ostrov Rudolfa	33. Gyda Yamo	45. Mys Shalaurova
10. Pond Inlet	22. Bukhta Tikhaya	34. Ust'Yeniseyskiy Port	46. Russkoye Uste'ye
11. Alert	23. Matochkin Shar	35. Ostrov Domashniy	47. Mys Shmidta
12. Thule	24. Malyye Karmakuly	36. Mys Sterlegova	48. Ostrov Vrangelya

tundra transition stations at the 95 percent significance level. For each station in each of the two groups, a discriminant value has been computed. These values have been ranked to indicate the degree of overlap between the two groups. Table 2.2 shows this overlap to be slight.

Charlier (1969, p. 1992) also noted an approximate correspondence between the southern limit of the polar

desert zone and the 40°F (4.4°C) July isotherm. Desert areas according to this definition are limited in figure 2.1. The 40°F factor was tested by means of a discriminant function. Twenty-one stations having July temperatures less than or equal to 40°F were compared, in terms of their group membership, with twenty-one stations having July temperatures greater than 40°F (table 2.1). Here the computed F-value is significant at the 99 per-

TABLE 2.1

Discriminant Analysis of Charlier (1969) and Fillipov (1964) Maps

Factor Tested	Stations in Desert Group (no.)	Stations in Transition Group (no.)	F-value for Separation	F-value Computed	Significance Level (%)
1. Charlier (1969) map of desert and desert-tundra transition soils	7	17	3.51	5.87	95
2. Charlier (1969) factor of 40°F July temperature	21	21	3.36	8.41	99
3. Soils and-vegetation maps in Fillipov (1964)	20	20	3.37	4.96	95

TABLE 2.2

Population Rank of Two Groups of Stations on Charlier (1969) Map

Polar Desert Group (N = 7)		Desert-Tundra Transition Group (N = 17)	
Rank	Station	Rank	Station
1	Nord		
2	Isachsen		
3	Alert		
4	Mould Bay		
5	Resolute		
6	Eureka		
		7	Arctic Bay
8	Craig Harbour		
		9	Sachs Harbour
		10	Pond Inlet
		11	Ostrov Dikson
		12	Mys Sterlegova
		13	Ostrov Domashniy
		14	Mys Chelyuskin
		15	Ostrov Belyy
		16	Ostrov Rudolfa
		17	Mys Shalaurova
		18	Ostrov Vrangelya
		19	Malyye Karmakuly
		20	Bukhta Tikhaya
		21	Thule
		22	Matochkin Shar
		23	Ostrov Vaygach
		24	Mys Zhelaniya

TABLE 2.3

Population Rank of Stations According to Charlier (1969) Temperature Criterion

Polar Desert Group (N = 21) July temp ≤ 40°F		Desert-Tundra Transition Group (N = 21) July temp > 40°F	
Rank	Station	Rank	Station
1	Ostrov Rudolfa		
2	Ostrov Domashniy		
3	Ostrov Uyedineniya		
4	Alert		
5	Mys Chelyuskin		
6	Bukhta Tikhaya		
7	Mould Bay		
8	Isachsen		
9	Nord		
10	Mys Sterlegova		
11	Mys Zhelaniya		
12	Eureka		
13	Ostrov Vrangelya		
14	Mys Shmidta		
15	Mys Shalaurova		
16	Resolute		
17	Ust'ye R. Taimyry		
		18	Barter Island
19	Svalbard		
20	Ostrov Belyy		
		21	Craig Harbour
22	Danmarkshavn		
		23	Ostrov Sagastyr
		24	Ostrov Dikson
25	Barrow		
		26	Sachs Harbour
		27	Grønfjorden
		28	Arctic Bay
		29	Pond Inlet
		30	Kazach'ye
		31	Thule
		32	Matochkin Shar
		33	Upernavik
		34	Mare Sale
		35	Malyye Karmakuly
		36	Yugorskiy Shar
		37	Ostrov Vaygach
		38	Gyda Yamo
		39	Bukhta Tiksi
		40	Bulun
		41	Ostrov Kolguyev
		42	Russkoye Uste'ye

cent significance level, although table 2.3 shows some overlap between the two groups.

From the climatological standpoint, the ranking of stations in tables 2.2, 2.3, and 2.4 can be interpreted as representing an environmental continuum from extreme Arctic conditions through to less severe Subarctic conditions.

As a final stage in the preliminary analysis, soil and vegetation maps from Fillipov (1964) were analyzed. Twenty stations falling in desert vegetation and soils areas were compared with twenty from Arctic tundra areas. The F-value is significant at the 95 percent level (table 2.1) but is lower than the corresponding values for items 1 and 2 of table 2.1. This is reflected in a greater degree of overlap between desert and nondesert groups (table 2.4).

The three examples of this section demonstrate that deserts and nondeserts may be statistically separated when a discriminant function is used with the given input variables. The statistically significant results suggest that a more rigorous physical climatological approach to the definition of aridity in polar areas is worthwhile. This line of inquiry is pursued in the next section. However it should be noted that the polar desert and desert-tundra transition zones used in the discriminant analysis were defined on small-scale maps.

TABLE 2.4

Population Rank of Stations Shown on Fillipov (1964) Maps

Polar Desert Group (N = 20)		Desert-Tundra Transition Group (N = 20)	
Rank	Station	Rank	Station
1	Ostrov Domashniy		
2	Ostrov Uyedineniya		
3	Ostrov Rudolfa		
4	Eureka		
5	Mys Chelyuskin		
6	Isachsen		
7	Nord		
8	Mys Shalaurova		
9	Danmarkshavn		
10	Bukhta Tikhaya		
11	Thule		
12	Resolute		
13	Mould Bay		
14	Ostrov Vrangelya		
		15	Mys Sterlegova
16	Mys Zhelaniya		
		17	Ostrov Sagastyr
18	Alert		
19	Pond Inlet		
20	Ust'ye R. Taimyry		
		21	Kazach'ye
		22	Myggbukta
		23	Ostrov Belyy
24	Craig Harbour		
		25	Mys Shmidta
		26	Barrow
		27	Sachs Harbour
		28	Ostrov Dikson
		29	Arctic Bay
30	Matochkin Shar		
		31	Grønfjorden
		32	Mare Sale
		33	Ostrov Vaygach
		34	Svalbard
		35	Russkoye Uste'ye
		36	Gyda Yamo
		37	Yugorskiy Shar
		38	Bukhta Tiksi
		39	Malyye Karmakuly
		40	Bulun

The degree to which cartographic extrapolation has been carried out in areas where soils and vegetation are poorly defined is not known. Furthermore, station data may reflect only local conditions. For example, nearly all stations have a coastal location (fig. 2.1), which may give little indication of conditions in the interior (or on adjacent highlands, where Charlier noted that polar desert soils were best developed); considerable coastal-inland contrasts are well known to exist during both summer and winter on Ellesmere Island, for example (Jackson, 1959; Barry and Jackson, 1969).

An Analysis of Aridity

Four methods were employed to estimate annual evaporation, of which three included a mean annual net radiation term. This was available for thirty-three of the

TABLE 2.5

Evaporation and Annual Water Budget According to Budyko Formula

Station	Evaporation (cm)	Budget (cm)
Aklavik*	14.8	4.6
Alert*	0.0	14.7
Arctic Bay	3.6	13.6
Baker Lake*	15.3	5.6
Barrow	6.1	4.5
Bukhta Tikhaya	1.8	9.9
Bulun	13.8	8.8
Cambridge Bay*	9.2	3.9
Craig Harbour	6.3	15.6
Clyde*	5.1	14.6
Danmarkshavn	5.4	9.3
Eureka*	2.3	4.3
Frobisher*	15.4	30.3
Gyda Yamo	7.9	13.2
Isachsen	3.3	6.6
Kazach'ye	12.1	3.1
Khatanga	11.7	11.4
Malyye Karmakuly	7.5	16.9
Mare Sale	9.2	10.6
Mould Bay	3.0	5.4
Mys Chelyuskin	3.8	7.7
Mys Sterlegova	4.7	11.1
Mys Zhelaniya	3.7	9.2
Nome	19.2	28.0
Ostrov Belyy	2.2	13.6
Ostrov Dikson	7.8	9.0
Ostrov Vaygach	7.9	10.6
Ostrov Vrangelya	8.3	2.1
Resolute*	4.5	8.5
Sachs Harbour	6.2	3.7
Scoresbysund	5.6	26.2
Svalbard (Isfjord Radio)	6.8	33.9
Thule	2.9	3.7
Vardö	20.6	39.1
Volochanka	9.8	20.1
Yugorskiy Shar	9.0	11.7

*Net radiation estimates from Hare and Hay (1971, fig. 3).

forty-eight stations (Gavrilova, 1966). Some additional point values were interpolated from Hare and Hay (1971, fig. 3).

Methods of Budyko and Thornthwaite-Mather

An excellent review of methods for evaluating annual evaporation in terms of energy budget is given in Sellers (1965, ch. 7). He discusses a formula proposed by Budyko in 1956, which is based on earlier equations of Schreiber. Budyko makes the assumption that all available net radiative energy is used in evaporation and that no other energy sources are available. Then, $E_o = R_o/L$, where E_o is annual evaporation, R_o is annual net radiation, and L is the latent heat of vaporization. Also, $R_o = (Q + q)(1 - \alpha) - I$, where $(Q + q)$ is the sum of the direct and diffuse solar radiation, α is the surface albedo, and I is the effective outgoing terrestrial radiation. The units are: cal cm^{-2} yr^{-1} for R_o, $Q + q$, and I; cm for E_o; $L \simeq 597$ cal gm^{-1}.

The Budyko formula is designed to estimate the ratio

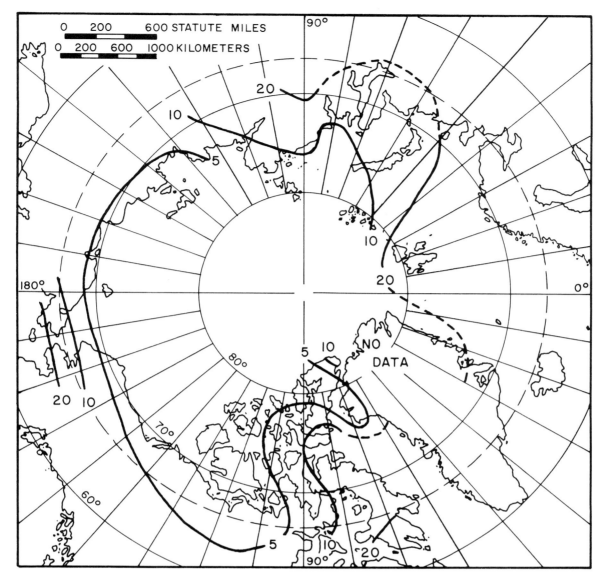

Fig. 2.2.　Annual water budget (in millimeters) according to Budyko (1956) formula.

$\Delta f/r$, where Δf is annual runoff and r is annual precipitation. With a rearrangement of terms however, the formula may be used to estimate evaporation since $r = \Delta f + E_o$, assuming that deep percolation losses are negligible on an annual basis. This is a reasonable assumption since permafrost would tend to inhibit such losses. Indeed, L'vovich (1961) shows that greater than 95 percent of total runoff occurs as surface runoff in tundra and taiga basins underlain by permafrost. By Budyko's formula,

$$\Delta f/r = 1 - [x(1 - \cosh x + \sinh x) \tanh 1/x]^{1/2} \quad (1)$$

where $x = R_o/Lr$. An estimate of Δf is obtained by multiplying through by r in (1) and hence annual evaporation may be estimated from the relation $E_o = r - \Delta f$. Table 2.5 shows the results of this analysis. The units of R_o, L, and r were adjusted to give E_o in centimeters. Mean annual precipitation in centimeters was used to compute the water budget (precipitation minus evaporation) shown in table 2.5.

The influence of oceanicity is apparent in the large values at Svalbard and Vardö in the Greenland Sea–Barents Sea sector. The lowest annual budgets are in the western Canadian Arctic Archipelago (fig. 2.2). Although no station has a negative budget on an annual basis, eight of the stations in table 2.5 have budgets of less than five centimeters. Most of these are located outside the area designated as polar desert according to the Charlier temperature factor (fig. 2.1), although with the exception of Aklavik, Barrow, and Kazach'ye they are within the zones of polar desert or desert-tundra transition soils (Charlier, 1969). The zone of Arctic desert vegetation shown in Fillipov (1964) contains two of the eight stations (Eureka and Ostrov Vrangelya); with Cambridge Bay and Kazach'ye in the tundra zone. Only Aklavik and Barrow are well outside of Fillipov's boundaries.

The dryness ratio (R_o/Lr) was also computed. This is the ratio of annual net radiation to the amount of heat required to evaporate the mean annual precipitation. Table 2.6 shows the computed values. The ratio is

TABLE 2.6

Dryness Ratio (Ro/Lr) and Thornwaite-Mather Index (I′m)

Station	Ro/Lr	I′m	Climatic Type
Aklavik	1.0	−3	Steppe
Alert	0.0		(Tundra)
Baker Lake	1.1	−11	Steppe
Barrow	0.7	39	Forest
Bukhta Tikhaya	0.2	537	Tundra
Bulun	0.8	26	Forest
Cambridge Bay	1.0	−2	Steppe
Craig Harbour	0.3	220	Tundra
Clyde	0.3	215	Tundra
Danmarkshavn	0.4	145	Forest
Eureka	0.4	161	Forest
Frobisher	0.4	167	Forest
Gyda Yamo	0.4	139	Forest
Isachsen	0.4	170	Forest
Kazach'ye	1.3	−24	Steppe
Khatanga	0.6	63	Forest
Malyye Karmakuly	0.3	205	Tundra
Mare Sale	0.5	86	Forest
Mould Bay	0.4	128	Forest
Mys Chelyuskin	0.4	174	Forest
Mys Sterlegova	0.3	215	Tundra
Mys Zhelaniya	0.3	224	Tundra
Nome	0.5	116	Forest
Ostrov Belyy	0.2	329	Tundra
Ostrov Dikson	0.5	86	Forest
Ostrov Uyedineniya	<0.0		(Tundra)
Ostrov Vaygach	0.5	106	Forest
Ostrov Vrangelya	1.4	−27	Steppe
Resolute	0.4	161	Forest
Sachs Harbour	0.8	19	Forest
Scoresbysund	0.2	429	Tundra
Svalbard (Isfjord Radio)	0.2	467	Tundra
Thule	0.5	98	Forest
Upernavik	0.1	1272	Tundra
Vardö	0.4	161	Forest
Volochanka	0.4	177	Forest
Yugorskiy Shar	0.5	102	Forest

TABLE 2.7

Evaporation and Annual Water Budget According to Turc Formula

Station	Precipitation (cm)	Evaporation (cm)	Budget (cm)
Alert	14.7	13.8	0.9
Arctic Bay	17.3	15.6	1.7
Barrow	10.7	10.6	0.1
Barter Island	19.3	16.9	2.4
Bukhta Tikhaya	11.7	11.5	0.2
Bukhta Tiksi	13.7	13.0	0.7
Bulun	22.6	18.7	3.9
Craig Harbour	21.8	18.2	3.6
Danmarkshavn	14.7	13.8	0.9
Eureka	6.6	6.6	0*
Grønfjorden	29.7	21.7	8.0
Gyda Yamo	21.1	17.9	3.2
Isachsen	9.9	9.9	0.0
Kazach'ye	15.2	14.1	1.1
Khatanga	23.1	18.9	4.2
Kistrand	43.2	25.1	18.1
Malyye Karmakuly	24.4	19.6	4.8
Mare Sale	19.8	17.1	2.7
Matochkin Shar	17.8	15.9	1.9
Mould Bay	8.4	8.4	0*
Myggbukta	22.1	18.4	3.7
Mys Chelyuskin	11.4	11.1	0.3
Mys Shalaurova	7.6	7.6	0*
Mys Shmidta	17.0	15.4	1.6
Mys Sterlegova	15.8	14.6	1.2
Mys Zhelaniya	13.0	12.5	0.5
Nord	20.3	17.4	2.9
Ostrov Belyy	15.8	14.6	1.2
Ostrov Dikson	16.8	15.3	1.5
Ostrov Domashniy	9.4	9.4	0*
Ostrov Kolguyev	25.1	19.8	5.3
Ostrov Rudolfa	9.7	9.7	0.0
Ostrov Sagastyr	8.6	8.6	0*
Ostrov Uyedineniya	11.4	11.1	0.3
Ostrov Vaygach	18.5	16.3	2.2
Ostrov Vrangelya	10.4	10.3	0.1
Peary Land	5.3	5.3	0*
Pond Inlet	15.8	14.6	1.2
Resolute	13.0	12.5	0.5
Russkoye Uste'ye	14.5	13.6	0.9
Sachs Harbour	9.9	9.9	0.0
Scoresbysund	31.8	22.4	9.4
Svalbard (Isfjord Radio)	40.6	24.5	16.1
Thule	6.6	6.6	0*
Upernavik	22.9	18.8	4.1
Ust' Yeniseyskiy Port	25.7	20.1	5.6
Ust'ye R. Taimyry	16.5	15.0	1.5
Volochanka	30.0	21.8	8.2
Yugorskiy Shar	20.8	17.7	3.1

*Evaporation is set equal to precipitation where $(P/L)^2 < 0.1$ (see text).

analogous to Budyko's radiational index of dryness (Sellers, 1965) which is a hypothetical value for wet surfaces with an albedo of 0.18. Numerical differences between the two are generally small (Hare and Hay, 1971). According to Sellers (*loc cit*) the limits of the Budyko index which correspond to major cover types are: 1.0 − 2.0, steppe; 0.33 − 1.0, forest; and ≤0.33, tundra. On this basis, the majority of stations in table 2.6 are forest, twelve stations are tundra, and five are steppe.

Computations using the Thornthwaite-Mather moisture index (Sellers, 1965):

$$I'_m = 100\{(Lr/R_o) - 1\}$$

give the same results since both indices include the ratio R_o/Lr or its reciprocal. The geographical distribution of climatic types as determined in terms of the two indices is given in figure 2.3. "Tundra" is confined primarily to islands in the Greenland Sea–Barents Sea

sector and to coasts around northern Baffin Bay. The latter feature, however, may well be an artifact of the available radiation data. Steppe areas are located in eastern Siberia and northwestern Canada.

Method of Turc

Penman (1963) discusses a method of estimating evaporation, formulated by Turc. An advantage of Turc's method in areas of sparse data is that it makes no

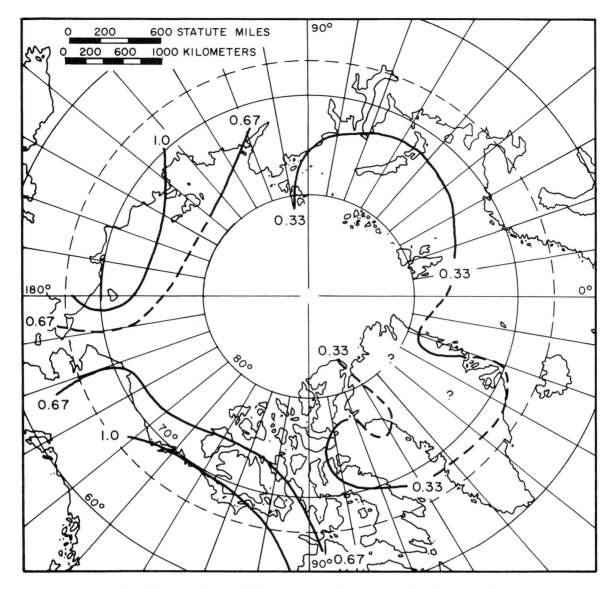

Fig. 2.3.   Distribution of deserts and semideserts, according to the Budyko
radiational index of dryness and the Thornthwaite-Mather moisture index.

assumption of an unlimited water supply at the surface to feed evaporation nor does it include a net radiation term. The latter is included in both the Budyko and Thornthwaite-Mather formulas as a factor which is not adjusted for mean surface moisture conditions, so that both of these methods are likely to overestimate annual evaporation for surfaces that are unsaturated for most of the year.

The Turc formula computes annual evaporation as a function of mean air temperature and mean annual precipitation by the following relation:

$$E = \frac{P}{[0.9 + (P/L)^2]^{1/2}}$$

where P = annual precipitation in millimeters, T = mean air temperature in °C, and $L = 300 + 25T + 0.05T^3$. If $(P/L)^2 < 0.1$ (which corresponds to P

< 95 mm for $T = 0$), E is set equal to P. Also, where the mean annual temperature is less than zero, T is set equal to zero so that $L = 300$. Computed evaporation and water budgets are given in table 2.7 for forty-nine stations. Brønlunds Fjord was included in the data set, since air temperature and precipitation data were available. Also, it was considered that this station would be more representative of conditions in northeast Greenland than Nord.

Seven stations have moisture budgets less than zero, and except for Ostrov Sagastyr all are located in areas previously defined by other workers as deserts and semideserts by soil and plant criteria. Kistrand and Svalbard, which have budgets exceeding 150 millimeters per year, both have pronounced maritime climates although there is a discrepancy between the latter station and Grønfjorden. Figure 2.4 shows the distribution of desert areas

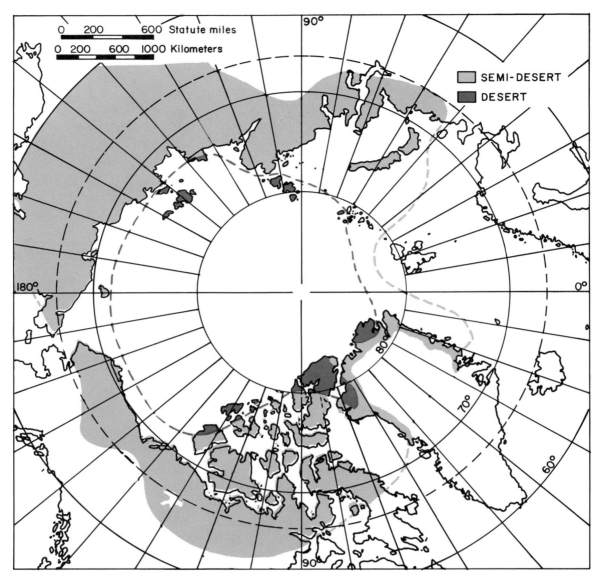

Fig. 2.4.   Distribution of deserts and semideserts according to the Turc evaporation formula.

(water budget less than or equal to zero) and semiarid areas using an arbitrary boundary value of 50 millimeters annual water surplus. Values for 16 additional stations (not included) were determined in order to delimit the semidesert boundary in North America and eastern Siberia.

Discussion

The water budgets calculated according to Budyko and Turc (figs. 2.2 and 2.4) show a broad similarity of pattern, although they differ considerably in detail. Also the surpluses as determined by the Budyko method are considerably larger. In the light of run-off records for the Arctic (Fillipov, 1964; Hare and Hay, 1971) the Turc values appear to be too low. However, evaporation measurements for the Arctic are almost nonexistent, and there is still considerable uncertainty over true annual radiation values. Moreover, it recently has been recog-

nized that measured precipitation totals in the Arctic are 10–30 percent less than the true amounts (Hare and Hay, 1971). This adjustment would displace the isolines as mapped according to Turc and Budyko poleward.

An alternative approach to evaporation estimates would be to define the evaporation "season" to include months for which the net radiation is positive. It would then be necessary to estimate what proportion of the net radiation is expended in snowmelt and evaporation from knowledge of surface conditions at specific stations. Even a crude index of soil moisture variations through the evaporation "season" would provide an estimate of the periods when evaporation proceeds at potential rates.

The extent of areas of limited moisture surplus in figures 2.2 and 2.4 seems reasonable on general climatological grounds, but the delimitation of climatic types by the dryness ratio (figure 2.3) provides no basis for identifying polar desert conditions. The unusual distribution shown in figure 2.3 probably reflects the departure of actual values of net radiation from the hypothetical Ro of Budyko's formulation as well as discrepancies in the ratio arising from quite large errors in estimated net radiation for annual values close to zero. Also the calculations used for table 2.7 take no account of the latent heat of snowmelt. It appears that at present a physical climatological approach to the problem of delimiting polar deserts is unworkable.

The results of the discriminant analysis were much more satisfactory. However, the employment of comparatively brief climatic records to determine the extent of arid and semiarid areas in the Arctic is a valid exercise only insofar as plant and soil zones are in equilibrium with the present climate. Indeed, Everett (1968) and Savile (1961) have attributed the paucity of plant species on islands within the Queen Elizabeth and Parry groups partly to the prevailing climate and partly to the relatively short time period during which these areas have been suitable for plant colonization. Under this interpretation, some polar desert areas would constitute relict landscapes. It is not known which other land areas within the Arctic might fall into this category, which serves to underline the possible dangers of delimiting polar deserts in purely climatological terms. The extent of aridity and semiaridity defined in previous sections, therefore, probably reflects historical rather than actual conditions for many areas.

BIBLIOGRAPHY

Alexandrova, V. D.
1960 Some irregularities in the distribution of the vegetation in the Arctic tundra. Arctic 13: 146–62.
Arctic, Desert, Tropic Information Center
1955 Glossary of arctic and subarctic terms. ADTIC, Research Studies Inst. Maxwell Air Force Base, Alabama.
Barry, R. G., and C. I. Jackson
1969 Summer weather conditions at Tanquary Fiord, N.W.T., 1963–67. Arctic and Alpine Research 1: 169–80.
Bird, J. B.
1967 Physiography of Arctic Canada. Johns Hopkins Press, Baltimore. 336 pp.
Blüthgen, J.
1966 Allgemeine Klimageographie, 2nd ed., pp. 507–46. Walter de Gruyter, Berlin.
Charlier, R. H.
1969 The geographic distribution of polar desert soils in the Northern Hemisphere. Bulletin Geological Society of America 80: 1985–96.
Dolgin, I. M.
1970 Subarctic meteorology. *In* Ecology of subarctic regions, pp. 41–61. UNESCO, Paris.
Everett, K. R.
1968 Soil development in the Mould Bay and Isachsen areas, Queen Elizabeth Islands, N.W.T., Canada. Institute of Polar Studies Reprint no. 24, Ohio State University, Columbus. 75 pp.
Fillipov, Y. V.
1964 Physico-geographical atlas of the world. Fisiko-geograficheskiy atlas mira, Moscow.
Fristrup, B.
1952 Wind erosion within the Arctic deserts. Geografisk Tidsskrift, Kjøbenhavn 52: 51–65.
Gavrilova, M. K.
1963 Radiation climate of the Arctic. Gidrometeorologicheskoe Izd., Leningrad (English translation:

Israel Program for Scientific Translation, 1966). 178 pp.
Hare, F. K., and J. E. Hay
1971 Anomalies in large-scale annual water balance over northern North America. Canadian Geographer 15: 79–94.
Jackson, C. I.
1959 Coastal and inland weather contrasts in the Canadian Arctic. Journal of Geophysical Research 64: 1451–55.
L'vovich, M. I.
1961 The water balance of the land. Soviet Geography, review and translation (New York) 2(4): 14–28.
Meteorological Office
1958 Tables of temperature, relative humidity and precipitation for the world. 6 parts. H.M.S.O., London.
Orvig, S. (ed.)
1970 Climates of the polar regions. (World Survey of Climatology, Volume 14). American Elsevier, New York. 370 pp.
Penman, H. L.
1963 Vegetation and hydrology. Farnham Royal, England. 124 pp.
Petterssen, S., W. C. Jacobs, and B. C. Haynes
1956 Meteorology of the Arctic. OPNAV PO3-3 Naval Operations for Polar Projects, Washington, D.C. 206 pp.
Savile, D. B. O.
1961 Botany of the northwestern Queen Elizabeth Islands, Canadian Journal of Botany 39 (4): 909–42.
Sellers, W.
1965 Physical climatology. University of Chicago Press. 272 pp.
Tedrow, J. C. F.
1966 Polar desert soils. Soil Science Society of America Proceedings 30 (3): 381–387.

CHAPTER 3

GEOMORPHIC PROCESSES IN POLAR DESERTS

Troy L. Péwé
Department of Geology, Arizona State University, Tempe

The arid regions of the polar areas have not been considered in classic studies of deserts of the earth. Yet, the polar deserts, like those in temperate and tropical areas, not only have a delicate balance between climatological, geological, and biological processes but also represent a geographical area of stress for occupation by man.

Definition, Distribution and Processes

In this chapter a polar desert is arbitrarily defined as a glacier-free terrestrial area where the mean annual precipitation is less than 25 centimeters and the mean temperature for the warmest month of the year is less than 10°C. In the northern hemisphere such areas include the north slope of Alaska, vast areas of northern Canada and Siberia, and the northern fringe of Greenland, plus parts of isolated polar islands (fig. 3.1). By such a definition the polar deserts occupy approximately 4.3×10^6 km² of the northern hemisphere. All glacier-free lowlands of Antarctica should be included and represent about 600,000 km² (Solopov, 1967); this area cited for glacier-free land includes both lowland "oases" and nunataks.

Similar to desert areas of the temperate and tropical zones which fall into categories of semiarid, arid, and extremely arid (Meigs, 1953; McGinnies, Goldman, and Paylore, 1968), the polar deserts logically grade

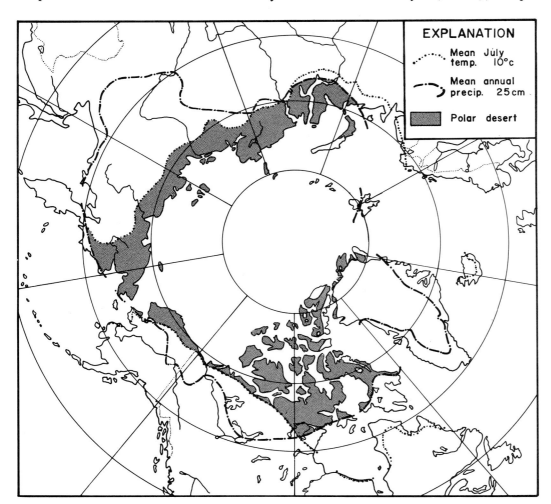

EXPLANATION

······ Mean July temp. 10°c

—·—· Mean annual precip. 25cm

▨ Polar desert

Fig. 3.1. Distribution of the polar deserts in the northern hemisphere.

from one end member (the tundra) on the "wetter" side to the other end member (rocky desert) on the extremely arid side. The wetter end member of the polar desert is characterized by the tundra regions of northern Alaska, Canada, and Siberia. These areas generally are treeless, covered with a thick mat of shrubs grass, moss, and lichens, and dotted with a myriad of lakes to produce in summer a paradox of a swampy, surface-soaked desert (fig. 3.2). The far northern islands of Canada, Peary Land of northern Greenland, and especially the oases of Antarctica present the essentially vegetation-free glaciated terrain of the extremely arid areas characterized by a wind-swept, boulder-strewn landscape (fig. 3.3).

Geomorphic processes in both polar and temperate-tropic deserts depend mostly on climatic control. Although precipitation is scarce in deserts, fluvial processes are prominent; however, the frequency of geomorphic events is considerably different in dry than in humid areas. For example, flooding may occur every 5 or 10 years, or more often, in humid areas and may be an important agency of erosion; in desert areas flooding may occur only every 50 to 500 years and yet may be the dominant erosional agency despite its frequent occurrence there.

The obvious differences in geomorphic processes between the polar and the southern deserts are: (1) cold versus hot environments, (2) precipitation in solid rather than in liquid form, (3) precipitation concentrated in annual spring runoff in the cold desert, and most important, (4) most soil moisture in the polar desert is in the solid state as ice. The most important feature of polar deserts is that the annual and diurnal temperature changes cross the freezing point of water and, therefore, both surface and shallow-soil moisture oscillate from a liquid to a solid state. The presence of seasonally and perennially frozen ground profoundly affects geomorphic processes in the polar deserts.

Fig. 3.2. Aerial view, from an altitude of about 200 meters, of polygonal ground formed by active ice wedges in the tundra polar desert near Barrow, Alaska. Polygons are 15 to 25 meters in diameter. Those on the right contain small ponds of water bounded by the raised edges of the polygons; those on the left are outlined by dark linear features which are trenches filled with water. Note markings of tracked vehicle which crossed the tundra some years earlier. (Photograph PK 14,676, by T. L. Péwé, July 6, 1970)

Fig. 3.3. Windswept and wind-truncated boulders in high-level glacial till on the south side of Miers Valley, McMurdo Sound, Antarctica. View looks up valley at Miers Glacier, with Victoria Range in background. (Photograph 1718, by T. L. Péwé, January 17, 1958)

Permafrost

Perhaps the most common result of long cold winters and short summers is the formation of a layer of frozen ground that does not completely thaw in the summer. This perennially frozen ground or permafrost affects many of man's activities in the Arctic and Subarctic and causes problems which are not experienced elsewhere. Permafrost is ubiquitous in the polar deserts and modifies all geomorphic processes.

Permafrost is natural-occurring material that has a temperature colder than 0°C continuously for two or more years (Muller, S. W., 1945). This layer of frozen ground is designated exclusively on the basis of temperature. Part or all of its moisture may be unfrozen, depending upon the chemical composition of the water or depression of the freezing point by capillary forces. Permafrost with saline soil moisture, for example, may be colder than 0°C for several years but would contain no ice and would not be firmly cemented. Most permafrost is consolidated by ice; permafrost with no water, and thus no ice, is termed *dry permafrost*. The upper surface of permafrost is called the *permafrost table*. In permafrost areas the surficial layer of ground that freezes in the winter (seasonally frozen ground) and thaws in

summer is called the *active layer*. The thickness of the active layer under most circumstances depends mainly on the moisture content; it varies from 10 to 20 centimeters in thickness in wet organic sediments and to 2 or 3 meters in well-drained gravels.

Permafrost, perennially frozen ground, or *vechnaya merzlota* is a widespread phenomenon in the northern part of the northern hemisphere (fig. 3.4); it is estimated to underlie 20 percent of the land surface of the world. (The term *vechnaya merzlota* means *eternal frost* and is being replaced in more recent Soviet literature by *Mnogoletnemerzlyy grunt*, which means *perennially frozen ground*.)

It occurs in 85 percent of Alaska, 50 percent of the U.S.S.R. and Canada, and probably all of Antarctica (Péwé, in press). In the northern hemisphere permafrost is more widespread and extends to greater depths in the northern than in the southern regions. It is reported to be 1600 meters thick in northern Siberia (Yefimonv and Dukhin, 1968), 650 meters in northern Alaska (Stoneley, 1970), and thins progressively toward the south. Permafrost can be differentiated into two broad zones: the continuous and the discontinuous. These terms refer to the lateral continuity of permafrost. In the continuous zone of the far north (fig. 3.4),

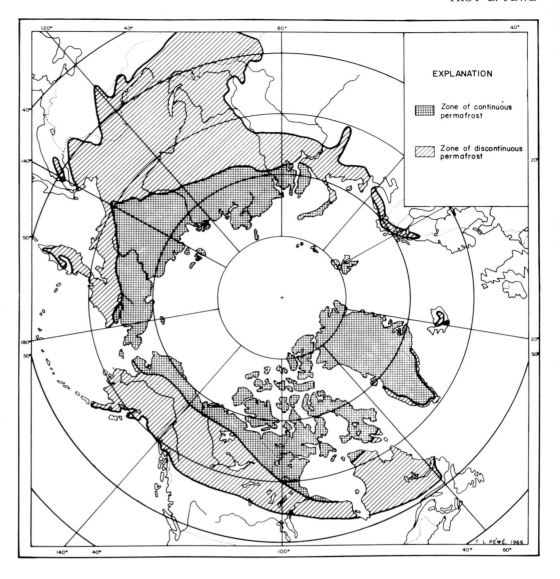

Fig. 3.4. Distribution of permafrost in the northern hemisphere. (From *The Periglacial Environment,* edited by T. L. Péwé, 1969. Reproduced through the courtesy of McGill-Queens University Press)

permafrost is nearly everywhere present except under the lakes and rivers that do not freeze to the bottom (fig. 3.5). The discontinuous zone includes numerous permafrost-free areas which increase progressively in size and number from the north to the south. Near the southern boundary of permafrost, only rare patches of permafrost exist.

Permafrost forms and exists in a climate where the mean annual air temperature is 0° C or colder. Such a climate is generally characterized by long cold winters with little snow and with short, relatively dry, cool summers. Therefore, permafrost is widespread in the Arctic, Subarctic, and Antarctic. There is a fairly good correlation between the southern boundary of permafrost and the position of the 0° C mean annual air isotherm.

Origin and Thermal Regime

In areas where the mean annual air temperature becomes colder than 0° C, some of the ground frozen in the winter will not be completely thawed in the

summer; therefore, a layer of permafrost will form and continue to grow downward in small increments from the seasonally frozen ground (Péwé, 1966b). The permafrost layer will become thicker each winter, and the thickness is controlled by the thermal balance achieved between the heat flowing upward from the earth's interior and that flowing outward into the atmosphere — a balance which depends upon the mean annual air temperature and the geothermal gradient. The average geothermal gradient is about 1° C increase in the temperature of the earth for every 30 to 60 meters of depth. Eventually the thickening permafrost layer reaches an equilibrium depth at which over several years the same amount of geothermal heat reaching the permafrost is lost into the atmosphere. A state of equilibrium takes thousands of years to be reached where permafrost is hundreds of meters thick.

An example of the change of temperature of frozen ground with depth and the upper and lower limit of permafrost is illustrated in figure 3.6. The annual fluctuation of air temperature from winter to summer is

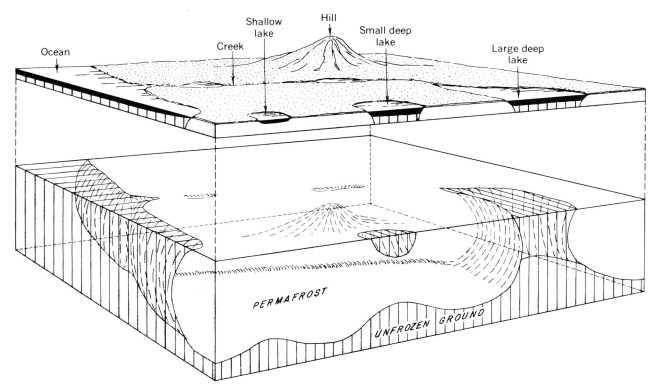

Fig. 3.5. The effect of surface features on the distribution of permafrost in the continuous permafrost zone. (From *Encyclopedia of Geomorphology*, by Rhodes W. Fairbridge, © 1968 by Litton Educational Publishing, Inc. Reprinted by permission of Van Nostrand Reinhold Company.)

reflected in a subdued manner in the upper few meters of the ground. This fluctuation diminishes rapidly with depth; it is only a few degrees at 8 meters and is barely detectable at 15 meters. The level at which the fluctuations are hardly detectable (10–15 m) is termed *the level of zero amplitude.* If the permafrost is in thermal equilibrium, the temperature at the level of zero amplitude is generally regarded as the minimum temperature of the permafrost. Below this depth the temperature increases steadily under the influence of heat from the earth's interior. The temperature of permafrost at the level of zero amplitude is close to the average temperature of the ground surface; however, it is 2° C to 6° C warmer than the mean annual air temperature determined from the U.S. Weather Bureau-type surface installations which are 1.5 m above the surface. The temperature of permafrost at the depth of minimum annual seasonal change varies from near 0° C at the southern limit of permafrost to −10° C in northern Alaska and −13° C in northeastern Siberia. In the continuous zone temperature of the permafrost is colder than −5° C.

As the climate becomes colder or warmer, but still with a mean annual temperature colder than 0° C, the thickness of the permafrost becomes correspondingly greater or less by changes in the base of permafrost. The position of the top of permafrost will be lowered by thawing. The rate at which the base or top of permafrost is changed depends not only on the amount of climatic fluctuation but also on the amount of ice in the ground and composition of the ground-factors which in part control the geothermal gradient.

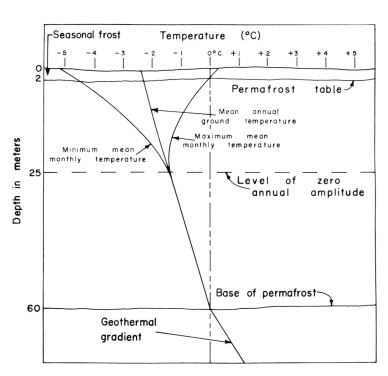

Fig. 3.6. Hypothetical thermal profile showing temperature and thickness of permafrost in central Alaska.

Therefore, if the geothermal gradient is known and if the surface temperature is stable for a long period of time, it is possible to predict from a knowledge of the mean air temperature the depth of permafrost in a particular area remote from water bodies.

Permafrost is the result of present climate; however, many temperature profiles show that permafrost is not in equilibrium with the present climate at the sites of measurement, and in such areas much of the permafrost is a product of a colder past climate. Some areas show, for example, that climatic warming during the late 1800s has caused a warming of the permafrost to a depth of 100 meters (Lachenbruch, Green, and Marshall, 1966). Here some of the existing perennially frozen ground would disappear with rising base of permafrost if present surface conditions were to persist for several thousands of years.

It is thought that permafrost appeared with the refrigeration of polar areas that began near the beginning of the Quaternary geologic period about two or three million years ago. However, the oldest documentation of former permafrost in North America is about middle Quaternary time (Péwé, in press). In the Subarctic at least, probably most permafrost disappeared during interglacial times and reappeared in glacial times. Most existing permafrost probably formed in the cold (glacial) period of the last 70,000 years.

Local Thickness and Ice Content

The thickness and aerial distribution of permafrost is directly affected by natural surface features such as snow and vegetation cover, topography, and bodies of waters, in addition to the earth's interior heat and temperature of the atmosphere mentioned earlier.

The most conspicuous change in thickness of permafrost is related to climate. At Barrow, Alaska, in the polar desert, the mean annual air temperature is $-12°$ C and the permafrost thickness is 400 meters. At Fairbanks, Alaska, in the discontinuous zone of permafrost in central Alaska, the mean annual air temperature is $-3°$ C and the permafrost thickness is about 100 meters. Near Yakoutsk, Siberia, the mean annual air temperature is $-6°$ C and the permafrost thickness is 230 meters. Near Kelsey, Manitoba, in Canada, the temperature is $-2°$ C and the thickness of permafrost is 17 meters (Brown, R. J. E., 1970). Near the southern border of permafrost the mean annual air temperature is about 0 or $-1°$ C and the perennially frozen ground is only a few meters thick.

Inasmuch as south-facing hill slopes receive more incoming solar energy per unit area than other slopes, they are warmer; permafrost is generally absent on these in the discontinuous zone and thinner in the continuous zone (see Péwé, 1954, fig. 72).

The main role of vegetation in permafrost areas is that it shields perennially frozen ground from solar energy. Vegetation is an excellent insulating medium; removal or disturbance, either by natural processes or by man, causes thawing of the underlying permafrost. In the continuous zone the permafrost table may merely be lowered by the disturbance of vegetation, but in a discontinuous zone permafrost may be completely destroyed in certain areas.

Snow cover also influences heat flow between the ground and the atmosphere and therefore affects the distribution of permafrost. If the net effect of timely snowfalls is to prevent heat from leaving the ground in the cold winter, permafrost becomes warmer. Actually, local differences in vegetation and snowfall in areas of thin and warm permafrost are critical for the formation and existence of the perennially frozen ground. Permafrost is not present in areas of the world with enormous snowfalls that exist throughout most of the winter.

Ground Ice

The ice content of permafrost is probably the most important feature of permafrost affecting human life in the North; it also is important in providing evidence concerning past climates beyond the range possible by geothermal calculations. It is deeply involved in most geomorphic processes in the polar deserts. Ice in perennially frozen ground exists in various sizes and shapes and has definite distribution characteristics. The forms of ground ice may be grouped into five main types: (1) pore ice, (2) segregated or "Taber" ice, (3) foliated or ice-wedge ice, (4) pingo ice, and (5) buried ice.

Pore ice is defined as ice which fills or partially fills pore spaces in the ground. It forms by freezing pore water in situ with no addition of water. The ground contains no more water in the solid state than the ground could hold if the water were in the liquid state.

Segregated or Taber ice is described as ice films, seams, lenses, pods, or layers generally 1 to 150 millimeters thick that grow in the ground by drawing in water as the ground freezes. Small ice segregations are the least spectacular and yet one of the most extensive types of ground ice. They have received much study from engineers and geologists interested in ice growth and its effect on engineering structures. Although the principle of bringing water to a growing ice crystal is generally accepted, there is not complete agreement as to the mechanics of the processes. Pore ice and Taber ice occur both in seasonally frozen ground and in permafrost.

Foliated ground ice or wedge ice is the term given to large masses of ice which grow in thermal contraction cracks in permafrost. Pingo ice is clear or relatively clear ice that occurs in permafrost in more or less horizontal or lens-shaped masses 3 to 15 meters in diameter. It originates from groundwater under hydrostatic pressure.

Buried ice in permafrost includes buried sea, lake, and river ice and recrystallized snow. Buried blocks of glacier ice in a permafrost climate also fall into this category.

World estimates of the amount of ice in permafrost range from 0.2 to 0.5 million cubic kilometers or less than one percent of the total volume of the earth (Shumskiy, Krenke, and Zotikov, 1964). On the basis of an examination of ice in the ground in many bore

Fig. 3.7. Foliated ground-ice mass (ice wedge) in organic-rich silt exposed in placer gold-mining operations on Wilbur Creek near Livengood, Alaska. (Photograph 474, by T. L. Péwé, September 19, 1949)

holes near Barrow, Alaska, and then extrapolation of this bore-hole information to the rest of the Coastal Plain by use of aerial photographs and geologic maps, Jerry Brown (1967) of the U.S. Army Cold Regions Research and Engineering Laboratory estimated that 10 percent by volume of the upper 3 meters of permafrost on the Coastal Plain of Alaska is composed of ice wedges (foliated ground ice). Taber ice is the most extensive type of ground ice — in places representing 75 percent of the ground by volume. It is calculated that the pore and Taber ice content in the depth between 0.5 and 2 meters (surface to 0.5 meters is seasonally thawed) is 61 percent; between 3 and 10 meters pore and Taber ice comprises 41 percent by volume. The total amount of pingo ice is less than 0.1 percent of the permafrost. The total amount of perennial ice in the permafrost of the polar desert of Alaska is estimated to be 1,500 cubic kilometers, and below 8.5 meters most of that is present as pore ice.

Ice Wedges

The most conspicuous and controversial type of ground ice in permafrost is the large ice wedges or masses characterized by parallel or subparallel foliation structures (fig. 3.7) (see Popov, 1969, figs. 1 and 2, for classic ice wedges in Siberia). Most foliated ice masses occur as wedge-shaped vertical, or inclined, sheets or dikes 1 centimeter to 3 meters wide and 1 to 10 meters high when seen in transverse cross-section. Some masses, when seen on the face of frozen cliffs, may appear as horizontal bodies a few millimeters to 3 meters in thickness and 0.5 to 15 meters in length. The true shape of these ice wedges can be seen only in three dimensions. Ice wedges are parts of polygonal networks of ice-enclosing cells of frozen ground 3 to 30 meters or more in diameter.

The origin of ground ice was first discussed in Siberia (Bunge, 1884). The origin of large ground ice masses

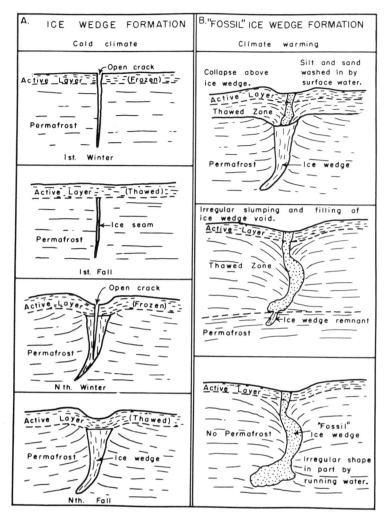

Fig. 3.8. Schematic diagram illustrating (A) the origin of ice wedges (after Lachenbruch, 1960) and (B) the subsequent formation of "fossil" ice wedges (ice-wedge casts). (From Péwé, Church, and Andresen, The Geological Society of America, Special Papers no. 103, 1969, p. 23. Reprinted with permission.)

in perennially frozen ground of North America has been discussed in print since Kotzebue recorded ground ice in 1816 at a spot now termed "Elephant's Point" in Eschscholtz Bay of Seward Peninsula (Kotzebue, 1821). The theory for the origin of ice wedges now generally accepted is the thermal contraction theory, which states that during the cold winter, polygonal thermal contraction cracks about two centimeters wide and 2 to 3 meters deep form in the frozen ground (Leffingwell, 1915). In early spring, water from the melting snow runs down these tension cracks and freezes, producing a vertical vein of ice that penetrates into permafrost. When the permafrost warms and re-expands during the following summer, horizontal compression results in the upturning of the frozen sediment by plastic deformation. During the next winter renewed thermal tension reopens the vertical ice-cemented crack, which may be a zone of weakness. Another increment

of ice is added in the spring when melt water enters and freezes. Over the years the vertical wedge-shaped mass of ice is produced (Lachenbruch, 1960) (fig. 3.8).

Ice wedges may be classified as active, inactive, and ice-wedge casts. Active ice wedges are defined as those which are actively growing. The wedge may not crack every year, but during many or most years cracking does occur and an increment of ice is added. Ice wedges require a much more rigorous climate to grow than does permafrost. The permafrost table must be chilled to $-15°$ C to $-20°$ C for contraction cracks to form. On the average, it is assumed that ice wedges generally grow in a climate where the mean annual air temperature is $-7°$ or $-8°$ C or colder (Péwé, 1966a). This area is limited today almost entirely to the polar desert (fig. 3.1).

The area of active ice wedges appears to coincide roughly with the continuous permafrost zone. From north to south across the permafrost area a decreasing number of wedges crack frequently. The line dividing zones of active and inactive ice wedges is arbitrarily placed at the position where it is thought most wedges do not frequently crack.

Inactive ice wedges are defined as those which are no longer growing. These wedges do not crack in winter; therefore, no new ice is added. There is, of course, a gradation between active ice wedges and inactive ice wedges represented by those wedges which crack rarely. Inactive ice wedges have no ice seam or crack extending from the wedge upward to the surface in the spring. The wedge top may be flat, especially if thawing has lowered the upper surface of the wedge at some time in the past (fig. 3.7).

Ice wedges in the world are of several ages, but none appear older than the last major cold period — the last 70,000 years or so. Wedges have been dated by radiocarbon analyses from 3,000 to 32,000 years old.

In many places in the now temperate latitudes of the world, in areas of past permafrost, ice wedges have melted and resulting voids have been filled with sediments collapsing from above and the sides (fig. 3.8). These ice-wedge casts, or fossil ice wedges, are important as paleoclimatic indicators and indicate a climate of the past with at least a mean annual air temperature of $-7°$ or $-8°$ C or colder.

Sand Wedges

Ice wedges are an ubiquitous physical phenomenon of permafrost in the wetter part of the polar desert, the tundra. It has only relatively recently been discovered (Péwé, 1959, 1962) that in the extremely arid parts of the polar deserts the microrelief pattern of thermal contraction crack polygons is not underlain with ice wedges as in the tundra but is underlain by sand wedges (Nichols, 1969). Under the furrow in most instances is a well-formed wedge-shaped mass of structureless fine-to-medium-grained sand extending 0.5 to 3 meters below the surface and 0.25 to 1 meter wide at the top, tapering down to a feather edge at the base (fig. 3.9). The sand is cemented by ice, and in many places a 10-to-20-millimeter wide open crack extends downward 0.5 to 1 meter into the wedge from the upper surface of permafrost. As in ice wedges, the sediments adjacent to the wedge have been deformed upward (fig. 3.10). The sand wedge and the deformed strata adjacent to the wedges duplicate in great detail the features and field relations associated with foliated ground ice wedges described from tundra areas of the polar deserts. Detailed measurements of sand-wedge growth have been made by Berg and Black (1966).

In the extremely arid regions of the polar desert it is believed that the thermal contraction crack in permafrost (fig. 3.8A) is not filled with water to gradually form an ice wedge, but because of the great aridity and lack of vegetation the cracks are gradually filled in part or entirely with clean windblown sand which filters down from above in spring and summer (fig. 3.9). Repeated cracking and filling with sand produces a wedge-shaped filling. A graph illustrating qualitatively the relationships of ice wedges and sand wedges to precipitation is shown in figure 3.11.

Surficial Manifestations and Processes

Many distinctive surficial manifestations of permafrost exist in the polar deserts, including such geomorphic features as polygonal ground, thermokarst phenomena, and pingos. In addition, many features caused in

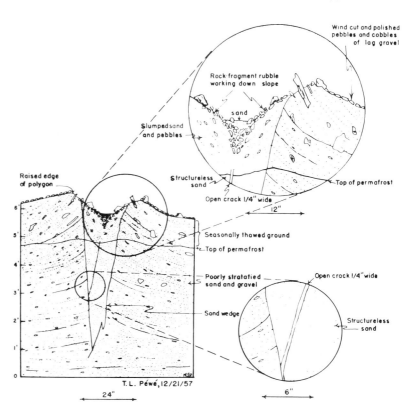

Fig. 3.9. Diagrammatic sketch of sand wedge, Taylor Dry Valley, McMurdo Sound, Antarctica. (From Péwé, *American Journal of Science,* vol. 257, no. 8, 1959, p. 549. Reproduced with permission.)

Fig. 3.10. Aerial view, from an altitude of about 200 meters, of sand–wedge polygons in the polar desert of northern Greenland. Polygons are about 15 to 30 meters in diameter. Small double ridges bound the thermal contraction crack. The polygons were formed in glacial outwash near sea level in the delta at the mouth of Borglum Elv, north shore of Brønlunds Fjord, Peary Land, North Greenland. Part of the fjord is shown in upper left corner. (Photograph by George Stoertz, July 15, 1957)

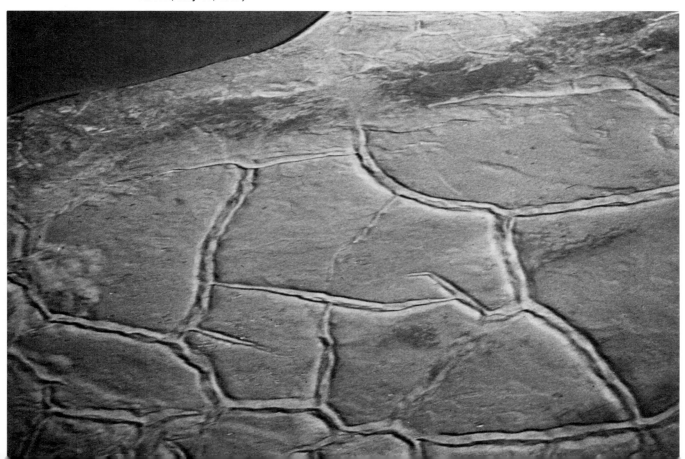

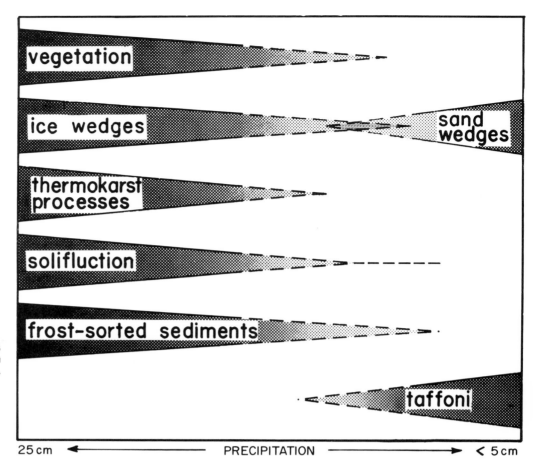

Fig. 3.11. Geomorphic processes and features of the polar desert in relation to precipitation.

large part by frost action are common in but not restricted to permafrost areas. Such features are solifluction (soil flowage) and frost-sorted patterned ground. There also occur features and processes common to both polar and temperate-tropic deserts.

Features Related to Permafrost

One of the most widespread geomorphic features associated with permafrost in the polar deserts is the microrelief pattern on the surface of the ground generally called polygonal ground or tundra polygons (fig. 3.12). This pattern is caused by an intersecting network of shallow troughs which delineate polygons 3 to 30 meters in diameter (see Jahn, 1970, figs. 38 and 39, for polygons in Spitzbergen). The troughs are underlain by more or less vertical ice wedges or sand wedges 1 to 3 meters across on the top that are joined together in a honeycomb network. These large-scale features are thermal contraction polygons and should not be confused with the small-scale polygons or patterned ground produced by frost sorting (Black, 1952; Washburn, 1956).

Ice-wedge polygons may be topographically low in the center or high in the center. Upturning of strata adjacent to the ice wedge may make a ridge of ground on the surface on each side of the wedge (figs. 3.9 and 3.13), thus enclosing the polygons. Such polygons are lower in the center and are called low-center polygons or raised-edge polygons and may contain a pond in the center. Low-center or raised-edge polygons indicate that

the wedges are actually growing and that the sediments are being actively upturned. If erosion, deposition, or thawing is more prevalent than the up-pushing of the sediments along the side of the wedge, or, if the material being pushed up cannot maintain itself in a low ridge, the low ridges will be absent, and there may be either no polygons at the surface or the polygons may be higher in the center than the troughs over the ice wedges that enclose them. Both high-center and low-center tundra polygons are widespread in the polar regions and are good indicators of the presence of foliated ice masses in the tundra; however, care must be taken to demonstrate that the pattern is not a relic and an indication of "fossil" ice wedges.

In many areas of the tundra polar desert, surface drainage follows the troughs of the polygons (tops of the ice wedges), and at ice-wedge junctions, or elsewhere, melting may occur forming small pools. The joining of these small pools by a stream causes the pools to resemble beads on a string. This type of stream form is termed "beaded drainage." Such drainage indicates the presence of perennially frozen fine-grained sediments cut by ice wedges.

The thawing of permafrost creates thermokarst topography, an uneven surface which contains mounds, sinkholes, tunnels, caverns, and steepwalled ravines caused by melting of ground ice (Péwé, 1954; Czudek and Demek, 1970). The hummocky ground surface resembles karst topography found in limestone areas. Thawing

Fig. 3.12. Aerial view, from an altitude of 200 meters, of sand-wedge polygons in the polar desert of Taylor Dry Valley, McMurdo Sound, Antarctica. Polygons are from 10 to 30 meters in diameter and pass under Canada Glacier. (Photograph PK 4600, by Troy L. Péwé, December 18, 1957)

Fig. 3.13. Raised-edge tundra polygons in the polar desert, 2 kilometers south of Barrow, Alaska. (Photograph 1779 by T. L. Péwé, July 24, 1958)

Fig. 3.14.   Large thermokarst pit in pasture land near Maya, 30 kilometers east of Yakoutsk, Siberia. Undulating topography on sides of thermokarst pit is an indication of continuation of melting of underlying ground ice masses in the loess. (Photograph PK 13,624, by T. L. Péwé, August 3, 1969)

Fig. 3.15.   Sorted stone circles in the bottom of a small drained pond along Denali Highway on the south side of the Alaska Range at Alpine Creek. (Photograph 1764, by T. L. Péwé, June 14, 1958)

may result from artificial or natural removal of the vegetation or from warming of the climate.

Thawed depressions filled with water (thaw lakes, thermokarst lakes, cave-in lakes) are widespread in the tundra polar desert, especially in areas underlain with perennially frozen silt. They may occur on hillsides or even on hill tops and are good indicators of ice-rich permafrost. Locally, deep thermokarst pits 6 meters deep and 10 meters across may form as ground ice melts. These openings may exist as undetected caverns for many years before the roof collapses. The thawed areas may enlarge to as much as a kilometer, forming a lowland which in Siberia is called an *alass*. Such collapse in agricultural or construction areas may be disastrous (fig. 3.14). Thermokarst mounds are polygonal or circular hummocks 2 to 15 meters in diameter and 0.5 to 3 meters high, separated by trenches 0.5 to 2 meters wide. Trenches are formed by the melting of a polygonal network of ground ice masses and subsequent subsidence of the ground, leaving mounds in the intervening areas.

The most spectacular landforms associated with permafrost are pingos, small ice-cored circular or elliptical hills of frozen sediments, or even bedrock, 2 to more than 60 meters high and 15 to 400 meters in diameter. They are widespread in the polar desert. Pingos are generally cracked on top, and the ice melts forming a summit crater. Pingos are grouped into two types based on origin: the closed system and the open system (Müller, F., 1959). The closed-system type forms in level areas when unfrozen groundwater in a thawed zone becomes confined on all sides by permafrost, freezes, and heaves the frozen overburden to form a mound. These form the larger of the two types and occur mainly in tundra areas of continuous permafrost. The open-system type is generally smaller and forms on slopes when water beneath, or within, the permafrost penetrates the permafrost under hydrostatic pressure. A hydrolaccolith forms and freezes, heaving the overlying frozen and unfrozen ground to produce a mound. It appears that present pingos are the result of postglacial climate and are less than 4,000 to 7,000 years old.

Features Related to Seasonal Frost

There are many microgeomorphic features common to the polar deserts that may or may not be associated with permafrost. Intense seasonal frost action, that is, repeated freezing and thawing throughout the year, produces small-scale patterned ground (Washburn, 1956). Cycles of freezing and thawing tend to stir and sort granular sediments forming circles, stone nets, and polygons a few centimeters to 7 meters in diameter. The coarse cobbles and boulders form the outside of the ring, and the finer sediments occur in the center (fig. 3.15). The features require a rigorous climate with some fine-grained sediments and soil moisture, but they do not necessarily need underlying permafrost. Permafrost, however, forms an impermeable substratum which keeps

the soil moisture available for frost action. On gentle slopes the stone nets may be distorted into garlands by downslope movement, or if the slope is steep, into stone stripes 25 to 50 meters wide and 30 meters long. In the drier parts of the polar desert frost sorting becomes rare (fig. 3.11); in the extremely arid regions, such as the west side of McMurdo Sound in Antarctica, and northern Greenland (Davies, 1961), it is essentially absent except near melting snowbanks or glaciers.

In areas underlain by an impermeable layer (seasonally frozen ground or perennially frozen ground) the active layer in the tundra is often saturated with moisture and is quite mobile. The progressive downslope movement of saturated detrital material under the action of gravity and working in conjunction with frost action is called solifluction. This material moves in a semifluid condition and is manifested by lobe-like and sheet-like flows of soil on slopes (fig. 3.16). The lobes are up to 30 meters wide and have a steep front 1 or 2 meters high. One of the outstanding features of solifluction is the mass transport of material over low angle slopes. Solifluction deposits are widespread in the tundra part of the polar deserts and consist of a blanket 25 centimeters to 2 meters thick of unstratified or poorly stratified, unsorted, heterogeneous, till-like detrital material of local origin. In many areas the terrain is characterized by relatively smooth round hills and slopes, with well to poorly defined solifluction lobes or terraces. If the debris is blocky and angular, and fine material is absent, the lobes are poorly developed or entirely absent. As shown in figure 3.11, solifluction becomes less prominent or absent in the extremely arid parts of the polar desert. However, solifluction is locally present in the very arid regions below melting snowbanks (Nichols, 1966).

In many areas the frost-rived debris contains few fine materials, little water, and consists of angular fragments of well-jointed, resistant rock. Under such circumstances solifluction lobes do not often occur, but instead striking sheets or streams of angular rubble form. These are called rock streams or rubble sheets.

Those parts of the polar desert that lie near snowline may have active altiplanation terraces and rock glaciers. Since these features are not common through the broad lowlands of the typical polar desert they will not be considered in this chapter.

Features Common to Polar and Temperate-Tropic Deserts

As mentioned earlier, despite the scanty precipitation, fluvial processes are predominant in both polar and southern deserts, although the frequency and magnitude are different from the more humid areas. Therefore, in both types of deserts there are the conventional alluvial fans and ephemeral streams, although pediments and playas are not seemingly common in the cold deserts.

Other, more distinctive, "desert" features which are common to both cold and hot deserts are sand dunes, ventifacts, and taffoni. Sand dunes are geomorphic features most commonly associated with deserts, yet dunes, both active and inactive, are common outside of the typical desert areas. Dunes depend upon source material, and the sand is picked up by the wind where the vegetation is absent, scanty, or "insufficient." This may be along beaches or braided streams, as well as in extremely arid areas where scanty vegetation permits such sand to be obtained from the weathering of bedrock.

Sand dunes are present in polar deserts but are not prominent as in some hot deserts, mainly the Sahara. Most polar deserts are near glaciated areas and are crossed by vegetation-free braided glacial streams whose floodplains provide a fine source of sand. Therefore, dunes are common, especially in northern Alaska, on the lee side of these major streams, even in the tundra areas.

In the extremely arid parts of the polar desert, blowing sand is common and areas of small dunes exist as reported from Antarctica (Péwé, 1960; Calkin, 1964; Nichols, 1966; Neall and Smith, 1967; and Webb and McKelvey, 1959). In the polar desert of Inglefield Land in northwest Greenland, Nichols (1969) mentions that there is a small amount of windblown sand that dribbles down into thermal contraction cracks, but for the most part, windblown sand is almost nonexistent.

The process of cutting and polishing of stones by wind-driven sand to form ventifacts is common to deserts but not restricted to such areas. Ventifacts are not widespread in the tundra part of the polar deserts. However, in extremely arid cold deserts they are ubiquitous (Fristrup, 1953; Péwé, 1960; Nichols, 1966, 1969; Calkin and Cailleux, 1962). Such deserts may be floored with a lag gravel in large part composed of ventifacts. In Antarctica it was discovered that the older the glacial moraine surface the better the ventifact development (Péwé, 1960).

One of the least understood processes in arid polar deserts, as well as in the temperate-tropic deserts, is that of cavernous weathering or formation of taffoni. Cavernous weathering is a process in which recesses, hollows, pits, niches, or taffoni are developed in rock faces. The pits may be pocket, purse, or U-shaped. The cavities may have nearly circular rounded openings, or the openings can be elongated, giving the cavity an ellipsoidal shape. The taffoni may be from a few centimeters in diameter to 10 meters high and 20 meters long, but generally smaller (fig. 3.17).

Taffoni have been reported in boulders and rock faces from many places in the world such as Antarctica

Fig. 3.16.   Aerial view toward the northeast shows headwaters of east tributary of Nome Creek, Circle Quadrangle, Alaska. Well-developed solifluction lobes are seen in the foreground. Glaciated Mt. Prindle occupies right background on skyline. (Photograph 2694, by T. L. Péwé, July 9, 1968)

(Taylor, 1922, fig. 58; Priestley, 1923; Avsyuk, Markov, and Shumskiy, 1956; Péwé, 1960; Calkin and Cailleux, 1962; Cailleux and Calkin, 1963; Neall and Smith, 1967), Australia (Dragovich, 1967), Chile (Segerstrom and Henríquez, 1964), Corsica (Kvelberg and Popoff, 1937), Greenland (Nichols, 1969), Sahara (Schwarzbach, 1954), and southwestern United States (Bryan, 1922, 1923, 1925; Blackwelder, 1929; Péwé, 1969, p. 14). The pits seem to be best developed and the most common in coarse-grained igneous rocks, especially granitic rocks. However they do occur in other types.

The origin of the taffoni in both the cold and hot deserts is a subject that needs more study as no clear-cut quantitative answer is available, especially in polar deserts. Sekyra (1970) strongly supports the eolian hypothesis for cavernous weathering in the polar desert of Antarctica. In fact, it has long been widely acclaimed that taffoni are formed by wind action (Taylor, 1922), although Blackwelder (1929) states that wind probably is effective only in removing the debris. In polar deserts, windblown ice crystals and salt are referred to, as well as sand, in the origin of taffoni. (The cover page of the Antarctic News Bulletin of the New Zealand Antarctic Society for September 1964 shows a person standing on a rock with well-developed taffoni, and it is stated that the erosion is "probably formed by wind-blown sand and salt erosion. . . .") It was noted by the writer in Taylor Dry Valley, and by Cailleux and Calkin (1963) in Victoria Valley, that the cavities in McMurdo Sound of Antarctica had no preferred orientation. In the Sonoran desert at Phoenix in southwestern United States, preliminary observations by the writer indicate some preferred orientation.

Kvelberg and Popoff (1937) and Cailleux (1953) believe that lowering the temperature of the rock by circulating cool air in cavities is important in taffoni origin.

In hot deserts solar heating and cooling of the rocks (plus some solution of cement between grains) has been suggested by Bryan (1922) as origin of taffoni from southern Arizona (fig. 3.18). The idea that thermal changes alone can cause cavernous weathering has been disproved by Blackwelder (1933) and more recently by Roth (1965). It would seem ineffective in the polar deserts. In Antarctica crystallization of salt from sea spray (Neall and Smith, 1967) and also frost action has been suggested as processes involved in cavernous

Fig. 3.17. Cavernous weathering (taffoni) in granitic boulders on a glacial moraine in the polar desert, Taylor Dry Valley, McMurdo Sound, Antarctica. (Photograph 1594, by T. L. Péwé, December 14, 1957)

Fig. 3.18. Taffoni in arkosic conglomerate, Papago Buttes, Tempe, Arizona. (Photograph 3233, by T. L. Péwé, October 2, 1971)

weathering. Frost action has also been suggested by Cailleux and Calkin (1963).

Most modern work (Dragovich, 1967) now seems to support the earlier ideas of Bryan (1923) and Blackwelder (1929) that the probable cause for the formation of taffoni seems to be chemical alterations of some of the minerals, perhaps mainly by hydration. Moisture evaporates rapidly on bare rocks in deserts but lasts longer in shady recesses or irregularities. In this initial moist, shady recess chemical weathering proceeds faster than in the unshaded part and the recesses enlarge and therefore the cavity grows.

In both cold and hot extremely arid deserts it would be well to know more about the origin of taffoni. It is especially important to know more about the rate of formation and the possibilities of using it as a dating mechanism. A start has been made on this in Antarctica (Calkin and Cailleux, 1962) and in Arizona (Péwé, unpublished).

The Polar Desert and Man

Development of the polar desert demands understanding and ability to cope with problems of the environment dictated by permafrost (Péwé, 1958, 1966b; Brown, R. J. E., 1970). The most dramatic, widespread, and economically important examples of the influence of permafrost on life in the North deal with construction and maintenance of roads, railroads, airfields, bridges, buildings, dams, sewers, and communication lines. Engineering problems are of four fundamental types: (1) those involving thawing of ice-rich permafrost and subsequent subsidence of the surface under unheated structures such as roads and airfields; (2) those involv-

ing subsidence under heated structures; (3) those resulting from frost action, generally intensified by poor drainage caused by permafrost, and; (4) those involved only with the temperature of permafrost causing buried sewer, water, and oil lines to freeze. The first three are common to the tundra part of the polar desert and less important in the extremely arid polar desert where there is less ground ice. The fourth point is important in both areas.

A thorough study of the frozen ground should be part of the planning of any engineering project in the polar desert (Brown, R. J. E., 1970). It is generally best to attempt to disturb the permafrost as little as possible in order to maintain a stable foundation for engineering structures, unless the permafrost is thin; then, it may be possible to destroy the permafrost. The method of construction preserving the permafrost has been termed the *passive method,* and alternately, the destroying of permafrost, the *active method.*

Since thawing of permafrost and frost action are involved with almost all engineering problems in polar areas, whether dealing with highways, buildings, or sewer lines, it would be well to consider the general principles of these phenomena (see Ferrians, Kachadoorian, and Greene, 1969). The delicate thermal equilibrium of permafrost is disrupted when the vegetation or snow cover, or active layer, is compacted. The permafrost table is lowered, the active layer is thickened, and considerable ice is melted, both lowering the surface and providing in summer a wetter active layer with less bearing strength. Such disturbance permits a greater penetration of summer warming. It is a common procedure to place a fill or pad of gravel under engineering works. Such a fill generally is a good conductor of heat.

and, if thin, may cause additional thawing of permafrost. It is necessary to make the fill thick enough to contain the entire amplitude of seasonal temperature variation, in other words, keep the annual seasonally freezing and thawing within the fill and the compacted active layer. Under these conditions no permafrost will thaw. Such a procedure is easily possible in the polar desert of the Arctic (fig. 3.19), but in the warmer Subarctic it is impractical because of the enormous amount of fill needed. Under a heated building profound thawing may occur more rapidly than under roads and airfields.

Frost action is the freezing and thawing of moisture in the ground and has long been known to seriously disrupt and destroy structures in polar latitudes. In the winter there is the freezing of ground moisture with upward displacement of the ground (frost heaving), and in the summer there is the loss of bearing strength due to excessive moisture in the ground brought in during the freezing operation. The intensity of frost action is regulated by temperature, texture of the ground, and amount of soil moisture. Frost action is best developed in silt — and silt clay — sized sediments in areas of rigorous climate and poor drainage. Polar latitudes are ideal for maximum frost action because most lowland areas are covered by fine-grained sediments, and the underlying permafrost causes poor drainage.

Piles are used to support many, if no most, structures built on ice-rich permafrost. In regions of cold winters many pile foundations are in ground that is subject to seasonal freezing and, therefore, may be subject to the damaging effect of frost heaving (Péwé and Paige, 1963). Frost heaving tends to displace the pile upward and thus to disturb the foundation of the structure. Expen-

sive maintenance and in some instances complete destruction of bridges, school buildings, military installations, and other structures have resulted from failure to understand the principles of frost heaving of piling.

The need for careful geological location study for highways, railroads, airfields, and pipelines (Lachenbruch, 1970) is very important anywhere in the world but absolutely essential in permafrost areas to avoid constant costly maintenance if not complete abandonment. Such location studies were not frequently considered in construction work prior to the 1950s in North America and perhaps prior to the 1930s in Asia. Even in the early 1970s many construction projects proceed with inadequate location studies that could minimize many permafrost problems.

Highways in polar areas are relatively few and mainly unpaved. They are subject to subsidence by thawing of permafrost in summer, frost heaving in winter, and loss of bearing strength in summer on fine-grained sediments. Constant grading of gravel roads permits maintenance of a relatively smooth highway. Where the road is paved over ice-rich permafrost, the roadway becomes rough and is much more costly to maintain than unpaved roads. Many of the paved roads in polar areas have been resurfaced two or three times in a period of ten years.

Railroads particularly have serious construction problems and require costly upkeep in permafrost areas because of the necessity of maintaining a relatively low gradient and the subsequent location of the roadbed in ice-rich lowlands which are underlain with perennially frozen ground.

Heated buildings in polar areas can have a conventional basement if built in areas of no permafrost or bedrock and gravel with little or no ice. However, con-

Fig. 3.19. Petroleum camp at Prudhoe Bay, Alaska, built over raised-edge ice-wedge polygons. Roads are on a 1.5 meters gravel fill, and buildings are constructed on piles frozen into permafrost. (Photograph 3088, by T. L. Péwé, July 1970)

struction of such buildings on ice-rich permafrost requires a technique which enables the cold winter air to circulate under the building to counteract the heat generated in the building. The most common way to build structures above the ground with large spaces under the foundation for air flow is to construct on piles. This technique has been perfected both in the U.S.S.R. (fig. 3.20) and North America and requires that the piles do not move. If the piles are jacked up in the winter by frost action, the building will be disturbed and can be destroyed. Therefore it is important that either the pile be adequately anchored in permafrost or the pile be isolated from the heaving seasonally frozen ground by a movable collar.

Both surface and subsurface water supplies in the North are beset by problems uncommon in temperate latitudes. Groundwater sources are above the permafrost, in unfrozen zones with the permafrost, and below permafrost (Cederstrom, Johnston, and Subitzky, 1953; Williams, 1970). Sources above permafrost may be seasonal and subject to contamination from cesspools. Sources from unfrozen zones within the permafrost are common in the discontinuous zones where water also can be obtained below permafrost, deep drilling (350 to 600 meters) is expensive, and the sediments are generally lacking in sufficient groundwater.

Distribution of water as well as sewage presents unique problems in permafrost areas (Alter, 1950a, b; 1952). In addition to requiring a heated distribution system to prevent freezing, either in permafrost or seasonal frost, utility distribution lines are subject to problems as the result of frost action and thawing of permafrost. The most successful construction method generally utilized in such situations is to place all services in heated distribution boxes called utilidors. These boxes enclose water, steam, gas, sewage, and other utilities. The utilidor may be either under or above ground.

In summary, it can be said that normal techniques must often be modified at additional costs because of permafrost in construction and maintenance of railroads, buildings, water and sewer lines, dams, roads, bridges, and airfields. But, despite special problems unique to the cold regions, development of the permafrost areas will continue at an ever-increasing rate. Man has already learned to cope with the problems, and improvements of scientific and engineering approaches, plus careful geological site selection and study of the permafrost problem, will allow successful expansion into polar areas.

Acknowledgment

The writer wishes to acknowledge the aid of Robert K. Merrill for his thorough review of the manuscript and for his compilation of figure 3.1.

Fig. 3.20.   Brick apartment house on concrete piles frozen into permafrost, Yakoutsk, Siberia, U.S.S.R. (Photograph PK 13,462, by T. L. Péwé, July 28, 1969)

BIBLIOGRAPHY

Alter, A. J.
1950a Arctic sanitary engineering. Federal Housing Administration, Washington, D.C. 106 pp.
1950b Water supply in Alaska. American Water Works Association Journal, pp. 519–32.
1952 Water problems in low temperature areas. Selected Papers of Alaskan Scientific Conference, Arctic Institute of North America, pp. 219–39.

Avysuk, G. A., Markov, K. K., and Shumskiy, P. A.
1956 Geographical observations on an Antarctic "oasis." National Commission International Geophysical Year 1957–58, Academy of Science, Antarctic Council, Moscow, U.S.S.R. 69 pp.

Berg, T. E., and Black, R. F.
1966 Preliminary measurements of growth of nonsorted polygons, Victoria Land, Antarctica. Antarctic Soils and Soil Forming Processes. American Geophysical Union, Antarctic Research Series, Washington, D.C. 8: 61–108.

Black, R. F.
1952 Polygonal patterns and ground conditions from aerial photographs. Photogrammetric Engineering 18: 123–34.

Blackwelder, E.
1929 Cavernous rock surfaces of the desert. American Journal of Science 5–17: 393–99.
1933 The insolation hypothesis of rock weathering. American Journal of Science 226: 97–113.

Brown, J.
1967 An estimation of the volume of ground ice, coastal plain, northern Alaska. U.S. Army Cold Regions Research Engineering Laboratory, Technical Note. 22 pp.

Brown, R. J. E.
1970 Permafrost in Canada. University of Toronto Press, Toronto. 234 pp.

Bryan, K.
1922 Erosion and sedimentation in Papago country, Arizona. U.S. Geological Survey Bulletin 730-B: 19–83.
1923 Pedestal rocks in the arid Southwest. U.S. Geological Survey Bulletin 760-A: 1–11.
1925 The Papago country, Arizona. U.S. Geological Survey Water-Supply Paper 499. 427 pp.

Bunge, A.
1884 Naturhistorische boebachtungen und fahrten im Lena Delta. St. Petersbourg Academy of Science Bulletin 29: 422–76.

Cailleux, A.
1953 Taffonis and alveolaire erosion. Cahiers Geologique Thoiry 16–17: 130–33.

Cailleux, A., and Calkin, P.
1963 Orientation of hollows in cavernously weathered boulders in Antarctica (translated title). Biuletyn Peryglacjalny 2: 19–28.

Calkin, P. E.
1964 Geomorphology and glacial geology of the Victoria Valley system, southern Victoria Land, Antarctica. Ohio State University Institute of Polar Studies Report Number 10. 66 pp.

Calkin, P., and Cailleux, A.
1962 A quantitative study of cavernous weathering (taffonis) and its application to glacial chronology in Victoria Valley, Antarctica. Annals of Geomorphology 6: 317–24.

Cederstrom, D. J., Johnston, P. M., and Subitzky, S.
1953 Occurrence and development of ground water in permafrost regions. U.S. Geological Survey Circular 275. 30 pp.

Czudek, T., and Demek, J.
1970 Thermokarst in Siberia and its influence on the development of lowland relief. Quaternary Research 1(1): 103–20.

Davies, W. E.
1961 Surface features of permafrost in arid areas. Geology of the Arctic, Proceedings of the First International Symposium on Arctic Geology, Toronto 2: 981–87.

Dragovich, D.
1967 Flaking, a weathering process operating on cavernous rock surfaces. Geological Society of America Bulletin 78: 801–4.

Ferrians, O. J., Jr., Kachadoorian, Reuben, and Greene, G. W.
1969 Permafrost and related engineering problems in Alaska. U.S. Geological Survey Professional Paper 678. 37 pp.

Fristrup, Børge
1953 Wind erosion within the Arctic Deserts. Geografisk Tidsskrift 52: 51–65.

Jahn, A.
1970 Azgadnienia strefy peryglacjalnej. Panstwowe Wydawnictwo Naukowe, Warszawa. 202 pp.

Kotzebue, O. von
1821 A voyage of discovery into the South Sea and Behring's Straits for the purpose of exploring a northwest passage. English translation, 3 volumes, London.

Kvelberg, I., and Popoff, B.
1937 Die Tafoni-Verwitterungserscheinung. *In* Riga. Acta Universitatis Latviensis, Faculty of Chemistry 4(6): 129–370.

Lachenbruch, A. H.
1960 Thermal contraction cracks and ice wedges in permafrost. U.S. Geological Survey Professional Paper 400-B: B404–6.
1970 Some estimates of the thermal effects of a heated pipeline in permafrost. U.S. Geological Survey Circular 632. 23 pp.

Lachenbruch, A. H., Greene, G. W., and Marshall, B. V.
1966 Permafrost and the geothermal regimes. *In* Environment of the Cape Thompson Region, Alaska, Oak Ridge, U.S. Atomic Energy Commission, pp. 149–63.

Leffingwell, E. de K.
1915 Ground-ice wedges: The dominant form of ground-ice on the north coast of Alaska. Journal of Geology 23: 635–54.

McGinnies, W. G., Goldman, B. J., and Paylore, P.
1968 Deserts of the world. University of Arizona Press, Tucson. 788 pp.

Meigs, P.
1953 World distribution of arid and semi-arid homoclimates. Reviews of Research on Arid Zone Hydrology, Arizona Zone Program, Paris, UNESCO 1: 203–9.

Müller, F.
1959 Permafrost or permanently frozen ground and related engineering problems. U.S. Army, Office Chief of Engineers, Military Intelligence Divi-

Müller, F. *(continued)*
    sion, Special Report, Strategic Study 62. 231 pp. (Reprinted 1947, J. W. Edwards, Inc., Ann Arbor, Michigan)

Muller, S.W.
  1945 Permafrost or permanently frozen ground and related engineering problems. U.S. Army, Office Chief of Engineers, Military Intelligence Division, Special Report. Strategic Engineering Study 62. 231 pp. (Reprinted 1947, J. W. Edwards, Inc., Ann Arbor, Michigan)

Neall, V. E., and Smith, I. E.
  1967 The McMurdo oasis. Tuatara 15 (3): 117–28.

Nichols, R. L.
  1966 Geomorphology of Antarctica. *In* Antarctica Soils and Soil Forming Processes, Antarctic Research Series. American Geophysical Union 8: 1–77.
  1969 Geomorphology of Inglefield Land, North Greenland. Meddelelser om Gronland 188(1): 1–109.

Péwé, T. L.
  1954 Effect of permafrost on cultivated fields, Fairbanks area, Alaska. U.S. Geological Survey Bulletin 989-F: 315–51.
  1958 Geologic map of the Fairbanks d-2 quadrangle, Alaska. U.S. Geological Survey Quadrangle Map Number 110 (with text).
  1959 Sand wedge polygons (tesselations) in the McMurdo Sound region, Antarctica. American Journal of Science 257: 542–52.
  1960 Multiple glaciation in the McMurdo Sound region, Antarctica — a progress report. Journal of Geology 68(5): 498–514.
  1962 Age of moraines in Victoria Land, Antarctica. Journal of Glaciology 4: 93–100.
        Oregon State University Press, Corvallis. 40 pp.
  1966a Ice-wedges in Alaska — classification, distribution and climatic significance. International Permafrost Conference, Washington, Proceedings of National Academy of Science, National Research Council Publication Number 1287. pp. 76–81.
  1966b Permafrost and its effect on life in the north. Oregon State University Press, Corvallis. 40 pp.
  1969 Colorado River guidebook. Lebeau Printing Company, Phoenix. 78 pp.
  In   Quaternary geology of Alaska. U.S. Geological
  Press Survey. Professional Paper 835.

Péwé, T. L., Church, R. E., and Andresen, N. J.
  1969 Origin and paleoclimatic significance of large scale polygons in the Donnelly Dome area, Alaska. Geological Society of America Special Paper 109. 87 pp.

Péwé, T. L., and Paige, R. A.
  1963 Frost heaving of piles with an example from the Fairbanks area, Alaska. U.S. Geological Survey Bulletin 1111-I: 333–407.

Popov, A. I.
  1969 Underground ice in the Quaternary deposits of the Yani-Indigirka lowland as a genetic and stratigraphic indicator. *In* The Periglacial Environment: Past and Present. McGill-Queens University Press, Montreal. pp. 55–64.

Priestley, R. E.
  1923 Physiography (Robertson Bay and Terra Nova Bay Regions), British (Terra Nova) Antarctic Expedition 1910–1913. Harrison & Sons Limited, London. 87 pp.

Roth, E. S.
  1965 Temperature and water content as factors in desert weathering. Journal of Geology 73(3): 454–68.

Schwarzbach, M.
  1954 Geologie in Bildern, eine Einfurung in die Wissenschaft von der Erde. Georg Fisher Verlab, Wittlich. 132 pp.

Segerstrom, K., and Henríquez, H.
  1964 Cavities, or "tafoni" in rock faces of the Atacama desert, Chile. U.S. Geological Survey Professional Paper 501-C: C121–5.

Sekyra, J.
  1970 Forms of mechanic weathering and their significance for the stratigraphy of the Quaternary in Antarctica. SCAR/IUGS, Symposium Antarctic Geology and Soil Earth Geophysics, Oslo. 13 pp.

Shumskiy, P. A., Krenke, A. N., and Zotikov, I. A.
  1964 Ice and its changes. *In* Solid Earth and Interface Phenomena, Research in Geophysics. Massachusetts Institute of Technology, Cambridge, pp. 425–60.

Solopov, A. V.
  1967 Oases in Antarctica (translated title). Moscow Academy of Science, Interdepartmental Geophysics Commission, Meteorology Number 14, Izdatel stvo "Nauka." (Translated, 1969, by Israel Program for Scientific Translations, Jerusalem. 146 pp.)

Stoneley, R.
  1970 Discussion. *In* Thermal Consideration in Permafrost, American Association of Petroleum Geologists, Pacific Section Geological Seminar on the North Slope of Alaska, pp. J2–J3.

Taylor, G.
  1922 The physiography of the McMurdo Sound and Granite Harbour region, British Antarctic "Terra Nova" expedition 1910–1913. Harrison & Sons Limited, London. 246 pp.

Washburn, A. L.
  1956 Classification of patterned ground and review of suggested origins. Geological Society of America Bulletin 67: 823–26.

Webb, P. N., and McKelvey, B. C.
  1959 Geological investigations in South Victoria Land, Antarctica, Part 1. *In* Geology of Victoria Dry Valley. New Zealand Journal of Geology and Geophysics 2–1: 120–36.

Williams, J. R.
  1970 Ground water in permafrost regions in Alaska occurs according to the same geologic and hydrologic principles prevailing in temperate regions. U.S. Geological Survey Professional Paper 696. 83 pp.

Yefimonv, A. I., and Dukhin, I. Y.
  1966 Some permafrost thicknesses in the Arctic (translated title). Geologiya i Geofizika 7: 92–7. (Abstracted in Polar Record, 1968, p. 68)

CHAPTER 4

GEOLOGICAL AND LIMNOLOGICAL FACTORS OF COLD DESERTS

William E. Davies
United States Geological Survey, Washington, D.C.

The Arctic Deserts

From a hydrologic viewpoint aridity in the High Arctic and possibly in the Antarctic is not a recent phenomenon. In northernmost Greenland, where three distinct glaciations are evident in the Pleistocene, observations indicate that the oldest glaciation was most extensive and that successive glaciations were each progressively less extensive. Also, in northern Greenland, large areas in Peary Land were free of ice cover throughout all of the three glacial periods. The progressive weakening of glacial advances and the presence of refugia are indicative of an increasing aridity in the Pleistocene.

At present aridity is responsible for the large area of ice-free land surrounding the north polar basin. So pronounced is this aridity, that as one goes northward glaciation and glacial activity decreases. In addition the aridity is accentuated by processes of natural desiccation from extremely low temperatures during winter.

In contrast to retardation of glacial activity, the hydrologic regimen of Arctic deserts is not curtailed very much by the arid conditions, and the area is unique among deserts in that there is a myriad of fresh water, permanent lakes, and large well-developed river basins. In many respects surface drainage has characteristics of a temperate humid climate rather than those of a desert. To put it in perspective, it can be safely said that man is more in danger of drowning than dying of thirst in the Arctic desert.

With so much water available in an area where precipitation is as low as 6 centimeters a year, the first question to be answered concerns the sources of water. In the High Arctic there are three major sources for runoff: precipitation, melt of glacier ice, and melt of ground ice. Direct runoff from precipitation is negligible because the amount of rainfall is extremely small and generally is in the form of mist or drizzle which seldom accumulates sufficiently to form channel flow.

Lag runoff from accumulation of winter snow is a major source of water in small stream basins that are independent of glaciers. Snowdrifts act as reservoirs, and the duration of flow in small streams depends on the amount of drift that accumulates (fig. 4.1). In valleys that trend across the direction of prevailing winds, the accumulation is generally sufficient to sustain flow in small streams throughout the brief summer (Fristrup,

1953). The amount of snowfall if uniformly distributed and not concentrated in drifts would sustain flow for only a few days or a week during early summer melt.

The wind in sweeping the snow from the surface and accumulating it in drifts reduces the amount of direct ablation which in Peary Land, northern Greenland, is great enough to remove most of the ground cover before any melt occurs. In addition the drifts concentrate the potential water supply directly along the streams, which cuts the losses from evaporation and seepage after melting. The concentration of snow in the valleys provides increased insulation and some protection from radiation. The protection of snowdrifts results in prolonging flow and making the discharge more uniform. Talus slopes also contain large quantities of drifted snow and act as reservoirs that aid in prolonging runoff.

The large streams in the northern cold desert are supplied primarily by runoff from melting of glaciers, ice caps, and ice sheets. These sources are large accumulators of water, and in melting they concentrate the runoff in relatively small areas. The effect is the increase by many fold of the area of drainage basins and the establishment of regulated flow as effective as that provided by vegetation and soil infiltration in more temperate areas. During the twentieth century this source of water has been operating at a deficit, with more runoff than accumulation, resulting in some dramatic changes in glaciers and in the margins of ice sheets.

The part melting ground ice plays in furnishing water for runoff in the Arctic deserts is difficult to assess. Seepages are present everywhere, but most of these probably are a result of complicated movement of water from the surface into the soil, resulting in saturation above the permafrost table with little disturbance to the permafrost (fig. 4.2).

The streams fed exclusively from snowdrifts follow distinct patterns of flow throughout the year. Mecham River on Cornwallis Island, northern Canada, is a stream of this type. Flow is initiated in late spring when residual ground cover of snow melts. The first flow is a mere trickle in mid- to late-May, and distinctive channel flow occurs a week or two later. By mid-June snow-bank melt greatly increases and flow in the Mecham steadily rises from 10 cubic meters per second to a peak of 50 cubic meters per second in early July.

Fig. 4.1.   Perennial snowbank in northern Greenland, a reservoir sustaining streamflow during arid summer months.

Fig. 4.2.   Small seep issuing from ground ice in a moraine on upland near Centrum Sφ in northeastern Greenland.

Fig. 4.3.   Large braided river on Polaris Forbjerg fed by melt of the Greenland Ice Sheet.

In late July flow dwindles to an average of 1.2 cubic meters per second until early August when it drops abruptly with depletion of the snow drifts (Cook, 1960). Freeze-up occurs at the end of August, but the underflow from residual water beneath the channel apparently continues into September and results in small-scale over-icing in the small channels. The beginning and end of flow of snowdrift-fed streams varies with latitude and altitude but peak flow is generally in early July regardless of location.

Rivers sustained by meltwater from glaciers and ice sheets generally are large and commonly flow in braided channels (fig. 4.3). Average discharge in the summer is in the order of 10 to 50 cubic meters per second with peak discharges up to 200 cubic meters per second. Flow is initiated in late May when surface snow melts and water saturates the snow on the river ice, causing slow percolation at first and shortly afterwards developing rills and channels in the ice. By the first week in June channels cut through the ice as the runoff increases from melt of snowdrifts. The channels are rapidly cleared of ice and peak flow is reached in mid-July. After this the flow recedes until late July when a slight increase occurs as runoff from melt of glacier ice becomes effective. During the period of glacial melt there are pronounced diurnal variations in flow within 30 kilometers of the glaciers. Flow is reduced for a quarter of a day in the early morning and increased for a quarter of a day after noon. In late August flow is gradually reduced by freezing of the surface of the glaciers and ice sheets.

By the middle of September surface flow ceases, and channels ice over. Underflow in the sand and gravel of riverbeds continues into mid-October, after which frost penetrates to a depth of 2 to 3 meters.

Large rivers fed by glaciers or ice sheets are found throughout Spitsbergen, Greenland, and the Canadian Arctic islands. They are commonly spaced 18 to 50 kilometers, and each drains ice-free land areas 1,200 to 2,500 square kilometers in size. The area of drainage of ice sheets and glaciers is difficult to estimate, but from evidence of melt streams on the surface of ice sheets, the area involved is in the order of one to three times as great as the ice-free portion of the drainage basin.

The rivers feeding Centrum Sφ in northern Greenland are examples of those carrying water discharged by glaciers and ice sheets. Dissolved solids are in the order of 50 parts per million, which is low. Turbidity varies considerably, but the amount of silt in one of the rivers discolors it throughout the summer. Since these rivers drain only ice sheets, their turbidity is much lower than those draining glacial tongues.

In the polar deserts in Alaska, western Canada, and the Soviet Union, runoff reflects subarctic rather than polar conditions. These regions are drained by major rivers that rise in temperate and subarctic areas and flow directly across the narrow segments of the polar deserts. Their pattern of flow, quality of water, and heat budgets are independent of the polar deserts. For the purpose of this discussion, these areas will not be considered, as to do so would only complicate and distort the picture of hydrology of cold deserts. One feature worthy of comment in the Alaskan and Soviet Union parts of the cold deserts is that of over-icing. The rivers crossing the gently sloping coastal plains in these areas flow in broad braided channels. During early fall the channels freeze and obstruct the flow of water received from the south. This causes overflow and additional buildup of ice which may attain a thickness of 3 meters or more. Lateral drainage is blocked and local heads of pressure are created in the area adjacent to the river. Water in these areas of pressure freezes to form large icing mounds (Lewis, 1962).

The land in the polar deserts is literally dotted with many thousands of lakes (fig. 4.4). Some are mere ponds while others are over 20 kilometers long and several kilometers wide. Lack of detailed thermal and chemical measurements makes it difficult to classify most Arctic lakes according to systems established in limnology. Roen in his studies of Greenland lakes has established a qualitative system that is applicable to lakes of all sizes in the cold deserts (Roen, 1962).

The first category is that of lakes with large quantities of material suspended in water. One group of lakes in this category are those in direct contact with glacial ice. There are many hundreds of such lakes adjacent to the Greenland ice sheet and smaller ice caps and outlet glaciers in Greenland and the Arctic islands of Canada. The water is cold; in many of the lakes ice is perennial but some have short periods when they are ice free.

Anguissaq Lake, north of Thule, Greenland, is one of the few large ice-contact lakes that have been studied in the area of polar desert. It abuts the Greenland ice sheet, is 13.5 kilometers long, and has a surface area of 45 square kilometers. At the height of the melt season ice normally covers 90 percent of the lake. Its greatest depth is 187 meters with a mean depth of 75. About 3.4 cubic kilometers of water and ice are in the lake (Barnes, 1960). The lake is nearly isothermal throughout the year, with temperatures of 0.15° to 0.26° C in early June and 0.35° to 0.40° C after snow cover has melted. The heat budget is 2,000 calories per square centimeter per year. At the height of the melt season a moat 25 meters wide lies along the shore; during winter, ice 1.5 meters thick covers the moat.

The ice cover on the lake during the annual melt is reduced from a thickness of 3.3 to 1.7 meters, most of which occurs by melting of the top side. The annual loss is between one-half and one-third of the total ice cover. This loss is made up by refreezing of the lower side of the ice cover, beginning late in August. The ice at the surface, therefore, is generally not more than three years old, even though the mass is perennial. At the height of the melt season in late June the lake level rises 50 centimeters, after which outflow causes a recession followed by a rise to 65 centimeters in early August. Dissolved salts are 6.77 to 7.14 milligrams per liter of inorganic ions, mainly sodium, calcium, and sulfate. Dissolved oxygen is 8.90 milligrams per liter beneath the

surface of the ice; in deeper water it is from 9.55 to 9.80 milligrams per liter, increasing with depth.

Barnes concludes that perennially frozen lakes require at least 5,000 degree-days of freezing coupled with low summer ablation. Such conditions occur in high latitudes, with elevations over 500 meters, with few or small cold influents supplying water to the lake, with large volume and great depth of water, with steeply sloping banks, and with glacial contact for deep cooling of lake water.

Another type of lake receiving large amounts of suspended sediment is that fed by rivers draining from a glacier or ice sheet. The temperature of the water entering such a lake and the amount of suspended sediment received depends on the distance the lake is from the glacial source. Centrum Sφ in northern Greenland, Lake Hazen in Ellesmere Land, Canada, and Lake Nettilling on Baffin Island are large lakes of this type. Normally these lakes are ice-free at the height of the melt season, but in some years over 50 percent of the ice cover persists.

Centrum Sφ was studied in 1960 (Krinsley, 1962); its regime is typical of large lakes of this type elsewhere in the Arctic. Centrum Sφ is fed by two large rivers that drain about 5,000 square kilometers of ice-free land and probably an equal area of the Greenland ice sheet. Outflow is by way of Saefaxi Elv, a large river flowing east to Hekla Sund. The lake is 20 kilometers long and averages 4 kilometers in width with depth up to 79.5 meters. Snow cover before the melt starts is in the order of 7.5 to 51 centimeters, with the greatest amount near the south and east sides of the lake. Visual melting begins in late May when flow from the large rivers spreads over the west end of the lake; by the end of May open water exists in the vicinity of the mouths of the rivers and moating along the shore is well under way. By early June the rivers pour large volumes of water with temperature of 3.8° to 8.0° C into the moats, and the level of the lake rises rapidly, reaching a maximum of 2.5 meters in mid-July. In the last quarter of July the lake is free of ice, with 75 percent of the ice removed by melting from the top and 25 percent from the bottom.

Before melt starts temperatures are 0.1° C at 2 meters and 3.5° C at the bottom; after melt the surface rises to 2.4° C but remains at 3.5° C at the bottom. Transient convection currents apparently form at depths of 30 to 33 and 60 to 63 meters during early June. Later in summer and during the period of ice cover the lake apparently is close to isothermal. The lake water is slightly alkaline, with pH of 7.2 to 7.5. The waters are well mixed chemically, and there is little vertical variation. Total dissolved solids are 60 to 64 parts per million, mainly calcium and bicarbonates with smaller quantities of chlorides, sulfates, magnesium, and sodium.

In his study of Nettilling Lake of Baffin Island, Oliver (1964) has postulated that insolation alone is not sufficient to clear ice from large lakes. Wind action is the

Fig. 4.4.   Small dimictic lake near Thule, Greenland.

ultimate destructive force after the ice has been weakened by melting. Wind-generated waves grind ice blocks into smaller pieces with greater surface exposed to warm water and also spread warm water over the upper surface of larger ice masses. Wind-generated currents counter the loss of heat sustained in melting by circulating warm water.

The second major category cited by Roen covers lakes containing clear water. Lakes of this type with low salt content are the most common type in the cold deserts of the Arctic (fig. 4.4). During ice-free periods lakes of this group have some outflow, and conductivity of the lake water is about 100 micromhos. Deep lakes of this type show little fluctuation in temperature throughout the year except for minor variation in the uppermost layers. There is no loss of oxygen toward the bottom, nor is there any distinct increase in dissolved solids in the water during freeze-up. in deep lakes. In shallow lakes, however, there is a change in salt content in freezing, a loss of oxygen near the bottom in summer, and a 2° to 6° C variation of bottom temperature during the year. Most of the clear water lakes are fed by snow melt, and except for a few in Peary Land, northern Greenland, they are clear of ice in late July and August.

Clear water lakes with high salt content are found throughout Greenland and the Canadian Arctic islands. They are most numerous in the northern part of these areas where aridity is maximum. The salt content of the lakes when they are free of ice is relatively constant, and specific conductance is between 200 and 700 micromhos Most of the lakes have outlets, but outflow is confined to short periods after spring thaw. The saline lakes are generally shallow, and temperature and oxygen distribution is similar to other types of shallow lakes.

Klaresø in the Brønlund Fjord area of northern Greenland is a common type saline lake. It is 300 meters long, up to 100 meters wide, and up to 3.5 meters deep. During winter, ice is 2.7 meters thick, but the lake is clear of ice in midsummer and temperature of the water rises to 8° C. The thermal change is almost entirely from insolation. pH ranges from 7.0 to 7.8 and specific conductivity is 300 to 600 micromhos at the time of spring melt. Salinity increases through evaporation during the summer, and after the freeze-up the water at the bottom of the lake is extremely salty with a specific conductivity of 10,000 micromhos. Content of sodium chloride then reaches 11 grams per liter with a magnesium-calcium content of 50 milligrams per liter (Roen, 1966).

It is of interest that lakes of this type with high saline content are generally in depressions in marine silt terraces within 90 meters elevation above sea level. The silt is a former lagoonal deposit, and much of the salt in the lakes is probably leached from these deposits. Streams flowing across the marine silt are generally saline during periods of low flow in mid- to late-summer. Salt efflorescence is common on the surface of the marine silt, and elements present are approximately the proportions in ocean water (fig. 4.5).

In contrast small lakes on the uplands in the vicinity of Brønlund Fjord with no outflow are generally low in salt content, even though they exist under climatic conditions similar to the saline lakes. It appears that direct leaching of salts from former lagoonal deposits along with possible influx of seawater carried by spray are primary in

Fig. 4.5.   Salt incrustation on silt, Jørgen Brønlund Fjord, North Greenland.

forming the saline lakes, and aridity is a complementary feature.

Clear-water salt-lakes with salinity up to 3.4 percent occur in southern Greenland but are outside of the area designated as cold deserts. These lakes have no outlets, and salts have reached high concentrations through long periods of evaporation (Hansen, 1970).

Roen includes lacustrine lagoons as a form of lake, but these would reflect seawater conditions to a great extent. Even though such lakes are present in the Arctic deserts, they have not been included in this discussion.

On the Alaska coastal plain in the area of cold deserts there are swarms of freshwater lakes that differ from those elsewhere. The lakes occupy oriented elongated basins up to several kilometers in length and width and cover 25 to 90 percent of the coastal plain. Most of the lakes are less than 3 meters deep, and in winter they freeze to a depth of 2 meters. During thaw, moats develop and winds generate strong wave and current action in them, causing considerable erosion along the shore. The lakes are in an isothermal state from June to September when they are ice free. Water temperature at this time is 2.39° C within the lake and 4.40° C at the surface. Once the lake is ice covered, temperatures may rise as much as 2° C, but after being blanketed by snow there is a sudden cooling followed by warming at and near the bottom (Brewer, 1958). The lakes have no inflow other than melt of snow cover. Some influx of water from melting

permafrost occurs. Evaporation is relatively low because of the high incidence of fog. Dissolved solids range from 35 to 159 parts per million.

In many respects the large fjords of northern Greenland are similar to large lakes. They are up to 300 kilometers long and 16 kilometers wide; depths are not known but are probably in excess of 200 meters. In Brønlund Fjord water is stratified with a layer of fresh water 1 meter or less at the top, beneath which is a zone of brackish water up to 5.5 meters thick. Below this is a zone of 13 to 30 percent salinity, increasing to 33.1 percent at 105 meters. Temperature at the surface in summer is −0.9° C rising to 0.2° C at 4–6 meters and dropping to −1.53° C at 36 meters. Melt of winter ice occurs in mid-July preceded by moating. Most of the melt is accomplished through heat from large rivers flowing into the fjord (Just, 1970).

The degree of melting is quite variable in different fjords. Frederick E. Hyde Fjord, one of the longest, generally is free of ice in most years from its head to the ice-covered Arctic Sea. Independence Fjord to the south is similar in size to Hyde Fjord but has not been known to be free of ice. Extensive areas of open water do develop in the vicinity of large rivers and adjacent to smaller tributary fjords that are clear of ice. Danmark Fjord, also a large one trending south at the mouth of Independence Fjord, is clear of ice in most years. Both Hyde and Danmark Fjords are fed only by drainage. In contrast several large glaciers flow into Independence Fjord. Possibly this contact with glaciers and large numbers of icebergs is enough to keep the temperature below the critical melting point.

Because of deep continuous permafrost groundwater is practically nonexistent in the regions of cold deserts. Without groundwater solution activity is extremely limited. At present carbonate rocks in cold deserts are subject to a high degree of surface corrosion from solution. The snow in contact with the carbonate rocks is apparently an effective solvent during the brief melt period, and rills, scallops, and grooves are etched out on the rock surfaces. This solution activity is confined to exposed faces and is absent on the underside of the rock (fig. 4.6). The etching is predominantly along weakness in the rock such as fractures, joints, and bedding. The exact rate and method of solution is not well understood and may include some activity by anaerobic bacteria (Davies, 1957).

Solution in the High Arctic in the past was not as retarded as now. In northern Greenland near Centrum Sφ is an area containing numerous cave systems (fig. 4.7). The passages in these caves are up to 10 meters wide and high. Some of the caves at low levels in the valleys are blocked with moraine, while caves at higher levels are free of moraine. Earth fill obtained from these caves was sterile and indicative of a desert condition at the time of origin of the fill and possibly at the time of

solution of the caves. Similar caves in limestone occur in Wulff Land in northwest Greenland (Davies, 1960).

Because of the lack of groundwater, there are few true springs in the cold desert area of the Arctic. Seasonal seeps have commonly been called springs, but the only springs are scattered hot springs, mainly in eastern and northern Greenland.

The Antarctic Deserts

Ice-free land within the area of cold deserts in Antarctica occurs in relatively small regions commonly referred to as oases or dry valleys. The largest and best known of these regions is on the west side of McMurdo Sound in the Taylor, Wright, and Victoria valleys. In many respects this region is similar to Peary Land in northern Greenland. Precipitation is low and is probably in the order of 6 to 12 centimeters per year; practically all of it is in the form of snow, much of which is blown away by strong persistent winds. Ablation is high, and as in Peary Land most of the snow cover except for protected snowbanks is removed before summer.

Flowing streams in summer are a rarity and are small in size. Onyx River, which feeds Lake Vanda in Wright Valley — apparently the longest stream — is about 24 kilometers long and seasonally carries meltwater from Wright Glacier to the lake (Nichols, 1962). Lake Miers, in a valley near the southern end of the McMurdo Sound

Fig. 4.6.   Rills etched into limestone, Thule, Greenland.

Fig. 4.7.   Caves, Grottedalen, North Greenland. Entrances are up to 15 meters in width.

dry valleys, is fed by short streams, a little over a kilometer long, draining from Adams and Miers Glaciers. Inflow from each of these streams during the melt season in December and January is about 0.03 cubic meters per second, dwindling to zero during cold days and rising about 0.3 cubic meters per second at the end of warm sunny days (Bell, 1967). The annual inflow to Lake Miers is in the order of 300,000 cubic meters, or a depth of 30 centimeters. Temperature of these streams reaches 8° C, but in general it is about 3° C, giving a heat input into the lake of about 100 calories per square centimeter of lake area. Similar short streams carry meltwater from glaciers to numerous lakes in the Taylor Dry Valley. Except for Lake Miers, most of the lake basins in the dry valleys are landlocked, being blocked from the sea by glacial deposits or existing glaciers. The outflow of Lake Miers, however, reaches McMurdo Sound via the Miers River and forms a swift-flowing stream that in some years may be as much as 30 centimeters deep and 3 meters wide (Bradley, 1967).

The lakes in the dry valley systems range in size from under a kilometer in length and width to 6 kilometers long and 1.5 kilometers wide (Lake Vanda, Wright Valley). Most of the larger lakes are in deep basins with depths ranging from 15 to over 70 meters deep. Ice cover is perennial and is in the order of 3.5 meters in late spring. By mid-December melt progresses to the point

that most of the lakes have moats up to 5 meters wide along their shores; where inflow from melt streams enters the lakes, the moats are expanded into small areas of open water.

All but one of the lakes are saline. Salt concentrations are as high as 31.40 percent, with pH down to 5.1 (Tedrow and Ugolini, 1963).

Dominant salts differ in various lakes. Calcium is high in all lake waters and overrides lesser quantities of sodium and magnesium salts. In some lakes calcium chloride and calcium sulfate are dominant (Tedrow and Ugolini, 1963); in others sodium and magnesium chloride along with calcium carbonate are dominant (Ball and Nichols, 1960).

Temperature distributions within several of the lakes are quite out of line with distributions found in most polar lakes. In Lake Vanda the temperature was found to increase with depth rising to 10° C at 30 to 60 meters, 20° C below 60 meters, and 21.6° C at 65 meters (Nichols, 1962). Similar rises have been described in Lake Bonney (Shirtcliffe, 1964) and Lake Fryxell in Taylor Valley (Angino and others, 1962, 1965). Shirtcliffe cites solar heating as adequate to explain the abnormal temperatures; Nichols and Angino trace the heat to the existence of hot springs beneath the lakes. Crude thermal and chemical stratification is present in the large salt lakes.

Lake Miers is a warm freshwater lake (Bell, 1967). To a depth of 15 meters the water contains less than 92 parts per million of dissolved solids; below this depth the contents are in the order of 90 to 110 ppm to 19.4 meters, where an increase to 188 ppm occurs and the rise continues to the bottom at 20 meters when there are 287 ppm. The dominant elements in the upper 12 meters of the lake are sodium, potassium, chlorine and oxygen. Below 12 meters the water is stagnating, and carbonates of calcium and magnesium are dominant. Distinct thermal stratification exists, with a uniform rise in temperature to 4° C to about 12 meters. Between 12 and 15 meters a rise from 4° C to 4.85° C occurs and conductivity rises 50 percent. Below 15 meters there appears to be two convection zones at 16.3 to 17.4 meters, and 17.4 to 18.3 meters. Below 18.3 meters there is little mixing, and conductivity rises sharply with little change in temperature. The break in stratification at 12 meters represents a region of major inflow, which after entering the lake settles into a zone at a depth of 10 to 12 meters.

The hydrography and limnology of ice-free cold deserts in Antarctica differ considerably from those in the Arctic. Thermal gradients, salinity, and stratification within large Antarctic lakes are greater; ice cover is more persistent on Antarctic lakes. Large, seasonal rivers prevalent in the Arctic are absent in Antarctica.

Summary

One can realize that the cold desert areas exist in a state of balance between supply and loss of water. At present they exist in a state of relative plenty by drawing heavily on natural reserves. Mankind would do well to appreciate this deficiency before he attempts to tamper with it through large-scale diversion of river water from Arctic arid areas to relatively humid regions and to respect the delicate balance before attempting to develop the surface and subsurface for his needs.

BIBLIOGRAPHY

Angino, E. E., and others
  1962 Chemical stratification in Lake Fryxell, Victoria Land, Antarctica. Science 138 (no. 3536, Oct. 5): 34–36.
  1965 A chemical and limnological study of Lake Vanda. Kansas University Science Bulletin 45 (no. 10, June 7): 1097–118.
Ball, Donald G., and Nichols, Robert L.
  1960 Saline lakes and drill hole brines, McMurdo Sound, Antarctica. Bulletin Geological Society of America 71 (no. 11, Nov. 1960): 1703–8.
Barnes, David F.
  1960 An investigation of a perennially frozen lake. Air Force Surveys in Geophysics, no. 129, December. 134 pp.
Bell, R. A. I.
  1967 Lake Miers, South Victoria Land, Antarctica. New Zealand Journal of Geology and Geophysics 10 (no. 2, May): 540–56.
Bradley, J.
  1967 Ice-cored moraines and ice diapirs, Lake Miers, Victoria Land, Antarctica. New Zealand Journal of Geology and Geophysics 10 (no. 2, May): 599–623.
Brewer, M. C.
  1958 The thermal regime of an arctic lake. American Geophysical Union, Transactions 39 (no. 2, April): 278–84.
Cook, F. A.
  1960 Periglacial-geomorphological investigations at Resolute, 1959. Arctic 13 (no. 2, June): 132–35.
Davies, W. E.
  1957 Rillestein in northwest Greenland. Bulletin National Speleological Society, no. 19, October, pp. 40–46.
  1960 Caves in northern Greenland. Bulletin National Speleological Society 22 (pt. 2, July): 114–16.

Fistrup, B.
  1953 High Arctic deserts. International Geological Congress, 19th, Comptes rendus, 1952, sec. 7, fasc. 7, pp. 91–99.
Hansen, Kaj
  1970 Geological and geographical investigations in King Frederick IX's Land, morphology, sediments, periglacial processes, and salt lakes. Meddelelser om Grønland, vol. 188, no. 4. 77 pp.
Krinsley, D. B.
  1962 Limnology. *In* Arctic Earth science investigations, Centrum Sø, northeast Greenland, 1960. Air Force Surveys in Geophysics, no. 138, pp. 47–55.
Lewis, C. R.
  1962 Ice mound on Sadlerochit River, Alaska. Arctic 15 (no. 2, June): 145–50.
Nichols, Robert L.
  1962 Geology of Lake Vanda, Wright Valley, South Victoria Land, Antarctica. Antarctic Research, American Geophysical Union, Geophysical Monograph no. 7, pp. 47–52.
Oliver, D. R.
  1964 A limnological investigation of a large Arctic lake, Nettilling Lake, Baffn Island. Arctic 17 (no. 2, June): 69–83.
Roen, U. I.
  1962 Studies on fresh water Entomostraca in Greenland: II. Localities, ecology, and geographical distribution of the species. Meddelelser om Grønland, vol. 170, no. 2. 249 pp.
  1966 Pearylands ferske vande og deres dyreliv. Grønland 1966, no. 3, March, pp. 90–102.
Shirtcliffe, T. G. L.
  1964 Lake Bonney, Antarctica: Cause of the elevated temperatures. Journal of Geophysical Research 69 (Dec. 15): 5257–68.
Tedrow, J. C. F., and Ugolini, F. C.
  1963 An Antarctic saline lake. New Zealand Journal of Science 6 (no. 1, March): 150–56.

CHAPTER 5

SOILS OF THE HIGH ARCTIC LANDSCAPES

J. C. F. Tedrow

Rutgers University, New Brunswick, New Jersey

If, during the early years of their investigations, naturalists had approached polar lands from the north rather than the south, the landscape descriptions probably would have been quite different from those generally depicted in the literature. Since it is quite common for authors to imply considerable homogeneity within polar lands, landscape elements are often poorly stated. However, investigators who work throughout polar lands for any length of time see that landscapes not only have a local mosaical pattern but that they also show broad changes with latitude — changes of soils, climate, vegetation, and animal distribution. This pattern was recognized over two centuries ago in Greenland by Egede (1745), who stated that in Greenland, soils and plant cover change with latitude.

At the beginning of the twentieth century the Far North began to be recognized as having its own set of properties. Accordingly, terms such as *High Arctic, Arctic desert,* and *cold steppe* came into existence. Nordenskjöld and Mecking (1928) recognized the importance of summer temperatures in establishing natural divisions of polar lands. Because of this, the 5° C July isotherm was used as the major criteria for separating the High Arctic from other polar sectors. Not only is the High Arctic subjected to low summer temperatures but annual precipitation values also are quite low — approximating 12 centimeters.

Grigor'ev (1930) and Gorodkov (1939) recognized that soil conditions of the Far North are extremely different from those of the main tundra region just north of the tree line, indicating that the area is mantled with polar desert soils. Gerasimov (1956) divided the polar region into (1) primitive soils of the polar tundra and (2) gley soils of the subpolar tundra. Earlier, my colleagues and I suggested a tundra soil zone and polar desert soil zone (Tedrow et al., 1958; Tedrow and Brown, 1962). Subsequent work in the Far North led me to believe that the original two soil zones of the northern polar lands would be more realistically divided into three zones: polar desert, subpolar desert, and tundra (Tedrow, 1972). Possibly the most xeric affinities are found on the northern coast of Greenland and, in particular, the western coastal sectors of the Queen Elizabeth Islands (Tedrow, 1966, 1970). Korotkevich (1967) published a map of the polar regions which listed a polar desert zone of moss-lichen, a tundra zone of moss-lichen, and a tundra zone of lichen-moss and moss-shrubs. Botanical zonation within polar lands has been discussed extensively by various investigators (table 5.1).

Soil zonation for the northern polar regions is shown in figure 5.1. Lines separating the zones cannot be defended with precision, but the general presentation is considered realistic. Most of the lines correspond to climatic as well as vegetative boundaries. Tundra soils are present within all three zones, but in high latitudes they occupy only a small percentage of the landscape. In central Prince Patrick Island, tundra soils are virtually absent (Tedrow, Bruggemann, and Walton, 1968).

Soils of the Arctic Desert Zone

The major genetic soils within the polar desert zone are shown in a modified drainage catena-landscape presentment (fig. 5.2). The uplands are generally free of snow much of the winter and spring seasons, but the depressions and stream courses receive considerable quantities of redistributed snow. Deep deposits of snow in the valleys persist into midsummer and later. Figure

TABLE 5.1

Some Approaches to Geobotanical Divisions of the Northern Polar Landscapes

Tedrow 1971 (pedologic)	Polunin 1951 (botanical)	Porsild 1957 (botanical)	Tikhomirov 1960 (botanical)	Targul'yan and Karavaeva 1964 (phytopedologic)
Polar desert	High Arctic	Rock desert or fell field	Arctic glaciers, polar tundra	Arctic
Subpolar desert	Midarctic	Stony sedge-moss-lichen-tundra	Arctic tundra	Tundra (Arctic)
Tundra	Low Arctic	Tundra zone of dwarf shrub, sedge-moss, etc.	Typical tundra	Tundra (typical)

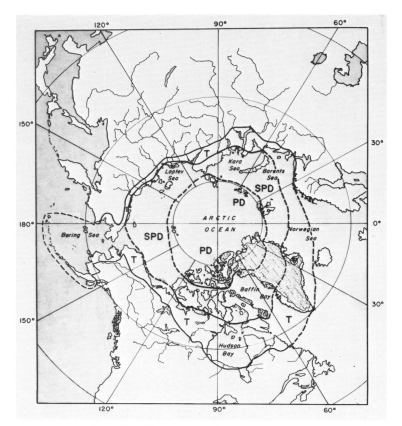

Fig. 5.1. The major soil zones of the northern polar regions. Polar desert is shown as PD, sub-polar desert as SPD, and tundra as T.

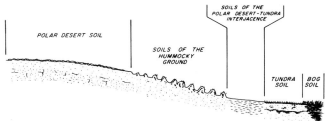

Fig. 5.2. Diagrammatic presentation of the major genetic soils of the High Arctic. The percentage of the landscape occupied by the various soils will depend upon relief, parent material, climate, and related factors.

5.3 shows a view on Prince Patrick Island taken in mid-July, 1965. The uplands within the polar desert soil zone probably have as little as three to five centimeters of water actually percolating into the soil during the course of a year. Higher exposed positions not only receive a small amount of precipitation but also are subjected to strong winds and considerable evapotranspiration.

Polar Desert Soil

Polar desert soil is usually found on the higher landscape positions but is also present in low-lying sectors, especially on gravelly and sandy material such as found on outwash, morainal, and fluvial deposits. Vascular plants cover only a small percentage of the surface, and in some situations they are absent. Clumps of *Saxifraga* or *Carex* often cover some five to ten percent of the ground surface, but under extreme xericity this value drops to less than one percent. Apparently the small accumulation of organic matter in the upper mineral horizons is contributed to by lichens, algae, and diatoms (Gorodkov, 1943).

The general appearance of polar desert soil is shown in figure 5.4. The soil has a desert pavement and has free drainage throughout which could even be designated as xeric. Such soil thaws to a depth of 60 to 120 centimeters by the end of June, and one can usually excavate to these depths without encountering frost or free water. The solum will usually have a brown to yellowish color with a grayish to yellowish colored A horizon (Tedrow, 1966; Tedrow, Bruggemann and Walton, 1968; Tedrow, 1970).

The soil is usually nearly neutral but commonly alkaline in reaction. With base-deficient sands, however, pH values may be as low as 4.5. Base saturation, especially in the case of loams and silt loams, is high; in some situations, the soils may be saline.

Authigenic carbonate encrustations commonly are present on the undersides of cobbles within the profile. At times thin travertine veneers coat cobbles and even sand grains. Efflorescence of salts at the surface of the soil during dry windy periods is also common, with thenardite (Na_2SO_4) being the main constituent. Crystallization of thenardite on bare surfaces of the

Fig. 5.3. View of the polar desert on Prince Patrick Island during mid-July 1965. The polar desert soil areas are free of snow. Snow-covered areas in the background remain completely frozen and are mantled with tundra and related hydromorphic soils.

Fig. 5.4. Polar desert soil in northern Greenland. The pick rests on well-drained material.

Fig. 5.5. View of the soils of the hummocky ground, northern Banks Island.

polar regions is well documented on a circumpolar basis. Thenardite appears to be the dominant efflorescing salt, irrespective of the mineral composition of the primary substrate.

There is a great deal of frost-stirring within polar desert soils as evidenced by active patterned ground forms and frost-altered morphology within the soil (Tedrow, 1966). There are other situations, however, in which frost action is minimal.

Soils of the Hummocky Ground

Soils of the hummocky ground present a most interesting set of problems which, up to the 1970s, have been studied very little. Several investigators have described the botanical and associated pedologic conditions of this area (Tedrow and Douglas, 1964). Beschel (1965) referred to such conditions on Axel Heiberg and Ellesmere Islands simply as *hummocks,* and Raup (1965) reported them in northeast Greenland as *turf hummocks.* They appear to be widespread throughout many sectors of the High Arctic (fig. 5.5).

Unlike *Eriophorum* tussocks of the main tundra belt which are comprised of vegetative matter, hummocks of the High Arctic are small domelike structures of mineral matter veneered with a 3-to-5-centimeter mineral-organic mat (fig. 5.6). Intensive frost action takes place within these soils with considerable quantities of humic substance smeared throughout the mineral matrix. *Soils of the hummocky ground* is an unsatisfactory term; as northern pedologic studies continue, it is hoped that a better term will be adopted. The hummocks nearly always occur on sloping land where there is a supply of water from snow, ice, or general seepage areas. By

virtue of their position, there is usually a reliable source of water throughout much of the summer season. As a rule, hummocks are quite small at the top of the slope but become as much as 25 to 30 centimeters high near the base (fig. 5.2). It is believed that the size differential is, at least in part, related to erosion, with considerable quantities of soil being removed from areas between the hummocks.

Fig. 5.6. Profile of soil of the hummocky ground, Prince Patrick Island. The scale rests on frozen ground. Photo was taken about July 10, 1965.

Soils of the hummocky ground usually do not have well-ordered genetic features. The mineral soil colors generally are a gray to yellowish brown, with a suggestion of gley formation in some instances. Hummocks themselves are usually stained with humic substances and have inclusions of fibrous organic material. The

Fig. 5.7. Soils of the polar desert-tundra interjacence. The area is very wet during early summer but becomes quite dry late in the summer. Salts commonly effloresce during the dry periods.

Fig. 5.8. View of tundra soil in northern Greenland. The meadow has a fairly continuous supply of water throughout the summer season.

hummocks usually have their highest content of organic matter in positions near the base of the slope (Tedrow, Bruggemann, and Walton, 1968). The pH values generally are near neutrality. Soluble salt content shows a seasonal amplitude with an efflorescence occurring on the surface after long dry periods. In fact, a muted crackling sound can be heard when one is walking over the dry salt-encrusted vegetation during the dry periods.

The hummocks themselves probably owe their genesis to a combination of frost processes and soil erosion. Soils of the hummocky ground have some affinities with upland tundra soils with respect to the wetness factor, but the two have little in common with respect to morphology.

Soils of the Polar Desert–Tundra Interjacence

Soils of the polar desert–tundra interjacence was a term introduced to describe a set of conditions in the High Arctic in which certain low-lying areas have a superabundance of moisture during the thaw season (spring and early summer) but become very dry during the summer months (Tedrow, 1970). It would perhaps be more realistic to describe sites as soil conditions rather than soils, and the suggested term is provisional. The soils occupy the bases of slopes where the terrain is virtually level (figs. 5.2 and 5.7).

Professor R. L. Nichols tells of the terrain in Inglefield Land, Greenland, just north of the Prudhoe Ice Cap, which during the early summer was a wet mineral matrix; if one stood still there, he would start to sink into the ground. The soils are in a supersaturated condition during the early months from local thaw and from melt water originating from higher positions.

During middle and late summer the soils become exceedingly dry and hard at the surface. A few scattered plants are present, but seldom are they in sufficient quantity to form a humus layer. By early July, after the soil shows a marked decrease in moisture content, one can walk over the area without difficulty. As drying continues, the soils become hard, with salts efflorescing on the surface (fig. 5.7). There are few instances of intense rainfall in the High Arctic, and because there is no dependable source of water during middle and late summer, these low-lying areas have a desert-like appearance. During the dry periods, the soils will develop saline conditions.

Day (1964), working in northern Ellesmere Island, recognized many soil conditions similar to those listed above; he described them as *subarctic orthic regosol* and *subarctic saline regosol*.

Tundra Soils

Tundra soils have been discussed by Douglas and Tedrow (1960), as well as many others, but most of these discussions are from the main tundra belt rather than the High Arctic. Tundra soils are present at the northern extremities of ice-free land, but in such sectors occupy only a small part of the landscape (figs. 5.2 and 5.8). In the High Arctic they occupy the low-lying areas where there is a reliable source of water throughout the growing season.

Tundra soils have similar genetic features in the High Arctic as they do farther south (fig. 5.9). Their morphology consists of a mineral horizon which usually grades into a buried organic layer at depth. The frost table is commonly at the 30 to 40 centimeter depth. With situations in which the sites are usually wet, a soil representing a northern variant of the meadow tundra is present (Tedrow et al., 1958). In case of the meadow tundra soil, the site commonly remains completely frozen until early July, and the active layer may be only some 20 to 30 centimeters deep.

Tundra soils of the High Arctic are usually mildly acid, but there are situations where the parent material is extremely base-deficient, and others where there is an abundance of bases, as is the case in which the parent material is limestone. In the latter case, the soils will be alkaline. In special situations where the low-lying tundra soils dry out, the soil may become saline and salts may effloresce on the surface.

The most primitive form of tundra soil I have encountered within the High Arctic was located near Tullett Point on the western edge of Prince Patrick Island. The tundra soil consisted of only a covering of black lichens over raw appearing water logged sand.

Bog Soils

Bog soils occur within the High Arctic, but they represent only extremely small, isolated cases (fig. 5.2). On Prince Patrick Island, organic deposits up to 60 centimeters thick were noted (fig. 5.10). No bog soil was recorded, however, on Cornwallis Island or in Inglefield Land, Greenland.

Influence of Textural Composition on Soil Distribution

Percentage distribution of various genetic soils within the polar desert landscapes is highly influenced by relief elements as well as by textural composition. Based on field experiences within the High Arctic, figure 5.11 has been constructed to show how texture of the substrate influences the percentage of various soils within the landscape. The diagram assumes a complete and adequate soil mantle on undulating to rolling relief under a "typical" High Arctic climate. It will be noted that soils of the polar desert–tundra interjacence are generally not present in situations where the materials contain considerable quantities of silt and clay. The reason for this condition probably lies in the fact that low-lying areas consisting of loams and silt loams have more water associated with them by virtue of greater surface exposure per unit of dry mass. Such sites, therefore, are not conducive to drying out so quickly during the summer, resulting in more favorable conditions for plant colonization.

Rockland, frost-shattered areas, rocky talus slopes, floodplains, and gravel bars are present throughout the

Fig. 5.9. Tundra soil in northern Greenland. The six-inch scale rests on buried organic fragments.

Fig. 5.10. Bog soil on Prince Patrick Island. The ice axe rests on clear ice. The whitish appearing background is from newly fallen snow (mid-July, 1965).

High Arctic. Soils on these landforms have received only minor attention from pedologists. It is pertinent to point out that many bare fluvial deposits along the streams develop saline conditions during dry periods.

Arctic brown soil occurs in the High Arctic, but such cases are rare and the soil is usually confined to the local

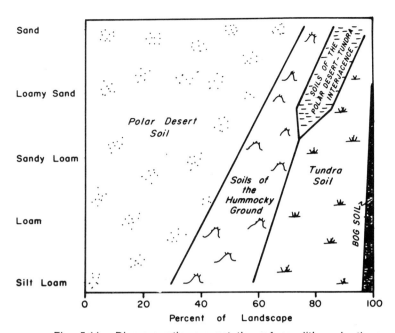

Sand

Loamy Sand

Polar Desert Soil

Sandy Loam

Soils of the Hummocky Ground

Tundra Soil

Loam

BOG SOIL

Silt Loam

0   20   40   60   80   100

Percent of Landscape

Fig. 5.11. Diagrammatic presentation of conditions in the High Arctic, showing that with more sandy material greater percentage of the landscape is mantled with polar desert soil. Soils of the polar-desert-tundra interjacence are usually restricted to the sandy textured materials.

Dryas mats in semiprotected spots of the uplands. The Arctic brown soil within the High Arctic has only a thin solum which may be alkaline throughout. Accordingly, it should be considered as a paravariety of the modal description (Tedrow et al., 1958).

Frost Processes

On steeper slopes, solifluction processes are quite active, resulting in many of the genetic soil features being deformed or largely obliterated. In preparation of soil maps, such mapping units have been described as *areas of active solifluction* with an approximation of the wetness factor (Tedrow, Bruggemann, and Walton, 1968).

Patterned Ground

The problem of frost action and patterned ground formation within the High Arctic is very complex. Solifluction processes are active on the slopes, and there is a great deal of physical mixing within the soil horizons. The drier higher land has, in addition to a network of ice-wedge polygons, a variety of other forms of patterned ground such as frost boils, stone circles, stone nets, stone garlands, stone stripes, and related features. Low-lying meadows with their wet mantle of organic-mineral mixtures are invariably highly polygonized with ice-wedges occupying the interpolygonal positions. Other patterned ground forms, such as frost boils and mounds, are also present in low areas. The problem of soil classification and patterned ground forms has been described in some detail elsewhere (Drew and Tedrow, 1962; Tedrow, 1962; Brown, 1966; Federoff, 1966; and many others) and is not further discussed in this chapter.

Cold Deserts of Antarctica

Turning briefly to Antarctica, the ice-free sectors make up only a small percentage of the continent, probably between one and five percent. Markov (1956) used the term *cold desert* to describe physical conditions on the continent; he reported the presence of weathering crusts, a variety of desert varnish forms, salt efflorescence, and saline conditions. Markov's work was expanded by Glazovskaia (1958), who reported on mineral alteration including minerals weathering to clay forms and the accumulation of salt deposits. McCraw (1960), Claridge (1965), and other New Zealand investigators provided some excellent information on the soil properties in Victoria Land; their reports clearly show the pedological-geochemical processes of the environment.

Tedrow and Ugolini (1966) referred collectively to all soils of the Antarctic continent as *soils of the cold deserts*. Antarctica is considered as a fourth (cold desert) polar zone, with the following genetic soils: (1) ahumic soils, (2) evaporite soils, (3) protoranker, (4) ornithogenic (guano deposits), and other minor units. Ugolini (1965) characterized Antarctic soils in some detail, particularly the problem dealing with soil moisture movement. Virtually all ice-free areas of the continent are subjected to soil processes lacking an organic component. Except for rocky sectors, most ice-free uplands are mantled with some variety of ahumic soil which generally is saline. In localities of negative relief, however, including closed basins, the soils are veneered with considerable concentration of soluble salts. A paravariety of protoranker soil is also present in rare occasions in Antarctica.

Pedogenic Gradients

If soils similar to those of the High Arctic are to be found in Antarctica, it had been believed that they would be located on the northern extension of the Antarctic Peninsula where climate is slightly more favorable for plant growth. This possibility has not been adequately explored. In the meantime, however, new information has become available from another sector of Antarctica. MacNamara (1969) reported from the coastal sector of Enderby Land that a paravariety of polar desert soil is present in this sector; accordingly, we are about ready to link genetically the soils from both north and south polar regions into a single pedogenic gradient. Some reports have already taken up the problem of relating pedologic data from both the north and south polar regions along a continuum (Targul'yan and Karavaeva, 1964; Tedrow, 1968). Everett (1968) has also provided similar interpretations within the Arctic sector of northern Canada.

It is believed that future soil studies of the north and south polar regions should be projected around four soil zones: (1) tundra, (2) subpolar desert, (3) polar desert, and (4) cold desert. It appears that the entire polar pedologic picture can be expressed as a spectrum of climatic, biologic, and pedologic conditions.

BIBLIOGRAPHY

Beschel, R. E.
1965   Hummocks and their vegetation in the High Arctic, *in* Permafrost International Conference Proceedings, National Academy of Science–National Research Council Publication 1287, pp. 13–20.

Brown, J.
1966   Soils of the Okpilak River Region, Alaska. Cold Regions Research and Engineering Lab (Hanover, N.H.) Research Report 188. 49 pp.

Claridge, G. G. C.
1965   Chemistry and clay mineralogy of some soils from Ross dependency, Antarctica. New Zealand Journal of Geology and Geophysics 8: 186–220.

Day, J. H.
1964   Characteristics of Soils of the Hazen camp area, Northern Ellesmere Island, Northwest Territory Defence Research Board, Ottawa, Canada. (Hazen 24) 15 pp.

Douglas, L. A., and Tedrow, J. C. F.
1960   Tundra soils of Arctic Alaska. Soil Science Congress, Proceedings of the 7th International Congress. Communication 5, vol. 4, pp. 291–304.

Drew, J. V., and Tedrow, J. C. F.
1962   Arctic soil classification and patterned ground. Arctic 15: 109–16.

Egede, H. P.
1745   A description of Greenland. (Translated from Danish.) C. Hitch, London.

Everett, K. R.
1968   Soil development in the Mould Bay and Isachsen areas, Queen Elizabeth Island, Northwest Territories, Canada. Ohio State University Institute of Polar Studies. Report 24. 75 pp.

Federoff, N.
1966   Les sols du Spitsberg Occidental. Spitsberg 1964 Centre National de la Recherche Scientifique, R.C.P. 42, chapter 10, pp. 111–28.

Gerasimov, I. P.
1956   Soil map of the world. Priroda 10: 5–13.

Glazovskaia, M .A.
1958   Weathering and primary soil formation in Antarctica. Naucnye Doklady Vysshei Skoly Geologo-Geograficheskie Nauki (1): 63–76.

Gorodkov, B. N.
1939   Peculiarities of the Arctic topsoil. Izvest iia Gosudarstvennogo geograficheskogo obshchestva 71: 1516–1532.

1943   Polar Deserts of Wrangel Island. Botanicheskii Zhurnal SSSR T. 28(4): 127–43.

Grigor'ev, A. A.
1930   Permafrost and ancient glaciation. Akademiia Nauk SSSR, Komissiia po izocheniiu estestvenn priozvoditel'nykh, Materialy 80: 43–104.

Korotkevich, Ye. S.
1967   Polar deserts. Soviet Antarctic Expedition Information Bulletin, vol. 6 (no. 65): 5–29.

MacNamara, E. E.
1969   Active layer development and soil moisture dynamics in Enderby Land, East Antarctica. Soil Science 108: 345–49.

Markov, K. K.
1956   Some facts concerning periglacial phenomena in Antarctica (preliminary report), Vestnik Moskovskogo Universitita 11, Geografiia 1: 139–48.

McCraw, J. D.
1960   Soils of the Ross Dependency, Antarctica. New Zealand Society of Soil Science 4: 30–35.

Nordenskjold, O. G., and Mecking, L.
1928   The geography of the polar regions. American Geographical Society Special Publication 8.

Polunin, N.
1951   The real Arctic: suggestions for its delineation, subdivision and characterization. Journal of Ecology 39: 308–15.

Porsild, A. E.
1957   Natural vegetation and flora, *in* Atlas of Canada. Canada Department of Mines and Technology. Surveys Sheet no. 38.

Raup, H. M.
1965   Turf hummocks in the Mesters Vig. District. Northeast Greenland, *in* Permafrost International Conference Proceedings, National Academy of Science–National Research Council Publication 1287: 43–50.

Targul'yan, V. O., and Karavayeva, N. A.
1964   Experience in the soil-geochemical classification of polar regions. Problems of the North, no. 8, pp. 213–24.

Tedrow, J. C. F.
1962   Morphological evidence of frost action in Arctic soils. Biuletyn Peryglacjalny 11: 345–52.

1966   Polar desert soils. Soil Science Society of America Proceedings 30: 381–87.

1968   Pedogenic gradients of the polar regions. Journal of Soil Science 19: 197–204.

1970   Soil investigations in Inglefield Land, Greenland. Meddelelser om Grønland 188 (3). 93 pp.

1972   Soil morphology as an indicator of climatic changes in the Arctic areas, *in* Climatic changes in Arctic areas during the last 10,000 years (Y. Vasari, H. Hyvärinen and S. Hicks, eds.). Acta Universitatis Ouluensis. Series A, Geologica no. 1, pp. 62–74.

In   Polar soil classification and the periglacial prob-
Press   lem. Biuletyn Peryglacjalny.

Tedrow, J. C. F., and Brown, J.
1962   Soils of the Northern Brooks Range, Alaska: weakening of the soil-forming potential at High Arctic altitudes. Soil Science 93: 254–61.

Tedrow, J. C. F., Bruggemann, P. F., and Walton, G. F.
1968   Soils of Prince Patrick Island. Arctic Institute of North America Research Paper 44, Washington, D.C. 82 pp.

Tedrow, J. C. F., and Douglas, L. A.
1964   Soil investigations on Banks Island. Soil Science 98: 63–65.

Tedrow, J. C. F., Drew, J. V., Hill, D. E., and Douglas, L. A.
1958   Major genetic soils of the Arctic slope of Alaska. Journal of Soil Science 9: 33–45.

Tedrow, J. C. F., and Ugolini, F. C.
1966   Antarctic soils, *in* Antarctica soils and soil forming processes (J. C. F. Tedrow, ed.). America Geophysics Union, Antarctic Research Series 8: 161–77.

Tikhomirov, B. A.
1960   Plantgeographical investigations of the tundra vegetation in the Soviet Union. Canada Journal of Botany 38: 815–32.

Ugolini, F. C.
1965   Soil investigations in the Lower Wright Valley, *in* Permafrost International Conference Proceedings, National Academy of Science–National Research Council Publication 1287, pp. 55–61.

CHAPTER 6

APPLICATION OF LOW-LATITUDE MICROBIAL ECOLOGY TO HIGH-LATITUDE DESERTS

Roy E. Cameron
Jet Propulsion Laboratory, California Institute of Technology, Pasadena, California

Field Approach to Desert Microbial Ecology

Although much can be learned through laboratory studies, an important approach to desert microbial ecology is through field studies, and some preliminary field measurements and observations should be made to determine the appropriateness of each site. "Blind" selection of a site is inappropriate and is not the same as random selection or selection of a specific sample. In all cases, considerations should be given to certain aspects of geography, geology, climatology (microclimatology), botany (macroecology), and soil science. This is necessary for the purpose of an ecological study of a microbial nature.

It should be remembered that microbiota are closely coupled to their environment (Gates, 1968), and therefore as many environmental and ecological features as possible should be measured or observed in the field before laboratory studies are begun. Some of these features include factors of topography, nature of parent materials, degree of slope, extent and direction of exposure, drainage patterns, surface features of microrelief, presence of desert pavement and varnish, hardpan, caliche, dunes, crusts (especially algal-lichen crusts), *in situ* soil moisture, relative humidity, temperature, heat flux, color, hardness, texture, structure, pH, Eh, the qualitative presence of specific chemical ions, and total salt concentration as determined by electrical conductivity.

Biotic factors to be considered in site selection should include at least the nature and extent (or absence) of macrobiota, such as the spacing and kinds of xerophytes and other plants and their phenology, quality, kind and state of decay of organic debris, and the associated animals, whether they are indigenous or domestic, permanent inhabitants or transients.

Previous data, if available, on climate and microclimate — for example, mean, maximum and minimum temperature, net and total solar radiation, degree of cloudiness, visible and ultraviolet radiation, relative humidity, dew point, seasonal and annual precipitation and its frequency distribution, evaporation rate, and degree of windiness — should be considered, with similar data collected on site, if possible.

For final site selection, a few preliminary microbiological analyses should be performed to determine the qualitative presence (or even the absence) and abundances of general microbial groups, including heterotrophic, autotrophic, coliformic, aerobic and anaerobic bacteria, yeasts, molds, algae and protozoa, especially in consideration of *in situ* algal-lichen soil crusts and possible algal and bacterial nitrogen fixers. These tests can be performed with a small amount of soil sprinkled on agar plates or inoculated into tube or capsule differential media, and subsequent reactions can be determined either at the site with a minimum of equipment, for example, a pocket field microscope, or later examined upon return to the laboratory. These tests are especially valuable before proceeding with detailed laboratory tests, as in the barren areas of the Antarctic.

Before leaving the site, as complete as possible photographic record should be made, not only of the general area but also of significant macro and micro features — for example, landforms, rock outcrops, drainage patterns, soil profile, spacing and kinds of plants, evidence of animal activities (burrows, tracks, droppings, vegetation perturbations, etc.), proximity to human habitations and activities, microrelief, algal, lichen, salt, and clay crusts (figs. 6.1–6.9). Desert regions have many features in common (Stone, 1967), as well as some distinctive features, as in the Antarctic polar desert (McCraw, 1967), and it is wise to carry pictorial descriptions of desert features into the field for the purpose of defining an area or site, and for later comparisons with similar or dissimilar areas or sites in the same desert or those located in other geographical regions. A site should also be well marked for future studies and its location indicated on a commercially available or hand-drawn map.

The monotony of desert terrain, changes brought about through weathering of a few or more years, or the perturbation of an area, such as from mechanical or animal disturbance, can make it difficult to return to an exact site location for subsequent studies. Time and care spent in the initial study and recording of area and site characteristics are therefore very important and should not be neglected; they are invaluable when data are integrated and correlated, and it may be impossible to return to the site for some needed measurement or observation.

Following or concurrent with the preceding measure-

Fig. 6.1. Scattered vegetation at International Biological Program (IBP) desert biome study site (soil samples 13U–14U), Sonoran Desert, near Silverbell, Arizona. Mesquite, *Prosopis juliflora* is seen at right; creosotebush, *Larrea tridentata* at left; gramma grasses in foreground. Soil algae crusts occurred in partially shaded and open areas between grasses and other vegetation.

Fig. 6.2. Close-up of *in situ* thin, algae soil crust, site 13U–14U. White quartz at left, dislodged from soil, serves as a protective "microgreenhouse" and shows subsurface coatings of algae material. Algae were primarily oscillatorioid forms, and included *Schizothrix arenaria, Schizothrix calcicola, Schizothrix rubella, Scytonema hofmannii, Nostoc muscorum* (as *N. humifusum*) *Chlorella vulgaris,* and *Navicula* spp. Protozoan associates included *Valkampfia limax, Peranema trichophorum, Amoeba guttula,* and *Bodo minimus.*

Fig. 6.3. Pebbly, cracked, low barren area covered with algae crusts (soil moisture tin in foreground), at Oregon Desert (Columbia Plateau), near Christmas Lake Valley, site 165. Vegetation in background includes sagebrush, *Artemisia* spp. and rabbitbrush, *Chrysothamnus* spp. Algae included *Schizothrix calcicola; Microcoleus vaginatus, Nostoc muscorum, Chlorococcum echinozygotum,* and *Navicula* spp. Nematodes also were present.

Fig. 6.4. Barren, eroded, ventifacted, and desert pavement-covered Antarctic Dry Valley, near McKelvey Valley site 506–509 (77°26′ south, 161°15′ east). Personnel are sterilizing hand trowel prior to sampling of surface soil for sprinkling on Petri plates of trypticase soy agar.

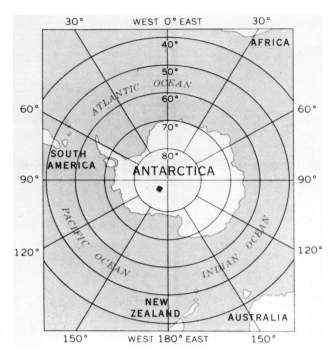

Fig. 6.5. Location diagram for farthest south soil microbial and ecological investigations at Mount Howe and La Gorce Mountains, Antarctica.

Fig. 6.6. Frozen pond at La Gorce Mountains, Antarctica (86°45′ south, 146°00′ west), near site 796, and location of farthest south algae. Algae included culturable *Schizothrix calcicola* and *Neochloris aquatica*. *Porphyrosiphon notarisii* was not recoverable in culture.

Fig. 6.7. Moraine, bluffs and peak of Mount Howe (elevation 2,800 meters, 87°22′ south, 149°18′ west). Farthest south exposed area of rock and soil in the world. Soil samples taken in this area, site 779 and near site 780, contained only a few diphtheroid bacteria or yeasts or no culturable microorganisms. Soil surface temperatures did not reach freezing, even during midsummer (see fig. 6.19).

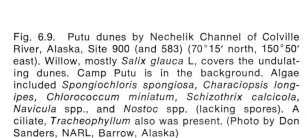

Fig. 6.8. Moss, lichen, and grass-covered frost-crack polygon at International Biological Program (IBP) at tundra biome study site 4 (soil sample 901) near Point Barrow, Alaska. Algae included *Chlorococcum Miniatum, Nostoc muscorum* (as *N. humifusum*), and *Navicula* spp. *Nostoc commune* was prevalent in the area, especially in depressed sites, including vehicular tracks and lemming runs.

Fig. 6.9. Putu dunes by Nechelik Channel of Colville River, Alaska, Site 900 (and 583) (70°15′ north, 150°50′ east). Willow, mostly *Salix glauca* L, covers the undulating dunes. Camp Putu is in the background. Algae included *Spongiochloris spongiosa, Characiopsis longipes, Chlorococcum miniatum, Schizothrix calcicola, Navicula* spp., and *Nostoc* spp. (lacking spores). A ciliate, *Tracheophyllum* also was present. (Photo by Don Sanders, NARL, Barrow, Alaska)

ments and observations, careful consideration should be given to the sampling and handling of soils for biological purposes, and also during the transport of samples back to the laboratory (Cameron, Blank, and Gensel, 1966a). Sampling, handling, and transport can have a great influence on the results of analyses. More than one sample aliquot should be collected, usually one kilogram per aliquot, not only in consideration of the variety of tests to be performed but also to insure the arrival of valid samples at the laboratory. For example, if at all possible, soil samples should be collected on a nonwindy day; if that is not possible, then be sure samples are collected downwind so as not to contaminate them with personal microbiota. Aerobiological monitoring, both upwind and downwind, during sampling is highly desirable; comparisons can be made later between distributions, abundances, and kinds of aerial propagules and soil microbiota.

Aseptic procedures should be used within reason, including sterilization of sampling tools and containers. More than one sample has been invalidated because of carelessness or neglect during sampling procedures, even to the extent of collecting samples with a hot shovel, or using a digging or other tool containing adherent residual materials from a prior sampling! Other soil samples have been invalidated because they were not collected in the proper container, that is, a sample for trace organics should not be put into a plasticized bag.

Additional samples have been "lost" when either moist or frozen samples were left in the field, "baking" in the sun. Precautions should be followed to protect samples from insolations whether in hot, cold, or polar deserts. Exposure of samples to thermal radiation can be extremely detrimental or even disastrous, as in the case of permafrost soils, where irreversible changes can occur in both abiotic and biotic soil properties.

If possible, and whenever samples are to be transported for some distance, a small aliquot of each sample should be handcarried; they should also be frozen, if from polar regions or collected during the winter in areas of below freezing temperatures. Upon return to the laboratory, storage conditions can vary, depending on the location, nature, and intended use of the collected sample. Although most of the soil samples collected for the JPL desert microflora program have been stored air-dry in air-conditioned rooms, it has been found essential to retain Antarctic samples at −30°C for viability of bacteria (Cameron and Conrow, 1971). This temperature (or −10°C) also has been found best for retaining viability of Antarctic blue-green and green algae (Holm-Hansen, 1963).

Laboratory Analyses of Soil Samples

After the return of soil samples to the laboratory and their proper storage, processing of samples is still necessary, and this should be performed under aseptic con-

ditions insofar as possible to reduce or eliminate influx of microbiota into the samples as well as outfluxes into the external laboratory environment. "Clean-room" procedures should be used whenever possible for sieving and subsequent grinding or homogenizing of samples. Final processing procedures usually result in at least four aliquots of the soil sample: (1) coarse materials above 2 millimeters diameter, (2) materials less than 2 millimeters diameter, (3) a separate, sterilized bottle or other container of sieved soil intended for microbiological analyses and research, and (4) soil particles less than 2 millimeters diameter which are subsequently powdered with mortar and pestle and are less than 105 microns diameter (number 150 mesh).

For samples collected from very dry and barren areas, precautions cannot be overemphasized in the handling of samples because the biotic component of the soil microbial ecosystem may be composed only of microorganisms, and these may be few in number or even absent. Some sites, such as the Chilean Atacama Desert, the Valley of 10,000 Smokes, Alaska, relatively recently volcanically formed materials from Surtsey, Iceland, cinder cones within Deception Island on the Antarctic Peninsula, or other areas on the Antarctic continent ranging from the dry valleys of South Victoria Land south along the Transantarctic Mountain Range to Mount Howe, have yielded few or no viable microorganisms (Benoit and Hall, 1970; Boyd, Staley and Boyd, 1966; Cameron, 1969a; Cameron, 1971; Cameron and Benoit, 1970; Cameron, King and David, 1970; Cameron et al., 1971). It is therefore extremely important to collect, transport, handle, store, process, and analyze such samples with great care so as to avoid contamination. For Antarctic samples, as well as other samples from similar "polar" environments, an isolation booth has been maintained at −30°C, for both processing and maintaining samples (Cameron and Conrow, 1968). In addition, this cold environment serves as a test chamber for polar equipment and instruments.

A number of physical, physicochemical, and chemical analyses have been performed on soil samples collected for the JPL desert microflora program. Some of these analyses are necessary to define the soil; others are desirable for the design and testing extraterrestrial life detection experiments; and others are needed to understand the nature and limitations of the soil as a microbial habitat. Most of the analyses have been performed by standard methods, although some modifications have been made for highly saline or acid soils or those containing low levels of organic matter (Cameron and Blank, 1963; Cameron, 1969b; Cameron, 1970; Chapman and Pratt, 1961; Jackson, 1958; Richards, 1954). Methods are given here because it has been found necessary for comparison of analytical data obtained for a large number of desert soils.

In general, the following methods were used to determine soil physical and chemical properties, some of which are presented in tables 6.1 and 6.2:

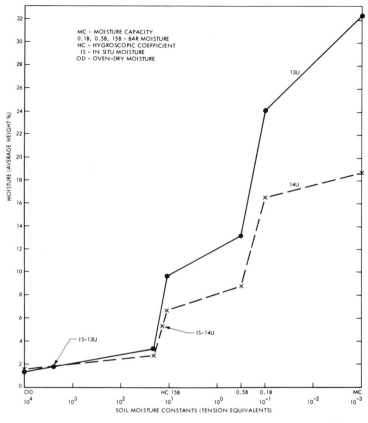

Fig. 6.10. Soil moisture retention-release curves for IBP desert biome site 13U–14U (surface 2, and 2–15 centimeters), Silverbell Experimental Area, Arizona.

1. Texture was determined by the hydrometer method.
2. Soil color and Munsell Notation were observed on the air-dry soil by comparison with Munsell soil color charts.
3. The *in situ* moisture content was obtained gravimetrically by drying the soil to constant weight at 105°C (± 5°C).
4. After one hour equilibration, pH and redox potentials (Eh) were determined on the soil: water (1:5) extract with a potentiometer.
5. Electrical conductivity (EC) values were obtained on the soil:water (1:5) extract.
6. Soluble cations and anions were obtained with a slightly acidified soil:water (1:5) extract followed by colorimetry, flame photometry, or atomic absorption spectrometry.
7. Analyses for organic carbon were by chromic acid digestion and gravimetric determination of evolved CO_2.
8. Organic nitrogen was determined by the Kjeldahl method.
9. Cation exchange capacity was usually determined by means of barium chloride-triethanolamine procedure.
10. Buffer capacity was determined by titration to the methyl orange or phenolphthalein end points.
11. Moisture constants, graphically presented for some of the samples, were determined by standard

methods for maximum water-holding capacity (free drainage at 0.001 bars), hygroscopic coefficient (30 days equilibrium under 3.3% H_2SO_4, or 30.6 bars), and at 0.1, 0.5 and 15 bars tension. Theoretical values for hygroscopic coefficient were determined from the moisture retention-release curves.

12. Thermoluminescence (TL) was performed for some of the soils (figs. 6.12–6.16) on approximately 10-milligram samples passed through a 100-millimeter sieve (number 10 mesh). Natural TL was determined, as well as TL following irradiation with a Co_{60} source. Relative peak heights of light intensity were plotted as glow curves versus temperature when heated from ambient (25°C) to approximately 425°C. Details of instrumentation and methods for analyses of soils have been given previously (Lawson, Ingham, and Landel, 1970; Nishita and Hansen, 1968) including analyses of Antarctic soils (Cameron, 1972c).

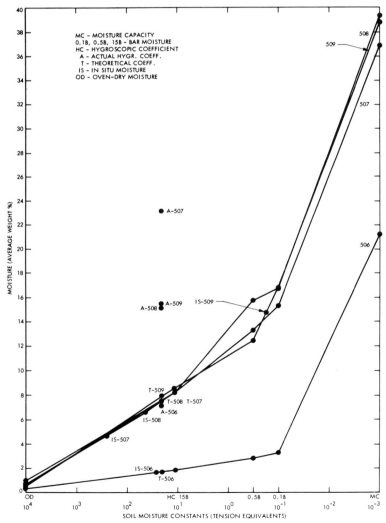

Fig. 6.11. Soil moisture retention-release curves for soil profile 506–509 (surface 5, 5–15, 30 and 60 centimeters), McKelvey Valley, Antarctica.

TABLE 6.1 — Physical and Chemical Properties of United States Arid-Zone Soils

Location	Soil No.	Texture	Color and Munsell Notation (air dry soil)	In Situ Moisture (wt %)	pH (1:5 extract)	Conductivity (10⁻⁶ mhos/cm at 25°C) (1:5 extract)	Cation Exchange Capacity (me/100 gm)	Buffer Capacity (me/100 gm)	Na+	K+	Ca++	Mg++	NH₄+	Fe+3	Cl−	SO₄=	HCO₃−	NO₃−	PO₄−3	Organic C (wt %)	Organic N (wt %)	Organic C/N (wt %)
Alaska Barrow tundra IBP site no. 4 (arctic)	901	Silty, peat	Very dark grayish brown 10yr 3/2	91.5	4.7	1,200	32	15	140	13	50	60	27	2	373	26	19	180	0.1	30.3	1.58	192
Putu, dunes (arctic)	900	Sandy, loam	Grayish brown 2.5yr 5/2	26.4	8.1	200	4	15	21	15	15	8	14	0.0	53	0	40	0.0	1.9	1.93	0.17	11.5
Putu, dunes (arctic)	583	Sand	Grayish brown 2.5yr 5/2	9.1	6.5	52	3	1.0	2	1	4	1	0.0	5	2	15	6	4	0.0	0.21	0.021	9.9
Valley 10,000 Smokes (volcanic cold)	115	Sandy, loam	Light gray 10yr 7/2	13.1	5.9	1.2	2.5	0.7	7.7	<5	<40	2	<0.1	1	9	<150	<1	1.3	<0.5	0.15	0.013	11.7
California High Mt. ("polar")	14	Stony, sandy, loam	Pale brown 10yr 6/3	9.2	6.3	16	10	1.6	5	3	9	1.1	0.8	0.08	4	11	15	28	1.1	0.55	0.070	1.3
California Great Basin Desert (cold)	3	Sandy, loam	Pale brown 10yr 6/3	0.42	6.8	100	4.5	2	12	6	1.3	1	0.2	0.03	4	6	34	1	2.1	0.14	0.011	12.7
Wyoming Red Desert (cold)	306	Loam	Reddish brown 5yr 5/4	3.18	7.0	1,980	3.5	8.0	5	13	520	48	4	0.0	4	1,120	30	2	0.08	0.52	0.006	86.6
	311	Silt, loam	Very pale brown 10yr 7/4	3.5	7.2	1,740	3.5	12.5	5	8	440	72	4	0.0	4	940	30	2	0.08	0.57	0.023	25.0
Colorado Dry land plains (cold)	130	Sand	Pale brown 10yr 6/3	0.35	6.4	113	0.5	0.5	1	8	2	0.5	1.75	1	7	6	24	3	1.0	0.02	0.219	14.6
Oregon Columbia Plateau (cold)	165	Sandy, loam	Light gray 2.5yr 7/2	24.9	8.4	315	3.2	16	76	11	0.5	0.3	1.60	0.0	9	21	204	1.5	4.0	1.39	0.072	19.3
Nevada Great Basin Desert (cold)	184	Loamy, sand	Brown 10yr 5/3	6.4	6.1	61	4	0.5	1	3	1	0.2	1.5	2	4	5	12	8	0.8	0.28	0.023	12.3
Arizona Painted Desert (cold)	355	Sand	Yellowish Red 5yr 4/8	0.23	8.9	140	3	2	13	6	11	1	3.2	2	20	0	70	5	1.3	0.10	0.006	16.6
Arizona Sonoran Desert (hot) Sahuarita IBP Site	9U	Loamy, sand	Yellowish brown 10yr 5/4	0.66	7.4	86	6	6.5	2	4	2	0.5	1.8	1	2	1	15	3	1.8	0.69	0.073	9.5
Sonoran Desert (hot) Silverbell IBP Site	13U	Sandy, loam	Yellowish brown 10yr 5/4	1.67	7.7	112	6	7.5	4	5	18	1	2.9	1	4	1	74	4	0.2	0.36	0.070	5.1
California Mohave Desert (hot) Hilgard Museum	H-11	Silt, loam	Grayish brown 2.5yr 5/2	—	6.8	213	4.5	10	36	2	8	2	0.0	2	54	5	61	0.0	0.0	0.44	0.020	21.8
Mohave Desert (hot)	75	Sand	Pale brown 10yr 6/3	0.60	7.0	200	6	18.5	7	13	28	1.5	5.6	0.04	2	60	76	0.0	2.0	0.62	0.045	13.8
Colorado Desert (hot)	1–2	Sand	Light brownish gray 2.5yr 6/2	0.36	8.0	138	6	15	9	9	7.5	1.3	0.1	0.04	5	5	61	4	0.8	0.25	0.026	9.6
New Mexico Chihuahua Desert (hot)	383	Sand	White 10yr 8/2	9.0	6.9	1,900	0	0.5	2	1	350	1.5	0.0	0.0	4	1,000	<10	0.0	0.0	0.10	0.003	32.3
Chihuahua Desert (hot) Jornada Range IBP Site	3U	Sandy, loam	Yellowish brown 10yr 5/4	2.1	8.0	146	18	7	4	10	9	0.7	1.7	0.0	7	1	64	3	2	0.93	0.109	8.5
Hawaii Kau Desert (volcanic hot)	37	Sandy, loam	Dark brown 10yr 4/3	31.6	6.8	99	10.5	2.5	5	2	1.5	0.5	0.5	1	10	2	15	0.0	0.0	2.09	0.183	11.4

Ions ppm (in 1:5 soil:H₂O extract)

[76]

TABLE 6.2 — Physical and Chemical Properties of World (except United States) Arid-Zone Soils

Location	Soil No.	Texture	Color and Munsell Notation (air dry soil)	In Situ Moisture (wt %)	pH (1:5 extract)	Conductivity (10^{-6} mhos/cm at 25°C) (1:5 extract)	Cation Exchange Capacity (me/100 gm)	Buffer Capacity (me/100 gm)	Na^+	K^+	Ca^{++}	Mg^{++}	NH_4^+	Fe^{+3}	Cl^-	$SO_4^=$	HCO_3^-	NO_3^-	PO_4^{-3}	Organic C (wt %)	Organic N (wt %)	Organic C/N (wt %)
									Ions — ppm (in 1:5 soil:H_2O extract)													
Antarctica Mount Howe	780	Sand	Pale brown 10yr 6/3	2.01	5.9	2,290	17	6.5	135	8	240	35	0.85	0.0	60	580	18	800	0.0	0.35	0.004	87.5
LaGorce Mountains	796	Sand	Olive gray 5yr 5/2	6.30	6.1	39	1.0	3.5	8	1	2.5	0.25	0.0	0.0	5	5	9	0.0	0.0	0.02	0.003	6.6
"Berg" Moraine	725	Sand	Reddish brown 5yr 5/3	0.92	4.8	1,700	2.0	1.5	90	2.5	240	35	0.2	0.0	75	700	18	140	0.0	0.02	0.091	2.3
Taylor Valley	600	Loamy, sand	Olive 5yr 5/3	0.15	8.2	4,560	2.5	12.5	200	75	55	100	0.5	0.0	835	8	30	5	0.0	0.02	0.003	6.6
Conrow Valley	638	Sand	Light olive brown 2.5yr 5/4	3.7	7.1	180	4.0	2.5	29	7	0.2	1.0	0.2	2	18	20	34	4	1.2	0.03	0.008	3.7
McKelvey Valley	506	Sand	Pale brown 10yr 6/3	0.84	6.8	2,150	8	1.5	340	3	95	32	0.1	0.02	385	130	21	320	0.2	0.09	0.006	14.2
Victoria Valley	799A	Loamy, sand	Light olive brown 2.5yr 5/4	2.28	7.0	3,800	1.0	5.0	325	11	210	24	0.0	0.0	657	250	27	230	0.3	0.05	0.010	4.7
Brown Peninsula	556	Sand	Gray 5yr 5/1	3.0	7.5	2,000	2.0	6.0	335	22	16	7	2.55	0.0	533	46	76	20	0.8	0.05	0.010	4.7
Deception Island	718	Gra-velly, sand	Grayish brown-very dark gray 2.5yr 5/2 & N3	21	6.9	170	2.0	0.25	8	0.05	1.5	0.6	0.0	18	7	4	18	0.0	0.5	0.02	0.002	10
New Zealand St. Mary's Range	577	Sandy, loam	Light gray 5yr 7/2	10.7	5.8	36	13	3.5	1	1	0.5	0.05	0.85	0.0	2	2	3	0.0	0.1	0.14	0.022	6.5
Colombia Andes Mountains	405	Loamy, sand	Light olive brown 2.5yr 5/4	43.5	5.7	60	1.5	0.5	1	1	0.5	0.4	0.0	0.0	7	5	12	0.0	0.1	1.44	0.109	13.2
Chile Atacama Desert (hot)	279	Loamy, sand	Pinkish white 7.5yr 8/2	1.95	8.4	3,100	0.0	4.0	135	195	5,750	130	10	0.0	585	12,000	45	850	4	0.05	0.002	26.5
Atacama Desert (hot)	268	Salty, sand	white 5yr 8/1	51.9	8.1	19,500	0.0	1.0	27,000	365	4,000	300	5	0.0	44,250	20,750	0.0	0.0	15	0.33	0.043	7.8
Argentina Gran Chaco (hot)	232	Silt, loam	Brown 7.5yr 5/2	3.9	7.8	225	11	5	5	5	125	1	5	2	35	300	30	20	0.5	1.15	0.139	8.3
Australia Simpson Desert (hot)	596	Sandy, loam	Red 2.5yr 4/6	0.67	6.4	150	8	7.5	2	0.4	0.2	0.1	1.9	0.0	5	0.0	9	3	0.1	0.78	0.103	7.5
Mexico Sonoran Desert (hot)	250	Loamy, sand	Dark gray 5yr 5/1	4.3	7.8	81	18.5	13.5	1.5	1	3.4	1.8	0.0	0.0	4	10	24	3	0.5	0.84	0.074	11.3
Morocco Sahara Desert (hot)	807	Sandy, loam	Light brown 7.5yr 6/4	3.9	7.0	26,500	24	140	6,200	400	1,160	20	2.8	0.0	10,280	300	31	5	0.1	0.3	0.013	22.8
Egypt Sahara Desert (hot)	293	Sandy, loam	Grayish brown 2.5yr 5/2	2.3	7.4	1,850	8	3.5	1,550	130	860	144	3	0.0	144	750	40	22	0.1	0.41	0.018	19
Israel Negev Desert (hot)	228	Sandy, loam	Very pale brown 10yr 7/3	1.2	6.8	350	14	40	39	11	15	3	0.0	0.0	83	10	42	1	0.5	0.91	0.037	24.5

[77]

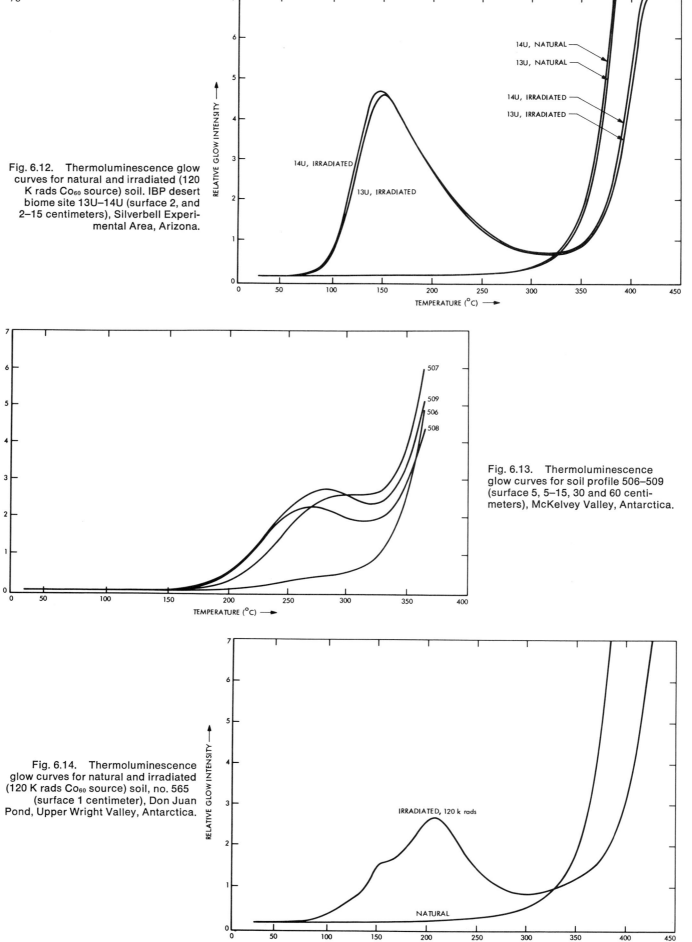

Fig. 6.12. Thermoluminescence glow curves for natural and irradiated (120 K rads Co60 source) soil. IBP desert biome site 13U–14U (surface 2, and 2–15 centimeters), Silverbell Experimental Area, Arizona.

14U, NATURAL
13U, NATURAL
14U, IRRADIATED
13U, IRRADIATED

14U, IRRADIATED
13U, IRRADIATED

Fig. 6.13. Thermoluminescence glow curves for soil profile 506–509 (surface 5, 5–15, 30 and 60 centimeters), McKelvey Valley, Antarctica.

507
509
506
508

Fig. 6.14. Thermoluminescence glow curves for natural and irradiated (120 K rads Co60 source) soil, no. 565 (surface 1 centimeter), Don Juan Pond, Upper Wright Valley, Antarctica.

IRRADIATED, 120 k rads

NATURAL

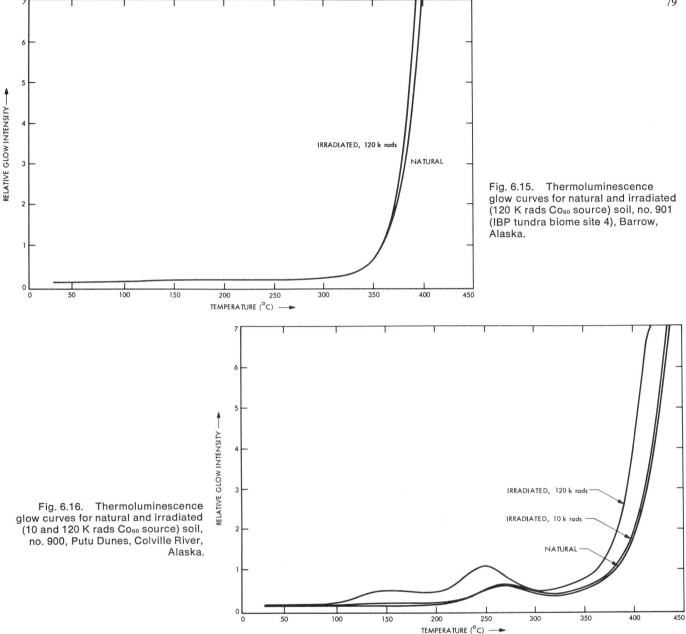

Fig. 6.15. Thermoluminescence glow curves for natural and irradiated (120 K rads Co_{60} source) soil, no. 901 (IBP tundra biome site 4), Barrow, Alaska.

Fig. 6.16. Thermoluminescence glow curves for natural and irradiated (10 and 120 K rads Co_{60} source) soil, no. 900, Putu Dunes, Colville River, Alaska.

Some of the other analyses performed but not included in these tables were:

1. "Total" analysis for major, minor, and trace elements determined by the semiquantitative cathode layer arc process. (O, C, N, P, and S must be determined separately.)
2. Predominate minerals determined by x-ray diffraction analyses, supplemented by data obtained for "total" analysis and water-extractable cations and anions.
3. The pH, Eh, and EC of saturated soil pastes.
4. Total loss on ignition determined by firing at 600°C for 30 minutes.
5. Additional values, such as "N-value" (for subsidence) bulk density, porosity, osmotic pressure, and reflectivity ratios were obtained by calculation from the above analytical data.

General groups of soil microflora were determined by cultural methods for bacteria, algae, fungi, and protozoa (Allen, 1954; Cameron, 1969b; Cameron, 1970; diMenna, 1966). A list of culture media and conditions used to obtain the various groups of microflora is given in table 6.3. However, only a few groups are listed in summarized form for comparison purposes. These are abundances of aerobic, microaerophilic, and anaerobic bacteria, possible nitrogen fixing bacteria, yeasts, molds and algae, as shown in tables 6.4 and 6.5. A summary of metabolic activity as determined by a radiorespirometric method versus abundances of culturable microorganisms in some Antarctic soils is given in table 6.6. Other tables of microbial groups and the properties of soils from which they were isolated have been presented in previous publications (Cameron, 1966; Cameron, 1969a; Cameron 1969b; Cameron, 1971; Cameron, 1972c; Cameron,

TABLE 6.3

Culture Media and Conditions for Determination of Microbial Groups in Antarctic Soils

Culture Medium	Microbial Test	pH	Eh + mv (uncompensated)	Electrical Conductivity (EC x 10⁻⁶ mhos/cm at 25° C)	Incubation Temperature (0°C)	Incubation Period (av. no. days)	First Observed Growth (av. no. days)
Actinomycete isolation agar	Aerobic bacteria and strepto-mycetes	7.8	124	3,680	20	21	14
Burk's "Ion" agar	Nitrogen fixing and non-chromogenic bacteria	6.9	172	2,800	20	21	14
Desoxycholate agar	Coliform bacteria	7.4	131	6,400	37	14	7
Di Menna's dextrose-neopeptone agar, pH 4.5	Yeasts and molds	4.5	160	880	5,20	42, 21	21, 14
Fluid thioglycollate	Microaerophiles, aerobic and anaerobic bacteria	7.1	5	7,300	20	56	16
Lactose broth	Lactose fermenters	6.8	155	2,180	20	42	6
Nitrate reduction broth	Nitrate reducers	7.1	158	3,020	20	42	7
Rose bengal agar	Fungi (molds and yeasts)	5.7	208	2,320	5,20	28	10
Salt - organic agar (stv.) simulated Taylor Valley extract, neopeptone, and yeast extract	Aerobic and chromogenic bacteria	7.1	153	2,420	5,20	42, 30	21, 14
Starkey's solution, modified	Sulfate reducers (anaerobic bacteria)	6.3	110	560	20	42	12
Thornton's salt medium, "Gro-lux" lights ~ 200 ft. c.	Algae and protozoa	7.8	158	2,670	20	180	14
Trypticase soy agar	Aerobic bacteria, streptomycetes and fungi; anaerobic bacteria in CO₂ or "gas pak"	7.5	140	5,680	5, 20, 45, 55; 20 or room temperature	42, 30, 5, 5; 40	21, 14, 2,2; 40
Trypticase soy broth	Bacteria (broad spectrum), halotolerants	7.4	142	12,800	20	42	4
Van Delden's sulfate reduction agar	Sulfate reducers, (microaerophiles), and non-chromogenic bacteria	5.8	176	5,120	20	21	14

King and David, 1970a; Cameron, King and David, 1970b).

Soil Properties

In general, regardless of geographical location, latitude, or elevation, desert soils do have some features in common as shown in tables 6.1 and 6.2. They are usually coarse-textured sandy or loamy, brownish or grayish materials, usually low in organic carbon and nitrogen, having a relatively narrow C:N ratio, and a pH of approximately neutral or above. However, lower pH values and higher concentrations of organic matter are found in polar (High Arctic) soils (Tedrow, 1966). A pedogenic gradient can be shown for polar zone soils, with progressive decreases in organic matter and increase in pH as climate becomes colder and precipitation also decreases (Tedrow, 1968). The organic matter in the driest parts of the Antarctic is derived essentially from anthracite coal (Bauman et al, 1970; Horowitz et al, 1969).

TABLE 6.4

Microbiological Determinations of United States Arid-Zone Soils

Location	Soil Number	Aerobic Bacteria (including Streptomycetes)	Microaerophiles Positives at Highest Dilution	Anaerobes	Nitrogen Fixers†	Yeasts	Molds	Algae Positives at Highest Dilution
Alaska								
Barrow, tundra IBP Site no. 4 (arctic)	901	1.8×10^6	$*10^6$	4.5×10^3	1.1×10^6	0	2.4×10^4	10^7
Putu, tundra (arctic)	900	1.6×10^6	$*10^6$	1.5×10^3	2.7×10^6	0	7.3×10^5	10^4
Putu dunes (arctic)	583	1.5×10^5	10^8	120	3.6×10^4	10	340	100
Valley 10,000 Smokes (volcanic cold)	115	4.7×10^3	10^3	1.3×10^3	60	0	190	10^5
California								
High Mt. ("polar")	14–2	8.5×10^5	10^6	1.5×10^4	1.2×10^4	0	225	10^3
California								
Great Basin Desert (cold)	3	2.1×10^4	1×10^5	1.6×10^4	5.1×10^4	0	150	10^3
Wyoming								
Red Desert (cold)	306	1.1×10^6	10^7	0	1.5×10^5	0	875	10^3
Red Desert (cold)	311	5.7×10^6	10^7	<10	1.4×10^5	0	300	10^6
Colorado								
Dryland plains (cold)	130	2.1×10^5	10^7	850	2.9×10^5	0	4.3×10^3	10^3
Oregon								
Columbia Plateau (cold)	165	1.8×10^5	10^7	4.8×10^4	3.6×10^5	0	2×10^3	10^7
Nevada								
Great Basin Desert (cold)	184	1.1×10^5	10^5	3.1×10^3	2.6×10^5	700	1.3×10^3	10^3
Arizona								
Painted Desert (cold)	355	1.2×10^3	10^5	4.8×10^3	7.5×10^4	25	400	100
Arizona								
Sonoran Desert (hot) Sahuarita IBP Site	9U	1.2×10^5	10^7	4.9×10^3	3.4×10^5	400	7.5×10^3	10^5
Sonoran Desert (hot) Silverbell IBP Site	13U	5×10^5	10^7	2.9×10^3	3×10^5	1.5×10^3	6.5×10^3	10^6
California								
Mohave Desert (hot) Hilgard Museum	H–11	3.6×10^5	10^7	830	1×10^5	0	0	10^5
Mohave Desert (hot)	75	3.9×10^6	10^6	8.4×10^3	3.2×10^5	50	475	10^3
Colorado Desert (hot)	1–2	5.5×10^5	10^6	2.6×10^3	7.5×10^4	120	250	10^6
New Mexico								
Chihuahua Desert (hot)	383	6×10^5	10^6	0	4.6×10^3	0	0	10^3
Chihuahua Desert (hot) Jornada Range IBP Site	3U	2.9×10^5	10^7	550	5.4×10^5	2.3×10^3	8.8×10^3	10^4
Hawaii								
Kau Desert (volcanic hot)	37	1.4×10^5	10^6	6×10^4	1.3×10^5	0	3×10^3	10^6
Culture Medium		Trypticase soy agar (TSA)	Fluid thioglycollate	TSA in CO_2 or "Gas-Pak"	Burk's agar	di Menna's agar	Rose bengal or di Menna's agar	Thornton's salt solution and $25 \rightarrow \sim500$ ftc.

*Includes sulfate reducers
†Includes soil diluent

Cation exchange capacity and buffer capacity also are usually low, as would be expected for coarse-textured soils low in fines and organic matter content. Moisture percentages of surface soils varied widely, but they were commonly air-dry, in equilibrium with the atmosphere above the soil surface, and commonly less than the hygroscopic coefficient (98% relative humidity), figures 6.10 and 6.11. Of course, following meteoric precipitation, or other moisture influxes such as from glacial melt and proximity to permafrost, moisture content could approach the saturation values and anaerobic conditions would result from the filling of soil capillaries with water. For one typical Arctic tundra soil (sample number 901), the *in situ* moisture retention was extremely high, which would provide a favorable milieu for anaerobic activity.

Electrical conductivity (EC) values varied widely, depending on the quantity and nature of salts in the soils. Only a few samples had unfavorable EC values. Extract EC values above 250×10^{-6} mhos/centimeter are high enough to be osmotically detrimental for macroplants under normal conditions of a favorable moisture-temperature regime (Richards, 1954). Values above $2,000 \times 10^{-6}$ mhos/centimeter indicate a "very high" proportion of total soluble salts (Metson, 1961). They constitute a "very high" salinity hazard in temperate arid areas (Smith, Draper, and Fuller, 1964), and the same is also true of polar arid areas (Cameron, 1972c). Depending on the moisture and temperature status of the soil, halotolerants or halophiles would be expected in some habitats of relatively high salt concentration.

As indicated by the range of EC values, the concentrations of chemical ions varied widely. This was not primarily a geographical or latitudinal factor but is related

TABLE 6.5

Microbiological Determinations of World (except United States) Arid-Zone Soils

Location	Soil Number	Aerobic Bacteria (including Streptomycetes)	Microaerophiles Positives at Highest Dilution	Anaerobes	Nitrogen Fixers*	Yeasts	Molds	Algae Positives at Highest Dilution
Antarctica								
Mount Howe	780	<10	10	0	0	<10†	0	0
LaGorce Mountains	796	160	100	0	90	0	0	0
"Berg" Moraine	725	9	0	0	0	5†	0	0
Taylor Valley	600	50	100	0	<10	0	0	0
Conrow Valley	638	6×10^3	10^3	0	1.7×10^3	0	0	200
McKelvey Valley	506	100	10^4	0	0	0	0	0
Victoria Valley	799A	560	100	0	0	0	0	0
Brown Peninsula	556	2.1×10^4	10^4	0	1.2×10^3	0.5†	0	10
Deception Island	718	1.6×10^5	10^7	<10	7.7×10^4	0	140	10^3
New Zealand								
St. Mary's Range	577	1.3×10^4	10^5	1.1×10^4	1.2×10^4	0	3.3×10^3	10
Colombia								
Andes Mountains	405	3.4×10^3	10^6	7.3×10^3	2.6×10^4	0	500	1×10^3
Chile								
Atacama Desert (hot)	279	3.5×10^4	10^3	600	0	0	10	10^6
Atacama Desert (hot)	268	20	10^3	5	0	0	0	0
Argentina								
Gran Chaco (hot)	232	8.4×10^5	10^8	5.3×10^3	3.3×10^6	0	500	10^3
Australia								
Simpson Desert (hot)	596	3.5×10^5	10^5	4.5×10^3	1.2×10^4	1.8×10^3	2.1×10^3	10^5
Mexico								
Sonoran Desert (hot)	250	1.9×10^5	10^7	4.5×10^3	2.5×10^4	0	2.3×10^3	10^6
Morocco								
Sahara Desert (hot)	807	1.1×10^4	10^6	1.9×10^3	330	0	0	10^3
Egypt								
Sahara Desert (hot)	293	1.9×10^6	10^7	0	9.5×10^5	0	75	100
Israel								
Negev Desert (hot)	228	4.5×10^5	10^8	5×10^3	1.7×10^4	0	4.3×10^5	10^3
Culture Medium		Trypticase soy agar (TSA)	Fluid thioglycollate	TSA in CO_2 or "Gas-Pak"	Burk's agar	di Menna's agar	Rose bengal or di Menna's agar	Thornton's salt solution and 25 → ~500 ftc.

*Includes soil diluent
†5° C only

to the parent materials, the nature and degree of weathering, leaching, drainage, and evaporative phenomena. The principal cations in polar (Antarctic) desert soils are Ca^{++}, Mg^{++}, Na^+, and K^+ (Tedrow and Ugolini, 1966), with CA^{++} and Na^+ usually dominating the exchange complex. This is also true for desert soils of lower latitudes, as indicated in tables 6.1 and 6.2. Ammonia usually is not prevalent in typical desert soils, although it is found in higher concentrations in tundra (for example, soil sample number 901). Principal anions for all of the desert soils were Cl^-, $SO_4^=$, HCO_3^- and sometimes NO_3^-. Concentrations of PO_4^{-3} were negligible or nil for many samples. Nitrate can occur in high concentration in soils of temperate as well as polar arid areas as shown in tables 6.1 and 6.2, even occurring in relatively high concentrations in tundra. A NO_3^- concentration of 20 parts per million is considered a "good supply" for temperate arid soils (McGeorge, 1940), but an excess can be toxic.

Microbial Abundances and Kinds

Abundances of general microbial groups in desert soils are shown in tables 6.4 and 6.5. As expected, aerobic and microaerophilic bacteria are in highest abundance, regardless of the desert region, but the Antarctic polar desert has the fewest recoverable numbers of microorganisms as determined by cultural methods. It is always debatable as to whether or not a significant number of microorganisms can be recovered through cultural methods, but the determination of metabolic activity by means of labeled substrates essentially substantiates this for Antarctic soils, table 6.6 (Horowitz, Cameron, and Hubbard, 1972; Hubbard, Cameron, and Miller, 1968). The C^{14}-assimilation studies indicated an excellent sensitivity for both bacteria and algae in Antarctic surface soils (Hubbard et al, 1970).

Moist soil incubations also can result in growth of some bacteria from Antarctic soils, but not in all cases (Cameron and Merek, 1971). Capillary enrichment methods, followed by scanning electron microscopy, may be useful (Gray, 1969). This approach has been utilized in the examination of desert soils in connection with exobiological research (Opfell, Zebal and Shannon, 1968). However, long-term incubations at high humidity of soil sprinkled on the surface of agar in petri dishes, as well as heavy inocula of soils into tubes of aqueous differential and enrichment media, can achieve similar results. It was determined early in work on Antarctic soils that pour plates were highly detrimental for obtaining growth of Antarctic bacteria, thus pretempered plates also are recommended. Sprinkle and spread plates have been subsequently used instead of pour plates for all our plate incubations of desert soils.

Among the groups of microorganisms, bacteria were the highest in abundance, and a number of aerobes and microaerophiles had the ability to grow in nitrate reduction broth, lactose broth, and trypticase soy broth as well as in fluid thioglycollate. Some had the ability to grow in nitrogen-free media, such as Burk's Ion Agar or Broth, regardless of the desert area from which they were isolated (R. M. Johnson, personal communication). Anaerobic bacteria were not usually abundant in arid mineral soils, and few, if any, were obligate forms. Anaerobes were most numerous in special habitats, such as volcanic environments or in tundra soils, where oxygen was limited. Although sulfate reducers are supposedly widespread in the Antarctic (Barghoorn and Nichols, 1961), this could not be confirmed for obligate forms when soils were tested with Starkey's medium. However, they were found in Arctic tundra soils, growing both in Starkey's medium and also subsurface in fluid thioglycollate, turning both media black.

Other groups of microorganisms occuring in desert soils include algae and fungi, but they were not found in any soil habitat unless bacteria also were present. Algae are sometimes quite evident in soil crusts, and the fungi are frequently associated with them, as well as protozoa and other microbiota. The biomass of algae and fungi is undoubtedly higher than indicated in tables 6.4 and 6.5, because many of them are filamentous forms and do not lend themselves well to dilution tube and plate count methods. Algae constitute the greatest biomass in the Antarctic (Llano, 1962). It also should be considered that depending on the past history of an area, especially in regard to duration of desiccation and time since the last period of available moisture, that incubation times should be lengthened to obtain growth

of desert microorganisms. Some algae, for example, may require at least six months under continuous incubation before they can be revived and grow out of desert soils (Cameron et al, 1971b), and a few from dry valleys of South Victoria Land have required more than a year! Longevity of microorganisms from stored air-dry bottles of museum soils 70 to 90 years old (for example, soil sample number H-11 from the Hilgard Museum, University of California, Berkeley) has been demonstrated as shown in table 6.3.

A determination of the kinds of microbiota in desert soils is complex, especially for comparative purposes, primarily because of taxonomic difficulties. Too many species of algae, for example, may be listed for the Antarctic (Koob, 1968), but a comparison of species, based upon the ecophene concept (Drouet, 1968), indicates a need to recognize the commonality of species, regardless of habitat and geographical location. Attempts to establish commonality of species of microorganisms from a wide variety of localities (Fehér and Frank, 1947; Fehér, 1948), are, however, quite essential for ecological as well as taxonomic purposes. A discussion on the ecology and list of Antarctic soil algae has been given in another publication (Cameron, 1972a); a similar presentation also has been given for algae in soils of temperate desert areas (Cameron, 1971b). A comprehensive list of Alaskan Arctic blue-green algae has indicated approximately forty species, many of them oscillatorioid forms (Maruyama, 1967). *Schizothrix calcicola* is probably the most widespread of all the blue-green algae in desert areas (Drouet, 1968), but also occurring in many other nondesert areas and a number of diverse habitats. *Nostoc commune,* another filamentous blue-green algae, also is widespread. It is especially important in all desert areas for its nitrogen fixing capability.

The bacteria in our desert soils have been identified in a number of progress reports (W. B. Bollen and R. M. Johnson). An attempt to classify and correlate over four hundred fifty strains of bacteria from seven desert areas has indicated that a few genera predominated in our soils. These included species of *Bacillus, Streptomyces, Arthrobacter* and *Corynebacterium,* with *Arthrobacter* spp. ubiquitous in desert soils. *Corynebacterium* spp. dominant in Antarctic soils, and sporeforming bacteria — *Bacillus, Streptomyces,* and *Nocardia* spp. occurring primarily in nonpolar regions (R. M. Johnson, personal communication). *Micrococcus* spp. and gram-negative bacilli were primarily limited to the colder deserts (Johnson and Holaday, 1970). In the nonpolar regions *Arthrobacter* spp. occurred primarily in sites without *Bacillus* spp., and conversely, *Arthrobacter* spp. were absent where *Bacillus* and *Streptomyces* spp. dominated (R. M. Johnson, personal communication). Both *Corynebacterium* and *Arthrobacter* belong to the diphtheroid group, and the taxonomy and relationships of these microorganisms are not well-defined, but, in general, they represent a pleomorphic group of aerobic, branched or nonbranched, cocci-rods that are gram-

TABLE 6.6

**Metabolic Activity Versus Abundances of
Culturable Microorganisms in Antarctic
Surface and Subsurface Soils***

Soil Distribution	Number of Soils	Range of Culturable Microorganisms per Gram of Soil	$C^{14}O_2$ Evolved (counts/min per hr per 10^3 viable cells)
Surface 2 ⟶ 5 cm	12	10 ⟶ 10^3	1,575
Surface 2 ⟶ 5 cm	5	10^3 ⟶ 10^4	665
Subsurface ⟶ ~30 cm	13	10 ⟶ 10^3	235
	4	10^3 ⟶ 10^4	25
	4	10^4 ⟶ 1.7×10^5	15

*Substrate mixtures contained 144 ng of U^{14} C-glucose (5 x 10^4 counts/minute) plus 20 ng U^{14} C-amino acids (3.9 x 10^4 counts/minute in 0.3 milliliters of water.

Source: Horowitz and others. Science, vol. 164, pp. 1054–56.

positive (or variable) catalase positive, sometimes acid-fast and forming pigment, and generally nonspore-forming. They may possess a glycoprotein which enables them to resist freezing as well as desiccation.

The fungi of desert soils are not well enumerated, although preliminary studies have been made of a few regions such as the Sahara (Fehér, 1945), or more extensively in the polar regions (Corte and Daglio, 1964; diMenna, 1966; Kobayasi et al, 1967, Kobayasi et al, 1969; Tubaki, 1961; Tubaki and Asano, 1965). Some species occur in both polar regions as well as having worldwide distribution, for example, *Chrysosporium pannorium* (Kobayasi and Sugiyama, 1969). It has been isolated from a number of our Antarctic samples which have shown viable molds (Cameron, 1971). *Penicillium* spp. also are worldwide in distribution and occur frequently in desert as well as nondesert areas. *Penicillium* spp. may or may not be endemic to the Antarctic, although they undoubtedly occur in some Antarctic soils and were found to be prominent in trappings of aerial borne plant propagules (Rudolph, 1970; Schofield and Rudolph, 1969). Among the yeasts, *Cryptococcus albidus* has been the most frequently recoverable isolant from our soils (diMenna, personal communication). Yeasts, as a group, can grow in relatively dry substrates, at high osmotic pressures, and they are cold-adapted, which presents tremendous advantages in high latitudes, such as the cold and drought-dominated Antarctic ecosystems (diMenna, 1966). A list of yeasts and other microorganisms cultured from Antarctic soils collected for the JPL desert microflora program has been presented previously (Cameron, 1971).

Ecological Considerations

In all desert regions, the environmental conditions become restrictive for various life forms, and in the most arid areas, macroplants cannot exist. The ecosystem therefore becomes simpler, and it is reduced to the microbial level of life forms. In the Antarctic dry valleys, and farther south, along the Transantarctic Mountain Range, the soil microbial ecosystem is the simplest of all terrestrial ecosystems. The Antarctic desert therefore provides a unique opportunity for studying soil microbial ecology at its least complex level in terms of gradients of the physical and chemical environment of the soil, terrain, and microclimate at increasing latitude and altitude. These gradients range from uninhabitable and relatively unfavorable to increasingly favorable environments. These conditions, both measurable or observational, are summarized in table 6.7. In essence, the solclime (hygrothermal regime) is primarily the most important factor.

Increasingly lower temperatures are found with increase in latitude along the Transantarctic Mountain Range, as shown by a comparison of soil and air temperatures for Taylor Valley (77°39′ south, 162°52′ east), figures 6.17 and 6.18, and Mount Howe (87°22′

south, 149°18′west), figure 6.19. Although soil surface temperatures during austral summer were frequently above freezing at some time during each diurnal period, as at Taylor Valley, there was still a diurnal freeze-thaw which would be detrimental for many microbiota. The soil surface temperatures at Mount Howe never did rise above freezing, even during austral midsummer, and any possible life forms were essentially incapable of growth or reproduction. Extended periods of temperature and moisture levels above freezing are necessary before increasingly complex groups and abundances of microorganisms can develop on the community level.

Along with temperature variations, the moisture status of the soil also changes, and soil relative humidity peaks are depressed when temperature peaks are elevated and vice versa (Cameron, King, and David, 1970a). It is therefore important to consider the integration of moisture and temperature for growth and activity of microorganisms. There is little evidence that microbial activity or growth takes place in polar soils when temperatures are below freezing and concurrent RH's are less than 65 percent.

Although moisture content can be determined in the field, it is useful to determine soil moisture constants on soil samples in the laboratory. Plotting of these constants indicates moisture activity on a soil moisture-retention release curve as influenced by texture, salts and other soil factors. As shown in figures 6.10 and 6.11 for a hot temperature desert soil and an Antarctic dry

TABLE 6.7

Environmental & Ecological Factors Determining Distribution, Abundance, & Kinds of Life Forms in Antarctic Terrestrial Ecosystems

Favorable	Unfavorable
Lower latitude and elevation	Higher latitude and elevation
N-S orientation	E-W orientation
Northern exposure and gentle north-facing slopes	Southern exposure and flat or south-facing slopes
High duration and intensity solar radiation (thermal)	Low duration and intensity of solar radiation (thermal)
Protected habitat; microclimate above freezing	Exposed habitat; microclimate below freezing
Absence of wind (low evaporation rate, negligible abrasion)	High winds (high desiccation rate and abrasion of surface)
Northerly winds	Southerly winds
High humidities	Low humidities
Slow or impeded drainage	Rapid drainage and leaching
Lengthy duration of available, good quality H_2O (presence of glaciers, lakes, streams, meltwater pools, snow and ice fields)	Short duration of available, good quality H_2O (absence of glaciers, lakes, streams, meltwater pools, snow and ice fields)
Translucent pebbles ("microgreen houses")	Opaque pebbles
Weathered geologic materials	Negligible or slow soil formation
Non-salty soils, balanced ionic composition	Salty soils, unbalanced ionic composition, soluble toxic ions
Approximately neutral pH	High (or low) pH
Organic contamination and accumulation (skuas, seals, penguins, man, etc.)	No organic contamination or accumulation (no large increments of organic matter by plants or animals; O.M. <0.1%)

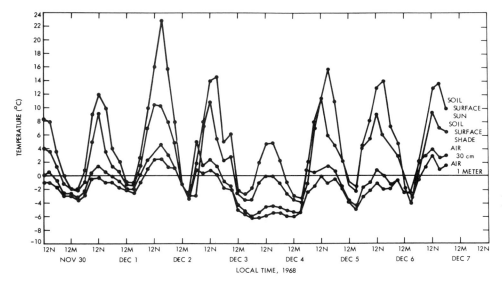

Fig. 6.17.   Air and soil surface temperatures, sites 600–603, Taylor Valley, Antarctica.

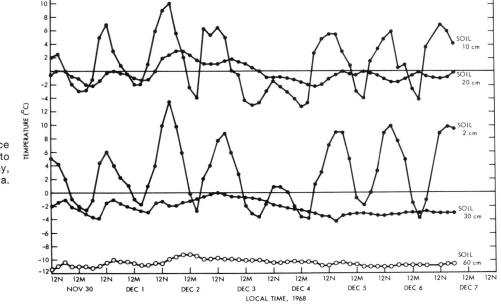

Fig. 6.18.   Soil subsurface temperatures, sites 600–603 (surface to 60 centimeters), Taylor Valley, Antarctica.

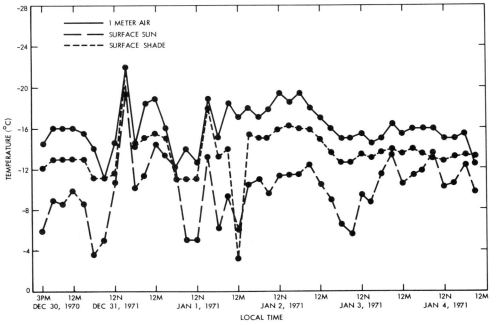

Fig. 6.19.   Soil and air temperature, Mount Howe, Antarctica (elevation 2,800 meters, 87°22′ south, 149°18′ west).

Fig. 6.20. Don Juan Pond, South Fork, Upper Wright Valley, South Victoria Land, Antarctica. This pond contains a saturated solution of calcium chloride, has a moisture activity of approximately 0.45, freezes at −45°C to −55°C, and contains few or no microorganisms.

valley soil, the *in situ* moisture content can be plotted on the curve and the possibility of microbial activity inferred from the curve. When the *in situ* moisture content value lies between the hygroscopic coefficient and the oven dry value, then growth and reproduction of most soil microorganisms is unlikely. Microbial activity also is unlikely at the *in situ* moisture content shown for subsurface soil number 507, figure 6.11, because this soil was at −11°C when sampled. For this same soil profile, 506–509, the displacement and elevation of the actual hygroscopic coefficient values from the theoretical values indicates the influence of moisture-absorbing salts. Microbiota would therefore have to overcome this salt effect, and any growth or reproduction would have to take place at an elevated osmotic pressure.

At the present time, there is no single instrument or analysis which can provide an overview of soil microbial ecology, but the use of thermoluminescence (TL) shows some promise in indicating geologic age, microclimate, mineral composition, and degree of gamma irradiation, as well as favorability of a habitat for soil microorganisms (Cameron, 1971; Cameron, 1972c; Ingham, Cameron, and Lawson, in press). For the Antarctic dry valleys, data have been obtained to show that there are distinct differences for individual sites and soils, and a rather consistent pattern for a given valley, its orientation, microclimate and soil characteristics. For Victoria Valley sites, there was an excellent correlation between TL and site exposure, slope, hygrothermal regime (heat and moisture), geologic age of morainic materials, derivation of minerals, nature of salts, and possibly soil texture and structure (Cameron, 1972c). Some soils, as found for McKelvey dry valley site 506–509, have natural TL, which changes with depth of profile, figure 6.13. Others show no natural irradiation, but a high capability for TL following irradiation with a Co_{60} source, as shown in figure 6.12 for IBP biome site 13U–14U in the Sonoran Desert. For Arctic

tundra biome site number 4, soil sample 901, Barrow, Alaska, natural TL was similar to irradiation with 10K rads, figure 6.15, but a dune site east of the tundra area, soil sample 900, showed essentially no natural or induced effects of irradiation, figure 6.16. A Don Juan pond sample from the South Fork of Upper Wright Valley, figure 6.20, had no natural TL, but it showed a broadly elevated peak following irradiation with 120 k rads, figure 6.14. The salty nature of this latter area and the difficulty encountered in obtaining viable microorganisms from the saturated calcium chloride pond water, have provided an important study from the viewpoint of possible Martian life detection (Horowitz, 1971).

Thermoluminescence also holds promise for determining the suitability of a site as a habitat for microorganisms. It appears to be more than coincidental that mineral soils which show relatively high natural TL also have reduced numbers of microorganisms (Cameron, 1972c; Ingham, Cameron, and Lawson, in press). A plot of natural TL versus numbers of culturable bacteria from Victoria Dry Valley shows an approximate correlation between increasing natural TL and decreasing numbers of bacteria, figure 6.21. Thermoluminescence of eleven samples collected from Mount Howe, the farthest south area of exposed rock and soil, showed that all samples had varying degrees of natural TL (D. Lawson, personal communication) and the samples had few (approximately ten) or no culturable microorganisms.

Concluding Remarks

The study of soil microbial ecology in desert regions has shown that there is a sequence of microbiota occurring in a given ecosystem, dependent upon environmental and associated ecological factors, as depicted in figure 6.22. This sequence is most easily observed in

Antarctic desert areas, which are relatively uncomplexed by the near absence of animals and higher plants, and also the disruptive influences of human activities. Along an environmental gradient, ranging from unfavorable to favorable, table 6.7, there are no life forms or cryophilic yeasts in even small abundance to start with. This is followed by a steady increase of species and numbers along the environmental gradient with more complex life forms occurring at the most favorable extreme of the gradient. This ecological sequence shows a surprising similarity to theories proposed for evolution of microorganisms, but it is only the environment and microbiota relationships which have determined the sequence shown in figure 6.22, especially in terms of quantitative measurements. It is an obviously important fact that terrestrial life forms do adapt in an ecological sequence along an environmental gradient, and a similar concept should be applied to possible detection of extraterrestrial life. There is a cutoff point at which life forms cannot adapt because of the characteristics of the natural environment. It also should be considered that simple ecosystems are easily disturbed or irreversibly destroyed, table 6.8, (Cameron, 1972b), and pollution and conservation of the ecosystem is important in polar deserts as well as in other desert regions. Influences of human activities in easily perturbed terrestrial ecosystems also can be applied to exploration of extraterrestrial bodies, and subsequent precautionary measures should be used as necessary to avoid disturbing a possible existing ecosystem or implanting an ecosystem where none existed previously.

Acknowledgments

This chapter presents the results of one phase of research carried out by the Jet Propulsion Laboratory, California Institute of Technology, under Contract NAS 7–100, sponsored by the National Aeronautics and Space Administration. Logistic support and facilities for the investigations in Antarctica and additional laboratory support at the Jet Propulsion Laboratory were provided

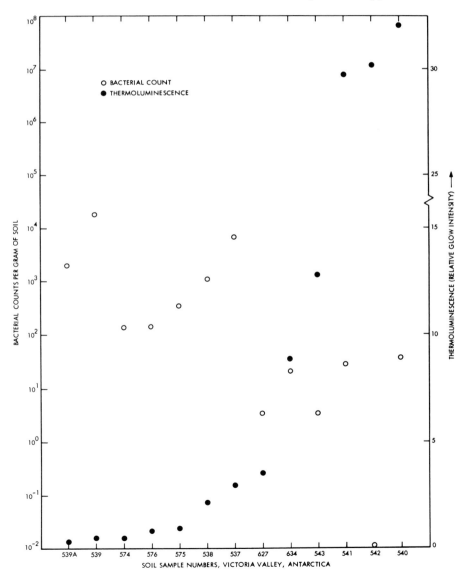

Fig. 6.21. Relationship between bacterial abundance and natural thermoluminescence of soil samples from Victoria Valley, Antarctica (numbers of bacterial colonies were determined following incubation at 20°C on trypticase soy agar).

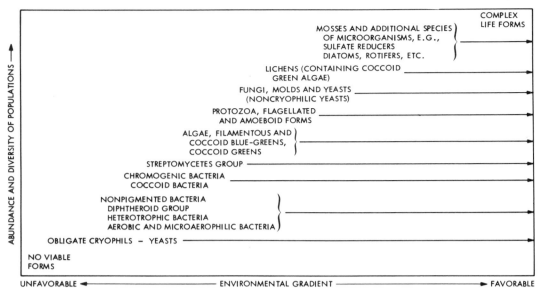

Fig. 6.22. Variability of population density and diversity with variability of environmental factors in undisturbed Antarctic terrestrial ecosystems.

under Contract NSF C–585 with the National Science Foundation.

Work in the Arctic was begun with field assistance and logistic support provided by Naval Arctic Research Laboratory, Barrow, Alaska. Tundra Biome Research was later supported by National Science Foundation Office of Polar Programs and The International Biological Program (IBP) through NSF Grant 323–431–1. At temperate desert biome sites, the work was partly supported through the US/IBP Desert Biome Program, under NSF Grant GB–15886.

During the years of research from the mid-1950s to the early 1970s on hot, cold, and polar deserts, especially for the Jet Propulsion Laboratory desert microflora program, a number of individuals have provided assistance in various ways. N. Horowitz has promoted the investigations of the Antarctic because of their value to extraterrestrial life detection, especially for Mars. The first JPL field trips were then undertaken to the Antarctic in austral summer 1966–1967, and these investigations have been subsequently encouraged by D. Le Croissette, Bioscience and Planetology Section Manager. G. Llano, Biology Director, Office of Polar Programs, also has provided valuable assistance and suggestions during the tenure of research on Antarctic microbial ecology.

Among the many others who have contributed in various ways, the following are extended special thanks for their field, laboratory, or technical assistance: S. Babcock, A. Bauman, R. Benoit, K. Bentley, G. Blank, D. Bogard, W. Bollen, W. Boyd, J. Brown, M. Cameron, G. Chapel, A. Cherry, J. Clark, H. Conrow, T. d'Arc, R. Dale, C. David, J. Devany, B. Dowling, F. Drouet, M. Frias, W. Fuller, W. Gardner, D. Gensel, D. Goodall, C. Hall, L. Hall, B. Hansen, R. Hansen, R. Harris,

E. Herbst, G. Hobby, J. Hubbard, J. Huffman, J. Ingham, H. Jaffe, H. Johnson, R. M. Johnson, R. W. Johnson, K. Kemper, J. King, Y. Kobayasi, G. Lacy, G. Laursen, D. Lawson, R. Lynn, H. Lowman III, S. Manatt, J. Marsh, E. Merek, F. Morelli, K. Moulton, B. Parker, R. Paterson, E. Rudolph, K. Sandved, A. Sasson, D. Sanders, W. Seelig, C. Shepherd, P. Smith, J. Sprague, E. Staffeldt, J. Sugiyama, J. C. F. Tedrow, F. Ugolini, K. Whitehead, R. Young, VXE-6 helicopter group and U.S. Navy Task Force 43.

TABLE 6.8

Influence of Contamination on Ecological Sequence of Microbial and Cryptogamic Populations in Antarctic Terrestrial Ecosystems

Microbiota Shifted From Natural Ecological Sequence	Microbiota Enhanced By Site Disruption	Microbiota Eliminated By Site Disruption
Nonpigmented bacteria	Heterotrophic, aerobic bacteria	Some bacterial groups, eg, fastidious red diphtheroid colonies
Chromogenic bacteria	Microaerophilic bacteria	Algae
Streptomyces group	Chromogenic bacteria, yellow and orange colonies	Some protozoa
Molds and yeasts	Lactose fermenters	Lichens
Protozoa	Sporeforming bacteria	Mosses
Heterotrophic, anaerobic bacteria	Molds and yeasts, including cryophilic yeasts	
Sulfate reducers	Heterotrophic, anaerobic bacteria	
Cryophils (yeasts)	Sulfate reducers	
	Bacteria capable of surviving 55°C incubation	
	Bacteria with shorter growth period	

BIBLIOGRAPHY

Allen, O. N.
1957 Experiments in Soil Bacteriology, Third edition, revised. Burgess Publishing Co., Minneapolis. 117 pp.

Barghoorn, E. S., and R. L. Nichols
1961 Sulfate-reducing bacteria and pyritic sediments in Antarctica. Science 134: 190–1.

Bauman, A. J., E. M. Bollin, G. P. Shulman, and R. E. Cameron
1970 Isolation and characterization of coal in Antarctic dry valleys. Antarctic Journal of the U.S. 5: 161–2.

Benoit, R. E., and C. L. Hall, Jr.
1970 The microbiology of some dry valley soils of Victoria Land, Antarctica. *In* Holdgate, M. W., ed. Antarctic Ecology 2: 697–701. Academic Press, London.

Boyd, W. L., J. T. Staley, and J. W. Boyd
1966 Ecology of soil microorganisms of Antarctica. *In* Tedrow, J. C. F., ed. Antarctic Soils and Soil Forming Processes. Antarctic Research Series 8: 129–59.

Cameron, R. E.
1966 Soil sampling parameters for extraterrestrial life detection. Journal Arizona Academy of Science 4: 3–27.
1969a Cold desert characteristics and problems relevant to other arid lands. *In* McGinnies, W. G., and B. J. Goldman, eds. Arid Lands in Perspective. AAAS and University of Arizona Press, Tucson. pp. 169–205.
1969b Abundance of Microflora in Soils of Desert Regions. Technical Report 32–1378. Jet Propulsion Laboratory, California Institute of Technology, Pasadena. 16 pp.
1970 Soil microbial ecology of Valley of 10,000 Smokes, Alaska. Journal Arizona Academy of Science 6: 11–40.
1971a Algae in soil crusts. *In* Desert Biome US/IBP Analysis of Ecosystems. Microbiological Specialists Meeting, New Mexico State University, Las Cruces, April 3–4. pp. 52; 53; 79–88; 98–105.
1971b Antarctic soil microbial and ecological investigations. *In* Quam, L. O., and H. D. Porter, ed. Research in the Antarctic. pp. 137–90. AAAS, pub. no. 93. Washington, D.C. 768 pp.
1972a Ecology of blue-green algae in Antarctic soils. *In* Desikachary, T. V., ed. First International Symposium on Taxonomy and Biology of Blue-green Algae. Centre for Advanced Studies in Botany. University of Madras, India. pp. 353–84.
1972b Pollution and conservation of the Antarctic terrestrial ecosystem. *In* Parker, B. C., ed., Conservation Problems of Antarctica and Circumpolar Waters. pp. 267–306. Allen Press, Kansas City.
1972c Microbial and ecological investigations in Victoria Dry Valley, Southern Victoria Land, Antarctica. *In* Llano, G. A. (ed.), Antarctic Terrestrial Ecology, Antarctic Research Series, vol. 20, pp. 195–260.

Cameron, R. E., and R. E. Benoit
1970 Microbial and ecological investigations of recent cinder cones, Deception Island, Antarctica — a preliminary report. Ecology 51: 802–9.

Cameron, R. E., and G. B. Blank
1963 Soil Organic Matter (in Desert Soils). Technical Report 32–443. Jet Propulsion Laboratory, California Institute of Technology, Pasadena, California. 14 pp.

Cameron, R. E., G. B. Blank, and D. R. Gensel
1966a Sampling and Handling of Desert Soils. Technical Report 32–908. Jet Propulsion Laboratory, California Institute of Technology, Pasadena, California. 37 pp.
1966b Desert Soil Collection at the JPL Soil Science Laboratory. Technical Report 32–997. Jet Propulsion Laboratory, California Institute of Technology, Pasadena, California. 153 pp.

Cameron, R. E., and H. P. Conrow
1968 Antarctic simulator for soil storage and processing. Antarctic Journal of the U.S. 3: 219–21.
1971 Survival of Antarctic Desert Soil Bacteria Exposed to Various Temperatures and to Three Years of Continuous Medium-High Vacuum. Technical Report 32–1524. Jet Propulsion Laboratory, California Institute of Technology, Pasadena, California. 6 pp.

Cameron, R. E., J. King, and C. N. David
1970a Microbiology, ecology and micro-climatology of soil sites in dry valleys of Southern Victoria Land, Antarctica; pp. 702–16 *in* Holdgate, M. W. (ed.) Antarctic Ecology, vol. 2. Academic Press, London.
1970b Soil microbial ecology of Wheeler Valley, Antarctica. Soil Science 109: 110–20.

Cameron, R. E. et al.
1971a Farthest south soil microbial and ecological investigations. Antarctic Journal of the U.S. 6: 105–06.
1971b Surface distribution of microorganisms in Antarctic dry-valley soil: a Martian analog. Antarctic Journal of the U.S. 6: 211–13.

Cameron, R. E., and E. L. Merek
1971 Growth of Bacteria in Soils from Antarctic Dry Valleys, Technical Report 32–1522. Jet Propulsion Laboratory, California Institute of Technology, Pasadena. 11 pp.

Chapman, H. D., and P. F. Pratt
1961 Methods of Analysis for Soils, Plants and Waters. University of California Press, Berkeley. 309 pp.

Corte, A., and C. A. N. Daglio
1963 Micromicetes aislados en el Antártico. Contributiones Instituto Antártico Argentin, no. 74. 27 pp.

diMenna, M. E.
1966 Yeasts in Antarctic soils. Antonie van Leeuwenhoek 32: 29–38.

Drouet, F.
1968 Revision of the Classification of the Oscillatoriaceae. Monograph 15. The Academy of Natural Science of Philadelphia. Fulton Press, Lancaster. 370 pp.

Fehér, D.
1945 Der Wüstenboden als Lebensraum. Erdezzetikiserletek 45: 213–336.
1948 Researches on the geographical distribution of soil mikroflora. II. The geographical distribution of soil algae. no. 21. 37 pp. Communications of the Botanical Institute of the Hungarian University of Technical and Economic Sciences, Sopron (Hungary).

Fehér, D., and M. Frank
1947 Researches on the geographical distribution of soil mikroflora. I. The geographical distribution of soil bacteria, no. 15. 39 pp. Communications of the Botanical Institute of the Hungarian Uni-

Fehér, D., and M. Frank *(continued)*
versity of Technical and Economic Sciences, Sopron (Hungary).

Gates, D.
1968   Energy exchange between organisms and environment. Australian Journal of Science 31: 67–74.

Gray, T. R. G.
1969   The identification of soil bacteria. *In* Sheals, J. G. ed. The Soil Ecosystem. Systematic Aspects of the Environment, Organisms and Communities. A Symposium. pp. 73–82. The Systematics Association, London, publ. no. 8. 247 pp.

Holm-Hansen, O.
1963   Viability of blue-green and green algae after freezing. Physiologia Plantarum 16: 530–40.

Horowitz, N. H.
1971   The search for life on Mars today. Bulletin of the Atomic Scientists 27: 13–17.

Horowitz, N. H., R. E. Cameron, and J. S. Hubbard
1972   Microbiology of the dry valleys of Antarctica. Science 176: 242–45.

Horowitz, N. H., et al.
1969   Sterile soil from Antarctica: organic analysis. Science 164: 1054–56.

Hubbard, J. S., R. E. Cameron, and A. B. Miller
1968   Soil Studies — Desert Microflora XV. Analysis of Antarctic Dry Valley Soils by Cultural and Radiorespirometric Methods. Space Programs Summary 37–52, vol. 3, pp. 172–175. Jet Propulsion Laboratory, California Institute of Technology, Pasadena.

Hubbard, J. S., et al.
1970   Measurement of $^{14}CO_2$ assimilation in soils: an experiment for the biological exploration of Mars. Applied Microbiology 19: 32–38.

Ingham, J. D., R. E. Cameron, and D. D. Lawson
In   Microbial abundance and thermoluminescence of
Press   Antarctic dry valley soils. Soil Science.

Johnson, R. M., and B. Holaday
1970   Physiology of desert bacteria. Bacteriology Proceedings Abstracts, p. 41.

Kobayasi, Y., et al.
1967   Mycological studies of the Alaskan Arctic. Annual Report of the Institute of Fermentation, Osaka, 3: 1–138.
1969   The second report on the mycological flora of the Alaskan Arctic. Bulletin of the National Science Museum, Tokyo 12: 311–430.

Kobayasi, Y., and J. Sugiyama
1969   Report on Fungus Cultures from Point Barrow, Alaska. Tokyo. Unpublished Report Submitted to Jet Propulsion Laboratory, California Institute of Technology, Pasadena. 9 pp.

Koob, D.
1968   Algae distribution. *In* Bushnell, V. C. (ed.), Antarctic Map Folio series, folio 5, pp. 13–15. American Geographical Society, New York.

Lawson, D. D., J. Ingham, and R. F. Landel
1970   Thermoluminescence as a forensic laboratory tool. New Technology Report, Case No. 2271. Jet Propulsion Laboratory, California Institute of Technology, Pasadena. 15 pp.

Llano, G. A.
1962   The terrestrial life of the Antarctic. Scientific American 207: 212–30.

Maruyama, K.
1967   Blue-green algae in the Alaskan Arctic. *In* Kobayasi, Y., compiler. Phycological Report of the Japanese Microbiological Expedition to the Alaskan Arctic, I. pp. 221–39 + 6 pl. Bulletin no. 10 of the National Science Museum, Tokyo.

McCraw, J. D.
1967   Some surface features of McMurdo Sound Region, Victoria Land, Antarctica. New Zealand Journal of Geology and Geophysics 10: 394–417.

McGeorge, W. T.
1940   Interpretation of Soil Analyses. Extension Circular No. 108. College of Agriculture, Agriculture Extension Service, University of Arizona. 9 pp.

Metson, A. J.
1961   Methods of Chemical Analysis for Soil Survey Sampler. Soil Bureau Bulletin 12. New Zealand Department of Scientific and Industrial Research, Wellington. 208 pp.

Nishita, H., and M. Hamilton
1968   Some thermoluminescent characteristics of gamma irradiated soils. Soil Science 106: 76–84.

Opfell, J. B., G. B. Zebal, and J. L. Shannon
1968   Applications of Capillary microscopy in exobiological research. *In* Brown, A. H., and F. G. Favorite (eds.), COSPAR, Life Sciences and Space Research 6: 157–69. North-Holland Publ. Co., Amsterdam.

Richards, L. A., ed.
1954   Diagnosis and Improvement of Saline and Alkali Soils. Agriculture Handbook no. 60, U.S.D.A., U.S. Government Printing Office, Washington, D.C. 160 pp.

Rudolph, E. D.
1970   Local dissemination of plant propagules in Antarctica; pp. 812–17 *in* Holdgate, M. W., Antarctic Ecology, vol. 2. Academic Press, London.

Schofield, E., and E. D. Rudolph
1969   Factors influencing the distribution of Antarctic terrestrial plants. Antarctic Journal of the U.S. 4: 112–13.

Smith, H. V., G. E. Draper, and W. H. Fuller
1964   The Quality of Arizona Irrigation Waters. Agriculture Experiment Station Report 223. University of Arizona, Tucson. 96 pp.

Stone, R. O.
1967   A desert glossary. Earth-Science Reviews 3: 211–68.

Tedrow, J. C. F.
1966   Polar desert soils. Soil Science Society of America Proceedings 30: 381–87.
1968   Pedogenic gradients of the polar regions. Journal of Soil Science 19: 197–204.

Tedrow, J. C. F., and F. C. Ugolini
1966   Antarctic soils. *In* Tedrow, J. C. F., ed. Antarctic Soils and Soil Forming Processes. Antarctic Research Series 8: 109–24.

Tubaki, K.
1961   On some fungi isolated from Antarctic materials. Biological Results of JARE, no. 14. Seto Marine Biological Laboratory, Nagao Institute, Sirahama, Wakayama-Ken, Japan. 9 pp.

Tubaki, K., and I. Asano
1965   Additional species of fungi isolated from Antarctic materials. JARE, 1956–1962, Scientific Reports, ser. E., no. 27. National Science Museum, Tokyo. 12 pp.

CHAPTER 7

MACROBIOLOGY AND ECOLOGY IN POLAR DESERTS

William S. Benninghoff

Department of Botany, University of Michigan, Ann Arbor

Polar deserts, with respect to their biological and ecological attributes, constitute a distinctive class of systems where stresses of the physical environment approach the ultimate extremes offered on the solid earth surface. Alpine tundras, which, for various reasons, cannot so readily be termed alpine deserts, are related systems; but alpine tundras are set in the context of different photoperiods, different shifts of seasons, rarified atmospheric gases, different spectral characteristics of solar irradiation, and different biogeographical setting with respect to biotic connections. In major biological and ecological features, polar deserts have many attributes in common with deserts at lower latitudes; there are the discontinuities of vegetation cover, short seasons for plant growth and reproduction, and various expressions of drought stress on both plants and animals. Beyond such general similarities, the comparison begins to fail with regard to biological and ecological details; yet, it is possible to point out some strong parallels in problems of development and management of these two kinds of deserts.

In this chapter I will attempt a brief review of the major biological and ecological features of polar deserts which I believe deserve consideration in planning the occupation, exploitation, and management of these regions. Against that background I shall try to evaluate the consequences of some current and anticipated human activity in relation to polar desert ecosystems.

Definition of Polar Deserts

For the purpose of this book, the following definition of a polar desert has been proposed: a glacier-free terrestrial area wherein the mean annual precipitation is less than 25 centimeters, and the mean temperature for the warmest month of the year is less than 10° C. It was intentional that this definition should include tundra areas, such as a considerable portion of the Arctic Slope of Alaska where the vegetation cover approaches the continuous cover state, as well as polar areas devoid of all macroscopic organisms, such as the Dry Valleys of Victorialand in Antarctica

In his *Desert Biology,* R. F. Logan (1968) defines "true deserts" as areas with a deficiency in the amount of precipitation received relative to water loss by evaporation. The term desert, then, refers basically to climatic phenomena. Logan (1968, p. 23) divides the

world's deserts, climatically, into five types, based upon the causes of their aridity: (1) subtropical deserts, (2) cool coastal deserts, (3) rain shadow deserts, (4) continental interior deserts, and (5) polar deserts. He does not provide strict climatic boundaries for polar deserts, but he mentions that the annual precipitation of the central and northern Greenland Ice Cap totals less than 13 centimeters water equivalent and that similar regimes of scanty precipitation prevail over much of the Canadian Archipelago and on the Arctic coasts of Canada, Alaska, and Siberia. The mean new snow depth over most of the Arctic Basin borderlands is less than 25 centimeters and is less than 50 centimeters everywhere except in the heavy precipitation areas of western Greenland, northern Baffin Island, Iceland, and the mountains of Norway, Svalbard, and Novaya Zemlya. Thermally, Logan has the Arctic desert bounded approximately by the isotherm of 15.5° C for the mean daily maximum for the warmest month. The vegetation must be lacking in arborescent forms and should consist of tundra (low bushes, grasses, mosses, and lichens) or be totally barren. The soils should have permafrost at shallow depth.

Logan and other authors ignore the Southern Hemisphere polar deserts, but in fact the most extreme examples are to be found in the interior of the Antarctic Continent. The Dry Valleys of Victorialand are the best known examples. The Antarctic Peninsula shares many of the attributes of polar deserts, but the climatic regime of the western slope does not agree with the qualification of aridity.

In general terms relating to vegetation, my definition of polar desert would center on dry tundra, fellfield tundra, and polar barrens, allowing for inclusion of local inclusions of sedge sod, mossy turf, and grassy turf in fertile protected valleys, and below late-melting snowbanks in favorable situations.

Polar Tundra Floras and Faunas

The polar tundra faunas and floras comprise the newest addition to the world's biota, having evolved during the climatic diversification and polar cooling since the Miocene. The paleobotanical record is meager for the vascular plants and completely lacking for mosses and lichens in the high latitudes from upper Miocene to mid- and late-Pleistocene. Arnold (1959) has postulated that high altitude areas during the early and middle Tertiary developed flowering plants adapted to alpine and then periglacial climates. With climatic change that engendered the polar climates during the Pliocene, these alpine plants invaded the polar regions. The several episodes of continental glaciations during the Pleistocene Epoch then forced plant and animal migrations in the high latitudes, on gigantic scales in the Holarctic, so that a more or less circumpolar arctic flora and fauna resulted. The isolation of the Antarctic continent greatly restricted colonization and development of a circum-south-polar flora and fauna.

It seems likely that the mid-Tertiary expansion of herbaceous flowering plants, especially of grasses and sedges, was in part a product of spreading arid climates. Perennial herbs, along with selected small shrubs, and dwarfed members of arborescent genera, could have migrated by way of arid grasslands and savannas into high latitudes as well as by way of alpine habitats. During the Pliocene and Pleistocene epochs there were a few genera of large mammals that invaded the Arctic tundra but did not survive with the bears, caribou, musk-ox, wolf, fox, and rodents which live there today.

The Arctic desert flora at Tanquary Fjord, on northern Ellesmere Island, comprises 119 species of vascular plants in 52 genera and 20 families (Brassard and Beschel, 1968). Fewer than 100 vascular species are known from Alert (Porsild, 1964). Axel Heiberg Island has 137 species, and Cornwallis Island has 51 species (Brassard and Beschel, 1968). In general the number of bryophyte and lichen species is often somewhat smaller than the number of vascular plants. We could assume, for the sake of argument, that those two plant groups roughly equal the number of vascular species. Thus, of mosses, lichens, and vascular plants, not more than about 300 species comprise the flora on areas of the order of 10,000 square kilometers. In the mid-temperate latitudes similar areas have floras of vascular plants alone numbering of the order of 1,500 species, and in the richest wet tropics 3,000 to 4,000 vascular species, an increase of 25- to 30-fold over the number in the High Arctic floras. This comparison serves to point out the restricted diversity in Arctic polar desert vascular plants, a condition that is paralleled in other major groups of terrestrial plants and animals of that region.

The small numbers of species in the floras and faunas of the High Arctic land areas are not a result of limitations on their dispersal. Seeds and other diaspores are transported considerable distances by wind with blowing snow over snow and ice surfaces. Whole lumps of turf are transported along shores by moving sea ice, and the widespread *Saxifraga oppositifolia, Phippsia algida, Stellaria laeta,* and six mosses and two lichen species were found, growing in glacial silt, on the floating ice island "Arlis II" in the Arctic Ocean in 1961 (Hultén, 1962). A number of species of algae grow on melting ice and snow in the High Arctic (Kol, 1968), but appar-

ently few have been found in the Antarctic. Mosses and lichens are rolled along in streams, or by wind on soil or ice, for long distances to new sites (Benninghoff, 1955). The fact is that a limited number of plant species are adapted to the polar desert environment around the Arctic Basin, and through successive glacial episodes and various modes of dispersal many of them have become widely distributed, and only a few are limited to a single region of a continent. Some members of the mammalian fauna are restricted to subcontinental areas, and geographic races of small mammals are common, so that, in spite of limited diversity, there is considerable endemism among the larger animals.

Ecology of Polar Desert Plants

The common characteristics shared by polar deserts and other deserts are aridity and extreme limitations of the length of growing season for plants. The short, cold tundra "growing season" is at the opposite end of an environmental gradient from the moist, warm, continuous "growing season" of a tropical rain forest (Billings and Mooney, 1968, p. 508). The plants of polar deserts are, like alpine plants, specially adapted to metabolizing, growing, and reproducing at low temperatures.

Plants of polar desert environments are small, close to the ground, and often widely separated with bare soil or rock in between. There is little modification of the microclimate by vegetation other than through effects on control of snow drifting. Control by the physical environment is dominant, and small features on the surface, a small knoll or a rock, can modify the wind effects, snow cover, or insolation and thaw depth. These conditions, especially the snow cover, determine the winter protection and growing season success of the plants. The extreme tundra environments are: (1) late-lying snowbank areas, where the growing season is extremely short, and (2) windswept, dry ridges, where dessication is the hazard. In both of these situations, at the limits of plant growth, the plants tend to be cryptogams — commonly mosses in the snowbeds and crustose lichens and occasionally mosses on the dry ridges and summits (Billings and Mooney, 1968).

Vascular plants of tundra are almost exclusively perennials. The woody ones are low bushes, recumbent, matlike, or espaliered on the surface. The perennial herbs have the larger part of their biomass underground, with root, rhizome, or bulb-storage organs. Perennial herbs commonly have a cushion form or basal rosette. The chief hazard to deciduous plants is winter-killing of exposed leaves by dessicating winds when soils are frozen. Evergreen plants are liable to damage from snow blast, as they are not dependent upon putting forth a new set of photosynthetic organs each year. There is some evidence that evergreen leaves may serve as food-storage organs, as lipids and proteins are mobilized and translocated from old to new leaves during the growing season (Hadley and Bliss, 1964). The herbaceous perennials, both monocot and dicot as well as the woody plants, nearly all form shoot and flower buds the year before, and in some instances the primordia are initiated the second season ahead of flowering.

Billings and Mooney (1968) provided a useful survey of the adaptations of vascular plants to severe tundra environments. They pointed to the occurrences of various combinations of the following characters:

1. Life form: perennial herb, prostrate shrub, or lichen. Perennial herbs have greatest part of biomass underground.
2. Seed dormancy is generally controlled by the environment; seeds can remain dormant for long periods of time at low temperatures because they require temperatures well above freezing for germination.
3. Seedling establishment is rare and slow, often requiring several years.
4. Chlorophyll content is not greatly different on a land-area basis from that in temperate herbaceous communities.
5. Photosynthesis and respiration are at high rates for only a few weeks when temperature and light are favorable; although annual productivity is low, daily productivity during the growing season can be as high as that of most temperate herbaceous vegetation.
6. Drought resistance, especially by plants of dry, exposed sites.
7. Breaking of dormancy controlled by temperatures near or above 0° C, and in some cases by photoperiod also.
8. Growth is very rapid, even at low positive temperatures; nitrogen and phosphorus often limiting in cold soils.
9. Food storage characteristic of all except annuals (which are rare).
10. Winter survival excellent after hardening.
11. Flowering: buds preformed year before.
12. Pollination: mostly by insects, but more by wind in the higher latitudes; Diptera more important than bees.
13. Seed production opportunistic.
14. Vegetative reproduction, by rhizomes, bulbils, or layering.
15. Onset of dormancy: triggered by photoperiod, lowering temperatures, and drought; dormant plant extremely resistent to low temperatures.

It is interesting to note that intrinsic dormancy of seed is not common among Arctic and alpine plants, and such that does exist is overcome by natural sequences in the tundra environment. Seeds of these plants retain their viability for relatively long periods, especially at low temperatures. There is some evidence that seeds and lichens from Arctic areas can survive for long periods, that is, several thousands of years, at below-freezing temperatures, as in permafrost. Porsild, Harington, and Mulligan (1967) describe the germina-

tion of Arctic lupine (*Lupinus arcticus*) seed that had been exhumed from a frozen deposit in central Yukon dated stratigraphically at 10,000 years B.P. and then stored dry at room temperatures for 12 years. The possibility of seeds of Arctic plants remaining viable for long periods in frozen soil or glacial ice led Billings and Mooney (1968) to speculate that this mechanism could help to explain some apparently rapid reinvasions of deglaciated areas and some puzzling distribution patterns of arctic species.

Ecology of Polar Desert Animals

Arctic polar desert animals may be grouped into the following categories with examples: (1) large carnivores, abroad all or most of the year (bear, wolf), (2) small carnivores, abroad all year (fox, weasel), (3) large herbivores, migrant (caribou, musk-ox), (4) small herbivores, local but surging populations (lemming, hare), (5) resident birds (ptarmigan, snowy owl), (6) migrant birds (geese, ducks, passerines), (7) flying insects, and (8) soil invertebrates (Acarina, Collembola, Tardigrades, Nematodes). In the Antarctic only the soil invertebrate and migrant bird categories are represented.

During the Arctic snowfree season, moist soils teem with invertebrates; these make up a whole subcycle based on detritus feeders, but with one or two levels of predators at several points in the chain. Dipteran larvae are abundant in every pool and in wet soil, constituting a considerable share of the animal biomass accumulated during the summer; they are food for birds and fish, primarily. Migrant passerine birds come into the Arctic tundra in considerable numbers to nest; waterfowl come to nest also, where lakes and marshes afford feeding grounds.

The small herbivores, notably the lemming, are cyclically abundant in the more productive tundra, where the vegetation cover is nearly continuous and comprised of a large proportion of herbs. In the less productive tundra the caribou and musk-ox can graze, especially on fruticose lichens, which grow at the rate of 3 to 5 millimeters per year and so constitute grazing plants with slow recovery. These herbivores are the base for the main portion of secondary productivity, and the large and small carnivores depend upon this food source. In winter, the lemmings and other small rodents work in galleries under the snow, whereas the larger grazers must scratch away snow to feed.

Polar seas are more productive per unit area than polar lands, and along the coasts there is a transfer of marine biomass to terrestrial systems. In the Arctic, sea-fishing birds, such as dovekies, terns, and puffins, roost and nest on land, leaving valuable nutrients and furnishing food for certain predators. In the Antarctic, penguins and skuas come on shore to nest and effect a similar enrichment of the terrestrial system.

The animal populations show wide fluctuations in numbers from year to year, with chain reaction relations between trophic levels. The fluctuations seem to begin with the small herbivores, especially lemmings, which build up their populations and then crash with a frequency of about five to seven years. Those fluctuations are passed on to the predators, the fox, snowy owl, and other predatory birds in this case, and the whole system is jolted to some extent. For example, some grasses which grow in standing water, such as *Dupontia fischeri,* grow much better when lemmings are regularly grazing the grass populations, thus preventing old dead growth of the *Dupontia* from burying its rhizomes in humus from which the nutrients are not readily released (Bliss, 1970). There are some indications that it is shortage in one or several essential elements in the ecosystem machinery that triggers the lemming crash, but the evidence available is still not conclusive.

Ecosystems of Polar Deserts

Polar terrestrial ecosystems are known especially for their relative simplicity owing to few species of plants and animals involved, the shortness of the food chains, the scarcity of alternate energy pathways, and the "boom-and-bust" oscillations of the member populations over periods of several years. There is a relatively small standing crop biomass per unit area. The growing season is short, and soils, except for short periods of warming at the surface, remain cold. These features conspire to make cycling of materials slow. Carbon-fixation rates by green plants may be rapid during the thaw season, and the chlorophyll content per unit land area is considered to be comparable to herbaceous communities of cool temperate regions.

Bliss (1970) notes that annual primary biomass production in tundra is known to range from a low 3 grams per square meter for a *Salix arctica* barren on Cornwallis Island through the values of 50 to 100 grams per square meter in wet tundra sites at Point Barrow and other sites in Alaska, Yukon, and the U.S.S.R., to a high of 190 to 224 for *Dupontia fischeri* in wet sites at Barrow. By way of comparison, table 7.1 shows summary figures for several major classes of vegetation from various regions.

TABLE 7.1
Productivity Data for Classes of Polar Vegetation*

Vegetation Class	Net Primary Productivity (dry g/m²/yr)	
	Normal range	Mean
Extreme desert, rock, ice	0–10	3
Desert scrub	10–250	70
Tundra and alpine	10–400	140
Boreal forest	400–2,000	800
Temperate forest	60–2,500	1,300
Tropical forest	1,000–5,000	2,000
Agricultural land	100–4,000	650

*Data from Whittaker, 1970.

Actual data on secondary productivity by herbivores in polar tundras are difficult to find and assemble in meaningful form, at least by a botanist such as I. We can use the commonly accepted harvest efficiency scale derived from food pyramid relations, that is, not exceeding one-tenth of the productivity of the supporting trophic level, for an upper limit. Thus, the extremely poor polar desert would yield 0.3 grams per square meter per year maximum productivity to the herbivore level, and 0.03 grams per square meter per year maximum to the first carnivore level, or, in more realistic terms for mammalian herbivores, 3 kilograms and 0.3 kilograms per hectare per year respectively. It is doubtful whether such productivity could support any mammals other than occasional migrants. On the other hand, the tundra and alpine mean for net primary productivity would yield 140 kilograms per hectare per year maximum to the herbivore level, and 14 to the first carnivore level — this is probably about the right magnitude for the more productive tundra areas near Barrow, where lemming, fox, and owl populations oscillate widely. With even the higher range of net primary production, herding of caribou or musk-oxen would require 50 to 100 hectares per animal, especially where sharing the range with the small herbivores, and this extent of range seems to me uneconomical if the herbs would have to be tended.

Cycling of nutrients in tundra ecosystems is even less well known than the production aspects. As noted, the short growing season and cold soils tend to inhibit the activity of decomposing organisms. The consequence is accumulation of dead organic material, largely in the form of raw humus or peat. Not only does the raw humus continue to hold a good share of the critical elements for plant nutrition but also it tends to bind up certain transient ions, including metallic ions such as lead and mercury. The directly apparent result is the progressive "paludification" of the surface by accumulating humus; the surface becomes more spongy and waterlogged, and the permafrost table moves closer to the surface (often to within 25 centimeters), and ice bodies in the ground grow to large wedges, sometimes marking out an especially striking form of polygonal ground as the surface expression.

Studies of lemmings on the Arctic Slope of Alaska near Barrow by Frank Pitelka and his colleagues and students have contributed importantly to knowledge of tundra ecosystems, including some indications of nutrient cycling. Bliss (1970) conveniently summarized recent developments in those studies. Peak standing crops of vegetation in 1959 and 1962 were followed by a lemming population peak in 1960 and 1963. In a peak population year, lemmings tear up a considerable portion of the tundra turf searching for roots and rhizomes as food. During the 1960 lemming peak, Schulz (1964) observed a 50 percent reduction in vigor and yield on one-half to two-thirds of the tundra, and nearly 90 percent reduction on the remainder from such lemming activity. Plant production for that year was reduced, but the nutrient content was high. The high level of plant nutrient was correlated with the flush of nutrients from fecal pellets and urine washed into the soil during the spring build-up of the lemming population. Pieper (1963, cited in Bliss, 1970) reasoned that with reduced plant cover and nutrients leached down into a deeper active layer and subsequently trapped by freeze-up, the lemmings the following spring have a reduced supply of phosphorus and nitrogen during lactation.

The heavy grazing and digging for roots by high density lemming populations constitute a kind of tilling of this tundra. Reduction in plant cover causes deeper thaw of the soil, allowing deeper root penetration and contact with downward leached nutrients. As plant productivity increases in subsequent years, and litter and humus accumulate again, the resulting insulation and shade causes the active layer to become shallower. The critical nutrient supply balance is again shifted into the standing crop of plants, and thence into a growing lemming population, as the cycle is begun again. Arnold Schulz (1965) has termed this postulated system as the "tundra homeostat." The IBP (International Biological Program) Tundra Biome group, working at the Barrow intensive site, has conducted subsequent investigations.

Decomposer cycles are less well known generally than the producer cycles, and this has been especially true for polar desert areas. Work by Roy Cameron, Robert Benoit, and others in the dry valleys of Antarctica and on the Arctic Slope of Alaska is illuminating some of the dark corners of this portion of ecosystems.

Every polar desert soil receiving some thaw season water appears to hold some nematodes, collembola, mites, or tardigrades. These probably feed upon fungi as well as humus, so one can postulate at least Actinomycetes and Phycomycetes, and perhaps molds of more advanced types (Hemiascomycetes and Euascomycetes, for example) as well. In polar desert areas such as Peary Land in north Greenland, it is conceivable that such soil-dwelling ecosystems can run on wind-imported humus, and at Cape Hallet near the Antarctic Circle, on penguin guano, which is marine production transferred to land. But in desert areas such as the interior dry valleys in Antarctica, it is difficult to guess what supports the faint glimmer of microorganism metabolic activity in those soils. We should look for specialized autotrophic soil algae and associated yeasts, among others, as some workers apparently have been doing.

Decomposer cycles and nutrient balance are keys to management of polar desert ecosystems, and we have only begun to investigate them. The empirical measures being tried for enriching or re-colonizing tundra to restore scarred areas will contribute relatively little until we can learn why a given measure does or does not operate as predicted.

Polar Deserts in the Global Ecosystem

As contributors of biological production to the global system, polar desert ecosystems are inconsequential. However, the sensitivities of at least certain of the polar ecosystems to changes in climate, in atmospheric chemistry, or in atmospheric pollution levels, are such that they should be examined for use as critical indicators of global change. It is conceivable that some species, or even some entire specialized ecosystems of these polar deserts, may be extinguished by man-induced changes started in the lower latitudes.

The global atmospheric circulation and the circulation of the world ocean effects transfers of particulate matter and gases from the low to high latitudes, and food chains further effect translocation of some materials within living matter to distant locations. The survey of DDT in the biosphere by Woodwell, Craig, and Johnson (1971) made the point well that the whole earth is a functional unit with respect to mobile pollutants. Concentrations of substances such as DDT in the carnivores at the tops of food chains remote from the origin; penguins in the Antarctic, for example, illustrate the problem.

Strontium-90 and other radionuclides have been given considerable attention in the Arctic, especially because the tundra ecosystem tended to channel concentrated loads into wild herbivores that are mainstays of the human diets of the region. Lodgment of materials of this kind in unleachable soils and in the long-lasting humus of tundra regions poses special problems because of the slow annual rates of ecosystem processes. On the other hand, these features may permit special kinds of monitoring of changes in global levels of pollutants.

The polar regions offer special environments for monitoring because of decreased thickness of the troposphere, low temperatures, descending air from upper levels, minimal convection, low precipitation as rain, and minimal pollution by man (Fischer and others, 1969). In these days when we are devising regional and global monitoring systems for better management of our environments, special attention should be given to the polar regions.

Vulnerability of Polar Desert Systems to Disturbance

Polar ecological systems have relatively little diversity in regard to total numbers of species, and the trophic levels of the production cycle of ecosystems are restricted to three or four, with only a relatively few species in each level. Thus there are few pathways for energy and materials, which is to say, few alternatives. On the other hand, the endless variation in the physical environment in space and time, through wind, snow depth, snow duration, slope, exposure, frost-susceptibility of soils, and so on, is countered by biological diversity expressed as side ecotypic variation by many of the species and by innumerable recombinations of the available species. The ecosystems may be saved by their relative instability, in that environmental forcing functions are detected fairly quickly and the old couplings are broken and replaced by new ones. This results in the "boom-and-bust" biological economy and makes management by man exceedingly difficult. Primarily because of this last quality, tundra ecosystems have been termed *fragile*. This term does have some applicability when a limited area is being dealt with over a limited time period; but, given extensive area and a number of decades, these ecosystems probably have relatively strong survival power. This matter of scale may be a clue to the estimate of how much of a stress we can safely apply to polar desert ecosystems in terms of human settlement, pollution, and other disturbance.

The instability of the soils because of the presence of permafrost beneath and intensive seasonal frost action in the upper layers provides distinctive environmental stresses for biological systems. Some of the relationships to soil nutrients have been noted. Underground organs of native plants are specially adapted to these stresses, and many species are able to live almost as if floating on top of the heavy and flowing soils. Vegetation furnishes shade and litter insulation against solar heating and promotes a high permafrost table and thin active layer. When the vegetation cover is broken, admitting solar radiation and warm summer air to the exposed dark soil, the permafrost table retreats to greater depth, leaving a waterlogged active layer which is then liable to intensive heaving by seasonal frost action (Benninghoff, 1952). Colonization by mosses, vascular plants, and even lichens does take place on these frost-disturbed areas, but there are many failures, and the process often takes many years. In instances where actual ponded water fills one of these "thermokarst" areas, the recolonization and filling by vegetation and transported mineral matter may take hundreds of years. Managed restoration of thermokarst areas requires precise thermal as well as ecosystem control, both of which are impractical in the early 1970s.

Thermal pollution becomes a critical matter in settlements on permafrost areas. Dwellings must not transfer heat to the soil, and utility pipes must be similarly insulated. Larger problems arise from sewage treatment plants and leaching fields, in which it is exceedingly difficult to keep the installation out of contact with frozen ground. Hard surfaced roads also tend to absorb heat and transfer it to the ground.

The fact that tundra ecosystems have relatively small standing crop biomass and low annual productivity also means that these ecosystems have little capacity to absorb extra loads of nutrients on the short term. The effects of eutrophication can be seen around bird roosts in the High Arctic. Furthermore, excessive addition of nutrients to soils is not relieved by leaching because of underlying permafrost; all is available to the plants on the area. Those species which can use the nutrients grow rapidly and lushly, and for reasons I cannot explain often do not go into dormancy early enough or deeply enough with onset of winter, so they suffer damage by freezing. It seems unlikely that terrestrial ecosystems in polar deserts will be found capable of absorbing any significant amounts of added nutrients, such as commonly result from the presence of human settlements.

"Natural" primary pollutants in polar desert ecosystems are limited to airborne dust. Air pollution is notoriously more severe in desert areas because of lack of scavenging by rain and entrapment by vegetation and surface water. Man-made pollutants from fossil fuel combustion, quarrying, cement-making, refining, chemical manufacturing, and highway dust can have different consequences in polar areas in contrast to temperate latitude areas, especially because of concentrating processes such as snowbed flushes, unleached soils, and simple ecosystems with few pathways. Without rain wash and other removal processes, pollutants coating vegetation will be ingested by wildlife browsers and thereby will be further concentrated.

Estimate of Limitations on Settlement and Development

In view of the composition of polar desert floras and faunas, the structure and functioning of the terrestrial ecosystems, and the physical environment relationships involved with the ecosystems, one is led to conclude that those biological systems are less resilient under stress than temperate ecosystems. On the other hand, they do not seem more *fragile* than many of the warm desert ecosystems or than the wet tropical forest ecosystems when placed against pressures of human disturbance. However, the responses to disturbance by the tundra ecosystems are widely different because of unique processes under the polar climate. The physical environment forces swing between wide extremes, so it is perhaps not surprising that the ecological responses swing widely as well.

We must assume some future settlement in the Arctic, because it already is in progress. Whether industrialization of the Arctic is inevitable, I do not have the means to guess; but it would seem only fair to require full justification and "environmental counseling" before such a program is begun. The question of how dense settlement can be in polar deserts without incurring excessive loss of biological resources or excessive maintenance cost can be answered to a degree out of present assessment of occupied areas. There seems to be little damage to the landscape beyond the limits of what we might call a "settlement" of a few dozen dwellings. With increase in size to the point of employing automobiles and building streets, the landscape is likely to suffer from motor traffic, eutrophication by wastes, and air pollution of various urban kinds.

We face the question of what is so precious about these polar desert landscapes that we would go to such efforts to preserve them. I believe the answers lie in the facts that we do not yet know how to maintain them in their natural condition in contact with pressures of Western culture, nor do we know how to convert them into useful or pleasant domesticated landscapes. Therefore, our choice is to try to protect them until our understanding is improved.

Stepping still farther beyond my own specialty, I would hazard the opinion that we are ready to raise esthetic qualities of landscapes into our valuation lists.

Polar landscapes in their natural states seldom fail to impress their beholder; therefore they have intrinsic esthetic value. This value might be expected to increase as the wilderness areas of lower latitudes undergo the continuing attrition and damage that show no signs of slackening. It is only fair to acknowledge, however, that often the human eye's delight in a wild landscape is heightened by a sign of harmonious human occupancy, a cabin, or a fishing boat, by people finding part of their sustenance in the land. We seem to have some innate appreciation for the human presence in a compatible relationship with the landscape.

BIBLIOGRAPHY

Arnold, C.A.
1959   Some paleobotanical aspects of tundra development. Ecology 40(1): 146–48.
Benninghoff, W. S.
1952   Interaction of vegetation and soil frost phenomena. Arctic 5(1): 34–44.
1955   "Jokla mys" [moss polsters on the Matanuska Glacier, Alaska]. Journal of Glaciology 2(17): 514–15.
Billings, W. D., and H. A. Mooney
1968   The ecology of arctic and alpine plants. Biological Review 43: 481–529.
Bliss, L. C.
1970   Primary production within arctic tundra ecosystems. IUCN Conference on Productivity and Conservation in Northern Circumpolar Lands, Edmonton, Alberta, 1969, Proceedings, pp. 77–85.
Brassard, G. R., and R. E. Beschel
1968   The vascular flora of Tanquary Fjord, Northern Ellesmere Island, N.W.T. Canadian Field-Naturalist 82(2): 103–13.
Fischer, W. H., J. P. Lodge Jr., J. B. Pate, and R. D. Cadle
1969   Antarctic atmospheric chemistry: preliminary exploration. Science 164: 66–67.
Hadley, E. B., and L. C. Bliss
1964   Energy relationships of alpine plants on Mt. Washington, N.H. Ecological Monographs 34: 331–57.
Hulten, E.
1962   Plants of the floating ice-island "Arlis II." Svensk Botansk Tidskrift 56(2): 362–64.

Kol, E.
1968   Kryobiologie. Biologie und Limnologie des Schnees und Eises. I. Kryovegetation. Die Binnengewasser, vol. 24. E. Schweizer-bart'sche (Nagele & Obermiller), Stuttgart. 216 pp.
Logan, R. F.
1968   Causes, climates, and distribution of deserts. *In* Desert Biology: Special topics on the physical and biological aspects of arid regions (G. W. Brown, Jr., ed.) vol. 1. Academic Press: New York & London. chap. 2, pp. 21–50.
Pieper, R. D.
1963   Production and chemical composition of arctic tundra vegetation and their relation to the lemming cycle. Ph.D. dissertation. University of California, Berkeley. 95 pp. (Cited by Bliss, 1970).
Porsild, A. E., C. R. Harington, and G. A. Mulligan
1967   *Lupinus arcticus* Wats. grown from seeds of Pleistocene age. Science 158: 113–14.
Schulz, A. M.
1965   The tundra as a homeostatic system. Paper presented at AAAS Symposium, "Polar Lore Since 1954," December, 1965, Berkeley, California.
Whittaker, R. H.
1970   Communities and Ecosystems. The Macmillan Company, Collier-Macmillan Limited, Toronto. 162 pp.
Woodwell, G. M., P. P. Craig, and H. A. Johnson
1971   DDT in the biosphere: Where does it go? Science 174: 1101–07.

CHAPTER 8

INDIGENOUS PEOPLES OF POLAR DESERTS

Graham W. Rowley

Department of Indian Affairs and Northern Development, Ottawa, Ontario, Canada

Deserts do not support large populations, and polar deserts are no exception. The Antarctic, of course, has no indigenous people. In the Arctic, man has managed to colonize, for a time at least, most of the land that is not covered by permanent ice. Usually he has not lived on what the land alone could produce, but, to a large extent, on the fish from rivers and lakes, and on fish and sea-mammals from the sea. It seems rather a paradox to speak of so much water in the context of deserts. In any event the difficulty of obtaining food, rather than the severity of the climate, appears to have restricted the size of the population and defined the area where man lived. Starvation, not cold, has been the control that imposed these limits.

Early History

In the Queen Elizabeth Islands north of Lancaster Sound, archaeological sites have been found as far north as the northern part of Ellesmere Island. However, no Eskimos were living in the Queen Elizabeth Islands when they were discovered, and it is only in recent years that they have returned there. The Eskimos do not appear to have occupied the Queen Elizabeth Islands for long. It may have been that they could survive there only so long as the musk-ox and caribou were numerous, and when they had killed too many they had to move on. The same may have been true of northern and north-eastern Greenland, where many old habitation sites have been found but where there has been no population for many years. In the polar deserts people and resources are in delicate balance, and it does not take much to tip the scales.

In North America the Eskimos are the only indigenous people who live north of the tree-line. Essentially they are a coastal people, hunters who have traditionally depended on seals, whales, and walrus for fuel, for most of their food, and for much of their clothing. In Canada the Caribou Eskimos in the District of Keewatin, and in Alaska the Nunamiut and the Eskimos of the Yukon and Kuskokwim deltas, were exceptions as they lived inland, but their country lies south of the boundary of the area of polar deserts as defined for this book.

Only the Ukusiksalingmiut, a handful of Eskimos on the Back River, used to live in and on the polar desert, existing throughout the year mainly on what it could provide. The rest spent most of their time on the coast, with some going inland to hunt caribou, particularly for skins for clothing in August. In the early 1970s about half of Canada's 16,000 Eskimos were living in the polar desert, and all had moved to the coast. In both Alaska and Greenland, the proportion was much smaller — under 2,500 or fewer than 10 percent of Alaska's 27,000 Eskimos, and much the same percentage of the more than 40,000 Greenlanders.

Among the characteristics of the North American Eskimos that have helped them survive on the shores of the polar desert are the following:

1. Skill in hunting. Long years of training and an intimate knowledge of the country and of the ways of the animals they killed were necessary to turn a boy into an effective hunter.

2. Skill in technology. The snow house, the kayak, the harpoon, the seal oil lamp, the sinew-backed bow were marvels of ingenuity, using the meager resources available in the North. The Eskimo's caribou skin clothing was lighter, warmer, and more comfortable than anything civilization has yet managed to produce.

3. Mobility. The kayak, the umiak, and the dog sled gave them the mobility that was essential in a country where a man had to cover a lot of ground or a lot of ice to find enough to eat, and the whole family had to move from one place to another from season to season.

4. The social structure. They lived in small groups, rarely as many as a hundred. The resources could not support a large population in any one place.

5. The mutual dependence within groups and between groups. Food was always shared within a group, and in times of scarcity groups who had food would help their neighbors.

6. Patience and control of the emotions. Living in small groups depending on and supporting one another, the Eskimos went to great lengths to avoid overt actions that would lead to disunity.

Turning to the other side of the world, we find a rather different situation. In Asia the polar desert forms a narrow strip along the Arctic coast, and the Siberian Eskimos live to the south of it, apart from a few families moved by the Soviet government to Wrangel Island. Three or four hundred miles of coast centered on Cape

Chelyuskin, the most northern part of the Siberian mainland, is uninhabited. The rest of the coast and the hinterland is the home, not of a single people, as in America, but of a variety of different races, people who belong to different language groups.

From west to east they are the Nentsy, the Entsy, the Nganasans, the Yakuts, the Evens, the Yukagirs, and the Chukchi. The northern Nentsy, the Entsy, and the Nganasans, to the west and south of Cape Chelyuskin, are all small related groups numbering only a few hundred. Their languages are Samoyedic, part of the Uralic family.

To the east of Cape Chelyuskin there are groups of Yakuts, who speak a Turkic language. They are one of the most numerous — if not the most numerous — of the Siberian native peoples, but the majority of the 300,000 Yakuts live in the Lena Basin, and only a few reach north into the area with which we are concerned. Then there are the Evens who number a few thousand and speak a Tungus-Manchu language. Among them live a few hundred Yukagirs who have an old language that is classified as a Paleo-Asiatic and was certainly spoken over a much larger area in the past.

Farther still to the east are the Chukchi, several thousand of whom live on or near the Arctic coast. Their language also belongs to the Paleo-Asiatic complex, but it is not related in any way to that of the Yukagir.

There is obviously a sharp contrast between the New and the Old Worlds. In North America the Eskimos spread from west to east across the top of the continent, producing a cultural uniformity along the whole Arctic coast. An Eskimo from Point Barrow can make himself understood, with some difficulty, all the way across the North to Greenland. In Siberia the different ethnic groups look southward for their origins, and there is a wide diversity in language. The diversity in culture is not so marked because the similarity in conditions and resources throughout the polar desert has often resulted in similar techniques and similar solutions to problems. The different groups have lived side-by-side for so long that there has been a considerable amount of borrowing of cultural traits, with complete absorption of some of the smaller groups by some of the larger.

Some of the Siberian northern people, notably the coast Chukchi, have, like the Eskimos, always been hunters first and foremost, but most of them have adopted reindeer herding to some extent. Hunting, trapping, and fishing have often remained important, but in most cases reindeer husbandry has become the main occupation. To this extent they had become capitalists, counting their wealth by the number of head of deer they owned.

The Eskimos of North America in contrast lived by hunting and were true communists, sharing what they caught and unable to amass capital, because an animal once killed is perishable, and possessions destroy mobility.

It is one of the ironies of history that the naturally communistic Eskimos have been faced with the problem of adapting to a capitalistic society, while the native people in Siberia with a more capitalistic background have met the opposite problem of adapting to communism.

Recent History

In North America since the end of World War II, there has been a great expansion of government services to Eskimos, with the provision of schools, nursing stations, housing, and other welfare measures. This has led to a great increase in population. The rate of natural increase among the Eskimos and Indians in Canada is about forty per thousand people, much higher than the national average, and one of the highest in the world. The government services, including the housing, have of necessity been concentrated at a few major settlements, and these have attracted the native people who have abandoned their small scattered hunting camps. The Eskimos do not like to be separated from their children at school, or from members of their family who are ill, and a warm house at a low rent is preferable to an igloo. These major settlements have now grown to be small towns, each with a population of several hundred.

These towns have no real economic base, and unemployment and underemployment have been the inevitable result. The young are much better educated than they were, but they have little to do and few profitable ways of using their new education. They are intelligent, energetic, frustrated, and growing rapidly in numbers. In this lies the most serious social problem in the North. In one or two places, it has taken the form of juvenile delinquency. In others, where the family bond is still strong, it has not yet reached this stage. This leads to another problem which is being found everywhere in the North — the gap between the old people, brought up in the traditional ways, and the young, whose whole outlook on life is different. The older people see their children drifting away from them; the young, while still respecting their parents, can find no common ground between them. The resulting strain within the family is tending to destroy family life. It can be said that a somewhat similar situation is common throughout the world. However, in the Far North all social life has been built around the family, and its destruction leaves a much bigger gap.

In Siberia the Russian revolution brought a great improvement in social services twenty years earlier than we have done in North America. There has probably been a considerable increase in the numbers of their native Siberian people, but this is difficult to demonstrate from the census figures. We hear little about the situation in Siberia because the Russians have always been reticent about the northern Siberian area, but all indications are that they have met, and are still meeting, social problems among their native people similar to those faced elsewhere in the Northern Hemisphere.

In both North America and Siberia, civilization, in the not very attractive form of extraction of nonrenewable resources, is forcing its way into the polar deserts. How is this going to affect the indigenous people? When we look around it is difficult to be optimistic. The Indians near Yellowknife, the Eskimos near Nome, the Lapps near Kiruna, the Entsy near Norilsk, do not appear to have gained much from the mineral wealth extracted from the area where they live, and few are employed at the mines which rely instead on immigrants from the south. The one thing that is obvious is that the higher standards of living and the other attractions of urban life make it more difficult for the native people to follow their old ways. They tend to move to the scenes of industrial activity and to live on the fringes, exposed to the vices of civilization but realizing few of its benefits.

The problem facing government in the polar deserts is how on the one hand to provide the amenities that will support and strengthen the traditional ways for those who want to follow them and, on the other hand, to help those who want to make the difficult transition to the technological age. The choice must be made by the people themselves, but the path must be made easier,

much easier, than it has been for those who wish to follow modern ways. It has always been the native people who have had to conform to the manners and practices of the more developed civilizations. It is also up to industry, and others who wish to exploit the northern resources, to adapt their practices to the needs and customs of the North. Government and industry are learning, and they have been slow to learn, that it is essential to consult the native people in regard to any measures that may affect them and to involve them fully in the planning of development. Unless this is done, the native people, who are now aware of the realities of politics, will remain detached and increasingly resentful spectators.

Scientists, too, have been slow to learn how to involve the native people. Many scientific parties go to the North, work there with or without the help of those who live there, and return to the South. The Eskimos are left wondering why the visitors came, what they have found out, and how this new knowledge of their country is likely to affect the natives. They have seen what happened to the whales and the musk-ox after the white men took an interest in them. They are beginning to feel that they have a right to know these things. Knowledge represents power. The Eskimos are not the only people who have felt uneasy about the export of power from their land.

BIBLIOGRAPHY

Armstrong, Terence E.
 1958 The Russians in the Arctic: Aspects of Soviet exploration and exploitation of the Far North 1937–57. Methuen, London. 182 pp.
 1965 Russian Settlement in the North. England: Cambridge University Press. 223 pp.
 1966 The Administration of Northern Peoples: The U.S.S.R. *In* R. St. J. Macdonald, ed., The Arctic Frontier. University of Toronto Press. pp. 57–88.
Birket-Smith, K.
 1936 The Eskimos. Crown Publishers, New York. 277 pp.
Bogoras, W.
 1904 The Chukchee: The Jesup North Pacific Expedition: Memoirs of the American Museum of Natural History, vol. 11. E. J. Brill, Ltd., Leiden; G. E. Stechert, New York. 733 pp.
 1913 The Eskimo of Siberia: The Jesup North Pacific Expedition: Memoirs of the American Museum of Natural History, vol. 12. E. J. Brill, Ltd., Leiden; G. E. Stechert, New York. pp. 417–56.
Collins, H. B.
 1954 Arctic area, indigenous period. Instituto Panamericano de Geografica e Historia, Mexico City. Comision de Historia, Publicaciones 68. Program of the History of America, 1: indigenous period, 2. 152 pp.
Dunn, Ethel
 1968 Educating the small peoples of the Soviet North: The limits of culture change. Arctic Anthropology, vol. 5, no. 1, pp. 1–31. University of Wisconsin Press.
 1970 Education and the native intelligentsia in the Soviet North: Further thoughts on the limits of culture change. Arctic Anthropology, vol. 6, no. 2, pp. 112–22. University of Wisconsin Press.
Dunn, Stephen P., and Ethel
 1963 The transformation of economy and culture in the Soviet North. Arctic Anthropology, vol. 1, no. 2, pp. 1–28.
Jenness, Diamond
 1962 Eskimo Administration. Technical Papers of the Arctic Institute of North America, nos. 10, 14, 16, 19, 21. Montreal.
Levin, M. G., and Potapov, L. P.
 1964 The Peoples of Siberia. (Translated from the Russian by Scripta Techniqua, Inc. English translation edited by Stephen P. Dunn. Originally published by the Russian Academy of Science, 1956. University of Chicago Press. 948 pp.
Nelson, E. W.
 1897 The Eskimo About Behring Strait. U.S. Bureau of American Ethnology. 18th Annual Report, 1896–97. pp. 3–518.
Popov, A. A.
 1956 The Nganasan. Indiana University Publications, Bloomington. 168 pp.
Rasmussen, K.
 1908 The People of the Polar North. (Compiled from Danish originals and edited by G. Herring.) K. Paul, Trench, Trubner & Co., Ltd., London. 358 pp.
 1927 Across Arctic America. G. P. Putnam's Sons, New York & London. 338 pp.
Reports of the Fifth Thule Expedition.
 Anthropological Volumes. Various dates.
Reports of the Canadian Arctic Expedition 1913–18.
 Anthropological Volumes, Ottawa. Various dates.

PART TWO

ECONOMIC BASE FOR DEVELOPMENT

PROCESSES AND COSTS IMPOSED BY ENVIRONMENTAL STRESS

Arlon R. Tussing

Institute of Social, Economic, and Government Research, University of Alaska, College, Alaska

"Processes and costs imposed by environmental stress" can be interpreted as referring either to the stress imposed by man and his works upon the polar environment, or to the stress imposed by that environment upon human activity. The two readings are closely related, however; in economic language, the distinction between them is one of *internal* against *external* costs of specific activities in a region with different physical and biotic characteristics from those encountered in the temperate heartlands of industrial society. The term *cost* denotes the consumption of resources, including human effort, that are scarce and have other human uses. The *measure of cost* is the value of these resources in alternative employments. The *internal cost* of an economic activity is the value of those resources expended by the enterprise or agency undertaking that activity — for instance, the cost of labor and materials directly consumed in Arctic oil and gas exploration. *External costs* are those imposed upon other parties; an example is damage in the course of petroleum exploration to wildlife or fisheries stocks used by the indigenous population.

External Costs in Polar Areas

The material in this chapter is not rigorously confined to the boundaries of the polar desert (as defined for this book) or to other zonal divisions that have been proposed, for instance the Far North and Middle North, or High Arctic and Subarctic. I have used all those terms broadly and have applied the term *North* to a broader zone; in the United States it coincides generally with the state of Alaska, in Danish territories with Greenland, in Canada with the Territories, and in the U.S.S.R. with those areas officially designated the North. Undoubtedly this loose usage will annoy some readers, but according to the hypothesis presented here, climatic indexes, the presence or absence of continuous permafrost, and location relative to the treeline turn out to be incidental, compared with the strength of transportation and cultural links to economic centers in the lower latitudes.

The polar areas are sparsely populated; relative to the temperate regions (and even to the "Middle North," which contains Fairbanks, Yellowknife, Godthaab, Tromso, Yakutsk, and Magadan), polar lands and resources generally have a limited number of potential human uses. Biotic productivity on land and in both fresh and salt water tends to be low (Bliss, 1970; Dunbar, 1970; Gulland, Tussing, and others, 1972; Alexander, 1972), so that the plant and animal resource potential is of little commercial significance. Accordingly, most of the scientific, engineering, and political attention to the costs of economic development in the polar regions has been directed at those expenditures for construction, mineral exploration, transportation, and human habitation that are internal to the actors involved.

The literature does show a concern for some of those environmental issues now associated largely with the conservation movement — for example, pollution and wildlife preservation — but the concern has typically been with "environmental" impacts and economic costs imposed by a single enterprise on itself, or those inflicted by small groups of people on one another by some shared activity. The waste disposal practices of isolated camps or villages generally create health and aesthetic problems only for the residents of those settlements; excessive hunting or whaling may jeopardize only the livelihoods of hunters or whalers; and it is oil and gas companies that have suffered most from poor engineering in their own roads, airstrips, and other alterations of nature in permafrost zones.

Only in the late 1960s did it become fashionable to look at the Arctic environment as a concern of anyone other than the few natives of the region and of the commercial enterprises that sought to "overcome" that environment in order to exploit its resources. In the earlier context the ability to discard wastes promiscuously and to disregard alterations in the landscape were considered, on the contrary, to be about the only cost advantages of working in the North compared with other places. The assumption that external costs were not significant was reflected in the mountains of trash and the land scars left by oil exploration teams of the United States Navy and Geological Survey on the Arctic Slope in the 1940s and 1950s (Klein, 1970).

Particularly since the Prudhoe Bay oil discovery, and growing out of the controversy over proposals to build a petroleum pipeline from the Arctic shore to a port in southern Alaska, the polar region is increasingly seen as a natural asset to non-Arctic man, and alteration of its wilderness status as constituting a cost to humanity. A substantial literature exists from this point of view. See, for example, Brooks (1971); Hemstock (1970);

Hill (1971); Holloway (1970); Klein (1970); Pruitt (1970); Rempel (1970); and Weeden (1972). However, neither the biologists nor the economists have yet specified the nature of the cost in a form by which the rate of exchange between net commercial benefits and net environmental costs can be defined, let alone be measured. As yet we have not even a satisfactory conceptual apparatus for finding the optimum level or mix of development and preservation that takes into account both the internal and external costs of commodity production in the Arctic. The attempts so far made to apply benefit-cost analysis to this issue (Cicchetti and Krutilla, 1971; Hill, 1971) tacitly assume that the weights given to environmental costs in such analyses are quite arbitrary.

I am not optimistic about ever finding the appropriate principles for evaluating wilderness. Differences in fundamental assumptions put limits on the usefulness and acceptability of any analytic concept for guiding policy. Even the proposition that the scholarly disciplines can improve decision-making is not part of everybody's ideological armory, and it is essentially beyond empirical demonstration. Neither the cost-benefit calculus nor the understanding of issues in terms of material "interests" (that is, in terms of the *distribution* of costs and benefits) is free of ideological bias, and either paradigm clearly serves some parties and some world views better than others. The use of such tools weights judgment toward measurable and commensurable values and particularly favors marketed or marketable goods. Quantitative analysis deals rather shabbily with transcendental values like national prestige, the permanence of social institutions, freedom, and wilderness. Not surprisingly, quantification has been a favorite intellectual weapon for those who would debunk such "ideals" as irrational or as hypocrisy serving some minority interest.

Ultimately the only value commensurable with other economic variables, that we may be able to assign to the *non-use* of any resource, is the net value of the commercial product society elects to sacrifice by that non-use. This imputation begs the very question we want to answer: just how much *should* society be willing to give up for this unpriced asset. The costs or benefits of cultural change to the indigenous peoples of the Arctic (and the costs or benefits to humanity of their transformation or disappearance as cultural entities) are also beyond the range of economic analysis except with similar circular assumptions and with similarly trivial results. In view of these difficulties most of this chapter is devoted to a review of those internal costs of human activity in the Arctic which are imposed directly on the actors as individuals, corporations, or agencies.

TABLE 9.1

Climatic Data and Cost-of-Living Information for Selected Cities of the United States*

Cities†	Heating Degree Days, Normal Year‡	Mean Daily Minimum, Coldest Month§	January Wind Chill Index (kg cal/ m² hr)§§	Cost of Family Consumption Other Than Housing — Moderate Income (U.S. = 100)# 1967	1970	Cost of Family Housing — Moderate Income (U.S. = 100)# 1967	1970	Median Contract Rent per Room** 1970	Construction Cost Index (Seattle = 100)†† 1971
Barrow	20,174	−31.0°C	1650	—	—	—	—	$39	350
Fairbanks	14,279	−29.6	1110	149	145	175	177	54	190
Anchorage	10,648	−18.3	1040	137	132	163	160	42	170
Duluth	10,000	−18.1	—	—	—	—	—	20	—
Juneau	9,075	−15.3	970	144	141	172	173	41	180
Minneapolis	8,382	−16.5	—	100	99	104	98	27	—
Milwaukee	7,635	−10.6	—	102	103	110	116	18	—
Portland, Me.	7,511	−11.2	—	103	103	99	98	17	—
Sitka	7,464	− 1.7	—	—	—	—	—	25	180
Ketchikan‡‡	7,069	− 0.9	940	134	132	153	157	25	—
Buffalo	7,062	− 7.6	—	105	106	104	108	14	—
Seattle	5,145	0.5	—	107	105	104	104	26	100
New York	4,871	− 2.8	—	109	112	118	123	25	—
Los Angeles	1,799	7.2	—	102	101	98	99	25	—
Honolulu	0	18.7	—	116	115	128	123	43	—

*Adapted and updated from Tussing (1969).

† Alaskan cities are in **italics**.

‡Source: U.S. Weather Service station summaries. Sum of deficiency in daily mean Fahrenheit temperatures below 65° F.

§Source: U.S. Weather Service station summaries.

§§Source: Johnson and Hartman (1969).

#Source: U.S. Department of Labor, Bureau of Labor Statistics data. Fairbanks, Juneau, and Ketchikan linked at Anchorage by method in Tussing and Thomas (1971).

**Source: 1970 Census of Housing.

††Source: U.S. Army Corps of Engineers, Construction Cost Index for Alaska, August 1971.

‡‡Climatic data are for Annette, Alaska.

Internal Costs in Polar Areas

Because of the small resident populations and the low level and scattered character of commercial activity in the regions with which we are concerned, there are no satisfactory indexes of the cost of living or of doing business in these regions compared to lower latitudes. For the United States Arctic, anecdotal evidence is available for Barrow and for North Slope petroleum enterprises, and those will convey some notion of the order of differential.

Table 9.1 puts a few variables for Barrow into a wider context. The 1970 Census of Housing shows a median monthly contract rent figure in Barrow of $109 and a median number of rooms per dwelling of 2.8. The ratio is $38.93 per room, which is 93 percent of the figure for Anchorage in south central Alaska, where, according to the information of table 9.2, rental costs for a moderate income family were 213 percent of the U.S. urban average.

Linking the two indexes gives a rental rate per room in Barrow of about twice the national average. This linkage was necessary because the U.S. Summary for the 1970 Census of Housing was not available at the time this chapter was written. This figure undoubtedly greatly underestimates the cost difference for comparable dwellings, as the typical room in Barrow is much smaller than average and the quality of housing is generally lower. A better indicator may be the U.S. Army Corps of Engineers Construction Cost Index for Alaska, in which Barrow costs are approximately twice those of Anchorage and three times those of Seattle, Washington.

The *Oil and Gas Journal's* 1971 drilling survey of active fields (McCaslin, 1971) shows the cost of a flowing well at Prudhoe Bay at $531 per meter, more than five times the unweighted average ($95) of 32 other instances in the United States and Canada, and 41 percent more than that ($377) of the second most costly example, a deep Texas offshore well. The daywork drilling rate at Prudhoe Bay is given as $21,000, about ten times the unweighted average of 32 other instances ($2,099) and 2.69 times the second highest rate, which is the Texas offshore instance.

Indications From the Subarctic

Better cost and price information is available for Subarctic or Middle North communities like Anchorage, Fairbanks, Whitehorse, Yellowknife, or Yakutsk than for the polar region itself. Arctic outposts and villages are generally supplied from transport and market centers in the Subarctic, and the labor force for remote northern petroleum and mining enterprises are often domiciled in such places and shuttled by air to the work-site in Alaska, Canada, and the U.S.S.R. alike (Tussing, Rogers and Fischer, 1971; Armstrong, 1970; Yanovskiy, 1969). For this reason, money wage rates, consumer prices, construction costs and other indicators of relative

TABLE 9.2

Comparison of Anchorage Family-Budget Costs With United States Averages, Spring 1970

Budget Categories	Lower Budget	Intermediate Budget	Higher Budget
Total family budget (in dollars)			
U.S. urban average	$ 6,960	$10,664	$15,511
Anchorage	10,783	14,535	20,301
Relative family budget (as % of U.S.)			
U.S. urban average	100%	100%	100%
Anchorage	155	136	131
Total family consumption	149	132	126
Food	121	116	113
Housing	205	160	148
Transportation	172	128	116
Clothing and personal care	119	118	115
Medical care	157	157	156
Other family consumption	95	95	96
Personal income taxes	231	175	159

Source: U.S. Department of Labor, Bureau of Labor Statistics.

costs from these Middle North communities provide a floor from which the costs of operating in more isolated and northern locations can be estimated.

Tables 9.2 and 9.3 illustrate living cost differentials between Anchorage and the United States urban average. At the intermediate budget level, 1971 family budget costs in Anchorage were 133 percent of the national urban average, and housing costs were 156 percent. These ratios had declined from 143 and 170 percent respectively in 1960. Tussing and Thomas (1971) made similar comparisons for Fairbanks and other Alaska communities based upon Bureau of Labor Statistics indexes. The Fairbanks budget cost differential in 1971 ranged from 137 percent of the national urban average for the higher level budget to 164 percent at the lower level; housing costs in Fairbanks were 158 to 214 percent of the national average.

Among the noteworthy patterns shown by these studies are that housing — especially rental housing — consistently has the largest differential among commodity groups; that there is a distinct bias in living cost differentials against low income households; and that in Anchorage, particularly, relative differentials with national averages have steadily declined over time. Touche and others (1968) estimated the cost of shelter in Yukon Territory at 30 percent higher than the Canadian national average, and household operation at 80 percent higher.

These differentials for the Yukon Territory are differentials for prices rather than for costs — the latter of which include differences in the composition of consumption as well as unit prices — and so are not precisely comparable to the figures for Anchorage cited in tables 9.2 and 9.3. It is tempting to pursue these exercises in other areas — for example, in southern Canada and northern United States — and project their results to the Arctic situation, but this approach is of course vulnerable to several objections. For example, Tussing in 1969 found a Spearman rank correlation coefficient of 0.36 between the number of heating degree days and total housing costs for 28 U.S. cities in the Bureau of Labor Statistics City Workers Family Budget. By a least-squares linear-regression function, climate expressed in heating-degree-days explained only about one-fifth of the variation of housing costs, and the standard error of estimate was greater than the entire range of cost variation in the sample. Deflating housing costs by an index of total consumer costs, or by SMSA — Standard Metropolitan Statistical Areas — per capita personal income allowed climate to explain about one-third of the variation in cost. Somewhat different fits

TABLE 9.3

Anchorage Intermediate-Level Family-Budget Categories as Percentages of United States Urban Averages, 1960–71*

(U.S. urban average = 100)

Budget Categories	1960†	1967 Spring	1969 Spring	1970 Spring	1971 April
Food: total	**138**	126	121	116	**112**
Food at home	**141**	129	126	122	**115**
Food away from home	**114**	107	106	104	**102**
Housing: total‡	**170**	163	164	160	**156**
Rent	**226**	203	213	**213**	207
Homeowner costs‡	**167**	168	166	152	153
Furnishings and operations	**137**	126	127	129	**126**
Apparel and upkeep	**128**	111	116	118	**119**
Men and boys	**136**	121	123	120	**124**
Women and girls	**119**	99	106	114	113
Transportation	**129**	138	128	128	**118**
Health and Recreation	**132**	123	124	126	**121**
Medical care	**167**	136	152	157	157
Personal care	**127**	134	128	130	**120**
Reading and recreation	**100**	100	90	**88**	89
Miscellaneous	**150**	..	134	126	124
Cost of Family Consumption	**140**	137	135	132	**128**
Renter families	**146**	140	140	**139**	133
Homeowner families	**137**	136	134	**129**	126
Other costs	..	122	122	..	..
Occupational expenses	..	100	100	..	..
Social security and disability payments	..	110	107	..	..
Personal taxes	..	191	186	175	..
Total Cost of Budget§	**143**	141	140	136	**133**
Renter families	**149**	144	145	**143**	138
Homeowner families	**140**	140	139	**134**	132

NOTE: Figures in lightface type are taken directly from United States Department of Labor, Bureau of Labor Statistics, **Annual Costs and Comparative Indexes for 3 Living Standards for a 4-Person Family,** Spring 1967, Spring 1969, and Spring 1970; and **Consumer Price Indexes,** United States and Anchorage, Alaska. Figures in **bold type** have been calculated by the authors by linking the **Consumer Price Indexes** to the **Annual Costs** figures in the following manner: The spring 1969 Anchorage-U.S. budget cost ratios were divided by the April 1969 **Consumer Price Index** for the United States, for the smallest commodity groups shared by the two sets of statistics. These coefficients were multiplied by the corresponding ratios between the Anchorage and U.S. **Consumer Price Indexes** for 1960, April 1970, and April 1971, to give price relationships for these years for each commodity group. The price relationships each year were aggregated into larger categories and into family consumption and total budgets using United States weights. 1967 weights were used for 1960, and 1969 weights for 1970 and 1971.

*The family consisted of a 35-year-old employed husband, a wife not employed outside the home, an 8-year-old girl, and a 13-year-old boy.

†United States price data for 1960 are annual averages; Anchorage data are averages of May and October.

‡Some distortion can be expected in the 1960 and 1971 total housing ratios and the 1960, 1970, and 1971 homeownership cost ratios because of substantial differences in definitions of homeownership costs in the two statistical series linked to calculate these figures.

§Total budget cost ratios for 1960 and 1971 utilize authors' estimates for items other than family consumption.

were obtained by omitting the southeastern United States and/or Honolulu, but in each case one thousand degree days added, on the average, only about one percentage point to the index of total housing costs. A projection of this function would suggest for Barrow total housing costs about 16 percent higher than the national urban average. The number of heating degree days for Barrow is more than twice that of the highest observation in the sample, however, and there is little ground for expecting a linear relationship with this one independent variable over the whole range or projection.

Indicators and analyses of construction and operating costs for residential and commercial buildings in urban Alaska are offered by Coxey (1968), Fischer (1969), and Massell and Massell (1972). All these studies find cost differentials of similar magnitude to those in the Bureau of Labor Statistics cost-of-living series. Aganbegyan (interview, December 1969) estimated construction costs in Yakutsk at four times the average for European Russia.

Not all of the indicated cost differentials result inexorably from climatic and other environmental differences with more temperate regions. Life and work patterns and the optimum mix of technology and materials are clearly different in the Arctic, and even in the Middle North, from their counterparts elsewhere. However, the permanent or inevitable sources of cost disadvantage may be limited in number. The only physical characteristic of the Arctic that comes to mind as an unmixed evil is the tendency toward formation of "ice fog" in the vicinity of human activity at temperatures below about $-30°$ C (Benson, 1965; Ohtake, 1970). One important distinction is of course the greater consumption of primary energy necessary to overcome cold and darkness, or the greater investment in insulation, enclosed spaces, and the like, to conserve energy. Within limits, heating and insulation are substitutes for each other, and the lowest cost combinations for a given performance will depend upon their relative prices.

However, the cost handicap of greater energy and/or insulation requirements may be offset by an abundance of oil, gas, and coal, related to the fact that the development of fossil fuels is a principal motive for economic and population growth in the North, so that primary energy will be one commodity obtainable there at lower money costs than elsewhere. The high cost of transport to markets at lower latitudes will assure that only those polar supplies of oil and gas with low unit costs are developed. The unit value of oil and gas in the fields will be low whether calculated by the inputs to their production or by the "netback" obtained by subtracting transport costs from their prices in their ultimate markets. See Adelman (1970) and Tussing, Rogers, and Fischer (1970).

The limitation imposed by pack ice on ocean shipping, usually the cheapest mode of bulk transport, may also be a fundamental cost disadvantage. But the most intractable cost handicap is probably the general disinclination of people, other things being equal, to live in the polar environment. The last disadvantage, that of people's reluctance to settle, is reinforced by the paucity of urban amenities that come — economically at least — only with relatively large absolute populations and rather dense population concentrations. The greater part of the indicated cost differentials between polar and temperate regions probably is caused directly or indirectly by isolation, that is, by the distance from those areas where the goods consumed in the North are produced, and by the small scale of local and regional markets. Distance and isolation operate to increase costs through the imposition of exceptional transport requirements; through inability to realize economies of scale in production, transportation and distribution; through requirements for greater inventories relative to the volume of production or consumption; through lack of competition; and through the lack of amenities mentioned, requiring incentive wage differentials and resulting in high rates of labor turnover.

Another powerful influence on costs is the fact that the polar regions are being developed with equipment, building methods, and materials largely developed for radically different environments. Complaints about the functioning of equipment and materials in exceedingly cold climates often relate to the operating temperatures for which the items were designed. As Northern markets grow, vehicles, construction machinery, modular housing, lubricants, and drilling compounds are being designed for these situations. Circumstances are found in which permafrost is an engineering asset, and ice promises to become a cheap and easily-worked building material; it is being used for docks, winter roads, and airstrips, and for building footings and foundations. The petroleum industry trade journals show a growing optimism about means of dealing with the engineering peculiarities of the permafrost region. See, for example, *Alaska Construction and Oil Report* (1970b), Anderson (1971), *Oil and Gas Journal* (1971a).

There is a substantial construction technology adapted to cold weather situations (bibliographies include Arctic Institute of North America, 1969; Crocker and Tibbets, 1960; CRREL, annual; Fulwider, 1965; and Griffiths and Griffiths, 1969). As previously noted, there are hazards in generalizing about the Arctic by projecting from Subarctic experience or from winter experience in the colder portions of the temperate zone. It is interesting that studies of construction seasonality (Bureau of Labor Statistics 1970) of weather-related costs in the northern United States and Canada (Arctic Institute of North America, 1969) and of building costs in Alaska (Coxey, 1968; Tussing, 1969; Fischer, 1969; and Massell and Massell, 1972) find either that climate costs are negligible or that they ought to be negligible if the appropriate technology were actually used; or else they strongly emphasize other factors such as transportation, the cost of capital, small markets, and uneconomic government contracting procedures.

Aganbegyan, in an interview with the author, estimated that half of Yakutsk's fourfold construction cost differential over European Russia was "objective"; this component included both climatic factors and transport costs. The "subjective" half of the differential included the rote application of southern designs and technologies, and rigid materials allocations coupled with uncertainty of actual delivery.

The cost of transport for heavy building materials such as cement and steel was estimated to increase their costs about 40 percent above that on points along the trans-Siberian railroad, but only if they arrived at southern river ports in time for shipment by seasonal barge traffic. If transport connections were not optimal, however, the construction enterprise was faced with a choice of transporting heavy materials by air or leaving a project uncompleted for an additional season. Either option, of course, increases implicit costs of the materials by far more than the 40 percent differential included in the category of "objective" costs.

Similar situations to the foregoing occur even in those parts of Alaska that have mild winters and year-round surface transportation. A construction boom in the summer of 1969 forced some contractors in Anchorage to import bathtubs and other heavy plumbing fixtures by air because local suppliers had run out. Numerous instances of a similar sort can be cited from Arctic Slope petroleum exploration; where the daywork rate on a drilling rig is on the order $21,000, the cost of relying on seasonal surface transportation even for bulky materials often makes aviation the only economical means of transport and increases average transport cost per ton far above the lowest common carrier tariff or lowest charter rate. Naturally, the cost of bottlenecks that are not or cannot be solved by larger outlays on transportation can be relatively even greater.

The preceding examples from Anchorage and Prudhoe Bay represent in part the absence or insufficiency of a wholesale trade sector. Such a sector would normally maintain optimum inventories of construction materials or drilling supplies acquired at minimum transportation costs and, by means of averaging, would reduce both the risks of bottlenecks and the costs of holding inventories. The building materials inventory problem at Anchorage is principally one of market size, while at Prudhoe Bay the effects of a small market are compounded by sharp fluctuations in exploration activity. The underdevelopment of wholesaling even in urban Alaska can be seen in table 9.4, which shows that the 1967 ratio of the gross volume of wholesale trade to personal income in the Anchorage area was only 38 percent of the comparable figure for the United States as a whole.

The absence of a wholesale building materials sector in Yakutsk is not a peculiarity of the Soviet North, however, but it creates serious problems throughout the U.S.S.R.

Labor costs tend to be substantially higher in the North than at lower latitudes. These costs include the

TABLE 9.4

Ratio of Gross Sales to Personal Income Received, in the Anchorage Area, as a Percentage of the United States National Average

Services	1958	1963	1967
Retail Trade			
Building materials, hardware, farm equipment			72
General merchandise group stores			84
Food stores			55
Automotive dealers			66
Gasoline service stations			53
Apparel and accessories stores			33
Furniture, home furnishings and equipment			57
Eating and drinking places			98
Drugstores and proprietary stores			85
Miscellaneous retail stores			66
Non-store retailing			23
Retail trade, total		51	65
Wholesale Trade	31	31	38
Selected Services			
Hotels, motels, tourist courts and camps	61	94	138
Personal services	43	44	60
Miscellaneous business services	24	26	46
Automobile repair, services, garages	43	44	60
Miscellaneous repair services	39	71	85
Motion picture theaters		25	36
Amusements and recreation		48	44
Selected services, total	37	46	65

Source: Calculated from U.S. Department of Commerce, Bureau of the Census, **Census of Business,** 1958, 1963 and 1967; and U.S. Department of Commerce, Office of Business Economics, **Survey of Current Business.**
NOTE: See note for table 9.3.

monetary differential arising from higher living costs, exceptional recruitment and termination costs owing to seasonal and cyclical instability in employment, and probably a substantial risk differential (Massell and Massell, 1972). Armstrong (1970), comparing differentials in the rate of labor compensation in Alaska, Canada's Northwest Territories, and the Soviet North, finds the purchasing power (the excess over the cost of living differential) of construction workers' hourly wages 17 percent higher than the national standard in Fairbanks; 33 percent lower at Yellowknife; and 9 percent lower to 24 percent higher in Yakutsk, depending upon length of residence.

Man-hour physical productivity is widely reported to be lower in Arctic and Subarctic environments. Some differential is understandable in outdoor work. The only investigation I have found of the actual relation between climate and manpower effectiveness is an Arctic Aeromedical Laboratory study (1963b) of the effect of temperature and wind upon aircraft maintenance crews in Arctic areas. The loss of crew effectiveness, under conditions of dry cold with no wind, was negligible down to about −18° C; performance fell to nearly zero for some crews at about −34° C, depending upon their levels of motivation. Similar findings related effectiveness to wind chill factors. However, climate alone can hardly explain low motivation and high turnover rates in a broad spectrum of indoor occupations.

A number of indicators suggest that the North is a severe environment for human life in some more subtle way. Among the United States, Alaska has the highest age-specific death rates, the highest rate of death by accidents, the highest suicide rate (U.S. Department of Health, Education and Welfare, *Vital Statistics of the United States,* 1967), and the highest alcohol consumption per capita (U.S. Treasury Department, Internal Revenue Service, *Alcohol and Summary Statistics,* 1969). The state also has the sixth highest homicide rate, 54 percent higher than the national average, and the sixth highest rate of forcible rape, 40 percent higher than the national average (U.S. Department of Justice, Federal Bureau of Investigation, *Uniform Crime Reports for the United States,* 1969). Yanovskiy (1969) offers a lurid picture of life in the Soviet North. Due to "the men's alcoholism and the women's unfaithfulness," the divorce rate in the North is twice that of Novosibirsk. In some areas, he indicates, the number of divorces is equal to the number of marriages. The turnover of population is very high; in the northeast during the 1960s, 80 percent of the entire population has been replaced, and those who leave do not return. In the oil towns in 1964–66, annual turnover was one and one-half times to twice the total population, compared to 10 percent in southern Siberia. The principal reason for leaving work is said to be discharge for misbehavior.

We do not know how much of the blame for dissatisfaction and demoralization to place on the physical environment. Doubtless, the abnormality of some social indicators is in part related to processes of acculturation among the indigenous peoples, and in part reflects a high proportion of deviant personalities among those who migrate into the North. But the backwardness of material and cultural amenities in remote regions must also play a major disturbing role. Despite Alaska's high rates among the states in the indicators of physical and mental illness, Alaska has the lowest ratio of physicians, of hospital beds, and of hospital personnel to population; it rates low in other indicators of health services available (U.S. Department of Health, Education and Welfare, Public Health Service, *Health Resources Statistics,* 1969). The backwardness of trade and services, even in Anchorage, Alaska's largest and most advanced community, is suggested by the ratios in table 9.4; the same community's relative poverty of housing standards is shown in table 9.5; in 1960, 21 percent of the dwellings in Anchorage were occupied by more than one person per room, compared to 3 percent of the United States as a whole. It must be pointed out that the tables show a rapid decline in the Anchorage/United States differentials in all but one of these indicators, just as table 9.3 shows a sharp decline in living cost differentials. Table 9.6 presents some indicators for Mirnyy in Yakutia; although we are not told how well the norms listed were fulfilled throughout the U.S.S.R., these figures do not suggest high levels of cultural amenities

TABLE 9.5

Selected Housing Comparisons in the Anchorage Area, 1960 and 1970

	Anchorage 1960	Anchorage 1970	United States 1960
Number of rooms, percent of units			
1 room or less*	8	3	2
2 rooms	16	9	4
3 rooms	20	15	11
4 rooms	28	26	21
5 rooms	14	20	24
6 rooms	6	10	19
7 rooms	2	6	8
8 or more rooms	2	7	6
Median number of rooms	3.6	4.6	4.9
Status, percent of total units			
Owner occupied	33	50	56
Renter occupied	57	41	34
Vacant, for sale	..	3	..
Vacant, for rent	4	..	2
Other	6	6	8
Number of occupants per room			
Less than 0.5	22	} 87	40
0.5 to 1.0	57		56
More than 1.0	21	13	3

Source: U.S. Department of Commerce, Bureau of the Census, **Population Census of the United States.**
NOTE: At the time of this writing, United States summaries were not available for 1970.
*More than one family in a room.

to compensate the immigrant population for the long, dark, and cold winter.

Conclusion

We do not know much about the direct, internal costs of economic activity in polar areas, except that they tend to be high. Much of the differential in costs between the Arctic and the temperate zones is not

TABLE 9.6

Indicators of Cultural Amenities at Mirnyy, Yakut A.S.S.R.

Indicator	Norm	Norm Fulfillment (%) at Mirnyy
Living space (square meters)	11 per person	38
Shop employees	7.6 per 1,000 inhabitants	50
Communal feeding space (square meters)	40 per 100 inhabitants	50
Hospital beds	10 per 1,000 inhabitants	14
Public baths space	8 per 1,000 inhabitants	55
Main water supply (liters per day)	300 per person	78
School places	190 per 1,000 inhabitants	39
Kindergarten places	90 per 1,000 inhabitants	21
Club places	100 per 1,000 inhabitants	30
Cinema seats	100 per 1,000 inhabitants	13

Source: Yanovskiy, 1969, p. 112.

directly related to climate and other physical factors and may not reflect these factors at all except through the influence of low population densities and low levels of economic development. Equipment, materials, and techniques used in the North were typically designed for a different physical environment; high rates of labor turnover and low manpower efficiency in the North probably result largely from the absence of cultural amenities that people in the United States, Canada, or the U.S.S.R. normally expect. In the United States' Subarctic (south central Alaska), cost structures are normalizing rapidly with the growth of population and economic activity. It is possible that settlement and economic development in the polar regions would bring similar results, but the necessary population and economic densities are not foreseeable in the early 1970s.

BIBLIOGRAPHY

Adelman, M. A. (ed.)
  1971 Alaskan Oil: Costs and Supply. New York: Praeger Publishers.
Alaska Construction and Oil Report
  1970a What Happens to a Well Casing as Permafrost Melts? Vol. 11 (8), August 1970, pp. 84–89.
  1970b Slip-Joint Casing: Questions and Alternatives. Vol. 11 (2), February 1970, pp. 73–80.
Alexander, V.
  1972 "Phytoplankton Primary Productivity as an Indicator of Biological Status in Alaska Freshwater Environments." *In* Tussing, Morehouse, and Babb (eds.), Alaska Fisheries Policy. University of Alaska, Fairbanks.
Anderson, Glen W.
  1971 "Near-guage Holes Through Permafrost," *Oil and Gas Journal* 69 (Sept. 20, 1971): 128–42.
Arctic Aeromedical Laboratory, USAF (AFSC)
  1963a Report no. AAL–TN–62–1. Water Supply and Waste Disposal; Problems at Remote Air Force Sites in Alaska. Fort Greely, Alaska.
  1963b Report no. ALL–TDR–63–18. Effect of Weather Factors on Aircraft Maintenance Crews in Arctic Areas. Fort Greely, Alaska.

Arctic Institute of North America
  1969 A Study of Technologies for Reducing Weather Costs. U.S.G.P.O.

Armstrong, Terence
  1967 "Labour in Northern U.S.S.R." *The Polar Record* 13(87): 769–74.
  1970 Soviet Northern Development, With Some Alaskan Parallels and Contrasts. ISEGR Occasional Papers no. 2. University of Alaska, Fairbanks.

Benson, C. S.
  1965 Ice Fog: Low Temperature Air Pollution. Geophysical Institute Report UAG R–173, 43. University of Alaska, Fairbanks.

Bliss, L. C.
  1970 Primary Production Within Arctic Tundra Ecosystems. Proceedings of the Conference on Productivity and Conservation in Northern Circumpolar Lands, Edmonton, Alberta, 15–17 October, 1969. Morges, Switzerland: International Union for the Conservation of Nature and Natural Resources.

Brooks, James W., and others
1971   Environmental Influences of Oil and Gas Development in the Arctic Slope and Beaufort Sea. U.S. Department of the Interior, Fish and Wildlife Service, Bureau of Sport Fisheries and Wildlife, Resource Publication 96. U.S.G.P.O.

Brown, R. J. E.
1967   "Comparison of Permafrost Conditions in Canada and the U.S.S.R." *The Polar Record* 13(87): 741–51.

Bureau of Labor Statistics, U.S. Department of Labor
1970   Seasonality in Manpower and Construction. Bulletin 1642. U.S.G.P.O.

Cicchetti, Charles J., and John V. Krutilla
1971   Prepared Statement on the Trans-Alaska Pipeline Environmental Impact Report. Filed with the Department of the Interior on March 5, 1971. Resources for the Future, Washington.

Coxey, Jerry G.
1968   Cost Factors of Alaska Construction. Unpublished Master's Thesis (civil engineering), University of Alaska, Fairbanks.

Crocker, C. R., and D. C. Tibbets
1960   Winter Construction. National Research Council, Division of Building Research, Ottawa.

CRREL
(an-   Bibliography on Cold Regions Science and Technology. CRREL Report no. 12. U.S. Army, Cold Regions Research and Engineering Laboratory, Hanover, New Hampshire.
nual)

Dunbar, M. J.
1970   "On the Fishery Potential of the Sea Waters of the Canadian North." *Arctic* 23: 150–73.

Ferrians, O. J., Jr., Reuben Kachadoorian, and
G. W. Greene
1969   Permafrost and Related Engineering Problems. Geological Survey Professional Paper 678. U.S.G.P.O.

Fischer, Richard W.
1969   "Comparative Housing Cost Analysis." *Alaska Review of Business and Economic Conditions,* vol. 6(5).

Fulwider, Charles W.
1965   A Bibliography on Winter Construction, 1940–1963. U.S. Army, Cold Regions Research and Engineering Laboratory, Special Report 83, Hanover, New Hampshire.

Griffiths, John F., and M. Joan Griffiths
1969   A Bibliography of Weather and Architecture. ESSA Technical Memorandum EDSTM9. Silver Spring, Maryland: U.S. Department of Commerce, Environmental Science Services Administration, Environmental Data Services.

Gulland, J. A., A. R. Tussing, and others
1972   "Fish Stocks and Fisheries of Alaska and the Northeast Pacific Ocean." *In* Tussing, Morehouse, and Babb (eds.), Alaska Fisheries Policy, University of Alaska, Fairbanks.

Hemstock, Russell, A.
1970   "Impact of Petroleum Activities on Arctic Ecology." *In* Rogers, George W. (ed.), Change in Alaska: People, Petroleum and Politics. University of Washington Press, Seattle.

Hill, Douglas
1971   "Cost-Benefit Analysis of Alaskan Development and Conservation." *Journal of Environmental Systems* 1(2): 161–82.

Holloway, C. W.
1970   Threatened Vertebrates in Northern Circumpolar Regions. Proceedings of the Conference on Productivity and Conservation in Northern Circumpolar Lands, Edmonton, Alberta 15–17 October, 1969. Morges, Switzerland: International Union for the Conservation of Nature and Natural Resources.

Johnson, Philip R., and Charles W. Hartman
1969   Environmental Atlas of Alaska. Institute of Arctic Environmental Engineering and Institute of Water Resources. University of Alaska, College (Fairbanks).

Klein, David R.
1970   The Impact of Oil Development in Alaska. Proceedings of the Conference on Productivity and Conservation in Northern Circumpolar Lands, Edmonton, Alberta 15–17 October, 1969. Morges, Switzerland: International Union for the Conservation of Nature and Natural Resources.

Kolb, Charles R., and Fritz G. Holmstrom (eds.)
1964   Review of Research on Military Problems in Cold Regions. Report AAL–TDR–64–28, Arctic Aeromedical Laboratory and Arctic Test Center, Fort Wainwright, Alaska.

Kossoris, Max D., and Reinfried F. Kohler
1948   Hours of Work and Output. U.S. Department of Labor, Bureau of Labor Statistics, Bulletin no. 917. U.S.G.P.O.

Lachenbruch, Arthur H.
1970   Some Estimates of the Thermal Effects of a Heated Pipeline in Permafrost. Circular 632, U.S. Department of the Interior, Geological Survey, Washington, D.C.

Mason, R. L.
1971   "SOCAL Learns About Alaskan Operations at Swanson River." *Oil and Gas Journal* 69(49): 77–84.

Massell, Benton F., and Adele P. Massell
1972   "Prices and Construction Costs in Alaska: An Analysis and Some Policy Guidelines." *Alaska Review of Business and Economic Conditions,* vol. 9(1).

McCaslin, John C.
1971   "Journal Survey of Active Fields." *Oil and Gas Journal* 69(38): 144–56.

Ohtake, Takeshi
1970   Studies on Ice Fog. Research Triangle·Park, North Carolina: U.S. Environmental Protection Agency.

Oil and Gas Journal
1971a   Prudhoe Permafrost Problems Can Be Licked. Vol. 69(25): June 21, 1971, pp. 115–19.
1971b   Prudhoe Production Scheme Revealed. Vol. 69 (21), May 24, 1971, pp. 62–64.

Pruitt, William O., Jr.
1970   Some Aspects of the Interrelationships of Permafrost and Tundra Biotic Communities. Proceedings of the Conference on Productivity and Conservation in Northern Circumpolar Lands, Edmonton, Alberta 15–17 October, 1969. Morges, Switzerland: International Union for the Conservation of Nature and Natural Resources.

Reed, John C.
1970   "Oil Developments in Alaska." *The Polar Record* 15(94): 7–17.

Rempel, G.
 1970 Arctic Terrain and Oil Field Development. Proceedings of the Conference on Productivity and Conservation in Northern Circumpolar Lands, Edmonton, Alberta 15–17 October, 1969. Morges, Switzerland: International Union for the Conservation of Nature and Natural Resources.

Simakso, D. L.
 1970 "Oil Industry in Alaska . . . Changeable as the Weather." *Alaska Construction and Oil Report* 11(2): 78–85.

Tibbets, D. C., G. C. Boileau, and Y. Fortier
 1969 A Bibliography on Cold Weather Construction. Ottawa: National Research Council, Division of Building Research.

Touche, Ross, Baily, and Smart
 1968 Yukon Territory Taxation Study 1968. Montreal.

Tussing, Arlon R.
 1969 "Alaska Regional Inflation: An Overview of the Problem from the Standpoint of the Federal Government." *In* Federal Field Committee for Development Planning in Alaska, Studies on Alaska Regional Inflation. Anchorage.

Tussing, A. R., and M. Thomas
 1971 "Prices and Costs of Living in Urban Alaska." *Alaska Review of Business and Economic Conditions,* vol. 8(3).

Tussing, Arlon R., George W. Rogers, and Victor Fischer
 1971 Alaska Pipeline Report: Alaska's Economy, Oil and Gas Industry Development, and the Economic Impact of Building and Operating the Trans-Alaska Pipeline. University of Alaska, Fairbanks.

U.S. Department of Labor, Bureau of Labor Statistics
 1970 Seasonality and Manpower in Construction, Bulletin 1642. Washington, D.C.: U.S.G.P.O.

Weeden, Robert D.
 1973 Wildlife Management and Alaska Land Use Decisions. ISEGR Occasional Papers no. 8. University of Alaska, Fairbanks.

Yanovskiy, V. V.
 1969 Chelovek i Sever [Man and the North], Magadan.

CHAPTER 10

REVIEW OF DEVELOPMENT OF ARCTIC RESOURCES

John C. Reed

The Arctic Institute of North America, Montreal, Quebec, Canada

The object of this chapter is to trace the history of the development of Arctic resources from the not-so-very-distant past up to the early 1970s. The use of the term "polar desert" instead of "Arctic desert" is not material insofar as this discussion is concerned. I do not care whether they are called polar-desert resources or Arctic resources.

Let us try to visualize Arctic resources in the broadest possible perspective, including both the tangible and intangible, for all are important for a proper and balanced impression of the Far North and of its problems and opportunities. The Arctic holds many resources; let us think of them in terms of three categories: the renewable, nonrenewable, and nonexpendable.

A nonexpendable resource is one that, although it may be intangible, is still real; it may be used again and again without affecting its availability and value for further use on and on into the future. In this category we may place such values as scenery, recreational use, or possibly running water. A stream may be sent through a power plant forever without affecting in any way the potential of the stream for producing more power.

This chapter will discuss all three categories of resources, but with emphasis on petroleum and gas resources, because that is where a great deal of the interest is now. Furthermore, I will be emphasizing the North American Arctic simply because I know it much better than other parts of the Arctic.

As pointed out by Terence Armstrong in his book on Russian Settlement in the North, "It is perfectly clear today that there is no nation with a better knowledge of, or more interest in, the development and exploration of Arctic lands than the Soviet Union" (Armstrong, 1965). Armstrong further is of the opinion that the pressure of world population will require the use of all marginal lands, of which the largest areas are in the polar regions. He feels that their use may be more necessary to exploit the resources than to accommodate the overspill of people.

Three factors have been outstanding in inhibiting the development of Arctic resources, ever since man from the lower latitudes has been probing the Arctic. These are (1) the lack of adequate transportation systems, (2) the limitations of communications systems, and (3) the inadequacies of a supply of reliable labor. These three factors have continued to be important, although of progressively lesser importance.

Transportation remains the outstanding limitation to Arctic resources development (Sater, 1969). First the canoe and other small craft could penetrate with difficulty only to the fringes of the real North by running down the large northward flowing rivers, with which the Soviet Union is much better supplied than is North America. North America really has only one, the Mackenzie, unless one chooses to count the Yukon, which flows into the Bering Sea and not to the real Arctic at all. Wooden ships under sail were outclassed as competitors with the ice of far northern seas.

As transportation vehicles became more sophisticated and more powerful, entrance to the Arctic and movement within it became a little easier, but by no means easy. Of help also are modern icebreakers and nuclear submarines. The development of air travel has made a great difference, of course. But the North is still woefully short of integrated transportation systems of roads, railroads, airports, and suitable over-tundra vehicles.

Much the same can be said of communications systems, although significant advances have been, and are being, made. Such systems are expensive, especially when designed to serve only a small number of people, and have generally been considered justified only in terms of a national need, such as in support of a defense system.

Local labor in the Far North is generally nonexistent, except for the Eskimos of North America and other native groups of northern Europe and Asia. These natives constitute a valuable and important resource indeed, but the numbers are small, and the natives are not yet fully integrated into modern development systems. It is even debatable whether or not in their own interest they should be integrated into the pattern of a developing North.

Nonexpendable Resources

Curiously, attempts to exploit a nonexpendable resource first brought men from lower latitudes to the Arctic; that resource is geographic position or location on the face of the earth. The attempts to exploit were the exploratory probings to find a shorter way through the Arctic to somewhere else. Geographic position is indeed a resource in this sense. This points up the groupings of the major populations of the northern hemisphere around the polar regions, and that over the Arctic is in many instances the shortest way from here to there. I do not suppose that John Cabot, or Martin Frobisher, or Sir John Franklin recognized that they were trying to develop a resource, but they were.

In more modern times, of course, that is why Anchorage is a major international airport, and why in 1971 the president of the United States met the emperor of Japan there. That also is why the DEW Line stretches around the Arctic of North America, and why one of the three BMEWS locations is at Clear, Alaska, and another near Thule.

In the Far North lie other nonexpendable resources of substantial value: for example, scenery — the open tundra, the midnight sun, the ice-flecked Arctic Ocean, sport fishing — resources to be sure, but most difficult to measure (Williams, 1958). Further, with the pressure of increasing populations and more abundant standards of living, such resources are recognized as having rapidly increasing value. Large numbers of tourists in Barrow are now a standard part of the summer landscape, and they talk knowingly of Deadhorse, Kotzebue, Nome, the Brooks Range, and the pollution problem.

Northern environments with their physical characteristics and their plant and animal assemblages constitute natural laboratories for study in many scientific fields, and they are being used as such — that is, are being used as resources — by such facilities as the Inuvik Laboratory in the Northwest Territories and the Naval Arctic Research Laboratory at Barrow (Reed and Ronhovde, 1971). The museum value of such environments is often cited as resources, and attempts are even made at appraising relative values.

Renewable Resources

The next step in the long course of invading the Arctic and the Subarctic for their resources was to obtain a renewable resource — furs. Of course the native peoples around the shores of the Arctic Ocean and southward over the tundra and into the forests had used the renewable resources of plants and animals from time immemorial for food, clothing, and shelter. Such use included those renewable resources provided both by the land and by the sea. The ingenuity employed in obtaining and using the products of the land and sea, and the efficiency and completeness of use were, and to some extent still are, marvels of the mastery of man over a fairly hostile environment.

Even before the long line of explorers searching for the Northwest Passage to China, some of the renewable resources of the Far North were tapped significantly. Through the Middle Ages the eastern Canadian Arctic was famous for two renewable resource items — falcons and polar bears. The Vikings exploited them, for the live birds and the bearhides were viewed as precious by royalty.

As pointed out by Armstrong, "Apart from her Alas-kan venture, Russia played no part in the colonization of overseas territories by European powers during the great period of expansion in the fifteenth to early nineteenth centuries. She colonized Siberia instead; a territory that happened to be adjacent to the motherland. The motive for its acquisition was the same as that which impelled the Western European powers to go overseas — the search for wealth" (Armstrong, 1965). The lure was furs, and Russian domination to that end spread rapidly, first northward in European Russia and then eastward across Siberia, clear to the Bering Sea.

In northern North America, the first significant step in the use of resources was fish; by the early 1500s the eastern Canadian seaboard was fairly well known. This interest expanded to furs also, and the beaver became the symbol of penetration of the continent. The spread of fur traders westward and northward is well known all the way to the Arctic and to the Pacific. So too is the long rivalry between "The Governor and Company of Adventurers of England trading into Hudson Bay," chartered in 1670, and the North West Company of Montreal.

After a pause, caused in part by reaching the sea, Russia pushed eastward along the Pacific coast of North America and eventually established a rich empire along the Alaska seaboard, managed, for the most part, from Three Saints Bay on Kodiak Island. That empire was, of course, based on a renewable resource, the gentle sea otter.

It was inevitable that the Russian and British fur trading interests would clash in western North America, and so they did, and the British won — at least until the closing out of Russian involvement in 1867 by the sale of Alaska to the United States.

Mention must be made also of the exploiting of the great sea mammals, mostly whales, both on the Atlantic side of North America and in the Bering Sea and the Arctic Ocean at the other extremity of the continent. Around 1600 the Dutch began to exploit the whale in the Greenland and Norwegian seas, but mostly around Spitzbergen and Jan Mayen. Minsky (1948) tells the story of blubber and bone, "of tons and tons of train oil and sperm oil needed for lubrication, for light, for soap; of pounds of spermaceti used as a base in ointments, cerates, cosmetics; of pounds of ambergris treasured for perfumes, spiced wines, aphrodisiacs; of hundredweights of baleen that stiffened parasols and corsets for modish ladies" until they "had the beauty of a pinched and blown water-bottle."

This went on until around 1670, until whaling had moved far to sea. During the Spitzbergen heyday, however, Holland and England had quarreled mightily over the rich bounty. And the Dutch were replaced by Russians on Spitzbergen, who hunted the land animals for fur, and later by Norwegians, who exploited the reindeer.

Later, as told by Brooks, "American whalers, by the middle of the nineteenth century, in spite of Russian prohibition, had made the Bering Sea and the adjacent portions of the Arctic Ocean their own hunting ground.

Here a lucrative industry developed, and the whalers did not hesitate to trespass on the domain of the company (the Russian American Company) by engaging in the fur trade along the shores of Bering Sea. The Russians were unable to prevent this, and it remained for the Confederate privateer *Shenandoah* to place the first check on this industry by a raid in 1864. This vessel appeared without warning and destroyed upward of thirty whalers without opposition, for there were no Union war vessels in this sea. She subsequently continued her voyage across the Pacific and was the only vessel to carry the Confederate flag around the world (Brooks, 1953).

So it went, and to a lesser extent, so it still goes. The taking of whales is no longer a commercial venture in the North land, but they are still used by the natives. Furs of land animals still constitute an important industrial item. But furs are not as highly prized relatively as they once were, and the abundance of animals is less. Big game hunting is an important item, including the taking of polar bears, mostly off Alaska and in the vicinity of Spitzbergen, or Svalbard, as it is known today. Sport fishing too is pursued, and even commercial fishing in a few places. Worthy of mention also is the taking of fur seals by Alaskans on the Pribilof Islands in a pattern of perpetual yield under international treaty.

Nonrenewable Resources

For all practical purposes, the nonrenewable resources of the Arctic and the Subarctic are the mineral resources (U.S. Geological Survey, 1964). For this brief review of their development in the North (Sater et al., 1971), consider them in four categories: (1) the nonmetals like sand, gravel, clay, fluorspar, and crushed stone, (2) the metallic ores, (3) coal, and (4) oil and gas.

Mineral resources are, of course, found in typical geologic environments; environments resulting from the action of geologic processes that produced both the environments and the mineral deposits. Thus, the mineral deposits of the Arctic and Subarctic generally have nothing to do with the fact that they happen to be in the Far North now.

In a gross way, it is sometimes convenient to think of the mineral resources of the North in terms of four overgeneralized types of geologic environments: (1) those of the shield areas, (2) those of the great belts of folded mountain systems, (3) those of the broad, more gently folded basins of marine deposition, and (4) surficial deposits. Each type of area, of course, contains mineral resources appropriate for the processes that have produced the geologic environment.

What is different about the North is the relatively higher cost of the exploitation of the mineral resources because of such factors as inadequate transportation, communications, and labor supply. That difference can be illustrated in several ways. First, it encourages, relatively, the exploitation of resources that require a small amount of manpower and have low volume and high unit value. Exemplifying this principle is the traditional placer-mining of gold and of the platinum-group metals in the North. Secondly, large high-grade deposits may also be mined in the North, if the volume to be removed, generally with little or no beneficiation, justifies the building of a transportation system. An example might be the iron ore of the Schefferfield area of northern Quebec. Thirdly, if the product is to be used locally, the resource is likely to be mined — rather than to bring the product in from elsewhere — because, in effect, it is developed under a price umbrella, the cost of transportation to import the needed product. An excellent example is the mining of somewhat inferior coal in the Alaska Railroad belt. Fourthly, special circumstances may result in mining in the North even at high cost if it is in a national interest to do so, or if the deposit happens to be especially favorably located, say near a deep-water port that is not icebound.

The normal pattern in the North, both in Asia and in North America, has been first the exploitation of high-grade gold deposits, then the larger scale development of somewhat lower grade, but larger deposits, with the use of equipment such as hydraulic giants and dredging. That phase is followed by the discovery and operation of deposits of base metals, usually sulfides, and, where such deposits are present, of large-scale iron ore deposits. Finally comes exploitation and development of oil and gas resources. This is the phase that is of special current interest. During the three phases mentioned, coal resources may be developed where there are satisfactory resources, and where a ready market is available. The coal of the Alaska Railroad belt already has been mentioned. To this might be added the example of the coal of Svalbard, which is readily transported to the Soviet Union.

So too, as development proceeds, there is more and more need for local building materials. These soon become an important factor. For example, in Alaska in the early 1970s, the sand and gravel produced each year were next to oil and gas in the value of minerals produced. In some instances, as in northern Alaska, gravel is a precious commodity indeed, and in some cases its lack is an important deterrent to development of other resources.

We have mentioned that development of oil and gas resources is of special interest (Reed, 1970). This is true both in northern Asia and in North America. It has long been known that favorable geologic conditions account for the accumulation of oil and gas deposits in northern Alaska and in northern Canada from the Mackenzie delta region northward and eastward over a substantial part of the northern islands. There was no really large oil or gas discovery in the far northern part of North America until the strike on the Kenai Peninsula of Alaska, not far from Anchorage, on July 19, 1951. Of course, Norman Wells, far up the Mackenzie drainage was known and developed long before that. So too, a little oil had been produced and a small refinery operated in southern Alaska near Cordova in the 1920s. The U.S. Navy carried on a $50,000,000 major oil exploration program in project NPR 4 in northern Alaska from 1944 to 1953, and one medium-sized oil field, several oil shows, and one fairly large gas field were discovered and partially tested (Reed, 1958).

The Kenai Peninsula discovery and the results of the exploration of NPR 4, plus the increasing need for more oil from North America, encouraged industry to begin to explore in northern Alaska in the 1960s. This resulted in the phenomenal Prudhoe Bay find in 1967, which was announced on July 18, 1968. Since then exploration has proceeded, although at a lower rate than would have been the case without the hurdles posed by objecting conservation interests, native claims, and various suits and injunctions. Several fields are now known, and the oil potential is large.

Meanwhile exploration was pushing northward in Canada, from the northern parts of Alberta into the Yukon and the Northwest Territories. That extension, of course, was influenced by continually increasing costs as distances became greater, transportation more difficult, the climate more severe, and labor less available.

However, the Prudhoe Bay discovery, and later developments, constituted an important spur. Eventually a substantial number of Canadian interests, plus the federal government, united into a consortium, termed Panarctic, under which exploration has proceeded on some of the Canadian Arctic islands, notably Melville Island and King Christian Island. Some, apparently small or moderate, oil strikes have been made in northern Canada, and at least three major gas strikes have occurred. The latter appear to be large enough, and indicative enough, to be of real potential for the future.

BIBLIOGRAPHY

Armstrong, Terence
    1965   Russian settlement in the North. Scott Polar Research Institute, Special Publication no. 3, Cambridge [England] University Press.

Brooks, A. H.
    1953   Blazing Alaska's Trails. University of Alaska, College (Fairbanks); Arctic Institute of North America, Montreal.

Minsky, Jeannette
    1948   To the Arctic! (revised edition). Adolph A. Knoff, New York.

Reed, J. C.
    1958   Exploration of Naval Petroleum Reserve no. 4 and Adjacent Areas, Northern Alaska, 1944–53: Part I, History of the Exploration. U.S. Geological Survey, Professional Paper 301.
    1970   Oil Developments of Alaska, *The Polar Record* 15(984): 7–17.

Reed, J. C., and A. G. Ronhovde
    1971   Arctic Laboratory. Arctic Institute of North America, Montreal. August.

Sater, Beverly F. (ed.)
    1969   Arctic and Middle North Transportation. Arctic Institute of North America, Montreal. December.

Sater, J. E., A. G. Ronhovde, and L. C. Van Allen
    1971   Arctic Environment and Resources. Arctic Institute of North America, Montreal.

U.S. Geological Survey, compiler
    1964   Mineral and Water Resources of Alaska. Published for the U.S. Congress, Senate Committee on Interior and Insular Affairs, 88th Congress, Second Session.

Williams, Howel, et al.
    1958   Landscapes of Alaska, University of California Press, Berkeley.

CHAPTER 11

RESOURCE DEVELOPMENT IN CANADA'S HIGH ARCTIC

George Jacobsen
Arctic Consultant, Montreal, Quebec, Canada

In the North American mythology, the undeveloped frontier and the land beyond were always thought to be the land of promise where great resources were supposed to bring great rewards. As far as the Canadian polar deserts are concerned, this belief is rather a recent one; the reward part of it has still been doubted by the majority even into the early 1970s.

Canada's High Arctic is the coldest, is the most distant, and has the longest period of darkness of the North American continent. Overland accessibility to the Arctic Coast of the mainland via roads, railroads, or other regular surface transport has still been nonexistent into the early 1970s. Access by sea to the coast and the islands is made difficult by pack-ice conditions, which even icebreaker-escorted shipping can penetrate for only a part of the year.

Renewable Resources

A small number of autochthonous people, the Eskimos ingeniously and precariously survived in the southern part of this region by exploiting its renewable resources through hunting and fishing. The northernmost islands were rarely visited by them except on hunting forays from the south or from Greenland.

Fishing, sealing, and whaling by Europeans comprised a sizable industry for centuries, until overfishing and lack of demand forced the industry to close down toward the end of the nineteenth century. It is fairly certain that early whalers regularly visited Lancaster Sound and Jones Sound and were familiar with a large part of the eastern Arctic wherever open water made their activities possible. However no written reports exist, as the know-how was regarded as a trade secret and kept away from competitors and the public.

The only renewable resource continuing to be exported is a small number of furs, mostly via the Hudson Bay Company, collected by their few posts.

Animal population surveys in the early 1970s indicate that certain species of whales have again been increasing, whereas others such as the Narwhal are just holding their own or are diminishing. Among the larger land animals, the polar bear is near extinction, the musk-ox exists in small numbers and is fully protected, and the caribou herds have greatly diminished. It seems that their reduction is not entirely due to over-hunting. Recent counts show some encouraging trends, but only the future will show any conclusive trends.

As our polar deserts have no trees or other plant life that can be exploited resourcewise, and as its fishes and sea and land mammals live in a precarious balance, one must say that from the traditional renewable-resource point of view this area has little to exploit.

From a wider renewable-resource point of view, however, the enormous empty space, yet unpolluted — except for atomic fallout and other human follies — is and will be a priceless asset for recreation and leisure activities and other industrial and human uses as yet unneeded and unthought of in a continuously crowded world.

Nonrenewable Resources

The nonrenewable-resource picture is rather a different one. Early explorers reported showings of galena, copper, oil seeps, and gypsum domes (the latter mentioned by Per Schei, the geologist of the Sverdrup expedition). However, not until the 1950s when aerial photography — which had commenced during World War II — had mapped the area, and parties of the Canadian Geological Survey had made some basic geological surveys, could one even think of resource extraction. It soon became evident that this large sedimentary basin must contain considerable deposits of hydrocarbons. Oil companies became interested, and exploration parties visited the area in ever-increasing numbers. Supported by small planes and helicopters their camps became a feature of the summer landscape of the High Arctic. When the Canadian government opened the area for claiming, against payment of a reasonable fee, the whole land and sea area was claimed within a few weeks.

The first well was drilled by a consortium headed by Dome Petroleum at Winterharbour on Melville Island in 1961; it was a dry one, although there was a small showing of gas. The cost was high, but valuable experience was gained. Two more dry wells were drilled by private interests, one on Cornwallis Island in 1963 and one on Bathurst Island in 1964.

It became apparent that large amounts of money would have to be spent in development of an oil industry. Private industry alone would perhaps spend the amount eventually, but the Canadian government was eager to exploit this potential resource as fast as possible. In 1966 a company called PanArctic Oils Ltd. was formed; it was a joint venture in which the Canadian government held 45 percent of the shares and twenty private oil and mining companies held the balance. A number of these twenty private companies had acreage in the Arctic Islands; with others, PanArctic had made drilling arrangements. Drilling began in earnest in 1968. After two dry wells the first gas discovery was made at Drake Point, Melville Island, in 1969. Then, after three dry exploratory wells, came the dramatic discovery of a gas well on King Christian Island in October 1970. This well, which blew wild and burned as a beacon that could be seen from the air up to 300 miles away until it was killed in March 1971, proved the existence of a potentially large gas reservoir. Not long thereafter, PanArctic reported another natural gas discovery at Kristoffer Bay on Ellef Ringness Island.

No commercial oil wells were developed in the Arctic Islands prior to 1972, but every indication has been that they will be developed soon. One must not forget that the Canadian petroleum industry drilled several hundred wells during forty years before establishing western Canada as a major producing area. There is every reason to believe that the Canadian High Arctic will become a major supplier of fossil fuel energy. However technically difficult and expensive it might be — and with automated operations and the ever-increasing demands of other oil-producing countries, Arctic oil from a friendly country might not be comparatively expensive — ways and means will be found to bring fossil fuels from the Arctic Islands to southern Canada and, in particular, to the United States, whose energy deficit in fossil fuels has been increasing yearly at an alarming rate.

The accelerated exploration activity has also produced many mineral finds, of which three are sizable enough that they could become mines in the not too distant future. Probably the first that might come into operation is the Mary River iron deposit on the northeastern part of Baffin Island. The enormous quantity of consistent high-grade iron ore in a location where construction is comparatively easy, plus the successful ship transport studies made by Canadian government icebreakers, has this deposit just waiting for the right economic moment to get into operation.

The second potential mining area consists of the long-known copper deposits on the Coppermine River. These deposits are not all high grade but stretch over many miles and are being proven through a continuous drilling program.

On the northern end of Cornwallis Island and at Strathcona Sound on northern Baffin Island, lead, zinc, and other base metals are being proven. Many other deposits are being explored, but the above mentioned might be the nearest to any commercial exploitation.

What are the aspects of this sudden surge of exploration activity in our polar deserts from the human, ecological, and transportation point of view? Except for small Eskimo camps and weather stations built since 1946, this area has been free from human habitation. Suddenly people from the South were moved to the North to work its exploration camps, oil rigs, and logistic support stations. In a post-industrial society where unemployment rates run as high as 10 percent in some areas, one would think that it would be easy to get all the personnel needed for activities of this kind. The fact of the matter is that in spite of high wages, excellent food, accommodations, and comfort, it is difficult to find the right personnel.

I believe this is due not only to lack of ambition brought on by our highly taxed welfare society, which rewards enterprise less and less and has not replaced financial rewards with other reward values, but through significant changes in our social structure and way of living. The late-twentieth-century man is a big town dweller, who for many reasons congregates in ever-larger urban communities. Living on a farm is contrary to present-day habit and trend. Furthermore the family unit is becoming smaller. The man who goes north today frequently leaves behind a wife with one or more young children who most often live by themselves. They miss the father's guidance and authority, which in the past would have become available from older family members when three or more generations lived in a big house together.

Various companies try to overcome this problem by flying the men back and forth every two or three weeks, with off time equaling working time. This is a temporary expedient and is disrupting to the life cycle of the worker and his family.

The answer obviously is to train the people who are used to living in the Arctic region, the Eskimos. Slow progress is being made in this direction. It probably will take several decades until enough Eskimos are trained to man the majority of available jobs. By that time the most able ones might have accepted so many of our own values that they might perfer to work in the South! On the other hand, highly automated operations will require fewer workers. In some places, like Resolute, larger communities might have developed by then, where people would want to work and live.

Everybody is aware of the danger of pollution and damage to the fragile Arctic environment by the activity of man. The new Northern Land Use regulations promulgated by the Canadian government in November 1971 should do much to hold these damages to a minimum, at least as far as oil and mining companies are concerned. These rules are enforced by a fee system, and a field inspection staff which will judge each case on its own merit, such as the question of access routes and whether summer operations should be allowed at the area in question. The rules restrict vehicle weight, and ground-pressure ratings are not to exceed five pounds per square inch. The oil industry has been trying to keep exploration and drill sites as clean as possible, even by flying nonburnable refuse out by helicopter, by adding incinerator sleds to their tractor trains on seismic traverses, by aerial reseeding of seismic trails damaged by summer work, and by experimenting with air cushion and low pressure tire vehicles — to name just a few procedures. There is a considerable amount of industry and government-initiated research in this direction, and many results will be applicable to other regions.

A really serious pollution problem concerns the sewage and garbage disposal from all permanent Arctic settlements. To prevent further damage, an extremely strictly enforced Northwest Territories Ordinance for existing and new Arctic settlements should be enacted as soon as possible.

Apart from the conventional pollution hazards, the most dangerous would be oil spills, whether through tanker damage by ice or oil pipeline breaks. About the latter, there is a lot of theory but no experience either in North America or in Russia where no large oil pipelines have been laid in permafrost areas. The main Siberian oil fields are in areas away from the permafrost, and gas transmission lines do not present the same hazards. Huge oil spills by tanker breakup or damage are too horrible to contemplate. Although pack ice presents an additional hazard, such disasters are not specifically confined to Arctic waters. However, it is probable that the damage to the whole biosystem in the cold Arctic Sea would be greater and longer lasting than in warmer seas, as the breakup of the oil globules would take much longer.

Gas pipelines will be built from Canada's Arctic Region within the 1970s. With the present state of technological know-how, ecologically safe oil pipelines can be built through any permafrost area — at a cost — if economic necessity and environmental consciousness demand it.

Conclusion

Apart from wildlife living in precarious balance, the two biggest conventional and nonconventional nonrenewable resources of the Canadian polar deserts are water, in liquid and frozen form, and space. Except as an area of leisure activity, of cold storage, and of possible food extraction from the ocean, other future uses of the area are open to speculation.

In the nonrenewable resource field, fossil fuels and to a lesser degree minerals will be of great importance, not only in the economic and political sense but through the new scientific and technological inventions and methods which they will force us to create to exploit them intelligently, and with due regard to the human and ecological aspect.

Many things found in this huge Arctic laboratory will be useful in other fields of mankind's activities.

PART THREE

PROBLEMS OF IMMIGRANTS

CHAPTER 12

TRANSPORTATION IN THE ARCTIC

Fletcher C. Paddison and Albert M. Stone

The Applied Physics Laboratory, Johns Hopkins University, Silver Spring, Maryland

Just traveling to the Arctic can be a difficult and thrilling experience. Travel in the North in the 1970s is convenient and safe by comparison with the end of the past century when 60,000 of the 100,000 South 48'ers and Southern Canadians, ill-prepared for the rugged terrain and the cold, either perished or turned back on the journey to reach the reported bonanza of the Klondike.

Fresh off the boat at Skagway in 1897, men and animals struck out from Skagway up over the coastal Rocky Mountains through the treacherous White Pass or, alternately, the higher Chilkoot Pass to Dawson and the gold fields on the Klondike River (the mispronounced Indian name of the Throndinck River).

Similarly, unsuspecting, unprepared for the much longer and harder Arctic trip, were the few thousand Canadians who, in the fall of 1897, left Edmonton and sailed down the Athabasca, then the Mackenzie River. From the broad Mackenzie River the Canadians labored up the twisting, ever-narrowing Laird River, some turning off on the South Nahanni River. The Nahanni River up the Headless Valley appeared to be a quicker, shorter path; however the rugged Mackenzie Mountains would not let the adventurers through to the gold fields. Only a handful of Canadians reached the gold fields after two winters in the brittle Canadian Arctic (Boyer, 1968).

Transportation can shape a society; just ask a remaining Husky dog what he thinks of his replacement, the snowmobile. Or ask the Eskimo, or the Indian, in a remote Alaskan village what he thinks about modern transportation, when he sees the Bureau of Indian Affairs boat, the *North Star,* forced to weigh anchor and depart without unloading its precious cargo. The *North Star* twice a year transports not only the absolute necessities of life, but, more important, some of the pleasures of modern life to some 50 coastal and island villages. The Northern Alaska ports of call can be difficult because of the shallow water, the lack of docks and the polar ice pack which is always nearby. For the last 68 years, with patience, the *North Star* has been able to unload at least part of her cargo; however, in 1970 she was not able to discharge any cargo at Barrow due to the proximity of the polar ice pack. The short season and the ever-changing weather do not allow extended stays. Many a ship has spent an extra year just past

Point Barrow, Alaska, trapped by the unpredictable ice. Transportation now means everything to the Northern man — oil worker, Eskimo, and Indian alike.

Early Arctic Exploration and Transportation

Throughout man's history — apart from the Eskimo and the Indian who feel at home in that hostile land — the Arctic has been ignored except by the explorers or by those searching for explorers, and more recently, by those who wish to develop the region's considerable frozen resources.

The principal exploration of the Canadian Arctic occurred when Martin Frobisher in 1577, John Davis in 1585, William Barents in 1595, Henry Hudson in 1607 to 1610, Robert Bylot and William Baffin in 1615, Vitus Bering (also spelled Behring) in 1725, James Cook in 1776, W. E. Parry in 1819, and Franklin in 1845, searched in vain for the Northwest Passage to Cathay. Franklin's ill-fated expedition resulted in unexpected but extensive exploration of the Canadian Arctic region by Scott, Rae, McClintock, and McClure in the middle of the nineteenth century, searching for traces of the Franklin expedition. The *New York Herald* newspaper, which sponsored the successful search for Livingston by Stanley in 1872, sponsored an ill-fated search for Franklin by sending Lt. G. W. Delong in 1879 on the *Jeannette.* All but two of that Arctic expedition perished. After being deserted, the *Jeannette* in three years traveled unmanned and alone from the Soviet Eastern Arctic to Southern Greenland, demonstrating to all that travel across the Arctic, drifting with the ice, is possible. Europeans searched in vain for either the Northwest Passage or the path to the North Pole, spurred on further by a prize of 20,000 pounds (divided by McClure and Rae) to the discoverer of the route or 5,000 pounds to the first who got within one degree of the pole.

Considerably more was known about the Asian side of the Arctic, whose exploration was planned and initiated by Peter the Great. He commissioned a Dane in the Soviet Navy, Vitus Bering, to explore the eastern regions of Asia to see whether Asia and America joined. Two expeditions, in 1725 and 1730, mapped the eastward extent of the northern Asian continent and most

(Paul Popper, Ltd.)

Fig. 12.1. Early snowmobile, used in Scott's Antarctic expedition in 1910-11.

(Paul Popper, Ltd.)

Fig. 12.2. Siberian ponies used to pull sleds in Scott's Antarctic expedition in 1910–11.

(Paul Popper, Ltd.)

Fig. 12.3. Men hauling sled in Scott's Antarctic expedition in 1910–11.

of its Arctic coastline and discovered the Aleutian Islands and Alaska. Bering was preceded in the Arctic by the Cossack Deshnett in 1648 and followed by Lt. Moroviot in 1734, Lts. Oftgin and Koskelef in 1734, Lt. Prontshistshef, a Yakutsk merchant Shalannof, in 1761–64, and Lt. Kotzeybue in 1815. As a result of these expeditions, the Arctic coast of Asia was rather well understood and mapped (Barrow, 1971; and Sater, 1969). The possibility of travel from one north-flowing Asian river to another through the Arctic was generally known and practiced.

During the First International Polar Year (1882–83), Otto Sverdrup explored much of the Canadian Archipelago on foot with sled transportation, just as Alexander Mackenzie had a century before when he worked his way to the mouth of the Mackenzie River. During this same time, in the late nineteenth century, Fridtjof Nansen almost got to the North Pole, striking out from the ship *Fram;* however, he left the triumph of reaching the Pole for Peary and Henson, who, in 1908, after many years of preparation, reached the North Pole. The Northwest Passage was confirmed by Amundsen, who, in 1903, in a 70-foot converted herring sloop, the *Ajöa,* threaded his way through the Canadian Archipelago over a period of three years. Later, after he beat Scott to the South Pole, he returned north and attempted to fly across the Arctic with amphibious aircraft. He succeeded with lighter-than-air craft in 1926. (For a brief resume of this later history, see Ley, 1962.)

Arctic and Antarctic explorers have experimented with each change in the state-of-the-art in equipment and methods of transportation, hoping that new developments would solve their Arctic transportation problems. In some cases they were successful, as with Amundsen and the lighter-than-air craft, but others met with disaster, such as Scott, whose lack of confidence in dog

teams resulted in his attempted use of an early mechanical snowmobile, Siberian ponies, and ultimately man as a pack animal (figs. 12.1, 12.2, and 12.3).

Although science and technology have moved far since Admiral Peary's trip to the Arctic, there is, incredibly, still no dependable integrated long-range year-round means of transportation in the Arctic, despite the fact that some of the major air routes of the world cross it at high altitude and several aircraft each day fly near the North Pole. The nuclear submarine has had successful but limited tests to prove its capability to operate in the Arctic seas. Technology could support the development of cargo submarines and dock facilities if the economic demand were there.

The Arctic and Its Significance

The Arctic (fig. 12.4) is a broad, deep ocean ringed by the Chukchi, Beaufort, East Siberian, Laptev, Kara, Barents, Norwegian, and Greenland seas. In the winter the grinding explosive fracture of the ever-present ice pack is heard as pressure ridges are heaved. In early

[126]

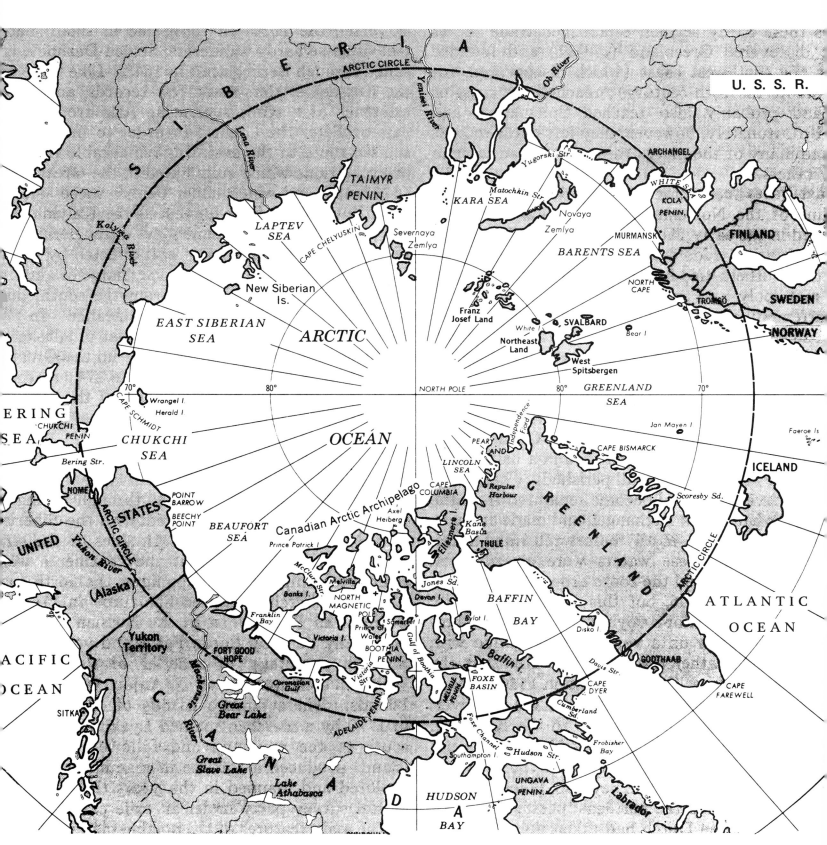

Fig. 12.4.   The Arctic regions.

(B. M. Buck, Delco Electronics Division, General Motors Corporation)

Fig. 12.5. The obstacle to ground travel on an Arctic ice pack.

(B. M. Buck, Delco Electronics Division, General Motors Corporation)

Fig. 12.6. A new pressure ridge.

(B. M. Buck, Delco Electronics Division, General Motors Corporation)

Fig. 12.7.   Arctic Research Laboratory Island (ARLIS V), spring, 1970.

spring this leaves a heritage of massive rubble fields of tortured ice covering the entire Arctic Ocean and its shores. The Arctic Ocean's shallow continental shelf is the most extensive found in any ocean and consequently limits underwater egress and ingress of boats and submarines to only a few relatively narrow passages, such as the Bering Strait and the Greenland Sea.

The Arctic Ocean's ice cover varies in thickness from approximately six feet in the brief summer to an average of 11 feet near the end of winter. During the winter the top of the ice is covered with only a thin cover of crunchy snow. This thin cover is a most effective acoustic absorber, damping all sounds except the ever-present whistle of wind. The fantastically ruptured surface of the ice pack is the nemesis of all travelers (fig. 12.5). The pressure ridges, often rising two and three stories high (fig. 12.6), one closely after the other, enforce a backbreaking, discouraging tortuous path. As if that were not enough, the ice pack frequently and unexpectedly fractures, and one part will move away from another, opening a lead — that is, a long stretch of open water (fig. 12.7). The traveler must either improvise a raft or wait for the water to freeze.

In the brief summertime the snow melts and pressure ridges are moderated; however travel is *more,* not less, arduous. The ice pack is covered with a myriad of lakes formed by the melted snow and ice. The ice is thinner and its surface is soft and will not support concentrated loads; open leads and expanses of open ocean are numerous.

The Arctic Ocean is ringed by two large continental land masses and spectacular glaciated islands. This land is in many ways less hospitable than the ocean. The permanently frozen land (up to several thousands of feet in depth) extends for hundreds of miles from the ocean. These permafrost regions, largely treeless,

are colder than the ice-covered Arctic Ocean in the winter and warmer in the summer and are populated with a number and variety of Arctic animals and insects. When man wishes to work, live, or arrange transport over the permafrost, he must isolate any structure or road he builds so that heat cannot be conducted into the permafrost region. If not, the structure will become unstable and will slowly settle into the surface. For example, shallow telephone poles are slowly and inevitably expelled. Not only does man have to insulate himself from the permafrost to stabilize structures and roads but he must also pay heed to his effect on the tundra if he is to return in subsequent times (fig. 12.8). The grass and moss that cover the tundra are easily affected, that is, removed or scarred, changing the local solar thermal input. In the summer this results in altered local thawing. Then in subsequent years, due to repetitive freezing and thawing, if the area is poorly drained, a puddle forms and slowly becomes a lake. In a well-drained area a canyon may be formed (Hok, 1969).

A list of resources in the land masses ringing the Arctic Ocean sound alike — oil, gas, coal, gold, phosphate, zinc, silver, molybdenum, uranium, beryllium, tin, platinum, antimony, copper — they vary only in degree from country to country. However, what is known is like the top of an iceberg — much more than the eye sees is hidden below. In addition to the aforementioned extractable resources, there is perhaps the most precious treasure of all, the renewable resource represented by the aquatic animals and the microorganisms which abound in the Arctic Ocean and its marginal seas and the animals which inhabit the land.

The location and extent of many of these frozen assets are well known and have been known for many years. For example, oil fields bordering on the North Slope

[129]

Fig. 12.8.   Indelible tracks left in tundra.

of Alaska were designated as a Naval Petroleum Reserve in 1923, although the extent and richness of the field were not established until the 1960s. The copper and oil shale deposits in the Northwest Territories of Canada also have been known for many years.

Another significance of the Arctic is the practical fact that it is in a unique position midway between the world's principal population and trade centers, and, with the advent of long-range jet aircraft, it is being traversed daily. Finally, it is the source region of much of the weather in the Northern Hemisphere.

Modern Arctic Transportation

Except in Scandinavia, to our knowledge, there are no year-round roads and no railroads north of the Arctic Circle in the early 1970s. The principal means of transport of bulk dry cargo and liquid cargo is by ship and barge, escorted by icebreakers. Important or perishable cargo is flown to or within the Arctic, and scheduled commercial aircraft daily fly to the edge of the Arctic Ocean.

Most people travel by air into and around the Arctic. In addition to the scheduled airlines, there are numerous small airlines and "bush" pilots. On the ground, people travel amazing distances with dogs or, more likely, snowmobiles in the winter and small boats in the summer. During the winter cargo is hauled by "cat trains," that

is, caterpillar tractors or similar tracked vehicles, pulling sled-like conveyances. During the summer most land transport over permafrost and muskeg regions essentially stops, other than in those regions where special roads have been prepared.

Air travel over the Arctic Ocean is possible year-round; but landing on the thin pressure-ridged ice pack is practicable only in the winter and then only with limited-weight aircraft and helicopters. The new air-cushion vehicles (hovercraft), which are truly amphibious, have the potential of year-round transportation and operation over the winter or summer ice.

Scandinavian Transportation

The northern European countries — the Scandinavian countries — although they physically project above the Arctic Circle, are warmed by the Gulf Stream current. The resultant moderation in climate results in little or no permafrost. Roads and railroads have, accordingly, reached into the northernmost regions of these countries.

Soviet Union Transportation

Murmansk is the only Arctic deepwater port in the U.S.S.R. It lies on the Kola Peninsula and is open most of the year as a result of the moderation of the Arctic climate by the Gulf Stream.

Siberia, much like the Canadian Arctic, with considerable permafrost, holds the record for the coldest area in the Arctic, −71.1°C at the town of Oymyakon (Conger, 1967).

Transportation has been a critical problem to the Soviet Union because of its size, its northern location on the Asian continental land mass, and the fact that it has only limited access to the sea. The southern sea access affords opportunities to export and import supplies from other continents; however, it affords little opportunity for intra-Soviet transport.

The Northern Sea Route — The Soviet Union has limited access to the open oceans through the Okhotsk and Bering seas on the far east, the Baltic and Black seas on the west and the frozen Arctic Ocean to the north. The Arctic Ocean holds promise of saving thousands of miles and a week of transit time to ships that can traverse the northern route around the perimeter of the Arctic Ocean. For example, Murmansk to Vladivostok by sea via the Arctic Ocean and Bering Sea is 11,000 kilometers (6,835 miles), while via the Suez Canal, when open, the trip is doubled. However, probably more significant is the fact that the Arctic Ocean allows access to and interconnection of the north-flowing Ob, Yenisey, Lena, Yana, Indigirka, and Kolyma rivers. The Ob, Yenisey, and Lena are large long rivers reaching far into central Siberia, and their headwaters cross the Trans-Siberian Railroad well inside the Soviet Union. The other rivers are connected to the Trans-Siberian Railroad and Okhotsk Sea by a road network.

Ships that ply the perimeter of Siberia through the Kara, Laptev, and East Siberian seas must of necessity be shallow-draft ships due to the extensive continental shelf. Ships of greater than 15,000 tons deadweight are not mentioned (Armstrong, 1968–70). These Soviet ships, however, are not all ice-strengthened. The shipping season is short, approximately 90 days, and support of an icebreaker is normally required. The Soviets have the world's largest fleet of icebreaker ships. Table 12.1 lists the United States, Canada, and Soviet Union icebreakers. Armstrong (1968–70) reported an offer made prior to the 1967 shipping season by the Soviets to escort any vessel across the northern sea route. This same reference indicated that no one accepted the offer and it was subsequently withdrawn that same year.

The mouths of the Soviet north-flowing rivers are for the most part large and reasonably deep. As a conseqence, the shallow-draft ships can progress upstream a considerable distance where protected docks are more easily maintained than on the perimeter of the Arctic Ocean.

Ground Travel — Tregubov (no date given) states that special trucks or cars have not been designed for Arctic land transport. Ordinary vehicles are used over frozen land in the Soviet Union with the application of the same techniques used in Alaska and Canada to

TABLE 12.1

Icebreaker Ships of the United States, Canada, and the Soviet Union

Ship's Name	Year Built	Where Built	Nation	Length O.A. (ft)	Beam (ft)	Draft (ft)	Displacement (1000 tons)	Speed (knots)	Machinery*	Power (1000 SHP)†
"Wind" Class	1944–47	USA	USA	269	64	26	5.3	16.0	DE	10.0
Abegweit	1947	Canada	Canada	372	61	19	6.9	16.0	DE	13.2
Edward Cornwallis	1949	Canada	Canada	259	44	18	3.7	13.5	Steam Uniflow	3.5‡
Thule	1951	Sweden	Sweden	204	53	16	1.9	15.0	DE	5.5
D'Iberville	1953	Canada	Canada	310	67	30	9.9	14.5	Steam Uniflow	10.8‡
Labrador	1953	Canada	Canada	269	64	30	6.5	16.0	DE	10.0
Gen. San Martin	1954	W. Germany	Argentina	278	62	21	4.8	16.0	DE	6.5
Voima	1954	Finland	Finland	274	64	22	4.4	—	DE	10.5
Glacier	1955	USA	USA	309	74	26	8.3	—	DE	21.0
William Carson	1955	Canada	Canada	351	70	19	7.7	15.0	DE	10.0
Montclam	1957	Canada	Canada	220	48	16	2.9	13.0	Steam Uniflow	4.0
Lenin	1958	USSR	USSR	440	90	30	16.0	—	Nuclear Turbo-Electric	39.0
Karhu Class	1958	Finland	Finland	243	57	19	3.4	—	DE	7.5
Moskva	1960	Finland	USSR	400	81	35	15.4	18.0	DE	22.0
John A. MacDonald	1960	Canada	Canada	315	70	28	8.9	15.5	DE	16.5
Tarmo Class	1963	Finland	Finland	276	69	20	5.8	—	DE	12.0
Dabjorn Class	1965	Denmark	Denmark	247	56	20	3.6	17.0	DE	10.5
Fuji	1965	Japan	Japan	328	72	27	8.5	15.0	DE	12.0
St. Laurent	1968	Canada	Canada	366	80	30	13.3	—	Steam Turbine	24.0
USS Manhattan	1969	USA	USA	1000	155	52	140.0	?	Steam Turbine	43.0
Arktika	1974	USSR	USSR	525	82	29	30.0	25.0	Nuclear Steam Turbine	80.0
WAGB–10	1974	USA	USA	400	84	28	12.0	17.0	DE	60.0

SOURCE: Polar Transportation Requirements Study Report — U.S. Coast Guard, November, 1968.

*DE = Diesel electric.

†SHP = Shaft horsepower.

‡IHP, or Indicated Horsepower.

keep them operable in the harsh environment; that is, engine start-up heaters, special radiator covers, independent cab heaters, special oils, greases, gasolines and protective shelters. In poorly drained permafrost regions, transportation ceased in the summer months, until recent years, when amphibious craft of small payload with airplane engines and propellers have been utilized. The native population still prefers the reindeer and dog sled to mechanical vehicles in the winter; however, things are apparently changing even there, and the snowmobile, or motor sleigh with ski-track propulsion, as they refer to it, carrying two passengers and pulling a 229-kilogram (660-pound) sled, are being tried.

There are connecting roads from the Trans-Siberian Railroad to the headwaters of the Lena, Indigirka, and Kolyma rivers. The Bolshoy Never to Yakutsk Road is 1,265 kilometers (786 miles) long. In the Chita region motor transport takes care of more than 40 percent of all goods shipped; in the Irkutsk regions 50 percent, Yakutia 80 percent, and Tuva 100 percent. Moscow-to-the-Far-East motor highway extends to Chita and eventually will be completed to parallel the railroad all the way to Magadan.

River Transport — The principal logistic route to Northern Siberia and intra-Siberia transport is by the interlocking system of north-flowing rivers connected at the top by the Arctic Ocean and at their headwaters by the Trans-Siberian Railroad (fig. 12.9).

Of the Eastern Siberian rivers, the Yenisey is one of the longest, 3,850 kilometers (2,400 miles), in the Soviet Union; in its lower reaches it is so broad and deep that seagoing ships can sail up to Igarka, 700 kilometers (440 miles), from its mouth.

The longest U.S.S.R. river is the Lena, 4,350 kilometers (2,703 miles); it is the most basic transport artery in Northern Siberia, with barges carrying goods to the Arctic. The shift of population and shipment of goods to Siberia are emphasized by the statistics of the percentage of goods transported by the river transport network of the Siberian Basin compared to the entire inland water transportation system of all the Soviet Union. At the end of World War I the percentage of goods by water transport was 6.7; 50 years later it was 23.5 percent; and by 1980 it may reach 50 percent or more (Demidov, 1970).

Air Transport — The Soviets have for many years had a program of operational and scientific research in the Arctic and on the floating polar ice cap, supported primarily by fixed- and rotary-wing aircraft. The Soviet technology is summarized in table 12.2, which lists and compares the large payload helicopters.

The aircraft, both fixed and rotary wing, have his-

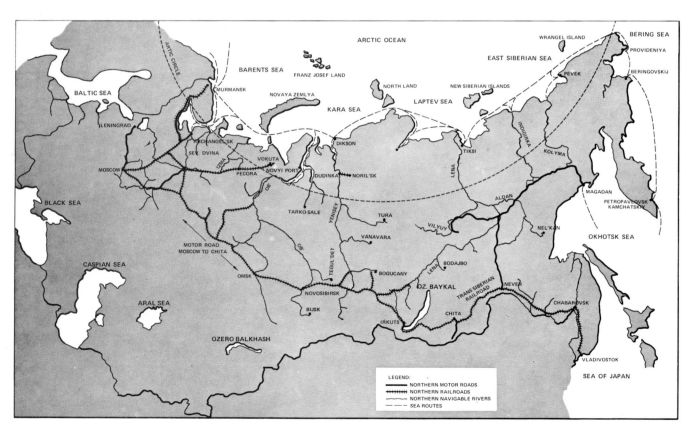

Fig. 12.9. Northern transportation routes of the U.S.S.R.

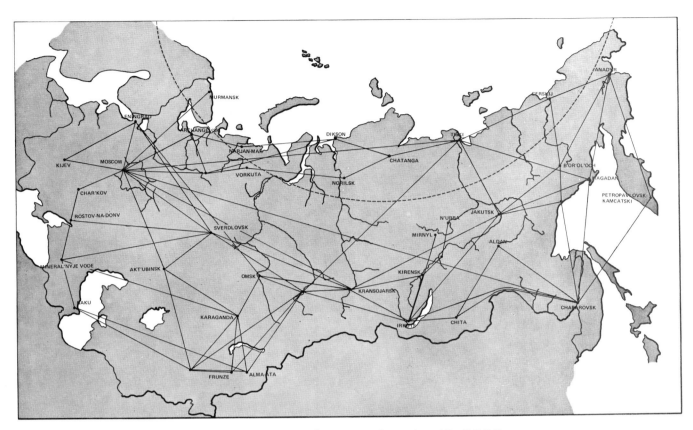

Fig. 12.10.   Northern air transportation routes of the U.S.S.R.

TABLE 12.2

Comparison of Large-Payload Rotary-Wing Aircraft

Designation	Name	Maximum Payload and Fuel (1,000 lb)	Normal Gross Weight (1,000 lb)	Range No Payload (100 N Mi)
U.S.A.				
212	Bell Helicopter	5.7	11.2	2.8
K-600 3	Kaman (Huskie)	4.5	9.1	2.7
S-61	Sikorsky (Sea Horse)	10.7	20.5	6.1
S-65	Sikorsky (Sea Stallion)	12.6	35.0	2.6
S-64E	Sikorsky (Skycrane)	22.4	42.0	2.3
107	Boeing (Sea Knight)	7.4	20.8	2.4
114	Boeing (Chinook)	25.5	46.0	4.0
France				
SA-321F	S-Frelon	10.8	27.5	3.7
U.S.S.R.	**NATO Names**			
Mi-6	Hook	44.0	93.7	3.3
Mi-8	Hip	9.0	26.4	1.9
Mi-10	Harke	33.0	95.8	2.3
Mi-12	Homer	88.0	231.0	(?)
Mi-24	Horse	9.0	35.0	2.0

torically been used for logistic support and in search-and-rescue missions in the Arctic Ocean and over the Arctic pack ice. The helicopter can, of course, be used year-round, but does have weather problems. The fixed-wing aircraft is usually restricted in use to September through June operations if landing is required.

The Russian *1967 World Atlas* shows a rather extensive network of air routes and landing fields throughout the U.S.S.R. Figure 12.10 reproduces most of the routes and shows that access is afforded to most of the Siberian Arctic.

Canadian Transportation

The Canadian northern provinces are a composite of all the geographic forms to be found in all the other countries extending into the Arctic. The Yukon has rugged rocky mountains similar to those found in Alaska. The river-eroded Mackenzie Basin is similar to several of the river basins in the Soviet Union. The Canadian Archipelago, reaching up to Pearyland and Greenland, is unique in that the polar ice mass, driven by the ocean currents and the Arctic winds, slowly rotates in a clockwise direction near Canada. As a result, the Arctic pack ice is driven into the channels between these Canadian islands. Consequently the outward channels to the Arctic Ocean, such as the McClure Straits, near the end of the winter have the worst accumulation of tortured twisted ice in the Arctic. This is the reason why passage through the Canadian Archipelago, the famed "Northwest Passage" to the east, was denied so long. In fact, even the more recent voyage of the *Manhattan,* specifically designed to operate in heavy winter ice, was forced during its 1969 trip (fig. 12.11) to return to an alternate route when she tried to pass through the McClure Straits.

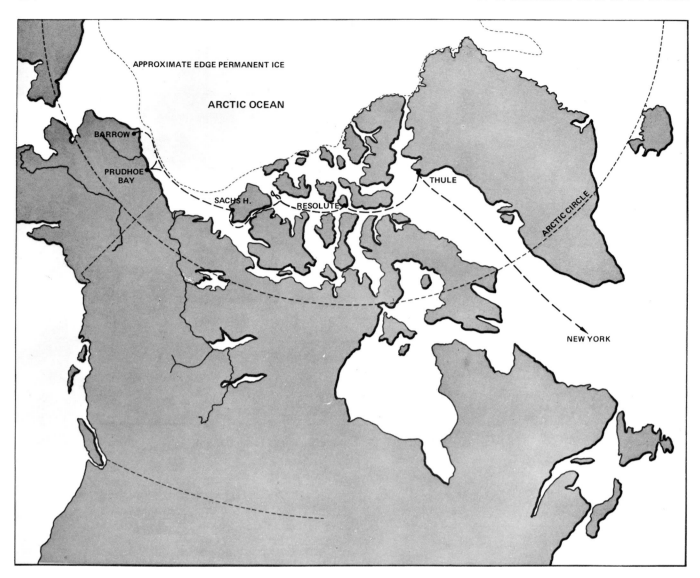

Fig. 12.11   Route of the SS *Manhattan*, fall 1969.

Ground Transport — Strategic problems of World War II forced the United States and Canada to build the Alcan Highway (fig. 12.12). This impetus led to the building of a road from the Hay River terminus of the railroad at Great Slave Lake to the mines and town of Yellowknife and then, later on, paralleling the Mackenzie up the Mackenzie Valley to Fort Simpson. Plans exist to extend this road to Norman Wells and eventually to Inuvik. The latter area, of course, will be in permafrost regions, so special techniques will be required for a year-round road. Currently a winter road exists along the Mackenzie (Ministry of Transport, 1970).

There are no railroads in the Canadian Arctic. The White Pass Railway, 175 kilometers (110 miles), from Skagway to Whitehorse was the first near-Arctic railroad built (1898) in North America, some 20 years before the U.S.S.R. Trans-Siberian Railroad was completed across Siberia. The Great Slave Lake Railroad, at about the same latitude as the White Pass Railroad, is 690 kilometers (430 miles) long. This railroad, a project of

the 1960s, goes from Edmonton to Hay River and serves as a logistic link to transport bulk cargo by barge up the Mackenzie River, and to ship ore from Pine Point.

The transport of oil by pipelines has received recently considerable political, economic, and technical analysis in Canada and the United States. The problem to be solved is the engineering design of a long pipeline system to transport the crude oil over some of the most isolated and rugged terrain in the world. A considerable portion of the pipeline must pass over the permanently frozen tundra, which requires special care to insure that stable construction is assured, while the occasional spills are controlled with tolerable damage. The prevalence of earthquake tremors forces an additional set of engineering problems. The well-drained permafrost regions require different construction techniques from the poorly drained regions. The effects of the various forms of pipeline construction on the migratory habits of the indigenous animals are also being determined.

Canada proposes oil and gas lines from the Arctic

paralleling the Mackenzie River and the roadway they hope to build. If the United States does not build its own lines, the oil may flow through Canadian pipelines.

Air Transport — Strategic considerations have been primarily responsible for development of much of the Canadian and American Arctic transportation techniques. Airfields were built on the tundra, and the barge, ship, and icebreaker support systems now so commonly used were organized.

Of recent years resource exploration has given added impetus to air transport of heavy cargo; for instance, complete oil-drilling rigs are designed so that they can be packaged in sections transportable by aircraft or helicopter.

The transport of people, important cargo, and perishables to native villages is by scheduled airlines to hub points, such as Resolute, Frobisher Bay, Churchill, Yellowknife, and Whitehorse. From these distribution points air service is available by bush feeder lines to many native villages. Figure 12.13 shows principal commercial airports in the Canadian Arctic (Ministry of Transport, 1970).

Marine Transport — Bulk, heavy cargo is shipped to the eastern Canadian Arctic during the brief summer by ships, and to the middle and western coast by barge coming up the broad Mackenzie River, much as is done in Siberia. Figure 12.12 shows marine routes to the Canadian Arctic.

The primary mode of transport to the Arctic is by ship, thence by barge and/or lighter craft, as required, to the beach. There are few docks at these ports, and consequently the lightering and off-loading is extremely time-consuming and expensive. The multiple handling of cargo results in much damage. Local ice conditions can simplify or greatly aggravate this situation, or make it impossible. Recently the Canadians have evaluated U.S. heavy-lift helicopters for the lightering job. They most certainly expedite the unloading and minimize damage

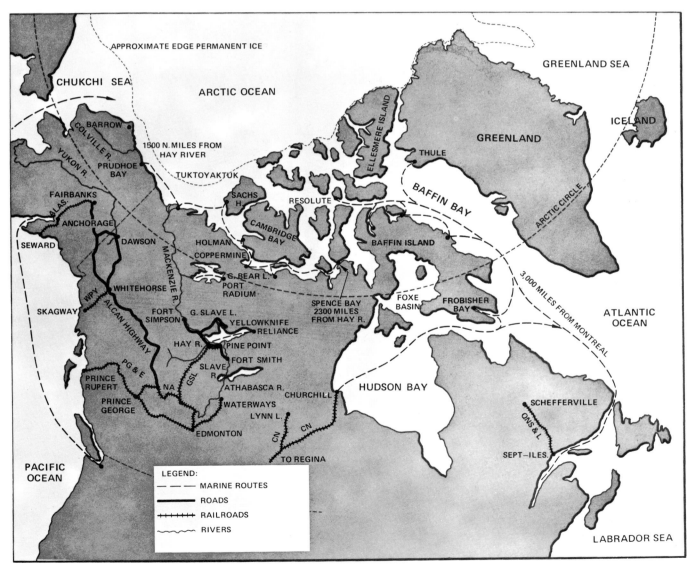

Fig. 12.12.   Transportation routes of Northern Canada.

and, in time, may pay their way for future continued usage. Figure 12.14 shows the helicopter in use for this service and illustrates the ice and shore problem.

Table 12.3 lists typical tonnage carried by barge and ship into the Canadian Arctic.

Alaskan Transportation

The northern portion of Alaska extends above the Arctic Circle and is separated from the lower portion by the rugged Brooks Range. The alluvial outwash plain and foothills of this east-west mountain range is called the North Slope. This treeless mountain range together with the permafrost are a formidable deterrent to transportation. There are no railroads or year-round roads to northern Alaska. There is a winter road, the so-called Hickel Highway, through the Brooks Range; however, in the early 1970s, it is not in use. The primary means of transport is by air to Point Barrow and the Prudhoe

Bay area, and by ship and barge through the Bering Sea. Figure 12.15 shows Northern Alaska Arctic air routes, and figure 12.16 shows Northern Alaska surface transportation routes.

TABLE 12.3

Marine Transport to the Canadian Arctic in 1970

Category	Cargo (tons)
Eastern Arctic	
Government (military and Indian affairs and northern development)	60,000
Non-government (Hudson Bay, O/L exploration, and general cargo)	70,000
Total	130,000
Western Arctic	
Athabasca, and Mackenzie River, Great Bear Lake, and Great Slave Lake: total cargo	275,000

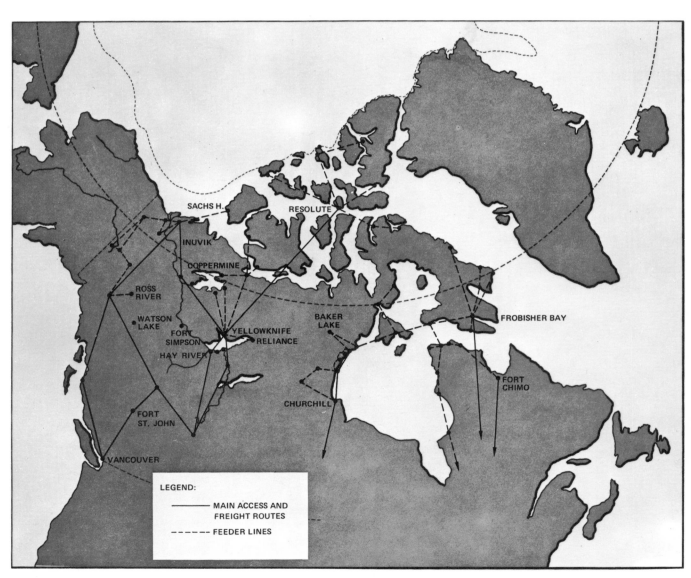

Fig. 12.13.   Commercial airline service of Canada.

(Sikorsky Aircraft)

Fig. 12.14.   Resupply in the Canadian East Arctic, using heavy-lift helicopter for lightering.

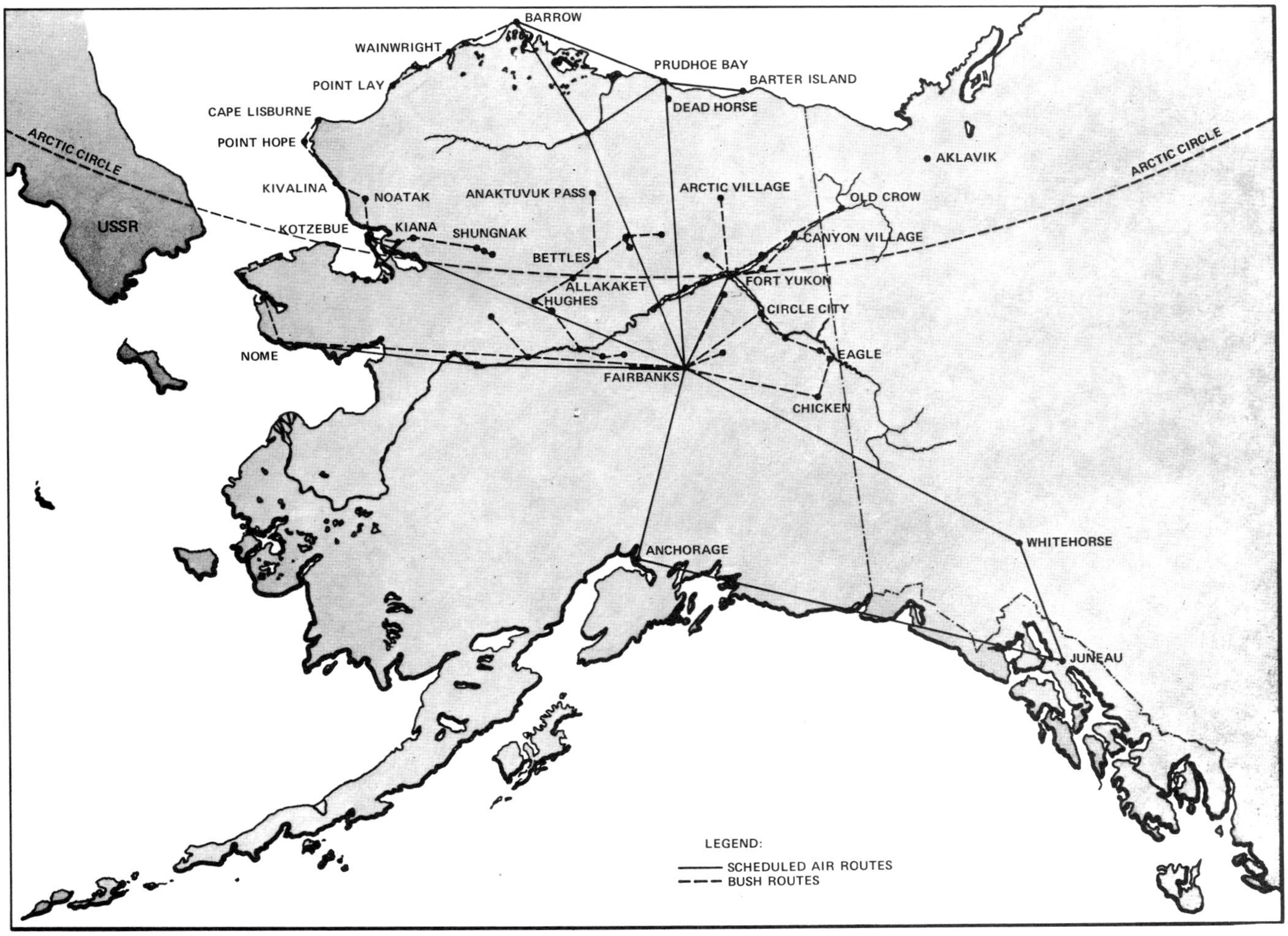

Fig. 12.15.   Northern Alaska air transportation routes.

Ground Transport — Although dog teams are still occasionally used in the winter in Alaska, the snowmobile has replaced them in most places for personal use and work (fig. 12.17).

The advent of leasing of the oil development rights at Prudhoe Bay has resulted in considerable experimentation and education with ground transport on the permafrost tundra. The winter appeared to offer no problems; however, when summer came, roads and drill-rig operating areas became impossible quagmires. From this experience, it was found that operating areas and roads could be insulated from the tundra by two meters (six feet or more) of thick gravel. This insulation results in little or no melting of the permafrost and provides a stable work platform or road. The limit to road systems that can be built is established by the availability of sand and gravel. Considerable planning is going into road construction techniques aimed at minimizing the amount of sand and gravel by use of alternative or better insulation materials. Road construction will always remain an exceedingly laborious task, but perhaps economically competitive in the long run.

In addition to developing road construction tech-

niques, the Prudhoe Bay development has resulted in the evaluation of many off-road vehicles, such as tracked vehicles, surface-effect vehicles, and low-pressure large-tire conventional and nonconventional power transmitters to the tire systems (fig. 12.18) (Burt, 1970).

Marine Transport — Marine transport to the northern slope of Alaska is the primary method of transportation of bulk and heavy cargo. Table 12.4 summarizes the tonnage transported to northern Alaska in 1969, 1970, and 1971. Marine transport is either around Alaska through the Bering Sea or up the Mackenzie River and thence along the coast. Historically and geographically, shipping to Point Barrow and the west is very limited in the time available. From mid-June to mid-September ships can normally find a period when the floating pack ice will move away from shore and the ship can travel in and unload. However, beyond Point Barrow is the dividing point between the Chukchi Sea and Beaufort Sea. These two seas have different currents, and consequently floating ice will have different paths, resulting in considerable turbulence when the two ice masses meet. The confluence of these two seas results in a hazardous

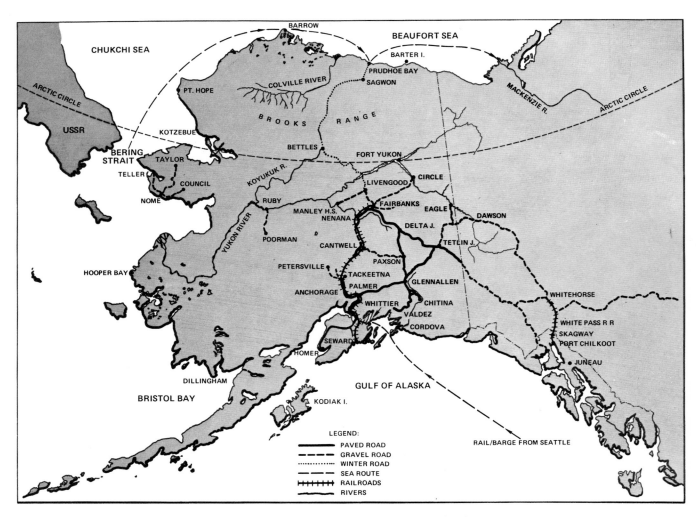

Fig. 12.16.   Surface transportation routes of Alaska.

(B. M. Buck, Delco Electronics Division, General Motors Corporation)
Fig. 12.17.   Snowmobile and sled on ARLIS V, spring 1970.

shipping situation. If a ship is to the east of Point Barrow and the ice shifts shoreward, the ship is trapped, which has happened many times, resulting in ships spending the entire winter there. Figure 12.19 shows a ship and barges in the Arctic Ocean.

The shallow water and the extensive continental shelf, together with the lack of dock facilities, considerably complicate marine shipping. Shallow-draft ships and barges are used as much as possible; however all cargo has to be lightered to shore. At Prudhoe Bay a causeway has been built and used with considerable success (fig. 12.20). Since the shallow ocean freezes solid to the bottom, the causeway is also frozen in and therefore is protected from damage from floating ice much of the winter. Large deep-draft ships, such as the *Manhattan,* have to stand off shore at least 19 kilometers (12 miles) to maintain anchoring depths.

In addition to handling commercial shipping, the Bureau of Indian Affairs runs a ship which yearly resupplies native village hospitals and schools around the coast of Alaska; the government contracts annually for a barge to resupply the DEW Line sites and other government installations. Table 12.4 lists the tonnage carried by these ships.

TABLE 12.4

Alaskan Marine and Motor Transport Tonnage North of the Arctic Circle, 1969–1971

Category	1969 (tons)	1970 (tons)	1971 (tons)
Marine (barge and ship) Government Bureau of Indian Affairs	7,000 approx.	3,600*	7,000 approx.
Other	13,000 approx.	13,000 approx.	12,700
Oil development and Pipeline companies †	110,000	253,000	23,000
Motor Freight (winter road) Oil development companies	‡	44,000	not used

*A total of 6,430 tons was planned for Barrow and Wainwright; however, only 3,600 tons were discharged due to ice. The balance of 2,800 tons was delivered at Seward for later air freight.

†SOURCE: Personal correspondence U.S. Department of Commerce, Maritime Commission, Western Regional Office, San Francisco, California, 13 December 1971.

‡No count is available prior to 1970, at which time a "check station" was established by the State of Alaska Transportation Commission (ATC). Personal correspondence ATC, 6 December 1971.

(Naval Arctic Research Laboratory)
Fig. 12.18.   Army land-train low-ground-pressure vehicle.

Fig. 12.19. A seagoing barge with tug and icebreaker support in the Arctic.

(Red Stack)

Fig. 12.20. The causeway at Prudhoe Bay.

(Red Stack)

Air Transport — The building of the DEW Line sites, their resupply, and now the Prudhoe Bay development show that tremendous amounts of goods can be transported into the Alaskan Arctic by aircraft. With landing strips, goods can be delivered any time of the year. In 1968 when oil companies were drilling at Prudhoe Bay, the entire drilling rig, fuel, and support equipment were flown in. The normal and stretched versions of the Hercules turboprop were used to transport 5,902,000 kilograms (13 million pounds) of equipment for the British Petroleum Oil Company from Fairbanks and Anchorage to the North Slope (Butler, personal correspondence). Table 12.5 lists the air cargo carried in the years 1967 to 1971.

The light aircraft is the true "family car" in Alaska. On wheels, floats, or skis, it can go anywhere.

The use of aircraft to support research at floating ice stations is an interesting example of Arctic transport. Since 1955 the United States has had a research group on a floating ice island, T-3 (Fletcher's Island), spawned by the ice shelves of Ellesmere Island or Greenland. This large thick block of ice is so substantial that large aircraft, such as the Hercules C-130 aircraft weighing 79,450 kilograms (175,000 pounds), can land safely during the winter. However, during the summer, from approximately 15 June to 15 September, the surface is so textured and rough with melted ponds that even small aircraft cannot land there. Consequently, the ice island is effectively isolated for three months of the year.

Greenland Transportation

Greenland is the only Arctic land mass which has an accumulation of thousands of feet of ice similar to the Antarctic ice mass. Transportation is by seasonal coastal marine craft, commercial aircraft, principally along the western coast, ski equipped aircraft, and helicopters. On the ice sheet, tracked vehicles are the principal means of transportation.

Summary of Transportation Techniques in the Arctic

Air Transport — The Hercules C-130 heavy cargo [900 to 22,700 kilogram load (2,000 to 50,000 pounds), depending on range] aircraft has had great impact on air freight to the Arctic. It would appear that the significance of air as a means of transport of freight will continue to grow as even larger aircraft become available. Since 1969 a stretched version of the Hercules 100-30 has been available. It can transport the 14.3-meter (50-foot) pipeline sections, previously only carried by barge. Jet airplanes, Boeing 727 and 737, are certified for gravel runways. The Lockheed C-5A and Boeing 747, if qualified for gravel runways, are attractive candidates in the Arctic during the winter when the ground is frozen and large concentrated loads can be tolerated. The Soviets are not laggards in cargo aircraft technology, having the world's heaviest lift rotary-wing aircraft.

There appears to be no competition to the fixed-wing airplane as a method of transporting people and precious or perishable cargo into and within the Arctic. The reliable jet or turboprop aircraft with ability for cold weather start has had considerable impact on Arctic aviation; consequently Arctic flying has become practicable and relatively safe. See table 12.6 for a list of large payload aircraft. Surveys have been made of ice-free Arctic airstrips, particularly in Greenland — dry lake beds, dry glaciated valleys, and so on.

The helicopter has been used extensively in the Arctic since 1955 by both the military and commercial airlines for transporting important cargo and personnel. The helicopter is coming into general use in the Arctic as a work platform. As has already been mentioned, the heli-

TABLE 12.5

Air Cargo to North of Brooks Range, Alaska, 1967–1971

	Year	Passengers	Mail (tons)	Freight (tons)
Commercial Carrier*				
Barrow	1967	5,489	724	982
	1968	5,976	835	1,106
	1969	7,549	877	1,073
	1970	12,976	1,145	1,750
Dead Horse/				
Prudhoe Bay	1969	8,880	—	2,621
	1970	14,466	—	1,579
Other Freight†	1969	—	—	42,000
	1970	—	—	100,000
	1971‡	—	—	72,000

*Personal correspondence: Mr. J. G. Barnes, Wein Consolidated Airlines, Inc., Anchorage, Alaska.

†Personal correspondence: Department of Commerce, Air Transport Commission, State of Alaska.

‡Ten months only.

TABLE 12.6

Characteristics of Large-Payload Fixed-Wing Cargo Aircraft

Designation	Name	Manufacture*	Power†	Gravel Runways#	Payload (1000 lb)	Maximum# T/O Wt. (1000 lb)	Maximum# Land Wt. (1000 lb)	Runway Length# (1000 feet) T/O	Runway Length# (1000 feet) Landing	Range Maximum Payload# (1000 nmi)
USA										
FH-227E	Friendship	FH	TP	—	11.2	45.5	45.0	3.6	4.1	0.6
C-123K	Provider	FH	Rec	Yes	15.0	60.0	60.0	1.2	1.8	1.0
C-119K		FH	Rec	Yes	20.0	77.0	77.0	1.5	3.2	0.9
C-130E	Hercules	L	TP	Yes	45.0	175.0	130.0	5.6	3.7	4.1
L-100-30	Super Hercules	L	TP	Yes	53.6	155.0	135.0	6.0	4.8	1.8
B-377SGT	Guppy 201	AS/B	TP	Yes	54.0	170.0	160.0	8.4	6.7	0.4
727-200		B	Jet	Yes	40.6	172.0	150.0	8.6	5.1	1.1
737-200C		B	Jet	Yes	36.3	115.5	103.0	5.6	4.0	2.1
747-200F	Freighter	B	Jet	No	257.8	775.0	630.0	10.9	7.2§	2.5
C-5A	Galaxy	L	Jet	Yes	220.0	728.0	635.8	6.5	4.0	3.0
DC-8/63CF	Trader	McD	Jet	No	118.5	355.0	275.0	11.5	5.9	4.5
DC-9-40		McD	Jet	No	34.2	114.0	102.0	8.0	4.8	1.0
C-141A (minuteman)	Starlifter	L	Jet	Yes	86.2	300.6	257.5	5.1	4.1	2.5
Japan										
YS11A-700		NAMC	Jet	NA	16.9	55.1	·54.0	4.2	2.2	0.6
Germany/France										
C-160		Transall	TP	—	35.2	108.2	108.2	2.6	2.1	1.1
USSR										
AN-22	Cock‡	—	TP	—	176.3	551.1	NA	4.2	2.6	2.7
AN-26	Curl‡	—	TP	—	11.0	53.0	NA	NA	NA	0.7
IL-18D	Coot‡	—	TP	—	30.0	141.0	NA	4.2	2.8	2.0
TU-114	Cleat‡	—	TP	—	66.1	377.0	NA	8.2	4.6	3.3

SOURCE: Jane's **All the World's Aircraft** 1972–73 and prior issues in the cases of older aircraft.

*FH = Fairchild-Hiller	AS = Aero Spacelines	‡NATO names.
L = Lockheed	Transall = French German Conglomerate	§FAA minimum.
McD = McDonnell Douglas	†TP = Turboprop	#NA = Not available
B = Boeing	Rec = Reciprocating	

Fig. 12.21.   The icebreaker tanker SS *Manhattan.*

copter has demonstrated its ability to lighter the entire ship's cargo to the storage site on the beach in the Canadian eastern Arctic.

Helicopters and small aircraft are the primary search-and-rescue vehicles in the Arctic. An example is the evacuation of an individual and the body of a second man from T-3 Island in the summer of 1970. T-3 Island at that time was close to the Pole; since it was summer, the aircraft normally used to supply the island could not land. Consequently, HH-3E (military version of S-61) Aerospace Rescue and Recovery helicopters equipped with an in-air refueling probe and trained crews were dispatched by Headquarters, Scott Air Force Base, to Thule, Greenland, and from there 600 nautical miles to T-3, refueling in air twice during the round trip (anonymous, Aerospace Rescue and Recovery Service).

The primary disadvantages of the helicopter are its short range, weather limitations, expensive maintenance, and problems in ice fog and blowing snow.

Marine Transport — Can an icebreaking ship be built to operate nearly year-round in the Arctic either through the Canadian Archipelago or across the top of Siberia? The answer undoubtedly is "yes." However, such critical characteristics as shaft horsepower, displacement, bow design, beam, and the type of materials to withstand ice-loading and intense cold are determined directly by the selection of the areas through which the ship must pass and the times of the year.

The experimental ship *Manhattan* (fig. 12.21) made two trips to the Arctic in 1969 and 1970; figure 12.11 shows the route of the 1969 trip. The *Manhattan* report (Mookhoek and Bielstein, 1971) indicates that Humble Oil designers know what would be required for an icebreaker tanker. Based on the *Manhattan* experience, the ship would probably be bigger, with considerably more power, and should make extensive use of high cold-strength steels. In particular, it should have sensors to detect the approximate ice course. The power required is probably close to that shown in table 12.7. It should be noted that table 12.7 does not include the effects of pressure-ridged or rough ice, which can considerably increase the impact loads.

Probably as significant as the ship's design are the practical solutions to the other ancillary, yet crucial, question which, when considered together with the ship design problem, affects its cost/effectiveness versus other transportation techniques. This ancillary problem is how to operate in the shallow waters of the Arctic without deep water docks and protected anchorages. An example of the problem is that the *Manhattan* would have to stand off Prudhoe Bay 19 kilometers (12 miles) at sea to take on oil, which must somehow be transported in a practical manner over or under 19 kilometers (12 miles) of wracked ice. This same problem applies also to the consideration of cargo submarines or towed submerged cargo.

Land Transport — Efficient year-round land transport in the Arctic still lies in the future. There are two possibilities in the future for off-road vehicles. The truly amphibious surface-effect vehicle, which is discussed at length in the following section, is one. Alternately, there are soft-tire vehicles with very low ground pressures, suitable for ice and snow, and low-ground-pressure tracked vehicles which are suitable winter and summer (but are so far barred from use on the tundra). An alternative to these is the building of insulated roads of reasonable thickness for heavier pressure conventional vehicles. Engineering and testing of various road construction techniques have been energetic only of recent years, and we may yet see a revolution in Arctic roads similar to those in urban areas after asphalt was developed.

Future Arctic Transportation

The air-cushion vehicle has been called the *fourth basic technique for transportation* that has been discovered since the dawn of civilization. The others are wheeled transportation, the boat, and the aircraft. Currently the air-cushion vehicles come in two basic varieties, the surface-effect ship (SES) and the truly amphibious surface-effect vehicle (SEV).

The Surface-Effect Ship

The SES is supported on an air cushion, but has rigid sidewalls and is generally powered by a water jet or a more-or-less conventional screw. Its chief virtue is its speed, which may well range up to 80 knots for a vessel of several thousand metric-ton weight. In applications in polar regions, it is restricted to regions where there is open water. If it ever plays a part in satisfying the

TABLE 12.7

Estimated Power Requirements for Large Arctic Cargo Ships*

Average Ice Cover Thickness (feet)	Estimated Shaft Horsepower Required† (200,000-ton deadweight ship)	
	3-knot speed	8-knot speed
0	—	5K
2	15K	30K
4	50K	75K
6	105K	145K
8	155K	245K

*SOURCE: Arctic Transport Conference Proceedings, Yellowknife, Northwest Territories, 1970. Comparable papers with approximately the same conclusions are to be found in Mookhoek and Bielstein (1971) and Voelker (1971).

†K = 1,000 horsepower.

transportation requirements in Arctic regions, it will be because of its rapid passage time and shallow draft. In the relatively short time that passages open in the polar ice in the regions near Alaska, Northern Canada, and Siberia, the vastly shortened round-trip time means that a considerable cargo can be handled in the short season of open leads. The second important point is the ability to save time because the vessel can come closer to shore to deliver cargo — simple shallow water causeways already in existence, for example, at Prudhoe Bay avoid the need for lightering and result in shorter turn-around time. However, there is no deliberate effort, to our knowledge, to develop the SES for polar or Arctic use.

The Surface-Effect Vehicle

On the contrary, there is a considerable effort devoted to the design of an Arctic SEV (ARPA, 1971), which has the potential of a near-ideal polar vehicle. It is driven by an air propeller or jet thrustor, and the supportive air cushion is restrained by a flexible skirt, not a rigid wall. The skirt itself does not usually make any contact with the surface. The consequences are that it can traverse ice, snow, water, land, mud, tundra and muskeg — the complete variety of Arctic winter or summer surfaces. In the latter cases, the relatively low cushion pressures (of the order of one to one and one-half psi) will do comparatively negligible damage to the terrain, a not inconsiderable advantage.

While these high prospects for the SEV are realistic, there are some negative features. The SEV has limited slope-climbing abilities, a factor which mitigates against or requires special designs for its use in rugged or mountainous terrain. It is expensive in fuel and, for that reason, is limited in range of operation. Its development for Arctic use is still far in the future, with a number of difficult technical problems to be solved, notably the skirt material problem, the obstacle-sensing and braking systems, and an efficient structural design.

Nevertheless, the SEV has a potential of speeds in the 80–120 knot range, ranges of several thousand miles in a multi-thousand metric-ton version, and the above-mentioned total amphibious capabilities. This makes it independent of season of the year, for its performance on ice is as good or better than over water; it is independent of port facilities, for it readily traverses from ice or water to shore; and it is probably the only large vehicle that can easily traverse frozen or soft tundra. For these reasons, we expect a revolution in the transportation system for the Far North, while the systems that ply the rivers from the interior, as in Siberia, may be affected as well, although to a lesser degree.

Principles of Operation — In view of the emerging importance of this revolutionary transportation system, a few words about its principles of operation may help to clarify the picture.

Figure 12.22 shows a highly schematic cross-section each of a canonical SEV and SES. The vehicle is sup-

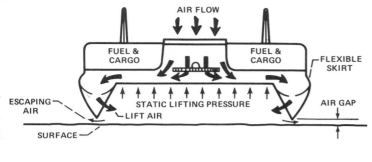

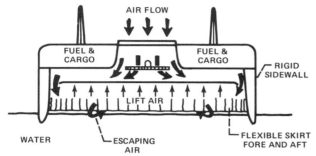

Fig. 12.22. Cross-section diagrams of the two basic types of air-cushion vehicles. *Top:* The SEV, or surface-effect vehicle (rigid wall type). *Bottom:* The SES, or surface-effect ship (flexible skirt type).

ported by the air trapped between the body of the vehicle, the skirt surrounding the vehicle, and the surface (ground, water, and ice). The air can escape around the periphery of the skirt, and this annulus is made quite small so that the air bubble can be replenished by means of fans or blowers. To get an order of magnitude, in the

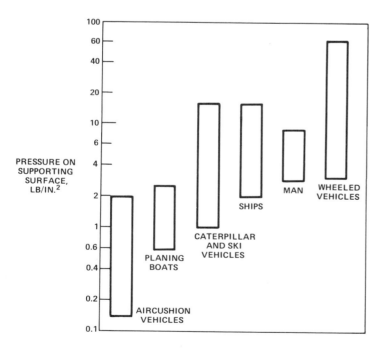

Fig. 12.23. Comparison of footprint pressures of surface transport vehicles.

case of the SEV, a vessel of two thousand metric-tons gross weight would be of the order of 1,860 square meters (20,000 square feet) in platform area, and consequently a pressure of about 0.11 kilograms per square centimeter (1.5 pounds per square inch) is sufficient to lift it clear of the surroundings. Figure 12.23 compares the footprint pressure of the SEV and other surface transport vehicles.

The SRN-4, or *Mountbatten* class, is the largest of the currently operational SEVs. It weighs 180 metric-tons (198 short tons) and has a disposable load, including fuel, of 69 metric-tons (75 short tons). It is currently in cross-channel service between England and France and carries 250 people and 30 vehicles, at a maximum speed of 120 kilometers per hour (75 miles per hour). The propulsion of the vehicle is by large standard swiveling aircraft-type propellers. By rotating the pylons, the direction of thrust can be altered to furnish steering without any contact with land or water.

Figure 12.24 shows the SRN-4 discharging its cargo at Calais. It has run up the beach directly from the water without a pause and scarcely slackening speed. Its reliability, in terms of making scheduled runs, currently exceeds 92 percent, the chief problem being skirt wear and consequently down-time for maintenance. Since its skirts are 240 centimeters (8 feet) high, it can traverse waves up to 180 centimeters (6 feet) in height, for the skirts simply tuck under to override the obstacles.

In general the skirts are flexible enough to tuck under for obstacles (rigid or water) up to about 75 percent of the skirt height. A two-thousand metric-ton craft would demand skirts of about 610 centimeters (20 feet) in height. Correspondingly, obstacles up to 450 centimeters (15 feet) can be passed over safely. This is a vital factor in crossing large pressure ridges and rubble fields (see fig. 12.5). Fortunately, the mean height of pressure ridges is about 275 centimeters (9 feet), and only in rare cases (less than 2 percent of the time) will ice mounds exceed 450 centimeters (15 feet). In such cases, the vehicle must detour this obstacle and find a more desirable path.

Operational Status — Reference has already been made to the cross-channel operation of the *Mountbatten* class in the English Channel. Smaller versions of this craft operate in regular service in the Solent in England. The French have a Nice-Cannes service in a somewhat different realization of an SEV. There is a Malmo-Copenhagen ferry run. In addition, craft development is going on in Japan, Italy, Sweden, Canada, the Soviet Union, and the U.S.A.

In 1970 four SRN-6 craft went north of the Arctic Circle for three months of trials. Based on the island of Andoya, off the coast of Norway, they were thoroughly evaluated in operational experience. Characteristically they were operated in the fjords, in sea states (roughness of water) up to 6, in blizzards, under icing conditions, across ice, and across ice-water interfaces. Temperatures ranged to −22°C. Basically there was no doubt of the ability of the craft to operate and perform its missions under these conditions.

Late in the spring of 1971, the U.S.A. operated an SK-5 craft (very similar to the SRN-6) in a series of trials in the Point Barrow, Alaska, area (fig. 12.25). While these were primarily engineering tests of obstacle sensing, stability, control, and dynamics, the exercise provided additional confidence that the SEV is of high potential use. Other SEVs were used to support the oil-drilling operations in Prudhoe Bay. We have no specific information, but all reports indicated relatively good performance.

One final mention should be made of the trip taken by the British SRN-6 up the Mackenzie River in 1970. Here the terrain was water, ice, snow-covered ice, and the interfaces among them. The craft performed well and provided river travel in the Far North at 40-knot speeds.

Table 12.8 shows some of the basic parameters of the three vehicles discussed. But more ambitious projects are in the offing.

TABLE 12.8

Comparison of Hovercraft

	SRN-4	SRN-6	SK-5
Gross weight (tons)	198	12	10.5
Length (feet)	130	48	39
Width (feet)	78	23	23
Payload, plus fuel (tons)	75	6	2
Maximum speed (MPH)	75	60	70
Cruising speed (MPH)	57	46	50
Passengers	250	37	14
Cars	30	0	0

Fig. 12.24.   The SRN-4 hovercraft at Calais, France.

Fig. 12.25   SK-5 hovercraft on fast ice off Point Barrow, Alaska.

(B. S. Walker, Applied Physics Laboratory, Johns Hopkins University)

ARPA Arctic SEV Program—In 1970 the Advanced Research Projects Agency (ARPA) embarked on an ambitious program aimed deliberately at providing high-speed all-area all-weather transportation suitable for the total Arctic region. Preceded by several years of study, planning and evaluation, the skirted SEV was selected as the prototype vehicle. Plans are to develop the technology and a test vehicle with the following gross characteristics: gross weight up to 1,000 metric-tons; length, in the 60-meter (200 feet) class; width, in the 30-meter (100 feet) class; payload, up to 350 metric-tons; maximum speed, up to 150 knots; and nominal range, up to 3,200 kilometers (2,000 miles). Figure 12.26 is one concept of what such a vehicle might look like.

The thrust of the ARPA program is to develop the necessary technology. Primary problem areas have been identified which include: skirt material, flexible and rugged in the Arctic environment; lift system, efficient and stable; sensory system, to provide safe passage in the region of ice and man-made obstacles; structures, to provide a safe structure with the lightweight characteristics of aircraft construction; and habitability, to provide a low-vibration environment for human occupancy.

A host of almost equally important other problems must also be solved — efficient propulsion, to curb the demand for fuel; sensors and controls, to ensure stability and trim; braking systems; efficient blowers and fans for the lift system; and integration of all subsystems for total vehicle operation.

It will take several years to carry the necessary development and engineering to the point where a reliable design handbook will exist. But eventually, one can foresee a test bed or engineering prototype vehicle undergoing serious trials in the polar regions.

What happens at the next stage is strictly a question of cost/benefit estimates. For year-round search-and-rescue in the remote polar regions, the SEV is almost certainly going to be the craft of choice. The aircraft is vulnerable in the summer, the helicopter suffers from short-range problems, ships cannot cut through the thick pack ice, and overland transportation is extremely arduous. For cargo use, there will be competition. In the coastal regions ships can operate during the summer season, but are costly.

The high speed of the SEV, and the absence of need for lightering, and therefore the shortened round-trip time of a factor of 5 to 10 over ships, may make it the most cost-effective means of transportation, even in coastal regions. For support of research effort in the area of the shelf in the Arctic Ocean or, indeed, to the floating island research stations, the SEV will have to be pitted against the helicopter and the fixed-wing airplane. A cost comparison of conventional techniques is shown in table 12.9.

All in all, the large logistics, SEV, when it arrives, will open up new options in travel that will surely be exploited, and the entire Arctic Ocean may well become

as accessible as Maine once was from Massachusetts in the hard January winter.

Summary and Conclusions

We have attempted a short but comprehensive description of transportation in the polar regions, but largely limiting ourselves to the Arctic Sea ice terrain, since the antipodal region does not yet appear ripe for habitation or exploitation, even though it is situated between the major populated regions. Tables 12.10 and 12.11 are terse summaries of Arctic transportation by geographical areas and transportation methods respectively.

Every conceivable means of transportation has had its day of evaluation — from dog sleds, horses, dirigibles, boats, aircraft, and cat trains to the new air-cushion vehicle, or hovercraft.

Two basic subdivisions in transportation requirements are evident, characterized by a nine-month winter and three-month summer.

In the winter, efficient and large-scale transport can be provided currently only by aircraft, mostly fixed-wing, but, in the offing, heavy-lift helicopters. No railroads exist. Hardly any auto roads exist, and there are formidable obstacles to developing a road network, notably the permafrost problem which requires thermal insulation of the roadway surface from the soil or grade. Frozen rivers are a possible route, but these are notoriously treacherous and more than one vehicle has perished through a weak shelf of ice.

Bulky cargo must hurry through the open leads in the

TABLE 12.9

Comparison of Arctic Transportation Costs to the North Slope of Alaska in 1971

Unit Costs	Distance (miles)	Costs (cents/ton mile)
Method of Transport		
Air, from closest railhead, Fairbanks	367	40.0
Marine barge		
Via Mackenzie from Hay River	1,300	7.9
Via Bering Strait from Seattle	3,000	4.0
Rail barge railroad		
Railroad cars on barge Seattle to		
Whittier, railroad Whittier to Fairbanks	1,590	2.4
Road		
Winter road Fairbanks to Prudhoe Bay		
currently not in operation		

Costs per Ton From Seattle to Prudhoe Bay	Distance (miles)	Costs (dollars/ton)
Method of Transport		
Barge	3,000	120
Railway car on barge to Whittier,	1,590	
railway to Fairbanks,	418	48
cargo aircraft to Prudhoe Bay	367	146
Total		194

SOURCE: Personal correspondence with Mr. O. G. Simpson (ARCO) and Mr. B. R. R. Butler (BP) of Anchorage, Alaska; and Lockheed Aircraft Publication "The Hercules Pipelines."

Fig. 12.26. One concept of ARPA Arctic surface-effect vehicle.

coastal regions during the all-too-brief summer. This is by no means the surest or safest ocean route imaginable. In some years the coastal waters never open up; in others the ice packs shift unpredictably and capriciously and the sturdy icebreaker is needed to effect passage. In all cases, approaching shore across the broad continental shelf is well-nigh impossible, and laborious and costly off-loading schemes must be employed. In Siberia and Canada, in the summer, however, a fortuitous group of north-flowing large rivers permits extensive tug-and-barge operation when overland transport is hopelessly mired in the thawed tundra. On the other hand, lateral transportation, except by air, is denied.

For oil, gas, or slurried materials, of course, the way is open to build pipelines into the Arctic, and there is every probability that this will occur, either in Alaska or Canada. But this is a specialized transportation system and far from general-purpose.

TABLE 12.10

Overview of Arctic Transportation by Area

Category	U.S.S.R.	Scandinavia	Alaska	Canada	Greenland	Arctic Ocean
Marine	Extensive use of river system, coastal ships, and barges; short season	Conventional shipping	Conventional coastal ships and barges; short season	Similar to U.S.S.R.	Conventional shipping limited season	Conventional shallow-draft ships and barges; near coast; icebreaker support; short season
Railroad	Integrated with rivers	Exist	Minimal	Moderate	None	
Ground	Roads between railroads and rivers	Road system exists	Short "thick" gravel road only	Sparse but growing	Tracked vehicles	Snowmobile, tracked vehicle, dog sled
Air	Extensive	Extensive	Extensive	Extensive	Adequate	Conventional fixed and rotary-wing aircraft for support of research stations and search and rescue
The Future	Unknown	Unknown	SEV (?)	SEV (?)	Unknown	SEV entire ocean; SES, coastal and rivers in open season

But looming on the horizon is a new technology in transportation that certainly on the face of it seems to surmount almost all of the problems unique to the Arctic. The air-cushion vehicle, or hovercraft, or surface-effect vehicle (to give it most of its names) is now considerably more than an inventor's dream. If it can be perfected to withstand the harsh and rigorous Arctic environment, if it can be made reliable, habitable, and not too costly to maintain and operate, then it offers speeds approaching helicopter speeds, cargo capacity akin to ocean-going ships, total terrain mobility, be it ice, water, snow, tundra — and therefore true amphibious performance.

TABLE 12.11

Overview of Arctic Transportation by Methods

Marine	Problem Areas	Future
Shallow-draft ships and barges	No deep-water docks in Alaska and Canada	Heavy lift helicopter for lightering
Carry own lightering equipment	No protected anchorage in Alaska and	and off-loading
Carry shore-handling equipment	Canada, except archipelago	High-speed shallow-draft ships
Get in and out in hurry	Short season	SES/SEV coastal water
Coast Guard icebreaker support	Harsh environment	SES/SEV in rivers
Coast Guard placement and retrieval	Ice-strengthening ship requirements	Year-round navigation aius in remote areas
of navigation aids	Icebreaker support requirements	
	High insurance	
	Not enough navigation aids	
	No unloading or handling gear	
	Shallow water	
Roads/Railroads		
Winter roads only	Summer travel on tundra only or muskeg	Greater use of very low ground
Short deep gravel roads	possible with very low ground	pressure amphibious craft
Large balloon tire vehicles	pressure vehicles	Development of inexpensive, high-bearing
Tracked vehicles	Any structure on tundra must be	strength, good insulation, road building
Amphibious craft	thermally insulated	materials and techniques
Aircraft		
Gravel runways	Lack of weather reporting network	Newer electronic landing instrumentation
Limited and old electronics landing	Lack of instrumented runways for	equipment and more places
instrumentation systems	poor weather operation	Longer runways
Don't fly when weather is bad	Lack of hard-surfaced runways; summertime	Hard-surfaced runways insulated
Visual flight rules (pilotage)	Essentially no long-range navigation	from permafrost
	capability above Arctic Circle	Installation of beacons and hyperbolic
		navigation aids
Search and Rescue		
Light slow ski-equipped aircraft in winter	Very long-range system required	Surface-effects vehicle
In-air refueled helicopters summer and winter	Quick reaction required because of climate	
Coast Guard icebreaker, summer	Travel and stopping on thin pressure-ridged	
	ice mantle	
	Limits size and type of ground system	

BIBLIOGRAPHY

Advanced Research Projects Agency
    1971 Arctic surface effects vehicle program. Fifth Canadian Symposium on Air Cushion Technology, Ottawa, Canada. September.
Armstrong, T. E.
    1965 Russian settlement in the North. Cambridge University Press.
    1970a Northern sea route. Inter-Nord no. 12, 1968–70.
    1970b Soviet northern developments with some Alaskan parallels and contrasts. ISEGR Occasional Papers no. 2. University of Alaska, College. October.
Barrow, John
    1971 A chronological history of voyages into Arctic regions 1818, [and supplement], Voyages of discovery and research within the Arctic regions from the year 1818 to the present (1846). Reprinted by Barnes and Noble, Inc.
Boyer, David S.
    1968 The Canadian North: emerging giant. National Geographic, vol. 134, no. 1, July.

Burt, G. R.
    1970 Travel on thawed tundra. Institute of Arctic Environmental Engineering, University of Alaska, College. Note 7005, September.
Butler, B. R. R., Operations Manager, BP Alaska.
    n.d. Report of 68–69 Move by James Moon. Seawest, Inc. Tustin, California.
Conger, Dean
    1967 Siberia: Russia's frozen frontier. National Geographic, vol. 131, no. 3, March.
Demidov, P.
    1970 Transport in Siberia and the Far East. Soviet News Release. November 20.
Director of Information, Headquarters, Aerospace Rescue and Recovery Service.
    n.d. Fletcher's Ice Island (T-3) Mission Narrative. U.S. Air Force. Scott Air Force Base, Illinois.
First International Arctic Aviation Conference
    1971 Office of the Mayor, Fairbanks, Alaska. May.

Hok, Jerome R.
    1969   A reconnaissance of tractor trails and related phenomena on the north slope of Alaska. U.S. Department of Interior, Bureau of Land Management.

Iverskoi, I. (Novosti Press Agency Correspondent)
    n.d.   Waterways in the U.S.S.R. Soviet News Release.

Kanin, Y. (APN correspondent)
    n.d.   Northern lights built in Tyumen. Soviet News Release.

Keating, B.
    1970   *Manhattan* makes the historic Northwest Passage. National Geographic, March.

Krypton, C.
    1956   The northern sea route and the economy of the Soviet north. Fredric A. Praeger, Publisher.

Ley, W., and the editors of Life Magazine
    1962   The Poles. Time Incorporated. New York.

Ministry of Transport and Department of Indian Affairs and Northern Development
    1970   Proceedings of the Arctic Transportation Conference, Yellowknife, Northwest Territories. 3 vols., December.

Mookhoek, A. D., and W. J. Bielstein
    1971   Problems associated with the design of an Arctic marine transportation system. Off-Shore Technology Conference Paper OTC–1426.

Polar Transport Requirements Study Report
    1968   3 vols. U.S. Coast Guard. November.

Sater, F. B. (ed.)
    1969a   The Arctic Basin. Arctic Institute of North America. August.
    1969b   Arctic and Middle North Transportation. Arctic Institute of North America.

Shevelyov, M. I. (Chief of the Polar Division of the Soviet Civil Air Service)
    n.d.   Soviet wings over the poles. Novosti Press Agency, Soviet News Release.

Sosnov, I. (First Deputy Minister of Transport Construction of the U.S.S.R.)
    1971   The development of Soviet railways. Soviet News Release, January 26.

Symposium on Arctic Logistics Support Technology
    1971   Proceedings Published by the Arctic Institute of North America, Montreal. November.

Transport Routes of Tomorrow
    1971   *Gudok*. Soviet News Release, July 6.

Tregubov, M. (Novosti Press Agency [APN] Correspondent)
    n.d.   Transport in the Soviet North. Soviet News Release.

Voelker, R. P.
    1971   Ships to transit the Arctic Ocean. Symposium on Arctic Logistics Support Technology.

CHAPTER 13

HEALTH AND SANITATION PROBLEMS IN THE ARCTIC*

J. W. Grainge
Department of Environment, Edmonton, Alberta, Canada

John W. Shaw
Environmental Protection Service, Department of National Health and Welfare, Edmonton, Alberta, Canada

The Arctic desert region of Canada, comprising about 1,500,000 square kilometers, is defined by the 25-centimeter annual isohyet and the 10-degree Centigrade isotherm of the average temperature of the warmest month. This is to say that it covers that area north of a line beginning at a point about 80 kilometers south of the coast on the Yukon-Alaska border and running through the Mackenzie delta, Amundsen Gulf and Bathurst Inlet, across Back River to a point about 160 kilometers south of Baker Lake, then through Chesterfield Inlet, Southampton Island and the Foxe Peninsula, across the center of Baffin Island, and then south along the northeastern coast of the Cumberland Peninsula.

Approximately eleven thousand people lived in this region at the beginning of the 1970s. The majority were native people living in about twenty-five settlements. There were fifty men in five High-Arctic weather stations and approximately one thousand men in the twenty or so military and government establishments — for example, the DEW Line stations, the Canadian Forces Station at Alert, and the airport complex at Resolute Bay. In addition, increasing numbers of people are engaging in scientific studies and in oil and mineral exploration. These people are, for the most part, short-term residents.

The extreme low temperatures in the Arctic are not much lower than those that occur during midwinter in the southern Subarctic and in the northern temperate regions, in which there are hundreds of cities and towns. However, the winter season is longer, and the periods of severe weather are more prolonged. This, plus associated thermal dependent phenomena, namely permafrost, snowdrifting, and frost heaving, and also the lack of sunlight in winter, cause the major problems in public health engineering.

History

The native people of the North were formerly nomadic. They lived in groups of ten to twenty people, or two to five families. These people were scattered

*The opinions expressed in this paper are those of the authors; they do not represent the policies of the departments of Environment and National Health and Welfare of Canada.

Fig. 13.1. Log cabin with sod roof at Tuktoyaktuk (lat. 69° N, long. 133° W, 20 miles beyond the mouth of the east channel [delta] of the Mackenzie River), Northwest Territories. Logs float down the river and are blown up on the beaches. In more recent years wood-frame houses have been supplied to the Eskimos.

throughout the Mackenzie River delta and all along the coast of the Arctic mainland, the southern Arctic islands, all around Baffin Island, and along the shores of the larger lakes and rivers in the tundra areas inland from Hudson's Bay.

The people in the Mackenzie River delta lived in tents and log cabins, but elsewhere the people lived mainly in tents in summer and in igloos and half tents (tents which have an excavated floor and are heaped with snow) in winter. Sod houses were common in northern Alaska and Greenland but were seldom used in Canada.

The people moved according to the availability of animals such as caribou, birds, fish, and sea mammals on which they depended for most of their needs. They had little contact with other people.

A construction period began in approximately 1949. Schools, nursing stations, and hospitals were provided at an accelerating rate by the federal government. During the years 1955 to 1958 the United States government built the DEW Line stations at 50-mile intervals along the mainland Arctic coast in Alaska and western Canada and through the southern islands of the Arctic

Fig. 13.2.   A winter scene at Tuktoyaktuk.

archipelago in eastern Canada. The construction of these stations provided airports, communications, and radar control for civilian aircraft as well as many jobs for the local people. A program of providing small wood-frame houses for the indigenous people was begun in Inuvik in the late 1950s and was practically complete in all settlements by the early 1970s.

As schools were built, there was a gradual migration to the communities. Although the intention was to keep the children in residence at the schools while their parents continued their nomadic way of life, the parents preferred to be with their children. The people began to live in permanent settlements, and most of them became dependent on welfare.

The indigenous people had few diseases until they were contacted by people from the outside world. They

had met a few whalers and explorers along the eastern coasts in the eighteenth century and throughout the Arctic during the nineteenth century. Traders and missionaries began arriving in increasing numbers at the larger traditional summer camps during the latter part of the nineteenth century. The people then began to gather to celebrate Christmas and Easter at the nearest settlement with church and trading post.

Health educators began training Eskimos to be community health workers in 1961. These Eskimos learned about the principles of sanitation and then began to teach the people in their communities. They have rendered a valuable service, but much work has remained to be done.

Diseases

Tuberculosis

Tuberculosis has been the most serious disease among the indigenous people. It was brought by people from the outside. It spread quickly because of the lack of immunity, the overcrowded living and sleeping conditions, the frequent visiting of people even to the extent of visitors sharing the family bed, and the complete lack of medical examinations and care. It was endemic in the Arctic by the turn of the twentieth century.

The first medical thrust was aimed primarily at controlling this disease. Resident physicians were established at Aklavik and Pangnirtung in 1920 and 1930 respectively. In 1952 medical x-ray teams began flying to the settlements in the western and central Arctic for Eastertime visits, and soon thereafter a medical ship started making annual visits to all the eastern Canadian settlements. Except for occasional small outbreaks, tuberculosis became controlled in northern Canada due to the comprehensive detection and treatment programs in effect in the early 1970s.

Medical care for tuberculosis was begun even earlier in Alaska and Greenland, and the disease has been brought under control in those countries.

Other Respiratory Diseases

Since the indigenous people began congregating in communities, other diseases, principally pneumonia, influenza, and bronchitis, and also otitis media, have become one of the most important causes of morbidity and mortality among them. In Alaska, influenza and pneumonia continue to be the number one cause of nonviolent deaths. Respiratory infections account for 75 percent of the post-neonatal deaths. About 35 percent of the children surveyed had at least one episode of pneumonia or bronchitis during the first year of life, and 15 percent of all hospital admissions were for respiratory diseases (Chin, 1970).

There appears to be an unusually high incidence of otitis media, particularly in children. For example, 30 percent of the children in Cape Dorset were found to have running ears. The extent of hearing loss due to this

Fig. 13.3.   A log cabin at the left, tents in the center background, the Hudson Bay Company outbuildings at the right, and sleigh dogs in the foreground comprise this scene at Tuktoyaktuk.

disease is not fully known but is judged to be serious.

The relationships between environmental, nutritional, and genetic factors and the incidence of respiratory disease are not established. There is evidence to suggest that poor sanitation, changes in nutrition, and the frequent changes from the warm dry atmosphere inside the houses to the exceedingly cold atmosphere outside all contribute to lowering the resistance to respiratory disease.

Gastroenteritis

Gastroenteritis stems primarily from the lack of sanitary facilities; the handling of garbage, sewage, and water; and the insanitary living conditions of the indigenous people. Their casual habits of waste disposal were not a problem while they were nomadic, but these habits constitute a grave public health hazard in the settlements. Gastroenteric disease is most common in children.

Fig. 13.4. Welfare house supplied to an Eskimo family at Inuvik (lat. 68° N, long. 134° W), Northwest Territories. Gravel is provided for the house and access road, but the surrounding ground is low, and puddles contain wastewater and spilled sewage.

In addition to bacterial infections, a large proportion of small children suffer from giardiasis and secondary infections due to the persistent diarrhea and malabsorption of food.

Amebiasis is rare. One or two cases have occurred, but in individuals who had traveled to the south and probably acquired the disease there.

Skin Diseases

Impetigo and other skin diseases are common. Health education, less crowded housing, and better medical care, particularly by public health nurses, have decreased the incidence of skin diseases. They will probably continue to be common until better water supplies and more sanitary conditions are established in the native communities.

Fig. 13.5. An Eskimo girl appears to be comfortably dressed at Cambridge Bay (lat. 69° N, long. 105° W), Victoria Island, Northwest Territories.

Fig. 13.6. Eskimo parents and children and others gather for a movie in a schoolroom at Coppermine (lat. 67° N, long. 115° W), Northwest Territories.

Fig. 13.7. Log cabin and sleigh dogs at Tuktoyaktuk. Ice in barrel is to be melted down for drinking water. In more recent years water has been hauled by truck.

Infectious Hepatitis

Infectious hepatitis is a relatively common and widespread acute or subacute viral infection. It is endemic in the Canadian Arctic, and periodic epidemics occur mainly in young children.

Infectious hepatitis is presumably spread by the oral-enteric route and in general is associated with overcrowded and unsanitary housing conditions. Although occasional outbreaks have been traced to water supplies, more than 99 percent of all outbreaks are spread by person-to-person contact.

Mental Illness

Mental illness is common among all groups of people in the North, particularly in the smaller communities. Acute depression, sometimes known as "Arctic hysteria" or "being bushed," occurs most commonly in people from the outside toward the end of winter. This problem has begun to receive more recognition and study. Isolation, restricted movement, and a lack of variety in recreation appear to be contributing factors. Such things as unsatisfactory sanitary facilities cause quarrels which are out of proportion to the original problems. There is a low standard of noise attenuation in the row housing and apartments that have been constructed in the North, with a corresponding lack of privacy.

The indigenous people seem to be frustrated by the changes in their life styles, the lack of gainful employment, and the apparent discrimination and segregation. Their settlement in permanent communities has brought with it a breakdown in morale and social structure and a decrease in friendliness.

Much could be done in a variety of ways to try to improve mental health. Improvements in the architecture of residences and in community planning are needed so that people can see the sun more, enjoy warm sheltered areas within the communities, and have more privacy in their residences, even though they may be closer together. Improvements in sports and recreation also may help to reduce tensions.

Botulism

Botulism, a type of bacterial food poisoning known as food intoxication, is usually fatal. The causative organism is a soil bacteria (*Chlostridia botulinus*) which multiplies in unrefrigerated food in the absence of oxygen and produces toxins. The toxin is heat liable (destroyed by heat). The spores of the bacteria are ubiquitous in the Arctic.

Spores of the bacteria contaminate the walrus, whales, and seals when they are dressed, cleaned, and stored on the ground. The meat is usually eaten raw or only lightly cooked. The most common foodstuffs involved have been "muktuk," which consists of flippers of beluga (white whale) preserved in seal oil, "utjak" (rotted seal flippers), dried seal meat, seal liver, and fluke (tail) of gray whale. The spores vegetate when the temperature is raised during the curing processes. Two deaths at Reindeer Station resulted from seal flippers being stored in plastic bags.

Echinococcosis (hydatid disease)

Echinococcosis, a parasitic disease of ruminants and canines, is widespread among indigenous people throughout the Arctic. It takes the form of cysts on the livers and lungs of infected humans. The excrement from infected sledge dogs contains the ova (eggs) which are picked up on the dog's hair and in turn infect the hands or mitts of the natives handling them. The ova may be transferred to ice which is to be melted to provide drinking water, or directly to drinking water or food. This disease occurs much less frequently than formerly due to the decrease in numbers of sledge dogs. It is not too important from a medical point of view, though on rare occasions complications such as an abscess formation or empyema (accumulation of pus) may develop. Occasionally, a huge liver cyst may require surgical removal.

Trichinosis

Trichinosis is caused by a round worm (*Trichinella spiralis*) and is contracted by eating the encapsulated larvae in the lightly or uncooked muscle tissue of an infected mammal. The disease is uncommon in the North, but it has occurred occasionally at places especially where walruses occur. Other animals which carry the disease are lemmings and the animals which prey on them, for example, foxes, wolves and bears. The disease spreads in lemmings because they tend to be cannibalistic, when they migrate. Freezing at minus

30 degrees Centigrade for a day and half will kill the trichinosis larvae.

Rabies

Rabies is endemic among the foxes and wolves, and the sledge dogs occasionally are affected. Unfortunately, the Greenland practice of cutting off the fangs of dogs has not reached Canada. This practice results in fewer cases of rabies in humans from dog bites because the remaining teeth do not penetrate clothing. In addition, this practice reduces the mauling of children by dogs and also the damage done by the dogs to one another.

Dental Problems

The dental health of the Arctic people is generally poor. A resident dentist has been established in the Inuvik-Aklavik area off and on since the early 1950s. Occasionally dentists are employed to make trips through the North, stopping at the larger settlements. Physicians who regularly visit all settlements make extractions when they are requested.

Fluoridation of water would be a great benefit. The water is fluoridated at Inuvik where there is a water plant and a distribution system.

In most settlements the water is hauled by truck from nearby lakes or rivers. A method of batch fluoridation, which is practicable for water distributed in this way, has been planned for a trial basis in ten communities.

Permafrost

Climate is basic to the formation and existence of permafrost. Permafrost or perennially frozen ground is defined as ground in which the temperature remains below 0 degrees Centigrade continuously for a number of years. Changes in climate and terrain can cause permafrost to thaw and disappear and also to develop.

In the Arctic desert zone, permafrost occurs everywhere beneath the ground surface but not below the larger lakes.

Local terrain conditions are responsible for variations in thickness of the active layer. Vegetation affects permafrost in various ways. It shields the permafrost from the thawing effects of summer air temperatures and sunlight. This protection is provided mainly by the insulating properties of the widespread moss cover. Removal or even disturbance of the surface cover results in degradation of the underlying permafrost or a lowering of the permafrost table.

The combination of permafrost and frost-heaving soils results in the formation of ice crystals and their agglomeration into ice lenses which in certain soil conditions may grow to a massive size, up to several meters in thickness. Ice lens growth occurs most readily in soil when the air temperature is only slightly below 0 degrees Centigrade. Moisture migrates through the soil from the bottom toward the top, that is, from the warmer to the colder layers. The moisture contents of such soils can easily approach 60 to 75 percent by weight. Thawing of these materials produces an unstable viscous mud.

Engineering and Sanitation Problems

Environmental factors influence almost all construction techniques and increase the cost of an urban development project throughout its life.

The extended periods of extreme low temperatures plus the related thermal-dependent phenomena, such as permafrost, extensive ice and snow buildup, and frost heaving, are the prime factors. The low temperatures cause brittleness and considerable thermal contraction in construction materials and consequently a higher rate of failure and breakage. Outdoor operations carried on by men and machines decrease in efficiency from 25 to 40 percent of normal in low temperatures. Furthermore, the decomposition processes in both sewage and garbage are slow.

Major problems occur with high-ice-content and frost-heaving type soils. If the protective moss cover is stripped, or heat is allowed to escape from pipelines and buildings, then the permafrost recedes. The ice crystals and lenses in the ground melt, and the ground slumps and settles as it becomes an unstable mud. Pipelines break and buildings tilt or fall apart.

The location and size of any community, permanent or temporary, in the high-ice-content soil areas are dictated by the availability of "dry" gravel (Lawrence, 1970).

Distribution systems for the Arctic require a complete thermal analysis, in addition to the normal hydraulic design considerations applied in temperate areas. Prevention of freezing is usually accomplished either by applying heat along the system, or by heating the water and maintaining a sufficiently high velocity of flow in a recirculation system. In some less sophisticated distribution systems, water is wasted from various points in order to maintain flows.

In many cases it is necessary to run pipelines above the ground surface in insulated boxing, which may also need to be heated, because burial of pipe systems within the active layer in certain soil types can result in disastrous vertical movement. The decision to place the system above or below ground is influenced by site topography, soil condition, economy, and the functional requirements of the community. In rocky areas also it may be necessary to build piped systems aboveground.

These utilidors, as the aboveground systems are known, cost from ten to thirty times as much as laying standard subsurface piped systems in the temperate regions. Moreover, the utilidors are costly to maintain because they are unprotected from the weather and vandalism and because heat losses are very high.

The remoteness of Canadian Arctic communities

Fig. 13.8. Utilidor under construction at Inuvik. The upper steel pipes distribute superheated water for heating buildings in the "serviced" section of the village. The lower asbestos-cement pipes are the water main and the sewer. The utilidor is supported on piles which are anchored in the permafrost. Removable asbestos panel siding is to be added.

from major cities and centers of supply and the general lack of locally available material and skilled labor require the expensive importation of both.

The North appears to be rich in natural resources, but, by almost any definition of poverty, the Northerners are extremely poor (Department of Indian Affairs and Northern Development, 1968).

This poverty must be kept in mind when considering sanitary servicing. Poverty together with the high costs of construction due to the climate and poorly-planned spread-out communities make servicing economically unfeasible for most places. In general, only those towns with major white populations have piped water and sewage services. The discrepancy between unserviced and serviced areas is quite apparent.

In the native communities, water and sewage are hauled respectively to and from the few residences which have internal-plumbing systems and holding tanks. Most people have water delivered to storage barrels, and toilet sewage in plastic bags is hauled away. Blizzards and heavy snowdrifting may interrupt the service for several days. Washwater is spilled outside of those residences without plumbing and sewage-holding tanks; and

because the ground surface is frozen for most of the year, the liquid does not seep away.

In the spring the melted waste washwater and runoff in a settlement form pools around the houses and bigger pools in the upper road ditches which are dammed by ice-filled culverts. Children often play in the puddles of melted waste washwater and surface runoff. Because of this, and also the fact that these pools provide mosquito-breeding grounds, they are an obvious public health hazard.

The cost of servicing some settlements would far exceed the total value of all the buildings in them. For example, the original Inuvik utilidor is quoted as costing anywhere from $650 to $1,650 a linear meter, and the more recent wooden utilidor construction costs from $200 to $230 a linear meter. Compare these costs with $23 to $26 a linear meter for a 150-millimeter (6-inch) water main, and $20 a linear meter for a 200-millimeter (8-inch) sewer for typical installations in urban sub-divisions in Alberta. The collection of domestic sewage is, therefore, the most difficult problem. Treatment of the sewage, once it is collected, is less difficult.

Fig. 13.9. An Eskimo community health worker observes a spill of sewage from a sewage haulage truck at Cambridge Bay.

Water Supplies

Inuvik has an all-season piped water distribution system. The source of water is the river. In winter the river water is used directly after chlorination and fluoridation. In summer, when the river water is turbid, it is pumped first to a lake in which the turbidity settles. It is then filtered, chlorinated, and fluoridated. People do not seem to object to the color, which varies from about 10 to 40 units. The Canadian Forces Station at Alert and the airport complex at Resolute Bay also have all-season piped water distribution systems. In both cases, water is pumped from a clear lake and chlorinated before distribution.

In summer in Aklavik, water is pumped from a delta lake. This lake is flooded in the spring, but within a few days the turbidity settles out, and the water is filtered, chlorinated, and then distributed by means of an above-ground summer piped system.

In winter, the water in the river is turbidity-free and is hauled throughout the settlement with a truck. Experiments are being made, using a complete-treatment package plant, to treat the river water in summer when it is turbid.

In the other larger settlements the water is truck-hauled mainly from lake sources but occasionally from rivers. The schools, nursing stations, and homes of government employees contain internal storage and distribution systems. Generally the rest of the people keep their water supply in 90- to 180-liter reservoirs; usually, under these circumstances, they use less than an adequate amount of water for cleaning and personal hygiene.

In the tundra areas the water in the lakes and the smaller streams is generally colored. However, usually a lake or stream can be found in which the water is either noncolored or low enough in color that it can be used with no treatment other than chlorination and also fluoridation if desired.

The conversion of seawater by a process of evaporation at ambient temperatures is being studied as a possible source of potable water for Upernavik, Greenland, and a few coastal communities in northern Canada, with inadequate freshwater resources.

Sewage Disposal

Inuvik, Alert, and Resolute Bay have the only piped sewer systems in the area. In Inuvik the sewage is treated in a makeshift long-retention sewage oxidation pond, which nonetheless provides satisfactory secondary treatment.

For small communities in the North, the simplest, least expensive and most foolproof method of sewage treatment has proven to be sewage oxidation ponds (Dawson, 1967). The ponds operate well even when overloaded or underloaded, and generally it is simple to increase the capacity of a system by adding cells or increasing the size of existing cells.

Fig. 13.10. Water intake and pump on a raft in the Mackenzie River at Inuvik. In winter a pumphouse is located on the ice. At spring breakup, the ice is lifted by the rising floodwaters and is jammed downstream. In the process, the ice and flowing water scour the river bed so that planning a permanent water intake is difficult.

Fig. 13.11. Water pump and a delta lake at Aklavik (lat. 68° N, long. 135° W), in the delta of the Mackenzie River, Northwest Territory. During the ice breakup in the channels, the water rises 4.5 to 6 meters and floods the delta lakes. The water, initially turbid, clarifies by natural sedimentation within a few days; it therefore requires only filtration to remove insects and floating matter. The pump is mounted on a platform above the high water level.

Fig. 13.12. A dog team hauls ice from the river for water supplies at Coppermine. Subsequently a water supply system has been built.

In winter when the sewage ponds are ice-covered, there is little biological activity in them. However, they provide low-cost storage of the sewage until the summer when there is algal growth 24 hours per day.

Package sewage treatment plants, based on biological processes, are subject to difficult operational problems in the North. It is almost impossible to attract competent operators to look after such small systems in these remote communities.

The communities along the shores of the Arctic Ocean are small, and the effects of sewage effluent on the ocean probably would be insignificant. Each community would need to be considered individually and a thorough investigation made before planning the outfall. Primary treatment to remove the solids would be required, because this is fundamental to the various current regulatory standards. Outfalls must be designed to avoid contamination of the beaches where people clean and cut up fish and sea mammals.

Refuse Disposal

The disposal of garbage is one of the most difficult problems in the Arctic. In a typical community, unsegregated garbage and toilet wastes are hauled to an open dump, usually on low-lying land. The refuse generally becomes strewn widely. The ravens, gulls, foxes, and lemmings feed upon the garbage, and if the dump is not almost a mile away from the community, the children play in it.

Some attempts are made to reduce the quantity of garbage either by burning it in the garbage cans in the settlement or in the open air at the disposal site. In either case, it is objectionable because of the lack of segregation of combustibles and noncombustibles, because charred waste meat attracts scavengers, such as bears and foxes, more readily, and also because of the

temperature inversions which persist for most of the winter throughout the Far North.

The regulatory authorities in Alaska have stated that burial of garbage or sanitary landfill is not satisfactory if the ground is cold. They are considering setting standards requiring that garbage be incinerated if the mean ground temperature is less than minus 3 degrees Centigrade (Alaska State Department of Health and Welfare, 1969).

Until the early 1970s, the common method of garbage disposal in coastal communities was to discharge it to the ocean in summer and lay it on the sea ice in winter. The reasoning has been that the quantity of garbage is small in these communities, which have populations from twenty to four hundred people, compared with the huge size of the Arctic Ocean. In a few of the communities the ice flows back and forth in the harbors, and garbage on it would be carried back to the settlement.

For the larger communities of the Canadian Arctic where the permafrost is close to the surface, it is suggested that the garbage should be discharged over the brow of the hill on a side which is not visible from the community. The refuse should be segregated into combustibles and noncombustibles, and the noncombustibles further divided into garbage and large pieces such as barrels and car bodies. The garbage should be compacted if mechanical equipment is available; even a garden bulldozer would be better than nothing for this job.

There is sound justification for restudying the matter of incinerating the organic matter. Perhaps the organic matter has value as fertilizer in the desolate and barren Arctic. For example, little vegetation grows around Resolute Bay on Cornwallis Island except in the areas of human activity or drainage from waste disposal.

Conclusions

By the usual standards of measurement, the disease rate among the people living in the Arctic desert is high. The causative conditions are understood, but the solutions are difficult because they stem from the basic environmental and socioeconomic conditions. Technological solutions are available for most of the problems.

Steps have been taken to produce improvements, such as a program of providing improved native housing, provision of hospital and medical care, organized distribution of potable drinking water, and organized garbage and sewage collection. An adequate supply of potable water and effective means of collecting and disposing wastes are essential to improving the general health of the indigenous people.

The people living in nonnative communities, such as mining camps, military stations, and weather stations, generally are in good health. In these establishments the people enjoy adequate housing, water, and sewerage services. However, improvements in waste treatment, community planning, and recreational facilities are required.

Acknowledgment

Appreciation is expressed for advice on the writing of this paper to C. K. Bridge, Regional Medical Officer, R. D. P. Eaton, Consultant Parasitologist, and O. Schaefer, Chief of the Northern Medical Research Unit of the Northern Region, Medical Services Director-ate, Department of National Health and Welfare, and to T. J. Orford, former Superintendent of the Charles Camsell Hospital, Edmonton.

The authors also wish to express their appreciation to R. E. Tait, Acting Director General, Regional Operations and Coordination, Environmental Protection Service, Department of Environment, and to A. H. Booth, Acting Director, Environmental Health Service, Department of National Health and Welfare for their kind support of the writing of this paper.

BIBLIOGRAPHY

Alaska Department of Health and Welfare
    1969   Solid Waste Management in Cold Regions. Scientific Research Data and Reports, vol. 2, no. 2. Office of Research and Academic Coordination. Alaska Water Laboratory, College, Alaska. 46 pp.

Canada Department of Indian Affairs and
        Northern Development
    1968   A Brief Analysis of the Human and Economic Resources of the Great Slave Lake Area — Northwest Territories. Ottawa, Canada.

Chin, T. D. V.
    1970   Communicable Disease Control. Conference on Arctic Health, College, Alaska, 1970, Issue Papers: 1–4.

Dawson, R. N.
    1967   Sewage Treatment in the Mackenzie District, N.W.T. Department of National Health and Welfare, Report 67–30, Ottawa, Canada. 73 pp.

Lawrence, N. A.
    1970   On the Human Aspect of Cold Climate Operations, 99th Annual Meeting of the American Institute of Mining, Metallurgical and Petroleum Engineers, Inc., Denver, Colorado, 1970, Paper No. SPE 2827, 10 pp.

CHAPTER 14
BEHAVIORAL DESIGN OF HABITATS FOR MAN IN POLAR DESERTS

William M. Smith
University of Wisconsin, Green Bay

The design of habitats, both housing and communities, has long been largely a product of planners' and architects' intuition. In the early 1970s, however, this process has begun to be increasingly questioned as a suitable or only way of arriving at habitat design. The principal criticism has been whether the housing and communities being produced are really habitable. Do they enhance the well-being of residents? Do they meet and support the day-to-day activities of people? Or, must residents make substantial and continued adjustments in all facets of their day-to-day living in order to accommodate themselves to the habitats that are provided?

In part these questions may be answered by examining the available types and styles of housing. It then becomes readily apparent that habitats in San Francisco are essentially the same as those in Chicago or in Dallas, Memphis, Minneapolis, and Fairbanks. Styles and designs are basically the same everywhere. One housing development is much like another, and dwelling floor plans are similar. Spatial arrangements both inside and out show little variation, and the layout of virtually all communities is a grid pattern that is duplicated everywhere.

The question of compatible designs for different geographical and climatic areas is only now beginning to be considered. The factors that have produced habitat similarity are of course very strong, and it is not easy to break into the ongoing production system. Probably the greatest single deterrent for new approaches is that of who will pay? This is an important problem that will have to be solved, but it is not within the scope of this presentation.

At one point, during the 1930s, social scientists attempted to show the ways in which our built-environment affected the health and well-being of people. Unfortunately, these initial attempts failed to show any direct relationship between specific parts of housing and communities and specific health or behavioral outcomes. The problem they were dealing with is now recognized as being extremely complex, in many ways similar to the event chains that make up certain ecosystems. Thus, it is not surprising that these early attempts failed. There were some exceptions, of course, most notably in the area of sanitary engineering.

These initial failures more or less stopped further work, and only in recent years has interest once again been reawakened. By recognizing that specific diseases or behavior problems are not directly tied to any specific part of the built environment — such as ceiling height — and by making their approaches at different levels, researchers are beginning to make some progress.

As an example, it is now generally recognized that for most families with children, vertical stacking of people in high-rise dwellings results in a variety of behavioral and health problems. Fanning (1967) has found that among mothers living in high-rise units, the higher one goes from ground level, the greater the incidence of psychoneurotic complaints. Mitchell (1970) has found that in high-density housing, those living on the higher floors report more psychological distress symptoms and that they socialize less with others.

Boyd (1965) has found significantly less social interaction among high-rise residents than among residents of two- and three-story low-rise buildings. These findings are supported by the work of Gunn (1968), who has found that in high-rise units many residents do not know their next-door neighbors.

In the North American Arctic and Subarctic, there are as yet only a few examples of high-rise dwellings — for example, Frobisher Bay in Canada, and Godthab in Greenland. But the number is growing, and problems similar to those found in temperate areas are already developing, with a few additional difficulties that are unique to the Arctic. At present, however, the prevailing type of northern habitat is not the temperate-area high-rise. Rather, there are three basic types of communities and four basic types of housing that can be classified as being of recent design and construction.

The three types of communities are (1) large towns and centers of government administration, (2) communities centering around industrial and/or extraction industries, and (3) small villages or basic subsistence settlements.

The four types of housing found in these communities are, first, government constructed single- or multiple-family dwellings of World War II or earlier design, with only the addition of more insulation and perhaps enclosed walkways to adapt them to northern use. Second are single-staff residences, which are essentially dormitory-style housing. These are also usually government housing, again using designs from another time and intended for another place. Third are shanties such as those found in the poorest sections around the outskirts of many major North and South American cities. Fourth and last are the so-called "Bold New Experiments," which are often advertised as model communities but which, except for indoor plumbing, are still of World War II vintage design. Often, but not always, these are newly established industry settlements or centers of government administration. In essence, they represent present-day suburbia transplanted to the North.

An examination of northern communities shows that housing is of generally low quality. In those instances where quality of construction and materials is acceptable, the designs do not meet northern requirements. In those rare instances where attention has been given to designing for this region, emphasis has been on engineering considerations rather than on human habitability.

Problems of northern settlement habitability may be divided into two major parts, those of the outdoor community environment and those of the indoor home environment. They are closely linked to one another.

In temperate climates, inadequate indoor living spaces are somewhat offset by the ready availability of outdoor areas. Strotzka (1961) has noted that in temperate areas, if a dwelling is not adequate, residents tend to stay outside. Because of climate, this solution is not available or will not be taken by many northern residents. For the greater part of each year outdoor living areas are avoided, and a majority of the population is constrained to essentially indoor activity.

Not surprisingly the full impact of deficiencies in both the outdoor and indoor built environments are felt by women and children. While husbands are away during the day, women who don't work or who have children, are confined to their houses. In most instances there is nowhere for them to go outside of their homes, as northern communities have few of the behavioral supports that women enjoy in temperate areas and virtually none of the facilities needed for children's activities.

Consider for example, shopping facilities that are customarily available in temperate areas. Designers and planners have not yet recognized that shopping is much more than just a means of obtaining goods and services. Indeed, in those areas of the world where open market places exist, it is *the* social and information transmitting center of the area. The acquisition of goods and services seems to be the least important part of what goes on in this setting. Deprived of this social and pleasurable activity, a woman is often left with little else to support and sustain her through each day. In those few settlements where shopping facilities are available, one usually finds most women who are not ill or required to remain at home for other reasons are visiting the Hudson Bay store or other shopping facility during the day. I have often speculated on what the effect would be in a village such as Inuvik, if the Bay were suddenly closed permanently. One outcome would in almost all probability be an even higher rate of population turnover and dissatisfaction among women who have families and who do not work outside the home.

Play areas for children outside the home are neglected in virtually every Arctic and Subarctic settlement. The burden this places on already inadequate facilities in the home has not been examined in detail, but sophisticated data gathering is not required to quickly gain the general impression that the burden is considerable. Among white immigrant non-native residents in many settlements along the Arctic coast, children are not encouraged to play out of doors during the winter because of the fear of a polar bear wandering in off the sea ice, heavy equipment such as tractors and graders that are often used to keep roads and paths within the settlement clear, and of course, the cold and darkness. We may quibble over whether any of these factors constitute a danger any greater than that of being hit by lightning, but the important point is that families feel there is a danger, and children's behavior is shaped accordingly.

Two additional factors in the community outdoor environment that demand systematic attention are village layouts and the exterior appearance of buildings. Most northern settlements faithfully follow a grid system. The question should be asked whether this pattern is the easiest for residents to use and to live in within these regions or whether other configurations, such as a star pattern with major facilities at a central point, might not be better suited.

The exterior appearance of buildings is overlooked almost everywhere, and one can find little attempt at making buildings more visually compatible with their physical environment. Parr (1965), commenting upon this problem, says:

Architectural adjustments to climate are almost universally treated as though they involved only the simple and obvious physical problems of heat, light, shade, insulation and air conditioning. Nevertheless, it seems beyond dispute that the perceptual image of a building has a lot to do with the sense of well-being it may generate. Houses and cityscapes that look cool and inviting during the hot summer may look chilly and forbidding in winter, adding to the psychological discomforts of the cold season. . . . The region around the Great Lakes, and especially around Lake Michigan, is particularly rich in striking, and often highly esteemed, examples of architectural disregard for the psychological effects of extreme seasonal ranges of climatic conditions. Responses to simulated and actual architecture and cityscapes should be obtained at different temperature and weather conditions. From such observations it should be possible to gain a rational approach to the problems of climate and environmental design.

If this is true for the Great Lakes region, it most certainly holds equally true for Arctic and Subarctic areas.

Most interior environments of northern housing are no different than those of low economic housing found anywhere in the United States. The question of whether interior environments, typical of temperate areas, are suitable for the rigorous climatic conditions of the

North, must be asked. We do not have sufficient data at this time to give a definitive answer to this question, but at least one design factor is frequently mentioned as causing problems. This is the overlapping of activity areas.

Few northern houses have sufficient space or are designed to permit visual and possibly auditory screening of adult and children's activity areas from one another. Both overlap. While this overlapping may cause minimal problems in temperate area housing, a supposition that is open to question, it presents a major problem when most of the day-to-day living is done indoors. This overlapping places a considerable burden on all members of the household, each having to accommodate his or her activity to that of other family members. As a result, no one can obtain the visual and auditory release from others that is necessary for everyone's well-being. This burden falls especially hard on women and children because they are usually at home more of the time than adult male members of the family.

Because we have so little data, the short- and long-term effects of such design deficiencies are not yet entirely clear. One outcome is the possibility of a reduction in emotional and activity levels of children (Smith, 1970). There is some indication that among very young children, motor and possibly muscular development may suffer some retardation. As an example, many young children find it difficult to walk distances that their peers, living in temperate regions, have no difficulty with.

Children of a wider age range often seem to show an apparent blunting of emotional effect. The differences between many children who are long-term residents and children recently arrived are striking. Unless ill or otherwise handicapped, recently arrived children show a typically high level of motor and verbal activity; running, jumping, shouting, yelling, laughing, and playing noisy games. Many long-time resident children do not show this activity level. Instead, it is common to find them playing quiet games in their homes. In contrast, newly arrived children generally show higher levels of motor activity. Within about three months after their arrival, however, impressions are that this begins to show a reduction and that some blunting emotional effect also takes place.

Reduced activity is encouraged by many parents. Being constrained to essentially indoor living in housing that has no visual or auditory separation of activity areas, parents find that they cannot tolerate what in temperate climates is an essentially normal child's level of activity. As a result, quiet play is encouraged and enforced.

Some families report that when they leave the Arctic, either on visits or permanently, their children are physically unable to keep up with peers. The full extent of these difficulties is not known, but it does seem to be related at least in part to habitat design, and it certainly should receive attention.

The magnitude of both health and social problems that inadequate habitat designs produce is not yet known because so little work has been done. As a beginning, the 1970 HEW Alaska Conference on "Man's Health in a Changing Arctic Environment," made the following recommendation:

A plan for the construction of Arctic communities should be developed: it should provide for the use of appropriate techniques in Arctic housing, consider social and health needs and include provision for ethnic representation; such a model community should be developed within the next 5 years.

This conference went on to suggest that at present, with few exceptions, man-made or man-built environments in the North do not satisfy the needs of residents even at a minimum level.

There seems to be little question but that as we learn more in this area, the high incidence of disease, mental illness, alcoholism, divorce rates, and population turnover that presently exist in the North will be found to be related in some measure to habitat design.

H. B. Brett (1971), of the Northern Regional Headquarters in Edmonton, has noted that:

There is a lot of misery in the North, misery for which the surgeon's knife and physician's medicine has little effect. It is at this point that the medical profession must accept its limitations and seek a multi-disciplined approach. . . . The main problem in the North today is not how to stop people from dying or how to bring new mines into production, it is how to make living more worthwhile for the living.

An important way of improving the quality of life for northern residents is through housing and communities that are designed to fit the living patterns of residents in this region, rather than reflecting life styles of more temperate areas.

BIBLIOGRAPHY

Boyd, D. W.
  1965 Selected social characteristics and multi-family living environment, a pilot study. Environmental Research Foundation, Topeka, Kansas.
Brett, H. B.
  1971 Quality of life in the North as seen from the health perspective. Presented at the Shell Program on the Canadian North, Scarborough College, Toronto. January 28–30.

Fanning, D. M.
  1967 Families in flats. British Medical Journal 4(5576).
Gunn, A. D. G.
  1968 The medical-social problems of multi-story living. Nursing Times 64: 468–69.
Mitchell, R. E.
  1970 Personal, family and social consequences arising from high-density housing in Hong Kong and

Mitchell, R. E. *(continued)*
    other major cities in Southeast Asia. Program
    Area Committee on Housing and Health, Ameri-
    can Public Health Association.
Parr, A. E.
    1965   In search of theory. Cited by H. M. Proshansky
            et al., *in* Environmental psychology, man and
            his physical setting. New York: Holt, Rinehart
            and Winston, 1970. pp. 15–16.
U.S. Department of Health, Education, and Welfare, Public
    Health Service, Environmental Health Service
    1970   Proceedings of a conference on man's health in a
            changing arctic environment, Fairbanks, Alaska,
            May 12–14, 1970.

Smith, W. M.
    1970   Environmental influences on interdependent
            groups. Symposium on assessing the environ-
            mental context of behavior. Presented at the
            meeting of the American Psychological Associa-
            tion, Washington, D.C.
Strotzka, H.
    1961   Cited in F. Chapin. The relationship of housing
            to mental health. Working paper 3A for the
            Expert Committee on the public health aspects
            of housing of the World Health Organization.
            Presented at a meeting in Geneva, Switzerland,
            June 19–26.

INDEX

Ablation, 14, 59; in Peary Land, 53
Adams Glacier, Antarctica, 60
Advanced Research Projects Agency, 146
Advection, 3, 7; and storage changes, 3
Advection, oceanic, into Arctic basin, 13
Advective cooling, 14
Aerobic bacteria, 82
Aerobic groups, 71
Aerobiological monitoring during sampling, 74
Aerological data, 10
Aerospace rescue and recovery service, HH-3E helicopters, 142
Ahumic soil, 68
Air cargo in Alaska, 141
Air inversion — upper, 8
Air pollution, 96
Air temperatures, annual and monthly mean, 6
Air transport: in U.S.S.R., 132–33; in Canada, 133, 135; types, 139, 140, 141; compared, 141
Aklavik, 157; evaporation and water budget-Budyko, 26; oceanicity, 27; dryness ratio, 28; resident physicians, 152
Alaska Railroad, mining along, 117
Alaska Range, 44
Alaskan pipeline, 105
Alass, described, 45
Albedo — snow, 6
Alcan Highway, 134
Alcohol and Summary Statistics, U.S. Treasury Department, 110
Alert, Alaska, 157; amplitude ratio, 4; station location, 24; population rank, 25, 26; evaporation and water budget-Budyko, 26; evaporation and water budget-Turc, 28; dryness ratio, 28; Canadian Forces Station, 151
Alexandria, variability of precipitation, 18
Algae crusts, 72
Algal-lichen soil crusts, 71
Alkalinity in lakes, 56
Alluvial fans, 45
Almirante Brown, Antarctica, 5
Amman, variability of precipitation, 18
Amplitude ratio: harmonic, in Arctic

station, 7; size, 7; of temperature, 7, 10, 12
Amplitude ratios: latitudinal variation, 7; and cloud cover, 9
Amundsen Gulf, 151
Anaerobic bacteria: activity in solution in rocks, 59; analyses, 71; in arid mineral soils, 83
Anchorage, Alaska: cost of living, 106; family budget costs, 107; family budget categories, 108; construction boom, 109; gross sales-personal income ratio, 110; trade and services, 110; selected housing comparisons, 111; airport facility, 116; oil and gas discovery, 117
Andes Mountains, Colombia: induced aridity, 17; soil properties, 77; microbiological determinations, 82
Angino, E. E., 60
Angstrom ratio relationship, 9
Anguissaq Lake, an ice-contact lake, 56
Animal populations, 119
Antarctic Dry Valley, 72
Antarctic ice-sheet, 10, 14; surface inversion, 10
Antarctic Peninsula, 13
Antarctic soil types, 68
Antarctica, coldest month, 6
Antarctica — permafrost, 35
Anticyclonic flow, 10
Antiplanation terraces, 45
Archaeological sites in Queen Elizabeth Islands and Ellesmere Island, 99
Arctic Basin, 9, 92; snow depth, 91
Arctic Bay: amplitude ratio, 4; station location, 24; population rank, 25, 26; evaporation and water budget-Budyko, 26; evaporation and water budget-Turc, 28
Arctic desert: area, 23; in Greenland, 23; first use of term, 63; animal types, 93
Arctic environment, changes in, 105
Arctic Ocean: seas, 126; ice cover, 129
Arctic resources: in broad perspective, 115; inhibiting factors, 115
Arctic Seas, 126
Arctic Slope of Alaska: tundra areas, 91; petroleum exploration, 109
Argentine Island, Antarctica, amplitude ratio, 5

Aridity in northern polar areas, an analysis of, 26–27
Arnold, C. A., 91
Atacama Desert, Chile: volcanic materials, 74; soil properties, 77; microbiological determinations, 82
Atmospheric advection, energy flux, 3
Atmospheric cooling, Arctic ice-pack and Antarctic ice-sheet, 8
Atmospheric heat advection, 7
Attenuation, winter temperature, 3, 6, 7
Authigenic carbonate encrustations, 64
Autotrophic groups, 71
Autotrophic soil algae, 95
Axel Heiberg Island: hummocky ground, 65; desert flora, 92

Back radiation — flux, 3
Bacteria, in desert soils, 83
Bacterial nitrogen fixers, 71
Baffin Bay, 28
Baffin Island, 151; base metals, 120
Baker Lake, 151; evaporation and water budget-Budyko, 26; dryness ratio, 28
Banks Island, soils in hummocky ground, 65
Barents Sea, 13, 27
Barnes, D. F., 56
Barrow, Alaska: amplitude ratio, 4; station location, 24; population rank, 25, 26; evaporation and water budget-Budyko, 26; oceanicity, 27; evaporation and water budget-Turc, 28; dryness ratio, 28; aerial view of tundra near Barrow, 34; mean annual temperature, 38; bore holes near Barrow, 39; raised-edge polygons, 43; microbiological determinations, 81; TL considera- tion, 86; lemming study, 94; cost of living, 106; contract rent, 107; tourism, 116; Naval Arctic Research Laboratory, 116
Barrow tundra biome site: soil prop- erties, 76; thermoluminescence curves, 79; microbiological determinations, 81
Barter Island: amplitude ratio, 4; station location, 24; population rank, 25; evaporation and water budget- Turc, 28

Bathurst Inlet, 151
Bathurst Island, well drilling, 120
Beaufort Sea, 138
Belet Uen, variability of precipitation, 18
Benson, C. S., 14
Bering, Vitus, exploration in Arctic Sea, 125
Bering Sea, 131
Bering Strait, 129
Beschel, R. E., 65
Biomass of algae and fungi, 83
Biomass production, 94
Biotic factors in site selection, 71
Biotic productivity, 105
Bird, J. B., 23
Biskra, variability of precipitation, 18
Blackwelder, E., 47
Black River, 99, 151
BMEWS locations, 116
Bog soils in High Arctic, 67
"Boom and bust" biological economy, 96
Borgium Elv, Greenland, sand wedge polygons, 41
Botanical zonation, 63
Botulism, 154
Braided channels, 55
Brea City, California, variability of precipitation, 19
British trading in Arctic areas, 116
Brønlunds Fjord: air temperature and precipitation, 29; polygons in delta, 41; lakes near the Fjord, 57; salt incrustations on silt, 58; stratified water, 58
Brown, J., 39
Brown Peninsula, Antarctica: soil properties, 77; microbiological determinations, 82
Budyko formula, 26, 27, 29
Budyko method, 26, 30
Buffalo, New York, cost of living, 106
Buffer capacity, 81
Bukhta Tikhaya: amplitude ratio, 4; station location, 24; population rank, 25, 26; evaporation and water budget-Budyko, 26; evaporation and water budget-Turc, 28; dryness ratio, 28
Bukhta Tiksi: station location, 24; population rank, 25; evaporation and water budget-Turc, 28
Bulk transport, costs, 108–109
Bull, C., 14
Bulun: station location, 24; population rank, 25, 26; evaporation and water budget-Budyko, 26; evaporation and water budget-Turc, 28; dryness ratio, 28
Burao, variability of precipitation, 18
Bureau of Indian Affairs supply ship in Alaska, 139
Bureau of Labor Statistics indexes: family budget costs, 107; cost-of-living, 108
Buried ice, 38
Burley, Idaho, variability of precipitation, 19

C¹⁴ assimilation studies in soils, 82
Cabot, John, 116
Calcium chloride in Antarctica lakes, 60
Calcium sulfate in Antarctica lakes, 60
Cambridge Bay: amplitude ratio, 4; evaporation and water budget-Budyko, 26; and Arctic vegetation, 27; dryness ratio, 28; Eskimo girl, 153; sewage spill, 156
Camp Michigan: net balance, 15; variability of precipitation, 17
Canada Glacier, 43
Canadian Arctic Archipelago, 91, 133; oceanicity, 27
Canadian Arctic islands: rivers fed by glacial melt, 55; clear lakes, 57
Canadian Geological Survey, mapping in Far North, 119
Cape Chelyuskin, 100
Cape Denison, turbulent heat flux, 11
Cape Dorset, children's diseases, 152
Cape Hallet, penguin guano, 95
Carbonate rocks in cold deserts, 59
Caribou Eskimos, 99
Casablanca, variability of precipitation, 18
Cations in soils: exchange, 81; in polar desert soils, 82
"Cat trains," 130
Cavernous weathering, 46, 47
Caves in Arctic areas, 59, 60
Census of housing, 1970, 107
Centrum Sφ, Greenland: seep from ground ice, 54; stream flow, 55; size and sedimentation, 56; numerous cave systems, 59
Charlier, R. H., 24, 26; soil maps for Arctic areas, 23
Chemical weathering, 13
Chesterfield Inlet, 151
Chihuahua Desert, New Mexico: soil properties, 76; microbiological determinations, 81
Chile, 47
Chilkoot Pass, 125
Christmas Lake Valley, 72
Chuchi Sea, 138
Claridge, G. G. C., 68
Clear, Alaska, BMEWS location, 116
Climate: in equilibrium with soil and vegetation, 23; and rental rates, 107
Climatic conditions: advective terms, 3; high latitudes, 3; surface-related terms, 3
Climatic records, analysis, 23
Climatic variables used in test of Krumbein and Graybill algorithm, 23
Cloud cover, 8–9; and amplitude ratios of temperature, 9; seasonal variation, 9
Clyde: evaporation and water budget-Budyko, 26; dryness ratio, 28
Coastal Plain, Alaska, permafrost, 39
Cold steppe, first use of term, 63
Coliformic groups, 71
Colorado Desert, California: soil

properties, 76; microbiological properties, 81
Columbia Plateau, Oregon: soil properties, 76; microbiological determinations, 81
Colville River, 72
Commodity production in North, costs of, 106
Commonality of species, 83
Communication systems, 115
Communities, housing types, 161
Community outdoor environment, 162
Conrow Valley, Antarctica: soil properties, 77; microbiological determinations, 82
Construction and operating costs, 108
Construction technology, 109; and permafrost, 48–49
Consumption of resources, 105
Coppermine, Canada, schoolroom in, 153
Coppermine River, Canada, 158; copper deposits, 120
Cordova, Alaska, oil production, 118
Coreless summer, 7
Coreless winter phenomenon, 6, 7
Coreless winters, 12
Corelessness, 12
Cornwallis Island: streams from snowdrifts, 53; lack of bog soil, 67; desert flora, 92; biomass production, 94; well drilling, 120; base metals, 120
Cost of living: in selected cities, 106; indexes, 107
Costs imposed by environmental stress: internal and external, 105; measure of, 105
Craig Harbour: station location, 24; population rank, 25, 26; evaporation and water budget-Budyko, 26; evaporation and water budget-Turc, 28; dryness ratio, 28
Cultural links to economic centers, 105
Culture media and microbial groups, 79, 80, 81
Cumberland Peninsula, 151
Cycling of nutrients, 94
Cyclonic circulation, 14
Cyclonic disturbances, 10
Cyclonic flow, 10, 11

Danmark Fjord, 58
Danmarkshävn: amplitude ratio, 4; station location, 24; population rank, 25, 26; evaporation and water budget-Budyko, 26; evaporation and water budget-Turc, 28; dryness ratio, 28
Davis, Antarctica: amplitude ratio, 5; monthly mean temperature, 6
Day, J. H., 66
DDT in biosphere, 95
Death rates, age specific, in Alaska, 110
Decepcion, Antarctica, amplitude ratio, 5
Deception Island, Antarctic Peninsula: cinder cones, 74; soil properties, 77; microbiological determinations, 82

Decomposer cycles, 95
Delong, Lt. G. W., 125
Denaii Highway, 44
Desert features, compared, 45–46
Desert flora, 92
Desert microbial ecology, 71
Desert pavement, 64
Desert perturbation, 71
Desert types, 91
Desert varnish, 68
Desert-tundra transition, 25; area, 23; zones, 23, 25
DEW Line, 116, 139, 140, 151
Dingle, R., 15
Discriminant analysis, 23, 31
Discriminant function: in comparison tests, 23; in 40°F isotherm test, 24; separation of desert and nondesert areas, 25
Diseases: tuberculosis, 152; respiratory, 152, 153; gastroenteritis, 153; skin, 153; infectious hepatitis, 154
Dissolved oxygen in lakes, 56
Dissolved salts in lakes, 56
Dissolved solids in rivers, 55
Djibouti, variability of precipitation, 18
Dog teams, 138
Dolgin, I. M., 23
Dome Petroleum consortium, 119
Don Juan Pond, Antarctica: thermo-luminescence curves, 78; described, 86; TL consideration, 86
Dormancy of seed, 93
Drainage catena — landscape, 63
Drake Point, 120
Dryas mats in High Arctic, 68
Dryland plains, Colorado: soil properties, 76; microbiological determinations, 81
Dryness ratio, 27, 28, 31
Dry Valleys, Victorialand, 91
Duluth, Minnesota, cost of living, 106
Dumont de Urbille, Antarctica: amplitude ratio, 5; turbulent heat flux, 11; ice-free conditions, 13
Dutch exploration in Arctic areas, 116

East Antarctica, 13; heat advection, 10; amplitude ratio, 12
Eastonville, Colorado, variability of precipitation, 19
Echinococcosis, 154
Ecological considerations and desert life forms, 84
Ecology of polar deserts, 92
Economic centers — cultural links, 105
Economic development — costs, 105
Ecosystems of high latitude barrens, 13
Eddy diffusion, 11
Eddy-flux, 3, 7
Efflorescence of salt.
    See salt efflorescence
Egede, H. P., 63
Electrical conductivity in soils, 81
Elephant's Point, Alaska, and ground ice, 40
Ellef Ringness Island, gas discovery, 120
Ellesmere Island: coastal-inland con-

trasts, 26; hummocky ground, 65; soils on, 66; archaeological sites, 99
Ellsworth land, 13
Enderby Land, 68
Energy consumption, 108
Energy flux, 3, 10
Engineering problems, 48; and sanitation problems, 155
Environment: microbiota, 71; pollution and damage, 120; man made; 163
Environmental and ecological factors, 84
Environmental counseling, 96
Environmental impact, 105
Environmental severity for human life, 110
Environmental stress — processes and costs, 105
Environmental stresses in biological ecosystems, 96
Ephemeral streams, 45
Erigavo, variability of precipitation, 18
Eriophorum tussocks in tundra, 65
Eschscholtz Bay, Seward Peninsula, 40
Eskimo: population in North America, 99; languages, 100; history of, 100, 151; job training, 120; schooling, 152
Eskimos: adaptation to polar areas, 99; in Siberia, 99–100; contrast between New and Old World groups, 100; economic base, 100; employment, 100; "generation gap," 100; Governmental services to, 100; population increase, 100; social services to, 100; ethnic groups, 100, 101; and white men, 101; as community health workers, 152
Esthetic values, 97
Etching in rocks, 59
Eternal frost, 35. See also permafrost
Eureka: amplitude ratio, 4; monthly mean temperature, 6; cloud cover, 8; potential isolation, 9; station location, 24; population rank, 25, 26; evaporation and water budget-Budyko, 26; evaporation and water budget-Turc, 28; dryness ratio, 28
Eutrophication in tundra ecosystems, 96
Evaporation: annual net, 26; and energy budget, 26; "season," 30
Evaporite soils in Antarctica, 68
Everett, K. R., 31
Exobiological research, 82
Explorers in Arctic, 125–26

F — distribution tests on precipitation, 18
Fairbanks, Alaska: mean annual temperature, 38; cost of living, 106; family budget costs, 107
Family budget: costs, 107; categories, 108
Features common to desert regions, 71
Fillipov, Y. V., 23, 25, 27
First harmonic, 7
Fixed-wing cargo aircraft, characteristics, 141

Fletcher, J. O., 8
Fletcher's Island (T-3 Island), 140, 142
Floating ice island "Arlis II," 92
Fluoridation of water, 155
Fluvial processes, 34
Foehn winds, 23
Foliated ground ice wedges, 38, 41
Footprint pressures of surface vehicles, 144
Fort Simpson, 134
Fossil fuel in Canadian Arctic, 120
Fourier series — analysis, 6
Foxe Peninsula, 151
Fragile tundra ecosystems, 96
Franklin, Sir John, 116
Frederick E. Hyde Fjord in ice-free state, 58
Fristrup, B., 23
Frobisher: evaporation and water budget-Budyko, 26; dryness ratio, 28
Frobisher Bay, 161
Frobisher, Martin, 116
Frost action and construction, 49
Frost boils, 68
Frost table depth, 67
Frost-sorted patterned ground, 42
Fungi: in Sahara, 84; in polar regions, 84

Gastroenteritis, 153
Gauge data values of climatological factors, 13
Genetic soils: in polar desert zones, 63; diagrammatic presentation, 64; distribution, 67
Geobotanical divisions in polar landscapes, 63
Geomorphic features in relation to precipitation, 42
Geomorphic processes in polar deserts, 34
Geothermal gradient, 36, 37
Geothermal heat, 36
Gerasimov, I. P., 63
Giovinetto, M. B., 14
Glacial melt, 55
Glacial outwash, Greenland, 41
Glacial till in Miers Valley, 35
Glazovskaia, M. A., 68
Global ecosystem and polar deserts, 95
Glycoprotein for resistance, 84
Godthab, Greenland, 161
Gorodkov, B. N., 63
Governing in polar deserts, 101
Gran Chaco, Argentina: soil properties, 77; microbiological determinations, 82
Great Basin Desert, California, 81; soil properties, 76; microbiological determinations, 81
Great Basin Desert, Nevada: soil properties, 76; microbiological determinations, 81
Great Slave Lake, 134
Great Slave Lake Railroad, 134
Greenland, 29, 33, 34, 41, 45, 46, 47; deserts, 23; snowbank, 54; rivers fed by glacial melt, 55; dimictic lake, 57;

Greenland (*cont'd*)
  salt incrustation on silt, 58; rills etched into limestone, 59; xeric affinities, 63; polar desert soil, 65; turf hummocks, 65; tundra soils, 67; Eskimos, 119
Greenland ice-sheet: inversion, 9; mean net balance of precipitation, 14; lakes on ice, 56; precipitation, 91
Greenland Sea, 27, 129
Grigor'ev, A. A., 63
Grønfjorden: station location, 24; population rank, 25, 26; evaporation and water budget-Turc, 28
Gross sales to personal income, ratio, 110
Grottedalen, 60
Ground transport: in Canada, 134; in Alaska, 138
Groundwater: in cold deserts, 59; solution activity, 59
Gyda Yamo: station location, 24; population rank, 25, 26; evaporation and water budget-Budyko, 26; evaporation and water budget-Turc, 28; dryness ratio, 28

Habitat, design, 161
Habitat design and social ills, 163
Hall Beach, amplitude ratio, 4
Hallet, Antarctica: amplitude ratio, 5; cloud cover, 8; potential isolation, 9
Halley Bay, variability of net balance, 16
Hargeisa, variability of precipitation, 18
Harmonic amplitude ratio, 4, 5, 9, 12
Harmonic amplitude ratios: in Arctic stations, 4; in Antarctic stations, 5
Harmonic analysis — air temperature, 6
Harvest efficiency scale, 94
Hay River, 134
Haynes, B. C., 23
Headless Valley, 125
Health resources statistics, United States Department of Health, Education and Welfare, 110
Health services in Alaska, 110
Heat, advection across latitudes, 7
Heat advection, 7–10
Heating degree days, and costs, 108
Hekla Sund, Greenland, 56
Herbivore productivity, 94
Hetrotrophic groups, 71
Heuristic attenuation — index, 6, 12
Hickel Highway, Alaska, 136
High Arctic, 119; runoff, 53; first use of term, 63; intense rainfall in, 66; tundra soils, 67; Arctic brown soil, 67; diagrammatic presentation of soils, 68; floral species, 92; eutrophication, 96
High Mountain, California: soil properties, 76; microbiological determinations, 81
High-rise dwellings, 161
Hilgard Museum, California: soil properties, 76; microbiological

determinations, 81; longevity of microorganisms, 83
History of flora, 91–92
Hochstein, C., 15
Homogeneity in polar lands, 63
Honolulu, Hawaii, cost of living, 106
Hope Bay, Antarctica, amplitude ratio, 5
Hot Springs, Antarctica, 60
Housing: comparative costs, 107; rental rate, 107; room ratio, 107; native, 151; quality, 162; exteriors, 162; interiors, 162–63; children and environment, 163
Hovercraft, 145
Hudson Bay Company, 119
Human activity and internal costs, 106
Human use — potential, 105
Hummock genesis, 66
Hummock size, 65
Hummocks, 66
Hummocky ground: soils in, 65; genesis, 66
Hyde Fjord, 58
Hydrocarbon deposits in Canada, 119
Hydrography in cold deserts, 61
Hydrolaccolith, 45
Hydrologic regimen of Arctic deserts, 53
Hydrological balance, 14
Hydrology of cold deserts, 56

Ice cover age, 56
Ice wedge formation, 40
Ice wedges, 34, 39, 94; age, 40; defined, 40; fossil, 40
Icebreaker ships: data, 131, 142; *Manhattan*, 142
Ice-contact lakes, 56
Ice-fog, 108
Ice-free barrens, 7, 10
Icelandic trough and air advection, 13
Ice-sheet slopes, 10
Ice-wedge casts, 40
Ice-wedge ice, 38, 39
Ice-wedge polygons: described, 42; in High Arctic, 68
Icing mounds, 56
Incubation, in moist soil, 82
Independence Fjord, 58, 59
Induced aridity, 17
Infectious hepatitis, 154
Inglefield Land, Greenland, 66–67; windblown sand, 46
Insolation — potential, 6, 7
Instability of soils, 96
Insulation, requirement costs, 108
Inuvik, 162; roadway to, 134; wood-frame housing, 152; welfare housing, 153; water fluoridation, 155; utilidor, 156; water intake, 157; sewage disposal, 157
Inuvik Laboratory, Canada, 116
Inversion: Greenland ice-sheet, 9; in ice-free barrens, 10
Inversion layer, 9
Isachsen: amplitude ratio, 4; station location, 24; population rank, 25,

26; evaporation and water budget-Budyko, 26; evaporation and water budget-Turc, 28; dryness ratio, 28
Isolation — costs, 109
Isotherm, 40°F July — location, 24
Isothermal: ice cover temperature, 56; balance in lakes, 56; in lakes, 58

Jacobs, W. C., 23
Jan Mayen, Dutch exploration, 116
Jeannette, three year voyage in Arctic Sea, 125
Jones Sound, whaling visits, 119
Jørgen Brønlund Fjord, 58
Jornada Range IBP Site, New Mexico: soil properties, 76; microbiological determinations, 81
JPL desert microflora program, 74
Juneau, Alaska, cost of living, 106

Karst topography and hummocky ground, 42
Kassala, variability of precipitation, 18
Katabatic flow, 11; and coreless winters, 12
Katabatic wind, 10, 12
Kau Desert, Hawaii: soil properties, 76; microbiological determinations, 81
Kazach'ye: station location, 24; population rank, 25, 26; evaporation and water budget-Budyko, 26; and oceanicity, 27; evaporation and water budget-Turc, 28; dryness ratio, 28
Keewatin, District of, 99
Kelsey, Manitoba, mean annual air temperature, 38
Kenai Peninsula, oil and gas in, 117, 118
Ketchikan, Alaska, cost of living, 106
Khatanga: station location, 24; evaporation and water budget-Budyko, 26; evaporation and water budget-Turc, 28; dryness ratio, 28
King Christian Island: oil exploration, 118; gas discovery, 120
Kistrand: station location, 24; evaporation and water budget-Turc, 28; moisture index, 29
Klareso Lake, Greenland, a saline lake, 57
Klondike, gold strike, 125
Klondike River, 125
Kola Peninsula, 130
Korotkevich, Ye. S., 63
Kotzebue, 40
Kristoffer Bay, 120
Kuhn, M., 15
Kuskokwim Delta, 99

Labor: costs, 107, 110; in the Far North, 115
Lacustrine lagoons as a lake, 58
Lag runoff in Arctic deserts, 53
LaGorce Mountains, Antarctica: location diagram, 72; frozen pond and algae, 72; soil properties, 77; microbiological determinations, 82
Laird River, 125

Lake: categories, 56; classification, 56; thermal gradient, 56; moating, 56, 58, 60; salt content, 57
Lake Bonney, Antarctica, temperature of water, 60
Lake Fryxell, Antarctica, temperature of water, 60
Lake Hazen, 56; net balance, 15; variability of precipitation, 16
Lake Miers, Antarctica: fed by short streams, 59; not a land-locked lake, 60; as a warm freshwater lake, 61
Lake Nettilling, Baffin Island, 56
Lake Vanda, Antarctica: fed by Onyx River, 59; in a "dry valley" system, 60; temperature of water, 60
Lakes — isothermal state, 58
Lancaster Sound: polar desert area, 23; whaling visits, 119
Land transport, 143
Landscape mosaical pattern, 63
Land-train low-ground-pressure vehicle, 139
Latent heat flux, 7
Lemming, tilling of tundra, 95
Lemming crash, 94
Lettau, H., 7
Lettau's proposal of amplitude ratios, 12
Level of zero amplitude, 37
Limitations on settlement and development, 96
Limnology: systems in classification, 56; in cold deserts, 61
Linear correlation, 11
Little America V: precipitation, 15; net balance, 15; variability of net balance, 16; variability of precipitation, 17
Living cost differentials, 107
Loewe, F., 12
Logan, R. F., 91
Long, W., 15
Long-wave energy flux, 3, 7
Long-wave radiation — downward, 8
Los Angeles, California, cost of living, 106
Low-center polygons, 42
L'vovich, M. I., 27

McClure Straits, 133
McGraw, J. D., 68
McKelvey Valley, Antarctica: soil moisture curves, 75; soil properties, 77; thermoluminescence curves, 78; microbiological determinations, 82; TL abundance, 86
Mackenzie Basin, 133
Mackenzie delta, 151
Mackenzie Mountains, 125
Mackenzie River, 125
Mackenzie Valley, 134
McMurdo, Antarctica: amplitude ratio, 5
McMurdo Ice Shelf: net balance, 15; variability of precipitation, 17
McMurdo Sound, Antarctica: frost sorting, 45; taffoni, 47; oases in dry

valleys near, 59; outflow from lakes, 60
MacNamara, E. E., 68
Macrobiotic refugia, 12
Malyye Karmakuly: station location, 24; population rank, 25, 26; evaporation and water budget-Budyko, 26; evaporation and water budget-Turc, 28; dryness ratio, 28
Mammalian fauna, 92
Man-made pollutants, 96
Manpower: effectiveness, 110; productivity, 110; turnover, 110
Mare Sale: station location, 24; population rank, 25, 26; evaporation and water budget-Budyko, 26; evaporation and water budget-Turc, 28; dryness ratio, 28
Marguerite Bay, Antarctica, amplitude ratio, 5
Marie Byrd land, 13
Marine biomas, 93
Marine silt terraces, location of lakes, 57
Marine transport in Far North, 135, 136, 138, 139
Markov, K. K., 68
Marrakech, variability of precipitation, 18
Martian life detection, 86
Mary River iron deposits (Canada), 120
Massaua, variability of precipitation, 18
Matochin Shar: station location, 24; population rank, 25, 26; evaporation and water budget-Budyko, 28
Maudheim, Antarctica: net balance, 15; variability of precipitation, 17
Mawson, Antarctica: amplitude ratio, 5; potential insolation, 9; ice-free conditions, 13
Maya, Siberia, thermokarst pit, 44
Meadow tundra soil, 67
Mean temperatures in high latitudes, 3
Mecham River, 53
Meeking, L., 63
Melchior, Antarctica, amplitude ratio, 5
Melville Island: oil exploration, 118, 119; gas discovery, 120
Men hauling sled, Scott expedition, 126
Mental illness, 154
Meridional advection of energy, 7, 8
Meridional circulation, 7
Metabolic activity in Antarctic soils, 83
Meteorological Office, 23
Methods for soil physical and chemical properties, 74–75
Microaerophilic bacteria, 82
Microbial groups: general, 71; in Antarctic soil, 80
Microbiological analyses in site selection, 71
Microbiological determinations: in United States arid-zone soils, 81; in world arid-zone soils except United States, 82
Microbiota: and environment, 71;

in desert soils, 83
Microgreenhouse — from quartz, 72
Miers Glacier, 35, 60
Miers Valley, glacial till in Valley, 35
Milwaukee, cost of living, 106
Mineral resources, types, 117
Mining: in North, 117; personnel difficulties, 120
Minneapolis, Minnesota, cost of living, 106
Minsky, J., 116
Miocene Epoch, 91
Mirny, Antarctica: amplitude ratio, 5; katabatic winds, 10; aerological data, 10, 11; ice-free conditions, 13
Mirnyy, Yakutia: living costs, 110; cultural amenities, 111
Mirogeomorphic features, 45
Mnogoletnemerzlyy grunt (permafrost), 35
Moats in Antarctica lakes, 60
Mogadiscio, variability of precipitation, 18
Mohave Desert, California: soil properties, 76; microbiological determinations, 81
Moisture balance: in polar desert areas, 23; in surface soils, 81
Molodezhnaya, Antarctica, amplitude ratio, 5
Mosaical pattern in landscapes, 63
Mould Bay: amplitude ratio, 4; station location, 24; population rank, 25; evaporation and water budget-Budyko, 26; evaporation and water budget-Turc, 28; dryness ratio, 28
Mount Howe, Antarctica: moraine, bluffs, and peak, 72; location diagram of site, 72; volcanism and soils, 74; soil properties, 77; microbiological determinations, 82; temperature considerations, 84; soil and air temperatures, 85; thermoluminescence, 86
Mount Prindle, 46
Müller, F., 14
Murmansk, U.S.S.R., 130, 131
Myggbukta: station location, 24; population rank, 26; evaporation and water budget-Turc, 28
Mys Chelyuskin: amplitude ratio, 4; station location, 24; population rank, 25, 26; evaporation and water budget-Budyko, 26; evaporation and water budget-Turc, 28; dryness ratio, 28
Mys Shalaurova: amplitude ratio, 4; station location, 24; population rank, 25, 26; evaporation and water budget-Turc, 28
Mys Shmidta: amplitude ratio, 4; station location, 24; population rank, 25, 26; evaporation and water budget-Turc, 28
Mys Sterlegova: station location, 24; population rank, 25, 26; evaporation and water budget-Budyko, 26; evaporation and water budget-Turc, 28; dryness ratio, 28

Mys Zhelaniya: amplitude ratio, 4; station location, 24; population rank, 25, 26; evaporation and water budget-Budyko, 26; evaporation and water budget-Turc, 28; dryness ratio, 28

Nasiriya, variability of precipitation, 18
Native poverty, 156
Natural primary pollutants, 96
Naval Arctic Research Laboratory, 116
Naval Petroleum Reserve, Alaska, 130
Nechelik Channel, Colville River, Alaska, putu dunes, 72
Negev Desert, Israel: soil properties, 77; microbiological determinations, 82
Nettilling Lake, Baffin Island, 56
New York, N. Y., cost of living, 106
Nichols, R. L., 60
Nitrogen fixing bacteria, 79
Nome: evaporation and water budget-Budyko, 26; dryness ratio, 28
Nome Creek, 46
Non-use of resources, net value, 106
Nord: amplitude ratio, 4; potential insolation, 9; station location, 24; population rank, 25, 27; evaporation and water budget-Turc, 28
Nordenskjold, O. G., 63
Norman Wells, oil and gas in, 117
North American Eskimo, characteristics, 99
Northern Land Use regulations, 120
Northern Sea Route, 131
Northwest Passage to China, 116
Northwest Territories Ordinance, 121
Norway, Antarctica: net balance, 15; variability of net balance, 16; variability of precipitation, 17
Norwegian Sea, 13
Novosibirsk, U.S.S.R., divorce rate, 110
Nunamiut, 99
Nunataks — ice-free areas, 33

Oasis: ice-free areas, 33; as "dry valleys" in Antarctica, 59
Oazis, Antarctica, ice-free areas, 13
Oceanic advection of energy, 13
Oceanicity, 27
Oil and gas resources, development of, 117–18
Okhotsk Sea, 131
Oliver, D. R., 56
Onyx River, Antarctica, 59
Oran, variability of precipitation, 18
Orcadas (Laurie Island), Antarctica: amplitude ratio, 5; cloud cover, 8
Oregon Desert, Columbia Plateau, 72
Organic component lacking in soil processes, 68
Organic matter accumulation in polar desert areas, 64
Ornithogenic soils in Antarctica, 68
Orographic uplift, 14

Orvig, S., 8, 9, 23
Os Chetyryekhstolbovy, amplitude ratio, 4
Ostrov Belyy: station location, 24; population rank, 25, 26; evaporation and water budget-Budyko, 26; evaporation and water budget-Turc, 28; dryness ratio, 28
Ostrov Dikson: station location, 24; population rank, 25, 26; evaporation and water budget-Budyko, 26; evaporation and water budget-Turc, 28; dryness ratio, 28
Ostrov Domashniy: amplitude ratio, 4; station location, 24; population rank, 25, 26; evaporation and water budget-Turc, 28
Ostrov Heisa, amplitude ratio, 4
Ostrov Kolguyev: station location, 24; population rank, 25; evaporation and water budget-Turc, 28
Ostrov Kotelny, amplitude ratio, 4
Ostrov Rudolfa: amplitude ratio, 4; cloud cover, 8; station location, 24; population rank, 25, 26; evaporation and dryness ratio, 28
Ostrov Sagastyr, 29; station location, 24; population rank, 25, 26; evaporation and water budget-Turc, 28
Ostrov Uyedineniya: amplitude ratio, 4; station location, 24; population rank, 25, 26; dryness ratio, 28; evaporation and water budget-Turc, 28
Ostrov Vaygach: station location, 24; population rank, 25, 26; evaporation and water budget-Budyko, 26; evaporation and water budget-Turc, 28; dryness ratio, 28
Ostrov Vize, amplitude ratio, 4
Ostrov Vrangelya: amplitude ratio, 4; station location, 24; population rank, 25, 26; evaporation and water budget-Budyko, 26; evaporation and water budget-Turc, 28; dryness ratio, 28
Over icing in rivers, 56

Painted Desert, Arizona: soil properties, 76; microbiological determinations, 81
Palmén, E., 7
Paludification, 94
PanArctic Oils Ltd., oil exploration, 120
Pangnirtung, residence physicians, 152
Parry Islands, paucity of species, 31
Particulate matter transfer into high latitudes, 95
Patterned ground: frost-sorted, 42; formation, 68; frost boils, 68
Peary Land, 133; ice-free area, 13; evaporation and water budget-Turc, 28; free of ice during Pleistocene, 53; lakes fed by snow melt, 57; similarity to Antarctic Dry Valleys, 59; soil-dwelling ecosystems, 95
Pediments, 45

Pedogenic gradients, 68
Penman, H. L., 28
Per Schei, geologist, 119
Percolating water, 64
Percolation zone, 14
Permafrost: active layer, 35; defined, 35; dry, 35; land area, 35; table, 35; vechnaya merzlota, 35; distribution in northern hemisphere, 36; origin, 36, 38; temperatures, 37; surficial manifestations, 37, 41, 42; thickness, 38; ice volume, 38, 39; history of studies in, 39–40; and man, 48; engineering problems, 48; highways, 49; railroads, 49; buildings, 49; sewage disposal, 50; and construction, 129; climatic causes of, 155
Petroleum development, 120
Petroleum exploration and environmental damage, 105
Petterssen, S., 23
pH values, 64
Phoenix, Arizona, variability of precipitation, 19
Pingo ice, 38, 39
Pingos — defined, 45
Pipelines, 134
Pitelka, Frank, 94
Plastic deformation and permafrost, 40
Playas, 45
Pleistocene, 53
Pleistocene Epoch, 91, 92
Pleistocene glaciation: and coreless winters, 12; glaciation in Greenland, 53; increasing aridity, 53
Pliocene Epoch, 92
Point Barrow, Alaska, 136, 139; tundra biome study site, 72; biomass production, 94; lay-over by ships, 125
Polar desert animals, types, 93
Polar desert tundra interjacence, soils in, 66, 67
Polar deserts, defined, 23, 33, 91; 23, 34, 45; temperatures, 34; development, 48, 49, 50; soil location, 63, 64; zones, 63; vegetation, 64; frost-stirring in soils, 65; herbivores, 93; invertebrates, 93; and nonrenewable resources, 101
Polar Lands — homogeneity, 63
Polar seas, reproduction of fauna, 93
Polar tundra fauna, 91
Polar tundra flora, 91
Polar zones and July isotherm, 24
Polaris Forbjerg, Greenland, braided river, 55
Pollution hazards: damage to environment, 120; hazards, 121
Pollution and wildlife preservation, 105
Polygonal ground, 94
Polygonal thermal contraction, 40
Polygons, 34, 39; low center, 42
Polynyas, 6
Pond Inlet: station location, 24; population rank, 25, 26; evaporation and water budget-Turc, 28
Population, demography, 105

Population rank: Charlier, 25; Fillipov, 26
Pore ice, 38
Port Martin, turbulent heat flux, 11
Port Sudan, variability of precipitation, 18
Portland, Maine, cost of living, 106
Potential insolation — lag, 6, 7, 12
Precipitation: energy and moisture flux, 13; and accumulation, 14, 15; variability in Arctic, 16; variability in Antarctica, 17; gauge networks, 18; global comparisons, 19; rates in ice-free barrens, 20
Predators in polar areas, 94
Pressure ridges in ice, 129
Pribilof Islands, hunting of fur seals, 117
Primary biomass production, 94
Prince Patrick Island: tundra soils in, 63; snow carryover, 64; soil profile, 65; tundra soil, 67; bog soil, 67
Producer cycles, 95
Productivity, biomass, 94
Productivity, man-hour physical, 110
Protoranker soils in Antarctica, 68
Prudhoe Bay, Alaska, 136, 138, 142; and raised-edge polygons, 49; oil discovery, 105; cost of oil production,107, 109; oil discovery, 118; causeway, 139, 140
Prudhoe Ice Cap, wet mineral matrix near, 66
Putnins, P., 9
Putu Dunes, Alaska: soil properties, 76; thermoluminescence curves, 79; microbiological determinations, 81
Putu tundra, Alaska, microbiological determinations, 81

Quaternary — geologic period, 38
Queen Elizabeth Islands: paucity of species, 31; xeric affinities, 63; archaeological sites, 99
Queen Maud land, 13

Rabies, 155
Radiation, seasonal penetration, 13
Radiation deficit, 7
Radiation input, 13
Radiation rate, 7
Radionuclides in Arctic, 95
Radiorespirometric method, 79
Raised-edge polygons, 42
Recreation, 162
Red Desert, Wyoming: soil properties, 76; microbiological determinations, 81
Refuse disposal, 158
Resolute: amplitude ratio, 4; station location, 24; population rank, 25, 26; evaporation and water budget-Budyko, 26; evaporation and water budget-Turc, 28; dryness ratio, 28
Resolute Bay, 157, 158; airport complex, 151
Resources: exploitation, 101; cost and consumption, 105; history of devel-

opment in Arctic, 115; inhibiting factors in Arctic, 115; nonexpendable, 115, 116; first use in North America, 116; renewable, 116, 119; mineral, 117; mining, 117; oil and gas, 117; nonrenewable categories, 117; nonrenewable, 119; natural, 129
Respiratory diseases, 152, 153
River, transport in USSR, 132
Rivers, in Polar Deserts: glacial fed, 55; in far north, 115
Rivers, in USSR, 131, 132
Roads, in USSR, 132
Roberts, C., 15
Rock desert, 23
Rock streams (rubble sheets), 45
Rockies, 17
Roen, U. I., 56, 57, 58
Roi Baudouin: net balance, 15; variability of precipitation, 17
Rotary-wing aircraft, data, 133
Roth, E. S., 47
Runoff in Alaska, Western Canada and Soviet Union, 55
Rusin, N. P., 10, 11
Russian exploration in Arctic areas, 116, 126
Russkoye Uste'ye: station location, 24; population rank, 25, 26; evaporation and water budget-Turc, 28
Rutbah, variability of precipitation, 18

Sachs Harbour: temperature, 3; advection, 3; summer air temperatures, 3; amplitude ratio, 4; angstrom ratio relationship, 9; station location, 24; population rank, 25, 26; evaporation and water budget-Budyko, 26; evaporation and water budget-Turc, 28; dryness ratio, 28
Saefaxi Elv River, Greenland, 56
Sahara Desert, Egypt: soil properties, 77; microbiological determinations, 82
Sahara Desert, Morocco: sand dunes, 46; taffoni, 47; soil properties, 77; microbiological determinations, 82; fungi identified, 84
Sahuarita IBP Site, Arizona: soil properties, 76; microbiological determinations, 81
Saint Mary's Range, New Zealand: soil properties, 77; microbiological determinations, 82
Salinity: and freezing in lakes, 57; in clear-water lakes, 58; in Antarctica lakes, 60
Salt content, in lakes, 57
Salt efflorescence, 66, 68; in marine terraces, 57; in soil surface, 64
Salt incrustation on silt, 58
Sand dunes in polar deserts, 46
Sand wedges: formation, 40; growth, 41; polygons in Greenland, 41
Sanitary landfill, 158
Sanitation: engineering problems, 155; and water, 155

Savile, D. B. O., 31
Scenery as a resource, 116
Schefferfield, Canada, mining, 117
Schultz, A. M., 94
Schwerdtfeger, W., 7, 9
Scoresbysund: station location, 24; evaporation and water budget-Budyko, 26; evaporation and water budget-Turc, 28; dryness ratio, 28
Seagoing barge, 140
Search and rescue vehicles, 142
Search for wealth, 116
Seas in Arctic Ocean, 126
Seasonal costs on transportation, 109
Seasons, generalized scheme, 7
Seattle, Washington, cost of living, 106
Second harmonic — amplitude, 7
Sediments in lakes, 56
Seed dispersal, 92
Seed dormancy, 93
Sekyra, J., 47
Sellers, W., 26
Sensible heat transport, 7
Settlement habitability, 162
Sewage, domestic, 156
Sewage ponds, 158
Seward Peninsula, 40
Shenandoah, Confederate privateer, in Bering Sea, 117
Ships, ice-breaker, 131, 142
Shopping facilities, 162
Siberia, 25, 33, 34, 37, 39
Siberian Eskimos, 99
Siberian oil fields, 121
Siberian ponies, Scott expedition, 126
Silverbell IBP Site, Arizona: scattered vegetation, 72; soil moisture curves, 75; soil properties, 76; thermoluminescence curves, 78; microbiological determinations, 81
Simpson Desert, Australia: soil properties, 77; microbiological determinations, 82
Site 2, Arctic: net balance, 15; variability of precipitation, 16
Sitka, Alaska, cost of living, 106
Skagway, gold discovery, 125
Skin diseases, 153
Slope stability, 13
Snow albedo, 6
Snow cover, influence on heat flow, 38
Snow melt and stream runoff, 53
Snow and ice facies, 14; and precipitation, 15
Snowmobile, Scott expedition, 126
Sodium chloride in lakes: in Lake Klaresco, 57; in Antarctica lakes, 60, 61
Soil: buffer capacity, 81; cation exchange, 81; electrical conductivity, 81
Soil alkalinity, 67
Soil bacteria, 79
Soil cations, 82
Soil conditions in Far North, 63
Soil microbiological ecology, 86–87
Soil microflora determined by cultural methods, 79

Soil moisture, 84
Soil moisture retention-release curves, 75
Soil properties, 80
Soil salinity, 67
Soil sample analysis, 74
Soil sample transport, 74
Soil sampling, 74
Soil types: in Far North, 63; in Antarctica, 68
Soil zonation in northern polar regions, 63, 64
Solar energy — incoming, 38
Solclime, hygrothermal regime, 84
Solid sublimation, 14
Solifluctuation, 42; defined, 45; processes in High Arctic, 68
Solum: in desert areas, 64; in Arctic brown soil, 68
Solution in High Arctic, 59
Sonoran Desert, Arizona: taffoni, 47; near Silverbell, Arizona, 72; soil properties, 76; microbiological determinations, 81; TL abundance, 86
Sonoran Desert, Mexico: soil properties, 77; microbiological determinations, 82
South Victoria Land: cinder cones, 74; algae incubation, 83
Southampton Island, 151
Spearman rank correlation coefficient, 107
Species diversity, 95
Spitsbergen: rivers fed by glacial melt, 55; Dutch exploration, 116; big game hunting, 117
Sponholz, M., 15
Springs in Arctic deserts, 59
Station 100, variability of net balance, 16
Station 2-0: net balance, 15; variability of precipitation, 16
Steppe areas, 28
Stone circles near Denaii Highway, Alaska, 44
Stone garlands, 68
Stone nets, 68
Stone stripes, 68
Stream discharge: sources of supply, 53; discharge in summer, 55
Stream flow: sources of stream flow, 53; variations in flow, 55
Stresses of physical environment, 91
Subarctic: 35, 36, 49; orthic regosol, 66; saline regosol, 66
Sublimation, 14
Sukkertoppen: net balance, 15; variability of precipitation, 16
Surface cooling rates, 8
Surface heat budget, 3
Surface inversion in Arctic Basin, 9
Surface-effect ship, 143
Surface-effect vehicle, 143, 144, 145
Surtsey, Iceland, 74
Survival of seeds and lichens, 93
Svalbard: station location, 24; population rank, 25, 26; evaporation and water budget-Budyko, 26; evapora-

tion and water budget-Turc, 28; dryness ratio, 28; oceanicity, 29; big game hunting, 117; mining, 117
Svalbard (Isfjord Radio), 24
Syowa, Antarctica, amplitude ratio, 5

'Taber' ice, 38, 39
Taffoni: as a desert feature, 45; formation, 46; need for study, 47; chemical alteration, 48
Tanquary Fjord, desert flora at, 92
Taylor Dry Valley, 60; sand wedges, 41; sand wedge polygons, 43; taffoni, 47
Taylor Valley: ice-free land area, 59; soil properties, 77; microbiological determinations, 82; temperature considerations, 84; subsurface temperatures, 85; air and soil surface temperatures, 85
Temperature, seasonal variation, 6
Temperatures: annual and monthly means, 6; monthly mean at Eureka and Davis, 6; in frozen ground level of zero amplitude, 37
Tertiary Epoch, 92
Thenardite (Na_2SO_4) in desert soils, 64, 65
Thermal contraction crack polygons, 40, 42
Thermal contraction cracks, 40
Thermal pollution, 96
Thermal tension and permafrost, 40
Thermokarst area activity, 96
Thermokarst, phenomena, 41
Thermokarst, pits: near Maya, Siberia, 44; described, 45
Thermokarst, topography, 42
Thermoluminescence: in soil ecology, 86; and bacterial abundance, 87
Thornwaite-Mather Moisture Index, 28, 29
Three Saints Bay, Kodiak Island, headquarters for Russian expansion, 116
Thule, Greenland: amplitude ratio, 4; station location, 24; population rank, 25, 26; evaporation and water budget-Budyko, 26; evaporation and water budget-Turc, 28; dryness ratio, 28; dimictic lake, 57; rills etched into limestone, 59; BMEWS location, 116
Transantarctic Mountains: ice-free areas, 13; volcanics and soils, 74; soil microbial ecosystem, 84
Transcendental values, 106
Transitional flow, 10, 11
Transport, Alaskan marine and motor tonnage, 139
Transport costs — heavy materials, 109
Transportation: strength of, 105; types, 115; limitation to Arctic development, 115; difficulties, 125; history of, 125; modern, 130; in Canada, 133; ground, 134; in Alaska, 136; future, 143; costs, 146
Trans-Siberian Railroad, 109, 131, 132, 134

Travertine veneers, 64
Trichinosis, 154
Trophic levels of production, 95
Tsavo, variability of precipitation, 18
T-3 Island (Fletcher's Island), 140, 142
Tuberculosis, among Eskimos, 152
Tucson, Arizona, variability of precipitation, 19
Tuktoyaktuk, Canada: native housing, 151; winter scene, 152; village scenes, 152, 154
Tullett Point, 67
Tundra, polygons, 42
Tundra, soils: prescence in all zones, 63; discussion on, 66; genetic features, 67; acidity, 67; base-deficient, 67
Tundras: area, 28; described, 34; as part of polar desert areas, 91; environments, 92
Turbidity, in streams, 55
Turbulent heat flux, 10, 11
Turc evaporation formula — desert and semidesert areas, 30
Turc Method, 28, 29
Turf hummocks, 65

Ukusiksalingmint Eskimo, 99
United States Geological Survey oil exploration in North, 105
United States Navy oil exploration in North, 105
Upernavik: station location, 24; population rank, 25; evaporation and water budget-Turc, 28; dryness ratio, 28
Upper air inversions, 8
Upper Ice (Station 11): net balance, 15; variability of precipitation, 16
Ust'Yeniseyskiy Port: station location, 24; evaporation and water budget-Turc, 28
Ust'ye R. Taimyry: station location, 24; population rank, 25, 26; evaporation and water budget-Turc, 28
Utilidors, 155, 156

Valley of 10,000 Smokes, Alaska: volcanic materials, 74; soil properties, 76; microbiological determinations, 81
Vanda, Antarctica, ice-free areas, 13
Vardo: evaporation and water budget-Budyko, 26; oceanicity, 27; dryness ratio, 28
Variation coefficient, precipitation and accumulation, 15
Vascular plant, adaption, 93
Vascular plants: of tundra, 92; adaption to tundra, 93
Ventifacts: common to hot and cold deserts, 45; described, 46
Vertical energy flux, 8
Victoria Dry Valley, 86, 87
Victoria Land, 68
Victoria Range, 35

Victoria Valley: taffoni, 47; ice-free lands, 59; soil properties, 77; microbiological determinations, 82; soil microbial ecology, 84; thermoluminescence relationship to bacterial activity, 87
Vikings, 116
Viscount Melville Sound, polar desert area, 23
Vladivostok, 131
Volochanka: station location, 24; evaporation and water budget-Budyko, 26; evaporation and water budget-Turc, 28; dryness ratio, 28
VonderHaar, T., 7
Vowinckel, E., 8, 9
Vulnerability of polar desert ecosystems, 95–96

Waste disposal practices, 105
Water percolation in soils, 64
Water supplies, 157, 158
Water temperature in lakes, 56, 57, 58, 60, 61

Water vapor, 9
Weathering crusts, 68
West Antarctica heat advection, 10
Whale population, 119
Whaling in Arctic waters, 116–17
White Pass, 125
White Pass Railway, 134
Wholesale trade sector, 109
Wilbur Creek, Alaska, foliated ground ice, 39
Wilderness — evaluation, 106
Wilkes, Antarctica: amplitude ratio, 5; angstrom ratio relationship, 9
Wilkes, S–2: net balance, 15; variability of precipitation, 17
Wind velocities, 10
Windspeed, 15
Winter temperature — attenuation, 8
Wrangel Island, 99
Wright Glacier, 59
Wright Valley: flowing streams in summer, 59; lack of natural thermoluminescence, 86
Wulff Land, Greenland, caves in area, 59

Xericity in polar desert soils, 64
Xerophytes, 71

Yakoutsk (See also Yakutsk), Siberia: mean annual air temperature, 38; buildings on permafrost, 50
Yakutsk (See also Yakoutsk), Siberia: construction costs, 108, 109; construction workers' wages, 110
Yeasts in polar soils, 84
Yellowknife, Canada, 110, 134
Yugorskiy Shar: station location, 24; population rank, 25, 26; evaporation and water budget-Budyko, 26; evaporation and water budget-Turc, 28; dryness ratio, 28
Yukon Territory, housing costs, 107

Zakharova, A. F., 13
Zone of Convergence, 12
Zones in polar deserts: moss-lichen, 63; moss-shrubs, 63
Zones in tundras: moss-lichen, 63; moss-shrubs, 63